THE ENVISIONED LIFE

THE ENVISIONED LIFE
ESSAYS IN HONOR OF EVA BRANN

Edited by Peter Kalkavage
and Eric Salem

Paul Dry Books
Philadelphia 2007

First Paul Dry Books Edition, 2007

Paul Dry Books, Inc.
Philadelphia, Pennsylvania
www.pauldrybooks.com

Text and display type: Berkeley
Composed by P. M. Gordon Associates
Designed by Willie•Fetchko Graphic Design

1 3 5 7 9 8 6 4 2
Printed in the United States of America

Library of Congress Cataloging-in-Publication Data

The envisioned life : essays in honor of Eva Brann / edited by Peter Kalkavage
and Eric Salem. — 1st Paul Dry Books ed.
    p.   cm.
  ISBN 978-1-58988-040-5 (hardcover : alk. paper) —
  ISBN 978-1-58988-041-2 (pbk. : alk. paper)
1. Philosophy. I. Brann, Eva T. H. II. Kalkavage, Peter. III. Salem, Eric.
  B29.E58 2007
  190—dc22

                                                        2007025343

Front cover: Eva Brann, ca. 1960. Photo by Marion Warren.
Back cover/flap: Eva Brann, 2004. Photo by Gary Pierpoint.

Contents

DEDICATION

*Peter Kalkavage, Christopher B. Nelson,
and Eric Salem*

THE FOLLOWING ESSAYS, poems, and painting are offered to Eva Brann on the occasion of her fiftieth year as tutor at St. John's College in Annapolis. They are intended as a tribute from Eva's colleagues, friends, and former students, but even more as an expression of admiration and gratitude. Herewith we celebrate Eva's passion for learning and her deep love of books, her breadth of knowledge and interests, her boundless energy, her mastery of the spoken and of the written word, her virtues of leadership, and her bright and generous spirit.

The title for this collection was inspired by a passage in Eva's *The World of the Imagination.* Cautioning against the narrow imageless thinking that forms "the exoskeleton of contemporary life," Eva writes: "And yet, if, as someone once said, the unexamined life is not worth living, neither is this unenvisioned life—at least not if it preponderates."

Eva T. H. Brann was born in Berlin in 1929 ("T. H." for the names of her grandmothers, Toni and Helene). In 1941, Eva came to the United States, where she and her family, Jewish refugees from Hitler's Germany, settled in Brooklyn. Reading comic books helped her to develop her English vocabulary—"sinister" was one of the first words she remembers acquiring.

After studying history at Brooklyn College, Eva imagined she would become an archaeologist. She earned a master's degree in classics and a doctorate in archaeology at Yale. As part of her doctoral studies, she was awarded a Phi Beta Kappa scholarship to attend the American School of Classical Studies in Athens, where her love for classical Greek culture deepened. But soon she learned that digging for pots was not for her. As she would write many years later, "My outward purpose was to study Greek antiquities, but my inward desire was to see the world through an air that was actively transparent, an atmosphere through which places and things assumed a beautiful clarity and a clarified beauty." Eva's archaeological odyssey culminated in a dissertation on the Athenian agora that was later published by the American School of Classical Studies: *Late Geometric and Protoattic Pottery, Mid 8th to Late 7th Century B.C.* (1962).

In 1957, Eva came to St. John's from Stanford University, where she had been an instructor in archaeology. Eva fell in love with this tiny college in Annapolis "at first sight." She once reported about her early years: "It was conveyed to me that [Jacob Klein] had described me as behaving like a fish in water, and that was just how I felt—like one who was disporting herself in her element, to whom understanding came as she breathed." So intent was she on teaching Greek in her first year that she threatened her language students with sudden death if they failed to learn their irregular Greek verbs —Jacob Klein, who was dean at the time, had to have a little talk with her about that.

Eva recently recalled some high points of her half-century as a tutor. Working her way quickly through the program, she was thrilled to teach junior seminar, mathematics, and laboratory all in the same year: "I began to see what world I was living in." Her favorite classes over the years have been freshman seminar, freshman mathematics, and junior mathematics. Her most beloved activity has been advising senior essays, which has gained her more "friends for life" than anything else she has done at the college. An experience Eva remembers with particular warmth and excitement: spending nearly three days with fellow tutors listening to Mr. Klein read his book on Plato's *Meno*. This, she recalls, "was exhilarating beyond anything." A more recent peak came when Eva sang portions of Bach's *St. Matthew Passion* with the St. John's Chorus. Thinking back over the time from her first days as a tutor to the present, Eva reflected: "It all seems like one day—like the *nunc stans* of heaven."

Eva became dean of the college in 1990 and served in that capacity for seven years. She brought to this office a much-needed mix of intellectual vigor, clarity of purpose, tough-minded practicality, and a spirit of just plain fun. She helped shepherd the college through hard financial times without compromising the program, and she educated a new president in the ways of the college. She promoted the intellectual life of students and tutors daily, and with disarming informality. In the days of Eva's "open door" policy, the dean's office was more than just a place for transacting business. It became a home for conversations of every kind—even a place where colleagues could translate Plato's *Sophist* together and read through Hegel's *Science of Logic*.

Students have always loved "Miss Brann." During her deanship, they asked her to play Yoda, the Jedi master, in a *Star Wars* skit that took place during "Reality weekend." (A group of cadets from the Naval Academy had agreed to represent the evil Empire!) Eva did not have to do any acting, or even speaking, in order to be persuasive as the wise elfin mentor of Johnnie "knights." She had only to appear.

Recalling that Mr. Klein once asserted that the college had no administrators, Eva liked to point out that administering means "ministering to." And so, she kept a box of tissues in her desk, ready for the students (and sometimes tutors) who were dealing with bad news. She also made sure that cookies were always served at instruction committee meetings, much to the delight of her colleagues.

Eva has always been a prolific spokesman for the college. But during these years especially, she wrote about and explained the college's unique program, defending it from its detractors and communicating to the alumni just how seriously she took her responsibilities to preserve and strengthen it. She also steered the college through a highly successful accreditation process.

When she left the deanship, she was praised for her many lasting contributions to St. John's. "With the college it's been one long love affair, starting from the day when, as a prospective tutor, I was up in Campbell and opened a closet door to find a red-painted skeleton with the Greek legend *Gnôthi sauton*, 'Know thyself,'" Eva recalled at a celebration honoring her service as dean. In the same speech, she linked her love of the college with that of her adopted country: "It has been one of the delights of my life that this college seems to be made by and for this country, that it is at the same time one of a kind and yet an expression of the essence of America as I see it."

Over the years, Eva has received many honors, most notably the National Humanities Medal, awarded to her in 2005 at a ceremony in the White House. The medal is given to those "whose work has deepened the nation's understanding of the humanities, broadened citizens' engagement with the humanities, or helped preserve and expand America's access to important humanistic resources." It was a pleasure to see how much this award meant to Eva, yet in characteristic fashion, she insisted that the real honors were due to St. John's. Her only disappointment was that a personal hero, Dolly Parton, who was to receive a National Arts Medal at the same ceremony, could not attend.

Eva has been a member of the Institute for Advanced Study; a member of the U.S. Advisory Commission on International Education and Cultural Affairs; a fellow of the Woodrow Wilson International Center for Scholars; and a fellow of the National Endowment for the Humanities. Yale University Graduate School recently honored her with the Wilbur Lucius Cross Medal, the highest honor it bestows on its alumni. In the citation to the honorary doctorate it awarded her, Middlebury College described Eva in the following way: "As a refugee from Nazi Germany, you have been a true friend of the Republic that has made it possible for you to pursue the good life. You have shown in word and deed that the careful study of great books is a republican, or conversational, activity among fellow students. You have also gently chided Americans not to pursue utility as the end of liberal education."

Eva's range of intellectual interests is evident in the dazzling variety of her many lectures. To name just a few: *The Music of the Republic* (her first lecture at the college, 1966), *The Venetian Phaedrus* (a reading of Thomas Mann's *Death in Venice*, 1971), *The Poet of the Odyssey* (1972), *What is a Body in Kant's System?* (1974), *The Perfections of Jane Austen* (1975), *Plato's Theory of Ideas* (1979), *Against Time* (1983), *Intellect and Intuition* (1984), *Mental Imagery: The College and Contemporary Cognitive Science* (1985), and *The Empires of the Sun and the West* (an exploration of the differences in character between the Aztec civilization and that of its Western conquerors, 2003).

Many of Eva's talks, especially her opening lectures as dean, are about education and reading: *Depth and Desire* (1990), *What is a Book?* (1992), *Why Read Books?* (1996).

The American republic and its founders hold a central place in Eva's lectures and writings, as they do in her heart. On this topic, Eva has written: *A Reading of the Gettysburg Address* (1968), *Concerning the Declaration of Independence* (1976), *Madison's "Memorial and Remonstrance": A Model of American Eloquence* (1981), and *Was Jefferson a Philosopher?* (1992).

Finally, there are Eva's reviews of everything from Paul Scott's *Raj Quartet* and Vikram Seth's *A Suitable Boy* to Pope John Paul's Encyclical *Fides et Ratio* and the movie *High Noon*.

Translating has been a special joy in Eva's intellectual life. Very early in her career at St. John's (1962), she translated Euclid's book on the mathematical construction of the musical scale (the *Sectio canonis* or *Cutting of the Canon*). A few years later, her translation of Jacob Klein's *Die griechische Logistik und die Entstehung der Algebra* (originally published in the thirties) made this foundational work known to the English-reading public as *Greek Mathematical Thought and the Origin of Algebra* (1968). Her translation of Heidegger's essay *What Is That—Philosophy?* (1991) is the penultimate reading in the senior seminar on the Annapolis campus. She has also translated, with colleagues, Plato's *Sophist* (1996) and *Phaedo* (1998). True to form, Eva has not only engaged in the activity of translation but also reflected on it in the delightful essay *On Translating the Sophist* (2000).

Eva is emphatically an author. Her concentrated inquiries into topics especially dear to her have become crystallized in a series of books, in which her luminous intelligence has reached a wider public: *Paradoxes of Education in a Republic* (1989), *The World of the Imagination: Sum and Substance* (1991), *The Past-Present: Selected Writings of Eva Brann* (1997), *What, Then, is Time?* (1999), *The Ways of Naysaying: No, Not, Nothing, and Nonbeing* (2001), *Homeric Moments: Clues to Delight in Reading the Odyssey and the Iliad* (2002), *The Music of the Republic: Essays on Socrates' Conversations and Plato's Writings* (2004), and *Open Secrets/Inward Prospects: Reflections on World and Soul* (2004). Soon to appear is her book on the passions: *Feeling Our Feelings: What Philosophers Think and People Know.*

These large-scale "Flowers of Eva" are a further blossoming of Eva as teacher and learner. They are the adventures of a mind striving to be fully awake. Eva's style is expansive and pointed, intricate and direct. Her tone is a summons to the reader: "Now let's get down to business—and enjoy!" As her friends know, Eva likes to write, and read, while taking a bath. Not since Archimedes, we are sure, has a tub been put to better use.

Eva is more than a prolific author and a beloved teacher. She is also a muse. For half a century, she has inspired her fellow tutors, her many friends, and generations of students to stretch their powers of thinking and imagining. She enthusiastically supports the projects of her colleagues and friends. An avid reader of anything her colleagues write, she has produced many appreciative and penetrating reviews of their work.

Taking aim at a trendy word, Eva once remarked that she was sure she had a life, and hoped she had a style, but did not have a "lifestyle." The many-sidedness of that life is evident in her eclectic, non-academic interests: sailing, woodworking, reading children's books, playing the flute, and occasionally singing. Reading remains her most beloved private activity. Whether it is Homer or Hegel or Louis L'Amour, "Give me a book, and I'm apt to swallow it whole," she once said.

To this Eva, then, teacher and learner, friend and colleague; woman of many ways, traveler in the world of spirit and the world at large; wily, resourceful, and circumspect; lover of books and words and wide-open spaces; light-bearer, cookie-bearer, sailor, and flute-player; multiplex and Yodaform—to this Eva, who has united so gracefully the examined and the envisioned life, we dedicate this feast of words and works.

PLATO'S *MENO* AND ARISTOTLE'S *NICOMACHEAN ETHICS*

Laurence Berns

The best introduction to the works of Aristotle are the dialogues of
Plato; and the best introduction to the dialogues of Plato are the works
of Aristotle.

—Philippidês

I. PRUDENCE, COURAGE, AND INTELLIGENCE

IN THE FINAL CHAPTER of Book VI of the *Nicomachean Ethics,* the book on the
intellectual virtues, Aristotle takes up the question of virtue and prudence
(*phronêsis*).[1] Socrates, he says, was "mistaken in thinking that all the virtues
are forms of prudence, but in saying that they cannot exist without prudence
he spoke well." Aristotle is probably referring to the passage in the *Meno*
where Socrates says,

> If then virtue is something in the soul and is itself necessarily beneficial,
> it must be prudence: since indeed all things that pertain to the soul are
> themselves in themselves neither beneficial nor harmful, but when pru-
> dence or thoughtlessness (*aphrosunês*) is added to them they become
> harmful or beneficial. According to this argument, indeed, virtue being
> beneficial, it must be some kind of prudence. (88C–D [388])[2]

Yet Socrates ends this section with a question that puts it almost the
same way that Aristotle put it, "Therefore do we affirm that prudence is
virtue, either virtue altogether or some part of it?" (89A [396]).

In the *Meno* this conclusion had been prepared for by the observation
that sometimes things called virtues, like courage, moderation, and readiness to learn, harm their possessors and at other times they benefit them.[3]
"For example, courage, if the courage is not prudence, but some sort of
boldness—is it not the case that when a human being is bold without intelligence (*nous*) he is harmed and whenever with intelligence he is benefited?"
Meno agrees here and also when next Socrates asks about moderation and
readiness to learn (*eumathia*). "When they are learned and trained for with
intelligence, they are beneficial, but without intelligence harmful?" (88B,
[382] and [384]). After these brief appearances, *nous* disappears from the

argument. It seems to have been absorbed into the more emphasized "prudence." *Nous* makes an even briefer but no less crucial appearance in Aristotle's fuller treatment of courage in *NE* III. (In Book VI *nous* reappears as the ultimate source of the links between virtuous inclinations and the prudent choice of means that issues in "authoritative virtue," or rightness of action.)[4]

In *NE* II courage was defined in general as a mean between fear and confidence. The presentation in Book III takes on the character of a dialogue:

> About what kinds of frightening things is the courageous man concerned? Would it not be about the greatest? . . . and the most frightening thing is death. . . . In what kind of death then? Would it not be in the most noble (*tois kallistois*)? And that is death in battle, for that is where the greatest and most noble danger lies. The honors bestowed by cities and monarchs are also in agreement with this. In an authoritative way then it might be said that the courageous man is he who is not afraid of a noble death even when the dangers that bring it on are close at hand; and such are the dangers of war.[5]

In this chapter courage comes to sight in its elementary and most conspicuous form, in the context of what starts off as something like a conversation between citizens and citizen-soldiers.

The next chapter begins by noting that the same things are not frightening to all people, but that there are some things beyond human endurance. And "this sort of thing is frightening for everyone, at least for anyone who has any sense (*tôi ge noun echonti*)"—"who has any *nous*." This word, which in its colloquial usage can be translated "sense," is the key theoretical term for Plato and Aristotle translated variously as intelligence, intellect, or intellectual intuition. With the almost parenthetical mention of the one who has *nous* a new unannounced perspective enters into Aristotle's discussion, the perspective of the prudently courageous man who endures fears and is bold towards those things which he ought, for the sake of what he ought, as he ought and when he ought. The word "prudence" does not occur in this chapter; we are not to be diverted from our consideration of courage. But we are introduced to the effects of prudence, and prudently prepared by anticipation for its thematic presentation later in Book VI.[6]

The final chapter of Book III's treatment of courage deals with the problem of the intrinsic pleasantness of virtue, where the virtue itself is primarily concerned with enduring pains. There is the briefest indication that true courage cannot be possessed in isolation from the other virtues: "The more a man possesses virtue in its entirety (*tên aretên pasan*), the more happy he is, and the more will he be pained by death; for life is most worth living for such a man" (1117b10–12).[7] This reference to virtue "in its entirety" brings us to the problem raised by Socrates throughout the *Meno*, the question he is never able to get Meno to inquire into seriously:[8] What is virtue itself, the one form of virtue, as distinct from the separate virtues, that which ultimately constitutes them as virtues? Plato, we hope to show, had much more success with his student, Aristotle.

II. Virtue Shattered

The chief complaint Socrates has with the accounts of virtue given to him by Meno is that he is being given swarms of many virtues and not that "one and the same form (*eidos*) [1] through which they are virtues, and [2] upon which one would somehow do well to focus one's gaze," in order to answer "him who has asked him to clarify that, namely what does virtue happen to be."[9] Socrates approaches this question in a variety of ways in the *Meno*. It is probably safe to assume that there is something special to be learned from each approach. Here, however, we will focus only on a few approaches.

In 79A [170] Socrates speaks of his asking Meno "not to shatter virtue or to change it into small coin." This remark was prepared for by Meno's adding acquiring gold and silver into a list of good things (78C) [153]. Meno does not object when Socrates restates it as Meno having declared that "to provide oneself with gold and silver, then, is virtue." And Socrates goes on to ask whether it makes any difference if the words "justly" and "piously" should be added "to this providing," but "if someone should provide himself with these things unjustly, would you still call these doings virtue?"(78D) [156]. Meno answers, "Surely not," and agrees that such providing is not virtue, but vice. Socrates then concludes, "It seems likely that one should add justice or moderation or piety, or some other piece of virtue to this providing," if it is to be virtue (78D and E) [160].[10]

In complaining about Meno's "piece" language Socrates speaks of having "begged you to talk about virtue as a whole."[11] What kind of whole is Plato's Socrates urging us to think of? Are justice, moderation, courage, and piety related to virtue as small change is to gold;[12] or as the different kinds of bees are related to their hive; or as circle, square, and triangle are related to figure; or as black, red, yellow, blue, and white are related to color; or as two, three, four, and five are related to number; or as the different classes of human beings are related to political society as a whole; or as the organs of a living body are related to the whole living body, the organism? There is one passage in the *Meno* that clearly seems to favor the organism model, where Socrates urges Meno to tell him what virtue is, "leaving it whole and healthy" (77A–B [112]).[13] "Healthy," as Aristotle informs us, is an analogous[14] term, the primary meaning of which is healthy animal.

III. VIRTUE AS A WHOLE

If we can regard Socrates' "exhibition" with the Slave-boy as a model for inquiry, a good inquiry should culminate in a solution or answer to the problem or question with which it began.[15] As we have noted, all the definitions of virtue attempted by Meno in answer to Socrates' question—What is virtue?—are shown to be inadequate. Socrates tells Meno and us in the final speech of the dialogue that we will not arrive at clarity about virtue unless "before we seek whatever way virtue comes to human beings" (Meno's opening question), "we . . . undertake to seek what virtue, itself in itself, is." How might the great definition of virtue in Aristotle's *Nicomachean Ethics* (II. vi. 1106b 36–1107a 6) measure up to Socrates' standards?

> Virtue then is a steady disposition for (*hexis*) deliberately choosing (*pro-hairetikê*),[16] which exists in a mean state (*mesotês*), a state relative to us, determined by reason (*logôi*) and as the prudent man (*phronimos*) would determine it.[17] And it is a mean state between two vices, one of excess and one of defect. And, further, it is a mean by some of the vices falling short and other vices exceeding what is appropriate in both passions and actions, while virtue both discovers and chooses the mean (*meson*).

At first glance, it would be easy to criticize this definition: it seems to be clearly circular. Prudence is the intellectual virtue that enables one correctly to choose what conduces to virtue. It is almost as if Aristotle had said virtue is behaving like a virtuous man. When a man who at the least was one of the greatest logicians that ever lived makes what could be taken for a beginner's logical slip, it might be prudent to take another look at our text and ask, "What might he be getting at?" The circularity, defining virtue in terms of a certain kind of virtuous man, points, I believe, to a most important consideration: for ethical *action* general rules are insufficient; given the variability of circumstances, there is no substitute for the good judgment of the human being on the spot.[18] Aristotle seems to suggest that when we exercise ourselves in steering clear of vices and finding the right mean, or proportion relative to our own particular nature and circumstances, something like the image of the perfectly prudent man should be guiding our judgment. As Aristotle says in his chapter (*NE* III, iv) on wishing or wanting (*boulêsis*), the serious ethical man (*spoudaios*) judges correctly; what seems noble[19] and pleasant to him is noble and pleasant: "he is himself, as it were, a standard (*kanôn*) and measure of these things."[20]

Before directly resuming our discussion of how Aristotle's definition meets Socrates' standards, "leaving [virtue] whole and healthy," it might not be inappropriate to indicate why one might assume that Plato's *Meno* was especially important for Aristotle's *Nicomachean Ethics*. Aristotle does seem to refer to the *Meno* a number of times in the *Ethics,* but he refers to many other dialogues of Plato as well. I propose to explore this assumption by considering the opening questions that give the dialogue its setting, and asking Aristotle, "What do you make of Meno's opening questions and Socrates' response to them?" Meno begins by asking,

> Can you tell me, Socrates, whether virtue is something teachable? Or is it not teachable, but something that comes from practice? Or is it something neither from practice nor from learning, but comes to be there (*paragignetai*) for human beings by nature, or in some other way?

Socrates saw at once, I think Aristotle might reply, that Meno's questions shatter virtue; they disjoin, as separated alternatives, what can only be understood as interrelated and interpenetrating powers working together in a unified whole. He knew that as far as human character is concerned nature provides the capacities; that teaching and learning aim at clarifying the ends, or goals, implicit in the natural capacities, preparing the learner, so far as he or she is able, to understand and to attain the goals; and repetitive practice develops the habits that bring about or impede the actualization of those goals.[21] In his own words (*NE* II, i), Aristotle remarks,

> Therefore, neither by nature, nor against nature are the virtues engendered, but [they are engendered] by our having been natured to receive them and by our being completed [or perfected] by habit (*ethos*). Furthermore, concerning those things that come to be there (*paragignetai*) for us by nature, we are first provided with the capacities for them, and later we render the actualities (*energeiai*) [being at work, activity].[22] (1103a24–28)
> . . . for it is by acting in dealings with people that some of us become just, and others become unjust; and by acting in dangerous situations we

also become habituated to be afraid or to be confident, and, for some, habituated to become courageous and, for others, to become cowards; and similarly it holds with regard to our desires and our getting angry. (1103b 14–19)

The questions, then, that set the framework for the *Meno,* rightly or Socratically understood, also set the framework for the *Nicomachean Ethics.*

The mean state determined by prudent reason in which virtue lives is a formative state, incompatible with excess or defect, an ordering form of being at work, which balances, limits, and shapes the materials of our feelings (or passions), practical dispositions, and actions.[23] This state is a "state relative to us"; that is, one must consider the distribution of one's own feelings, dispositions, and habits and one's own particular circumstances, as one moves toward and then lives in the rationally determined, appropriately proportioned distribution of those materials that constitute the mean state of being, in which one who most perfectly attains those ratios and proportions, the prudent one, the *phronimos,* lives.[24]

There is one place in the *Meno* where Meno seems to assert the unity of virtue as encompassed by justice: "For justice, Socrates, is virtue." But Socrates quickly convinces him that justice is one particular virtue among other virtues.[25]

In Book V, chapter i, of the *Nicomachean Ethics* Aristotle explores the sense in which justice might be said to be all virtue in sum. It is, insofar as justice is keyed to the law, the written and the unwritten laws, which includes religious law,[26] for "the laws pronounce on everything," ordering the virtues and forbidding their opposites. But this justice, he explains, is not justice unqualified, justice "simply," it is justice "in relation to another," it is justice in relation to our treatment of other people. And it does depend on whether the law has been laid down rightly or not (1129b11–34).[27] Law, decently laid down, then, by encouraging certain tendencies and discouraging others, might be said, along with family life,[28] to begin the ordering of feelings, predispositions, and practices that might later be brought into conscious thought, and, for those capable of it, be perfected by right reason and prudence.

Aristotle has discussed the natural and elementary predispositions from which moral and ethical education begins. Spiritedness (*thumos*) that manifests itself most conspicuously in anger and bravery is the elementary source of courage; shame-respect (*aidōs*)[29] the elementary source of temperance or moderation; and righteous indignation (*nemesis*) of justice.[30]

Each of these natural predispositions, left to itself, can go wrong. Can any of the virtues be realized in the absence of the others? Can courage subsist without the moderating of fear and love of self that is the proper office of moderation, without the sense of justice that should control the resistance it presents to what it takes to be a danger? Can justice be served without the courage to oppose dangerous malefactors? Can moderation deal with the not always comic problem of human self-importance[31] in others and especially in oneself without something of the playful nimble-witted sense of humor described by Aristotle as the mean between boorishness and buffoonery (1127b33–1128b4)? It would seem that every genuine virtue has some role to play in the constitution of each of the others, each an organic part in the ethical organism of all the virtues, of Virtue.

Aristotle may seem to have presented "a swarm of virtues," Stewart notes, but they are ultimately to be understood as facets of the "symmetry of the whole man."[32] People do differ naturally in their capacities for "the natural virtues," the steady disposition to want or wish for correct ends, Aristotle says, but for someone who is simply good, the possessor of "authoritative virtue," this lack of symmetry, or due proportion, in the possession of the virtues is not possible. "For when the one virtue practical wisdom (*phronêsis*) is present all the other virtues together will be present" (1144b32– 1145a3). While for most, if not all men, this state of *phronêsis* remains primarily an object of aspiration, Aristotle here seems to insist that it is an attainable human possibility. The ethical organism of all the virtues is the ethical nature or soul of the *phronimos,* the man or woman of practical wisdom.[33]

IV. Sense Perception and Experience

The usual word for sense perception in Aristotle and Plato is *aisthesis.* But Aristotle also argues that the universals derived from particulars do depend on *aisthesis,* perception; and "intellect (*nous*) is this perception" (1143b 4–5). Aristotelian induction (*epagôgê*—leading or bringing to, as the Latin *inductio*) does *not* proceed by way of abstraction[34] and the collecting of instances for the formulation of generalizations or universals, according to the usual modern accounts of induction, but, as Sachs put it, by being "brought face to face with the universals . . . through a contemplative act whereby the same activity that holds a perceptible thing together works directly on our souls."[35] This can happen through any number of examples, or even just one example.

Sensation and appetite presuppose *phantasia,* the presentation of appearances to the soul, which is usually translated "imagination." The existence of memory makes clear that imagination can also present appearances when the things that have appeared are no longer present. Objects of appetite cause movement by being imagined, by appearing to the soul. We judge or reason on the basis of what appears in our souls. The appearances may be illusions, they may be images or likenesses, or, Aristotle argues, if the soul is well constituted and rightly ordered, they may be true. In this case the things that appear would *be* as they appear.[36] In *The Movement of Animals,* Aristotle speaks of how "the feelings (*pathê*) fittingly prepare the organic parts [of animals] for movement, the appetite fittingly prepares the feelings, and the imagination the appetite, and this latter [preparation] comes about either through intellection or sense perception. The simultaneity and quickness [of these activities] stem from the active and passive elements being in relation to one another according to nature."[37] There are, Aristotle says, two kinds of imagination, sensory imagination, which all animals share, and rational, or calculative (*logistikê*), imagination. This difference is interestingly (if not in an altogether Aristotelian way[38]) described by Thomas Aquinas, who distinguishes two ways of apprehending sensible particulars: in animals an "estimative power," in human beings what he calls a "cogitative power." The cogitative power "apprehends the individual thing as existing in a common nature, and this because it is united to intellect in one and the same subject. Hence it is aware of a man as this *man,* and a tree as this *tree.*" The other animals, Thomas argues, are not aware of an individual thing as in a common nature, but apprehend them instinctively as terms of some action or passion. "Thus a sheep knows this particular lamb, not as this lamb, but simply as something to be suckled; and it knows this grass just in so far as this grass is its food."[39]

Many years ago in Chicago, before his commentary on the *Meno* was written, Jacob Klein began a conversation on the *Meno* with, "Plato's *Meno* is all about seeing and hearing." Let this be my introduction to sense perception in the *Meno.*

Aristotle could not have missed the great proliferation of words in the *Meno* inviting Meno to look, to watch, to observe, and to see.[40] The word *eidos,* for the form through which many things of the same kind are what they are and to which one should look in order to answer someone who asks about what they happen to be, is connected to the verb *eidenai* (usually translated "to know"), but *eidenai* and *eidos* are also connected to the sense of sight, for the elementary meaning of *eidenai* is "to have seen" and the elementary meaning of *eidos* is "looks," as it is used once in the dialogue by Meno to describe Socrates' resemblance to the torpedo-fish.[41]

In the model inquiry[42] that Socrates exhibits for Meno with the Slave-boy, hardly any step is taken without reference to diagrams drawn in the sand at which they are looking as they speak. But, despite his ease in following the geometrical argument, Meno seems to have little respect for looking. When (before the Slave-boy scene) Socrates, in practice for the virtue question, defines "shape," in terms of our fundamental experience of shapes, "that which alone of all the things which are which always happens to accompany color,"[43] Meno finds this too "simple-minded." He then argues, what if "someone should declare that he does not know (*eidenai*) color," which in Greek has the collateral meaning, "suppose someone should affirm that he has not seen a visible surface." As Klein puts it, Meno refuses the practice of defining shape in terms of his own experience, the phenomenon, of shape, "he wants to be *told* what *schema* [shape] is" (Meno *Commentary,* p. 58). Socrates obliges him with the authoritative geometrical definition of figure: "*schema* is the limit of a solid." As Meno rejects *looking*, his untamed spirit plods on with "what about color . . . . , Socrates?" Socrates has learned his lesson and "dialectically" accommodates himself to what Meno has been habituated to, a fancy Gorgian and Empedoclean doctrine that applies to all sense perceptions and distinguishes none. He applies it mechanically to color and ends up with this high-flown and deep-sounding ("tragical") definition: "color is an effluence of shapes commensurate with sight and perceptible." Meno praises this "best possible" response. Socrates returns to the question of virtue, but not before suggesting that he still thinks his first account of shape was better. Meno much prefers *hearing* about what shape and color are without considering the *looking* from which our primary experience of them becomes intelligible. He can, however, rest with the abstractions of geometry.

The relation between experience and knowing is explored in many places in the *Meno,* especially where bad habits come into play, but words for experience (*empeiria*) occur rarely.[44] There is one place where that relation is explicitly discussed, but the word used is the word for being "without experience" (*apeiros*). Socrates wonders why Anytus is so down on the Sophists, he wonders if any of them has wronged him. It turns out that Anytus and everyone under his influence "never associated with any of them."

SOCRATES: Then you are altogether without experience of these men?

ANYTUS: I am and may I remain so.

SOCRATES: How then, my daemonic one, could you know about this business, whether there is anything good or worthless in that of which you are altogether without experience?

ANYTUS: Easily: I still know what these people are, whether I am without experience of them or not.

SOCRATES: You are perhaps a diviner (*mantis*), Anytus, for how else, I might wonder, do you know about them, from what you yourself say about them. (92A–92C [427–434])

One can hear from others, but one can only see and experience for oneself. Experience, then, would seem to be not the cause, but rather the condition of natural knowledge.[45]

V. INCOMMENSURABILITY AND JUSTICE

After Socrates presents the Slave-boy with a square based on a two-foot line, and they have already figured out by observation that the number for the area can be determined by multiplying the numbers for the lines, and the area number for the square based on the two-foot line is, therefore, two times two feet, that is, four feet,[46] Socrates asks whether there could not come to be a square "two times as large as this one." The Boy says, "Yes," and then in response to Socrates' question, about how many feet the new area will be, says, "Eight." Socrates, then, shifting from the language of numerable quantity (*posoi*—how many?) to the language of continuous magnitude (*pêlikê tis*), asks him how *large* each line of that new area will be. After reconsidering the square with the two-foot line and the four-foot area, the Boy responds, naturally enough, "It is clear, Socrates, that the line is two times as large." Socrates goes along with the Boy, trying the only two numerable lines left, the four-foot line and the three-foot line, and seeing by their drawn diagrams that both are too large. At this point the Boy has earned a decisive hint from his teacher, "But from what sort of line [does the eight feet area come to be]? Try to tell us precisely: and if you don't want to count (*arithmein*), show us rather from what sort of line" (83E–84A [274]). "If you don't want to count" has the sense "if you don't want to do it arithmetically."[47] Socrates here hints that the line that would provide the eight-foot square might better be discovered by a showing, that is by pointing to some geometrical construction that gives up counting linear units, but does count area units. When the sought-for line is finally constructed by Socrates, it turns out to be incommensurable with any of the numerable lines they have been using. It is the diagonal of the four-foot square.[48]

> Underlying this conversation between Socrates and the Boy is the great discovery of Incommensurability and the fundamental distinction between discrete (numerable) and continuous quantities. Incommensurability refers to the fact that there are definite magnitudes (lines, surfaces and solids) that do not have to one another the ratio of a number to a number. They are said to be "irrational," *alogoi,* to one another, in that their relation cannot be expressed by a ratio between numbers, or in that both cannot be measured exactly by a common measure of their own kind, although they can be distinguished and ordered in terms of the numerable areas of the squares built upon them (in terms of "square roots"). The favorite example of incommensurability has long been that seen in the relation of a diagonal of a square to the side of the same square. . . . See also Plato, *Theaetetus,* 147D ff.[49]

There is much to be explored in Socrates' model prelude to inquiry, but for the purposes of this essay we confine ourselves to examining how the underlying theme of the Slave-boy scene, incommensurability, enters into the *Nicomachean Ethics* in two instances, both in connection with justice.

Aristotle begins his treatise on justice in the *Nicomachean Ethics,* Book V, by arguing dialectically and critically from generally accepted opinion:

> We see indeed that in speaking of justice everyone means that sort of steady disposition from which people are apt to do just things and from which they act justly and want just things: the same with injustice, a disposition from which they act unjustly and want unjust things. (1129a 7–11)

The first four chapters articulate the rational targets of the disposition for justice: general justice connected with lawfulness (discussed above, section III) comes first. It is distinguished from fairness, that is, particular justice, aiming at different kinds of equality, which is then divided into distributive (*dianemêtikon*) and rectifying (*diorthôtikon*) justice, the justice that "sets things straight."[50]

Distributive justice (chapter three) pertains to all the divisible assets of a society, honors and offices as well as material assets. It implies that no political society exists without some way of distributing the advantages and disadvantages, rewards and punishments, entailed in living together. It comprehends what we usually separate into social, political, and economic spheres. Some ranking of the values of goods exchanged or distributed works itself out in every society. Implicit in these rankings are rankings of the activities productive of the goods and, most importantly, rankings of the men and women who produce the goods and receive the distributions. These rankings reflect the goals or ends that predominate in the different societies: freedom in democracies, wealth in oligarchies, and virtue in aristocracies. (In mixed regimes like ours with serious electoral systems the debates between contending principles are, as it were, institutionalized.) In every political community some such order of distributive justice is operative, even where there might be no explicit expression given to the general idea of justice. Indeed, Aristotle suggests, the political community is constituted by the order of distributive justice it shares (*Politics,* 1253a14–18). The polity, the regime, the "constitution," the "soul" of every community is the order of distributive justice at work in that community. It carries into practice the notions of what is appropriate and fitting that dominate society and are reflected in its laws. The secondary order of rectifying justice (the subject of chapter four), which includes the civil and criminal law, is derived from the more fundamental order of distributive justice: that is, laws are laid down in accordance with the operative principles of distributive justice. Civil and criminal laws promote those principles and rectify their violations.

The mean of distributive justice must be distinguished from the mean of the other ethical virtues, which is a mean between two vices, of excess and of defect, which steers between contrary states of character and passions, and is concerned with internal goods and evils. The mean of distributive justice, however, concerns itself with persons, things, and external actions; it is found in correct relations of equality, proportional and arithmetic, between persons and their merits and external things, especially those external goods and evils that are distributable and exchangeable within the political community.[51]

The argument here takes an interesting mathematical turn (1131a10 ff.). Let capital letters represent persons and their merits and lower-case letters things or shares distributed. Aristotle begins with the just distribution, $A : B :: c : d$, shares distributed in the same ratio as personal merits (1131b5). He then alternates the ratio to $A : c :: B : d$, which seems to say that the same reason for A getting c gives d to B. But, as I assume Aristotle knew, these ratios violate the homogeneity (*homogenôn*) requirement for mathematical ratios: the magnitudes in mathematical ratios must be of the same kind (Euclid, V, definition 3, see also proposition 16). Aristotle, then saying "the whole [A + c] is to the whole [B + d]," composes the ratios A + c : c : : B + d : d (Euclid, V, definition 14 and proposition 18). He then alternates the ratios to A + c : B + d : : c : d, but since c : d : : A : B, this amounts to saying that A + c : B + d : : A : B, A and his share is to B and his share as A is to B, ending up with the original ratio between persons. This, he says, is the just distribution, a mean between what is "contrary to the proportional" which is "unjust." Letting > represent greater ratio and < lesser ratio (Euclid, V, definition 7), the just proportion then is a mean between A + c : B + d > A : B, where A gets more than he or she deserves and B less, and A + c : B + d < A : B, where A gets less than he or she deserves, and B more. Why does Aristotle, the supreme analyst of common sense, turn here to a mathematical treatment?[52]

In the fifth chapter Aristotle turns to that justice in exchanges that holds together the political community, that is, proportional reciprocity. The word translated reciprocity, *antipeponthos,* means literally to have suffered or undergone and be suffering or undergoing in return. It is a technical term in mathematics and physics, meaning inverse or reciprocal proportion, for example, the famous law of the lever in Archimedes's *Equilibrium of Planes* (Propositions 6 and 7): weights in equilibrium are said to be in reciprocal, or inverse, proportion to the lengths of their lever arms. That is, a big weight is to a little weight as the little weight's lever arm is to the big weight's lever arm (bw/lw = lwla/bwla). In equilibrium, it is as if the little weight gets reciprocity for its littleness by the bigness of its lever arm and vice versa for the big weight.

Reciprocity is like rectifying justice because it is primarily giving a thing for an equal thing, but it partakes of and reflects the principle of distributive justice, proportional distribution based on a hierarchy of personal qualities. Aristotle illustrates his fundamental principle of exchanges, proportional equality, by explaining that as a housebuilder is to a shoemaker, so is a house to shoes. The values of commodities are set primarily by the values of the works and of the producers of the commodities. Some way must be found to equalize products of different worth, so that one can say n shoes equals 1 house: money is invented to provide a conventional commensurability based on need for the exchange of intrinsically incommensurable goods. It is clear that this notion of reciprocity includes (but is not exhausted by)[53] the entire commercial life of society.

Aristotle's own manner of talking about these things, as well as the substance of his argument, is worth noting.

For it is not out of two doctors that a community arises, but out of a doctor and a farmer, and, generally, between those who are different and not equal: but these must be equalized. Everything, therefore, of which there is exchange must be comparable.[54]

For this purpose money (*nomisma*) has been introduced, and it becomes a measure (*meson*) somehow (*pôs*)[55] because it measures everything, so that exceeding and falling short [in value] also are measured, just how many shoes, then, are equal to a house or to [some amount of] food. Therefore, whatever a builder is in relation to a shoemaker, so must that many shoes be in relation to a house or to [some amount of] food. For if this is not the case, there will be neither exchange nor community. And this will not be unless the things exchanged can be somehow equal. It is necessary, therefore, for everything to be measured by some one thing, as was said before. And this is, in truth, need (*chreia*) which holds everything together. For if people were to want nothing, or not want in similar ways, there would be either no exchange or not the same kind of exchange. And money has by agreement and compact come to be a sort of exchangeable representative of need.[56] Because of this, money has the name *nomisma*, because it is not by nature, but by convention [*nomos*, also translated custom and law], and it is in our power to change it and to make it useless.

The deeper significance of Aristotle's remarks about this apparently mundane subject is often unnoted. J. A. Stewart is an exception: "It is only this or that particular monetary system which is by convention and can be changed and disused; the institution of money itself is by nature, just as speech is by nature; *i.e.*, like speech, it is essential to the realisation of that political community in which man attains his true nature. With a system of barter, as with a system of dumb signs, man could never have become a *politês* [a citizen, an active member of a political community], but would have remained an isolated savage."[57] Particular combinations of sounds forming particular words vary from place to place and from time to time: they are by convention. The impulse to form such conventions arises naturally whenever human beings come together, fed by the natural purposes of learning from and communicating with one another. The natural sociality implicit in this process manifests itself also in the invention of money, serving a natural human need for mutual exchange and political communion. Human beings, it seems, are convention-making animals by nature. "[In] the case of man *nomos* [convention, law], which expresses itself through the development of *logos* [speech, reason], is as indispensable an end for *physis* [nature] as *physis* is an indispensable ground for *nomos,* . . . *physis* provides the potentialities, *nomos* the actuality of man, and . . . therefore, *nomos* comes to be *the* key to a final understanding of man's *physis.*"[58]

Aristotle sums up this argument:

> Money indeed, as a measure making things commensurable, equalizes them. For if there were no exchange, there would be no community, nor would there be exchange if there were no equality, nor equality if there were no commensurability. Now then in truth it is impossible for things differing so much to become commensurable, but with reference to need they may become so sufficiently. There must then be some unit, and this is set down on the basis of a supposition (*ex hypotheseôs*), which is why it is called *nomisma,* for this makes everything commensurable, for everything is measured by money. (1133b16–23)[59]

Aristotle knows that not everything is measured by money. Besides the fundamental incommensurability discussed here, in his books on friendship (*NE,* VIII and IX) he discusses a number of necessarily unequal exchanges, for example, between parents and children, people of outstanding virtue and those of lesser virtue who benefit from that virtue, and others. In such cases honor is often due, but it is not thought of as being commensurable with that for which it is "paid." Jewish, Christian and Islamic theologians extend this thought to its limits by arguing for the utter incomparability of love and reverence due to the Creator with that due to any of his creatures.

The word "sufficiently" in the previous quotation seems to mean "for practical purposes." In truth the things evaluated by money do not possess the natural or intrinsic commensurability that perfect justice in distribution would require. The homogeneity required in mathematical ratios, referred to above, which would ground an intrinsic common measure in societal exchanges does not exist. Nevertheless, the *need* for different kinds of goods, although not being unqualifiedly rational and not a measure of the intrinsic worth of the goods, does provide a kind of homogeneity and commensurability reflected in monetary values that is sufficient for most purposes of exchange and for the social life that exchange supports. The conventional monetary units that roughly measure needs make possible that exchange and reciprocity that civil society requires. Aristotle clarifies, but does not emphasize, the theoretical insufficiencies of this conventional commensurability: he emphasizes its practical sufficiency. Both by the substance and the manner of his treatment he exhibits the inseparability of the genuine search for justice from moderation.

VI. NATURE, OR SOME OTHER WAY

Meno does not seem to find Socrates' way of inquiring and conversing particularly congenial. But there are a few places in the dialogue where he does seem to exhibit a more passionate interest in what Socrates is saying. At 81A-E [189–194] Socrates says, "I have heard from both men and women wise about things divine—," when apparently Meno interrupts with "What was the account they gave?" Socrates keeps Meno on the hook with "A true one, it seems to me, and a beautiful one." Meno repeats, "What was it and who are those who say it?" Those who say it are priests and priestesses who are concerned with giving an account of divine things, and what they speak about turns out to be the immortality of the soul and the doctrine of recollection. The prospect of wisdom about things divine does stir Meno's soul.

At 87D [366] Socrates forecasts his turn at the end of the dialogue to divine dispensation (*theia moira*) rather than teaching, knowing and nature as the source of virtue:

> Then, if there is something good and it is something else separated from knowledge, it may be that virtue would not be some sort of knowledge; but if there is nothing good which knowledge does not encompass, then we would be right in suspecting what we suspected, that it is some sort of knowledge.[60]

The treatment of nature in this dialogue is objectionable; it would seem, intentionally objectionable.[61] In the long discussion with the democratic politician Anytus (93C–94E [440–458]) about how the great Athenian political leaders, Themistocles, Aristides, Pericles and Thucydides (not the historian) were unable to pass on their political virtues to their sons, Socrates seems to be exhibiting the lack of natural political capacity in these sons. But he uses these descriptions simply to conclude that virtue is not teachable, which prepares the way for disconnecting virtue from knowledge.[62]

At 89A–C [398–402] accepting the separation of nature and teaching in accordance with Meno's opening question, Socrates makes a rather bizarre argument from which he concludes, "then the good become good not by nature." Setting up what is taken for a contrary-to-fact conditional, Socrates argues,

> If the good were to become so by nature, we would, I guess, have people who recognized those among the youth with good natures, whom, after we took them from those who had revealed them, we would guard on the Acropolis, setting our seal on them much more than we do with gold, so

that no one could corrupt them, and that when they should come of age, they could become useful to their cities. (89B [400])[63]

Meno agrees, and Socrates draws the above-mentioned conclusion.

The theme of nature and natural endowment also comes up implicitly in Socrates' discussion with Meno of Theognis' poetry (95C–96A [468–474]). He charges Theognis with "saying opposite things about the same things [i.e., the teachability of virtue] to himself." But, as R. S. Bluck notes,[64] "there is no real contradiction, and Plato can hardly have been unaware of this. . . . In the first four lines that Plato quotes a satisfactory native endowment (*noos* [intellect]) is assumed to be present," in the other lines quoted "the necessary native endowment [*noêma*, intelligence] is assumed to be either absent or perverted." This discussion began with the question about whether the Sophists are or are not teachers of virtue, and Socrates, Bluck suggests, is here deliberately mimicking the Sophists' usual manner of taking words out of context in interpreting poetry. The evidence for the power of nature is presented, while that evidence is rhetorically undermined to make way for the more popular, and, for Meno, more convincing substitute for nature, divine dispensation.

The "other way" of Meno's opening speech, anticipated at 87D [366], by which "virtue comes to be there for those for whom it may come to be there (*paragignêtai*)" (100B [564]), is divine dispensation and divine possession. It can be said to be the opposite of the previous arguments, because through it, Socrates says, the divinely inspired set straight many great affairs without intelligence (*nous*) or knowledge of what they do or say (99C–100A [554–562]).[65]

There are echoes of Plato's *Meno* throughout the *Nicomachean Ethics*, but nowhere more than in the book's final chapter, Chapter Nine of Book Ten, the introduction to Aristotle's *Politics*. Aristotle there explains why, after his *Ethics*, "in order that to the best of our power the philosophy of human things may be completed," a book on "legislation" and "polity as a whole," the *Politics*, is required. The argument is straightforward: "If words and arguments (*logoi*) [like those found in the *Nicomachean Ethics*] were sufficient in themselves to make men decent, many and great would be the fees they would justly bear away, as Theognis says." In Theognis, the if-clause of this hypothetical is: "If god granted this to the physicians, to cure vice and blindly ruinous sentiments of men."[66] As Burnet puts it, Aristotle's "quotation is suggested by Plato, *Meno*, 95E,"[67] where Socrates' if-clause is: "If intelligence (*noêma*) could be put into a man." Some rare, noble young people, it seems, can be moved by words and arguments, but most people are moved more by passion, especially by fear of punishment, than by the shame that accompanies respect and operates preventively against vice. Passion, in general, Aristotle argues, is thought to yield not to reason and to argument, but to force.

The echoes from the *Meno*, both from its beginning and its end, are loudest at 1179b20–23:

> Some suppose that people become good by nature, others that it is by habit, and still others that it is by teaching. Now while it is clear that what characterizes nature does not belong to those things that are in our power; but that it does belong to those who are truly fortunate through some divine cause.

Aristotle here disjoins the conjoined just as Meno did, but as he did before in the *Ethics*, he shows in the ensuing discussion how they work together. And here, he also connects nature and divinity, but not as opposites as Socrates did at the end of the *Meno*, but more moderately, as cooperating causes (cf. *NE*, 1099b9–24).

Aristotle goes on to say, "And argument and teaching are perhaps not effective with everyone, but what is needed is for the soul of the hearer to have been worked up beforehand by habits just as the soil is in order to nurture the seed, so as both to enjoy and to hate nobly." This working up beforehand is to be accomplished through the impersonal, but necessitous, authority of the laws, making what was originally unpleasant for the young become customary and no longer painful.[68] As a matter of fact, he goes on, this will be needed throughout adult life too: "For most people are moved to obedience by compulsion rather than by argument and by punishments rather than by the noble."

Whether one might acquire virtue and knowledge about virtue from the Sophists, especially from Gorgias or Protagoras, also seems to be a genuine concern for Meno,[69] yet there is nothing in the *Meno* like the extended critiques of the sophists found in Plato's *Protagoras* and *Gorgias*.[70]

Aristotle's themes in this chapter, the insufficiency of *logoi* and the need for laws enforced within a political order, require him to say something about "the Sophists who advertise themselves as teachers of politics, [but] appear to be very far from teaching it." For, if they knew what it was about, they "would never have set it down as the same as, or subordinate to, rhetoric." They lack political skill and political experience; "for those with experience in particular matters rightly judge the works there produced and understand through what and how they are brought to completion, and what kinds of things harmonize with what."[71]

When Aristotle argues that it is impossible, or at least not easy, to carry out noble actions if one is unequipped with external goods like "friends," wealth or political power,[72] he seems to be making what Socrates ironically disparaged as Meno's special contribution to the discussion of virtue.[73] Is this to be understood as a departure by Aristotle from the teachings of his teachers, Socrates and Plato? Perhaps, but could not Aristotle respond, "Did not the same Plato who wrote Socrates' speeches also write Meno's?"

The intractability of human nature, not in all people, but most people ("the many"), is presented in the final chapter of the *Nicomachean Ethics* as a fundamental condition calling for compulsory legislation and political life. This account, however, must be supplemented by what is said in Aristotle's books on friendship and in the *Politics* about human beings as social, political and rational animals by nature, prompted by that nature to yearn, moderately, for a community that might do justice to that rationality.[74] Near the beginning of the *Politics*,[75] speaking of the self-sufficient political community, Aristotle remarks that although it *comes into being* for the sake of life, it *is* for the sake of the good life. The fulfillment of a more primitive potency opens the way for an eventually even more fulfilling potency, all according to nature.

NOTES

The author is grateful to George Anastaplo, Gisela Berns, and Joseph Cohen for helpful comments on early drafts of this essay.

1 *Phronēsis* is the virtue of practical thoughtfulness, good practical judgment, practical intelligence, practical wisdom. "Prudence" comes from the Latin *prudens,* a contraction for *providens,* "looking ahead." In the preceding chapter prudence is distinguished from cleverness, that is, prudence presupposes good natural predispositions for virtue, its more specialized work is discerning and choosing the right means for achieving those good ends.

2 Plato, *Meno,* translated by George Anastaplo and Laurence Berns (Newburyport, Mass.: Focus Publishing/R. Pullins Co., 2004). The numbers in brackets are speech numbers. In the Anastaplo-Berns translation every speech is numbered. See 87C–89A [356 (end)–396].

3 Cf. Aristotle, *Nicomachean Ethics* (hereafter, *NE*) 1094b18–19 and 1144b8–9.

4 *NE,* 1143a35–1143b6. *Nous* opens us to the ultimate units of intelligibility contained in the particulars of sense perception, as well as in the ultimate terms of philosophical and scientific demonstrations. The intellectual power that is

most visible in practical reasoning is *dianoia*, linking thought (often translated understanding). *Dia-* is a linking prefix: consider dialogue and dialectic. (*Dianoia*, linking thought, in a negative sentence, links subjects and predicates by unlinking their meanings.) For the units to be linked meaningfully they must at the same time be distinguished, i.e., their differences recognized. The activity of *dianoia* combines the intelligible and sensible units into the meaningful conceptions and judgments of rational discourse, e.g., "That [unit 1] is a dog [unit 2]." Cf. the account of "dianoetic eikasia" in Jacob Klein, *A Commentary on Plato's Meno* (Chapel Hill: The University of North Carolina Press, 1965), 115–25.

5   *NE*, 3.6.1115a25–35.

6   Aristotle's treatment of courage in Book III is discussed in greater detail in Laurence Berns, "Spiritedness in Ethics and Politics: A Study in Aristotelian Psychology," *Interpretation: A Journal of Political Philosophy* (May & September 1984): 343–45.

7   This ending of chapter viii returns to and calls into question chapter vi's beginning in common opinion, for the "courage" discussed in chapter vi is now listed as first among the *likenesses* of courage.

8   *Meno*, 72A–72D [12–18], 86C–86E [354–356 beginning], 100B [564]. The fact that Socrates is never able to arrive at a solution with Meno, as he could in his "exhibition" inquiry with the Slave-boy, could suggest that the most fundamental problem of the *Meno* is the problem of inquiry itself. Consider the two occasions that move the Slave-boy to swear oaths. (*Meno*, translated by Anastaplo and Berns, Appendix A [Oaths in the *Meno*], 77.)

9   *Meno*, 72A–72D [12–16]. We note that Socrates' statement about the *eidos* presents one and the same *eidos* as constituting the being of the things of which it is the *eidos* and as functioning as a cognitive principle for the percipient of the *eidos*. That which the knower knows is in some way the same as that which constitutes the object known, that is, if there is genuine knowledge of that object.

10   "Piece" translates *morion*, derived from the word *meros*, part, and *-ion*, a diminutive suffix, meaning then "small part," or "small portion," or "piece of." There is more on the language of this section in *Meno*, trans. Anastaplo and Berns, note on 79A [170], 59.

11   *Meno*, 77A [112], 79B–D [172, 176].

12   Alfred Mollin and Robert Williamson, *An Introduction to Ancient Greek*, 3rd ed. (Lanham, Md.: University Press of America, 1997), 339. This volume contains the Greek text of the *Meno* with extensive grammatical and interpretive annotation.

13   I am grateful to Eva Brann for encouraging me to pursue this line of inquiry.

14   Strictly speaking, Aristotle refers to it as a special kind of equivocal term which points to one primary meaning, among others. See *Metaphysics*, 4.2.1003a32–b6.

15 Socrates' "model" in the Slave-boy scene is a mathematical model. In more complicated subject matters we may have to reconcile ourselves to the fullest possible clarity about serious alternative solutions.

16 *Hairesis* is simple choosing, which all animals, including irrational animals, engage in. It is also the political term for election. The *pro* in Aristotle's *prohairesis* points to the engagement of intellect in deliberate or rational choice. Someone can have a right opinion about something and yet choose wrongly: the opinion did not form or shape the choice. See NE 1112a10–11 and 1113a17–20, where choice is not made correctly and the *pro* disappears. But see 1151a5–7, where choice is deliberate, but wrong. (A very old translation nicely translates *prohairetikê* as pre-elective.) Cf. NE 1139b4–5, "*Prohairesis,* therefore, is either appetitive *nous* or dianoetic appetite"—or, we note, both. See note 4 above.

17 Joe Sachs (*Nicomachean Ethics,* translation [Newburyport, Mass.: Focus Publishing/R. Pullins Co., 2002]) joins Burnet (*The Ethics of Aristotle* [London: Methuen & Co., 1900]) and Bywater (*Aristotelis Ethica Nicomachea* [*Oxonii:* Oxford University Press, 1949]) in accepting the emendation (*hôi*) "by the means by which" for the manuscripts' (*hôs*) "as," and in translating *logôi* as "proportion." I do not disagree with the interpretation conveyed by Sachs's and Burnet's moves, but find it implicit in the manuscripts' more natural language. Sachs's translation of *phronêsis,* "practical judgment," is easily understandable as good practical judgment, but, Aristotle cautions us (*NE* 1179b8–21), much, if not most, "practical judgment" is bad practical judgment. Cf. note 1 above.

18 This is not to argue that general rules are altogether useless, but that if, in any particular situation, rules are to be used, the question becomes what rule, or principle, is appropriate? This depends upon a correct assessment of the situation, an assessment "as the prudent man would determine it."

19 *Kalon,* beauty; the word noble focuses on that special form of beauty that is ethical beauty. (There is another word in Greek for what is called nobility of birth, *gennaion.*) Joe Sachs, who consistently translates the word as beautiful, argues (op. cit., xxi) that "noble" probably first brings to mind a kind of hopelessly impractical high-minded naiveté. This was also Shakespeare's Edmund's view in *King Lear,* "a brother noble, / Whose nature is so far from doing harms / That he suspects none; on whose foolish honesty / My practices ride easy" (1.2.186–87). This was always the view of the more cynically minded. But by the end of the play Edmund is killed and his noble brother prevails. It seems to me that in the context of current talk "beautiful" is subject to even more corruption than "noble." The advantage of translating *kalon* as "beautiful" is connecting the word with the other associations beauty has. But that advantage does not overweigh the loss of the grand old word that especially distinguishes the kind of ethical beauty that Aristotle and Shakespeare talk about. (See the four and one half pages of small print under "nobility" and "noble" in Bartlett's *Complete Concordance to Shakespeare's Dramatic Works.*)

20 *NE,* 1113a29–33, see also 1176a16–23.

21 The "other way" will be discussed below in Section VI.

22   Burnet notes that here Aristotle relies on his understanding that "nature" has both its "principle of motion," potency, capacity, and its "principle of rest [or standstill]," goal, or end, in itself (op. cit., 76 [note 17 above]). See Aristotle, *Physics*, 192b8–193a2. Despite common usage, it is not difficult for thoughtful readers of English to see the "act" in "actuality." "Actuality," based on the Latin adjective for being in activity and, in Aristotle, keyed to a specific capacity or potency, has, with reference to its potency, a sense of "fulfilling activity," pointing to the more explicit Aristotelian word *entelecheia*, holding on in fulfillment, or in completion (*Metaphysics*, 1015a11–19). Concerning habit in *Meno*, see 70B [2], 75A [70], 76D [106], 82A [197], and 86D [356].

23   By disposition I mean tendency to act. Sachs (op. cit. [note 17 above]) translates *hexis* as active condition, getting the "holding" in *hex* (from *exô*) with condition and the action in -*sis* with active. I think of the "holding" in the disposing and the action in the -tion (-*sis*) suffix. The differences, it seems to me, concern how the English words will be understood: both disposition and condition could, mistakenly in these cases, be understood as implying passivity. Cf. John Burnet, *Plato's Phaedo* (Oxford: Clarendon Press, 1956), 106, on *Phaedo*, 99B 3.

24   "The *mesotês* [mean state] is 'rationally determined,' or 'determined according to the proper ratio or proportion'" (J. A. Stewart, *Notes on the Nicomachean Ethics of Aristotle*, vol. 1 [Oxford: Clarendon Press, 1892], 200). The word *logos*, which means reason, meaning, argument, speech and selection, is also a mathematical term meaning ratio or proportion. The *logos* in our definition can properly be rendered reason, or ratio or proportion, or, perhaps, rationally proportioned.

25   *Meno*, 73D–E [45–49].

26   See Aristotle, *Politics*, 1322b12–37 and 1328b11–13. These passages are discussed by Leo Strauss, *The City and Man* (Chicago: Rand McNally & Co., 1964), 32–34. See also 22–23. Religion, Thomas Aquinas argues, is attached (*adjungitur*) to justice. See *Summa Theologiae*, II-II, Q. 80; Q.81, A. 2; see also Q. 94, A.1.

27   In the *Politics*, Aristotle, conceiving of the most perfect form of law, says, "The law is intellect (*nous*) without appetite." But this has been qualified: "He that orders the law to rule seems to be ordering god and intellect alone to rule, but he that orders man to rule also adds a beast: for such is desire (*epithumia*), and spiritedness too perverts rulers, even the best men (*andras*)" (1287a16–32).

28   See *NE*, 1180b3–13.

29   Shame-respect is praiseworthy and usually operates preventively against vice. There is another word for shame in Greek connected with the word for ugly, shame-disgrace (*aischunê*), that is felt when one is caught in some disgraceful action.

30   *Nemesis* is from the same verbal root as the Greek word for law, *nomos*, namely *nemô*, to distribute or to deal out. It is aroused by the presence of something that is "not right!" In the middle or reflexive voice of its verbal form (*nemessô-mai*), where its meaning is referred to the subject of the sentence, or to the

speaker him- or herself, it can convey the dissatisfaction or displeasure with oneself that we tend to speak of as "conscience."

31 See Plato, *Laws,* 731D–732A.

32 Stewart, op. cit., 200–04 (note 24 above).

33 Again, for Aristotle, nature is not only the primitive beginnings *out of which* a natural being develops, but even more the *active fulfillment* of what the natural being is meant to develop into. Cf. note 23 above. For this linking of nature and soul, see Joe Sachs, trans., Aristotle, *On the Soul* (Santa Fe, N.M.: Green Lion Press, 2001), introduction, especially 8–10; and Leon R. Kass, M.D., *The Hungry Soul: Eating and the Perfecting of Our Nature* (New York: The Free Press, 1994), chapter 1. Both of these recent essays present the fundamental evidence for the scientific and philosophical conception of the soul with more than competent critical analysis of the philosophical and scientific objections to that conception.

34 Abstraction, *aphairesis,* "taking away," according to Aristotle, is used only by mathematicians to take away or to neglect all perceptible qualities in natural bodies in order to theorize solely about the numerical and continuous geometrical quantities found in them (*Metaphysics,* 1061a28–1061b3). In Plato's *Crito* (46C 6), the word is used for *confiscations* of money. See also Aristotle, *Politics* 1281a26.

35 *NE,* Sachs translation, 108, n. 155. See also note 9 and accompanying text, above. Sachs avoids the usual misconceptions by translating *epagôgê* as "example." See the glossary in his translation of Aristotle's *On the Soul,* 192–93. See also in his *NE* translation the remarkable note 168, p. 114. The prospect held out in the penultimate sentence of that note is amply clarified by pp. 31–38 of his Introduction to *On the Soul.*

36 See the text quoted at note 20 above.

37 *De Motu Animalium,* 702a15–21.

38 See Sachs's glossaries under "abstraction" in his translations of Aristotle's *Physics, Metaphysics,* or *On the Soul.*

39 Thomas Aquinas, *Commentary on De Anima,* translated by Kenelm Foster and Sylvester Humphries (New Haven: Yale University Press, 1959), §§395–98. Controversies in connection with such distinctions are still very much alive. See, for example, Paul Bloom, "Can a Dog Learn a Word?" in *Science,* vol. 304 (11 June 2004): 1605–06; and Raymond and Laura Coppinger, *Dogs: A New Understanding of Canine Origin, Behavior, and Evolution* (Chicago: University of Chicago Press, 2001), 217–20 (a new border collie mother retrieves a tape recorder sending out a puppy's "I am lost" signal and puts it in the nest with her puppies).

40 *Meno,* 72C [16], 78C [150], 80D [184], 81B [194], 82C [212], 82E [226], 82E [232], 84C [288], 86D [356], 86E [356], 87B [356], 87C [362], 87D [363] (Meno speaking), 87E [374], 88A [378], 88A [380], 88B [382], 89D [408], 90B [412], 91A [422], 93B [440] (4x), 94A [452], 94A [454], 96D [489] (Meno speaking), 96E [490].

41 *Meno*, 80A [179]. The word is used three times by Socrates between 72C and 72E, speeches 16, 18, and 20.

42 This requires qualification. The inquiry is a model for Meno: to show him how the careful exposure of one's own ignorance furthers inquiry and benefits him who is so exposed. But in itself it is perhaps rather a model prelude to inquiry, for in that whole Slave-boy scene the "What is . . . ?" question is never raised.

43 *Meno*, 75B [78]. The word for color, *chrôma*, also means visible surface. Edmund Husserl, it seems, would have appreciated Socrates' definition. See *Die Krisis der Europäischen Wissenschaften und die Transzendentale Phänomenologie*, edited by Walter Biemel (The Hague, Netherlands: Martinus Nijhof, 1976), Part II, §9, c, 32–36: *The Crisis of European Sciences and Transcendental Phenomenology*, translated by David Carr (Evanston: Northwestern University Press, 1970), Part II, §9, c, 34–37.

44 E.g., 89E [412]. See the end of note 22 above.

45 See Plato's *Phaedo* 99B2–4. See also the reference to *NE* in note 62 below.

46 The words for "foot" and "feet" in classical Greek can be used to measure both lines and areas, that is, both linear units and area units. They know the difference, but (certainly in the *Meno*) they do not say "square feet." *Meno*, 82B–E [204–225].

47 Numbers in classical times are restricted to what modern mathematicians call positive whole numbers. They are always numbers of things, either perceptible things or the pure monads or units of arithmetical science. Euclid, Book VII, definition 2, defines number as a multitude composed of units, which means that the first number is two, although the unit, "1," is perfectly usable in arithmetic calculations.

48 *Meno*, 84E–85A [302]. See Anastaplo and Berns translation, Appendix B, [Geometrical Diagrams], Figures 47–50 and 64, pp. 84–85. Socrates does not mention the Pythagorean Theorem, but his diagrams and the argument he makes to show that the line he constructed is indeed the sought-for line could be used to explicate the Pythagorean Theorem.

49 Ibid., note on [274] 83E–84A, p. 63. Theaetetus calls these lines which we might call square root lines, "powers (*dunameis*)," meaning straight lines capable of allowing certain specified squares to be constructed on them. Euclid says that, while the diagonal of a square is incommensurable in length with the side of its own square, those lines are "commensurable in square." In *Theaetetus* 147D Theodorus probably used the Pythagorean Theorem and an isosceles right triangle with sides equal to one to derive the square root of two line, then a right triangle with one side equal to one and the other equal to the square root of two line to derive the square root of three line, the square root of two line and the square root of three line to derive the square root of five line, etc.

50 *NE*, Sachs translation, 83. Other translations are "corrective" or "commutative" justice.

51 Aristotle does begin this discussion by reference to that steady disposition of the soul from which people are apt to seek, to do, and to want just things. The "mean" for the truly just *human being* does fit the general definition despite its difference from the mean of the just distribution.

52 Cf. Plato, *Republic*, 545D–547A.

53 See, for example, *NE*, 1132b34–1135a5. These two paragraphs are taken from Laurence Berns, "Aristotle and Adam Smith on Justice: Cooperation Between Ancients and Moderns?" *Review of Metaphysics* (September 1994): 71–90.

54 How these arguments about comparability and equality apply to political functions is discussed in Aristotle, *Politics,* 1282b14–1283a22.

55 What seems to be behind Aristotle's gentle but potent "somehows" is the fact, soon to be made explicit, that the intrinsic commensurability between persons, work and products that the standard of absolutely perfect justice would require does not exist.

56 Cf. Plato, *Republic*, 369A–372A.

57 Stewart, op. cit., vol. 1, p. 463 (see note 24 above).

58 Gisela Berns, "Nomos and Physis (An Interpretation of Euripides' Hippolytos)," *Hermes*, Bd. 101 (1973): 186. See Aristotle, *De Anima,* 415a16–22; Leo Strauss, *Natural Right and History* (Chicago: University of Chicago Press, 1953), 145–46; and Laurence Berns, "Rational Animal—Political Animal: Nature and Convention in Human Speech and Politics," in *Essays in Honor of Jacob Klein* (Annapolis, Md.: St. John's College Press, 1976), 29–35. The distinction between natural and unnatural exchange is developed in Aristotle's *Politics* 1256b27–1257b5.

59 "Everything is measured by money" seems to have been set down here as a generally accepted opinion expressing what is said about money. "Everything" seems to mean here every good, evil or service for which equal exchange of external goods is expected.

60 For the first alternative, consider 99A [548] to the end of the dialogue, for the second alternative, consider, among other places, 88A–D [380–388].

61 Meno never objects to these arguments. Anytus gets angry; perhaps he senses the antidemocratic implications of an argument based on natural inequalities (he may well fancy himself to be the successor of one or more of those famous statesmen).

62 Cf. *NE,* 1180b28–1181a13.

63 Socrates speaks here as if they were living in the city in speech of Plato's *Republic.*

64 R. S. Bluck, *Plato's Meno* (Cambridge University Press, 1961), 28–29 and 395.

65 In Plato's *Timaeus* (71A–72C) the diviner (*mantis*) "who utters oracles while not in his right mind but in a state of divine frenzy" is distinguished by Timaeus from the prophet (*prophêtês*) who in his right mind judges and interprets such oracles. The word *mantis,* but not *prophêtês,* does occur in the *Meno.*

George Anastaplo suggests that the fact that this is an "opposition" is indicated very early in the dialogue, 71B [2], where Socrates imitates Meno's disjoining of conjoined powers in his opening speech by asking whether "someone who has no cognizance of Meno at all, who he is, could know whether he is handsome *or* rich *or* well-born *or* the opposite of these" (emphasis added). We learn, he argues, "in the course of the dialogue that Meno himself is indeed handsome *and* rich *and* well-born (in the conventional sense of these terms), not 'the opposite of these'" (*On Trial: From Adam and Eve to O. J. Simpson* [Lanham, Md.: Lexington Books, 2004], 138).

66 See Bluck, op. cit., 394 (note 64 above).

67 Burns, op. cit., 468 (note 17 above). Aristotle adds "justly" to "bear off" in the otherwise common then-clause.

68 There is a distinction between habit as understood here in relation to incomplete childlike or youthful souls, and the completing or perfecting habits that persons of more advanced understanding need in order to bring their actions in line with what they are capable of understanding. See, above, the text of Aristotle containing note 22. In regard to childlike or youthful souls, consider *NE*, 1094a6–13: "And it makes no difference whether one is young in age or immature in character, for the defect is not a matter of time, but of living and pursuing each thing according to feeling. . . ."

69 See 70B–71D [2–10], 95B–C [462–469].

70 Meno, Callicles (of the *Gorgias*), and Hippocrates (of the *Protagoras*) all seem to be primarily practical men who have been impressed by and attracted to the intellectual fireworks of the sophists in a much more powerful way than they were ever attracted to Socrates' dialectical arts. They might be called intellectuals, even somewhat educated men (e.g., Meno's knowledge of geometry), but not scholars. Why did Plato devote a good-sized dialogue to the ways and ideas of each of them, to Protagoras and to Gorgias? They might be brought to function in ways uncongenial to Socrates himself as intermediaries between Socratic philosophy and practical life, between philosophy and spirited and intellectual men like Meno, Callicles and Hippocrates.

71 See *NE*, 1181a12–b11, and *Metaphysics*, 981a12–b 9.

72 See *NE*, 1099a30–1099b25.

73 See *Meno*, 78C–D [148–156], and Aristotle, *Politics*, 1260a25–28.

74 In the *Politics* too the opening of the *Meno* is reflected in Aristotle's introduction to his extended discussion of education where (1332a38–b11) he asserts, "But surely men become good [*agathoi*] and seriously good [*spoudaioi*] through three things, and these three are nature, habit and rational speech [*logos*]." In the sequel he makes clear that his *logos* embraces Meno's teaching and learning, and that "these [nature, habit and *logos*] are required to harmonize [*symphōnein*] with one another."

75 Aristotle, *Politics*, 1252b27–31.

THE ELEATIC STRANGER AND PARMENIDES IN PLATO'S *SOPHIST*

David Bolotin

AT THE CENTER of Plato's *Sophist* the Eleatic stranger undertakes an examination of being and non-being in order to refute the claim of his teacher Parmenides that it is impossible for (the) things that are not, to be. The stranger must attempt to refute this claim in order to defend his own assertion that the sophist is a producer of falsehood, for falsehood first comes to light as the opinion that the things that are not, are, which opinion would be impossible without the being, at least in some sense, of non-being (240d2–e4; cf. 237a3–9, 241d1–242a4).[1] Yet it is noteworthy, and surprising, that before turning to this refutation, the stranger first attempts to *support* Parmenides' claim with arguments of his own. Why does he do this? From the character of his arguments, it appears that he is concerned to rule out non-being in one particular sense of the term, which he will later speak of—in contrast to otherness, or the non-being that he claims to have shown to be—as the "opposite" of being (258e6–259b1). He argues, first, that the term "non-being," since it cannot refer to anything that is, cannot refer to anything at all, and so cannot enter into meaningful speech. He then adds the argument, which he presents as the first and greatest of the perplexities about non-being, that non-being itself is unthinkable and unsayable, on the grounds that one could not even think it without thinking of it as one (or else as many) and that one and many, like anything else that is, can be attributed only to being, or that which is. These arguments, however, prove to undercut themselves, for the stranger is compelled to admit that in his own claim that non-being (in the singular) is unthinkable and unsayable, he has violated his own prohibition by presuming to speak of it as being and as one. And thus he finally confesses that for a long time, as well as now, he has been defeated "concerning the refutation of non-being" (239b2–3; cf. 237b10–239a12). To this difficulty we might add the consideration, which the stranger alludes to later, that even if non-being is indeed unthinkable and unsayable, this does not necessarily mean that Parmenides' original claim is true, for it is not simply evident that the unthinkable and unsayable cannot be (259a1). And so we are left with our original question, of why the

–27–

stranger prefaces his refutation of Parmenides with an effort to support his claim, together with the further question of the implications of his failure in this effort.

Let us return for now to the former question. Since the stranger presents his arguments as support for a claim by Parmenides, it may be helpful to look to the extant fragments of Parmenides' poem itself in order to understand why a philosopher might seek to refute non-being. What we find there is that Parmenides had also asserted that non-being is unthinkable and unsayable, using this assertion as grounds for his rejection of the way of inquiry which claims that "it is not" (fragment 2, v. 6). For to assert that "it," or being, is not is to have made a claim about what is not, but such a claim presupposes a conception of what is not, or of non-being, the possibility of which Parmenides here denies. Still, why would anyone even be tempted to assert that being is not? Parmenides suggests an answer to this question in another of his fragments, where he argues that being, or being as a whole, is ungenerated and imperishable. For if it were generated, it would presumably have to have been generated from non-being; but Parmenides forbids the assertion of such an origin on the grounds that it would involve the inconceivable thought of a prior state in which being is not (fragment 8, vv. 1–9). In other words, Parmenides argues that there are only two fundamental alternatives, either the conceivable one that being is, and that it is necessary and eternal, or else the inconceivable one that being is not. What might seem to be a third alternative, that being is, but only as a consequence of having first come into being, is by this argument just another version of the second. And although it is hard to imagine anyone even trying to assert the absurdity that being is not, the claim that it has come into being has in fact been made by serious thinkers.

The most important of these thinkers, from the perspective of both Parmenides and the Eleatic stranger, is the poet Hesiod, who tells us in his *Theogony,* or rather whose Muses tell us there, that "at first Chaos came into being," followed by Earth, Tartarus, and Eros, and in each case from nothing at all, so far as we are told (*Theogony* v. 116–122). Hesiod or his Muses further tell us that all the gods, though they have come into being, are nevertheless immortal and continue to live forever (*Theogony* vv. 21, 33, 43, 74, 118, 120, 128, etc.). Hesiod's acceptance here of the traditional view that the gods have come into being and yet continue to live forever does more than anything else, I think, to explain his bold suggestion that there were first gods who came into being from nothing. For if the gods are generated but immortal, then even though they are not necessary beings, that is, even though it is possible in principle for them not to be, as their origin shows, this possibility will never manifest itself in the future. But this implies that in a decisive sense, despite the fact that they are said to have parents, they do not come *from* anything at all: they do not come from any material, for any material of beings like these, which are presumed not to have always been, would for that reason have to have inherent tendencies that do not simply serve their being, and that would eventually destroy them. Accordingly, Hesiod's suggestion that there were first gods who came into being from nothing is meant as an indication of what must be presupposed by those who accept the Olympian gods.

There are further consequences of this supposition. For if something can come from nothing, then anything can come from anything. Any kind of fruit, for instance, could come from any kind of tree (cf. Lucretius, *De Rerum Natura* Book I, vv. 159–166). Men and women who are born as mortals could become immortal through the help of the gods, as in fact Hesiod says that some do (cf. *Theogony,* vv. 940–955). And in general beings, or kinds of beings, would not have unchanging natures, or limits to what they can do and what they can suffer. And if the beings, or kinds of beings, have no fixed limits to what they can do and what they can suffer, there could be no knowledge of what they are, as distinct from mere acquaintance with them. No wonder, then, that a philosopher, or a seeker of such knowledge, would attempt to refute Hesiod's suggestion, since if it were true philosophy itself would be a vain endeavor.

Parmenides' claim, however, that it is impossible for (the) things that are not, to be goes well beyond a denial that being as a whole could have come into being from nothing. For one thing, his use of the plural form in the expression "(the) things that are not" helps call our attention to the fact that he never speaks of what truly is, in the extant fragments at any rate, except in the singular. And he later tells us explicitly that the fundamental error of mortals is a version of the belief in multiplicity, namely, in the duality of opposite forms as perceived by the senses (fragment 8, vv. 50–59). Accordingly, his denial that (the) things that are not can be is also a denial of multiplicity, or a denial that there can truly be beings that are not one another (cf. *Sophist* 242d4–7). And in addition to this, there is a further sense in which things that are not might be thought to be, and there is explicit evidence that Parmenides' denial extends to it as well. For beings that come into being and perish, or that undergo change in any respect, are not, or not of some particular character or in some particular place, at one time, though they are at others. And Parmenides asserts in a later passage that coming into being and perishing, as well as change of place and change of color, are mere names (fragment 8, vv. 36–41). For him to say, then, that it is impossible that (the) things that are not are—or, as we can also translate his words, that (the) things that *were* not are—is to assert the illusoriness not only of multiplicity, but also of change (fragment 7, vv. 3–6; cf. fragment 6, vv. 4–9).

But why does Parmenides attempt to deny the apparently obvious facts of multiplicity and change? In order to begin to answer this question, it is helpful to consider the first book of Aristotle's *Metaphysics*, in which Aristotle presents the denial of change, at any rate, as a response by some of the early philosophers to a difficulty in the teachings of their philosophic predecessors. Most of the early philosophers, according to Aristotle, thought that the only principles of all things were of the material kind, such as water or air, out of which all things come into being and into which they perish. More precisely, they thought that this principle (or these principles, if there are many) is the true underlying being, and that what we speak of as coming into being and perishing are in fact only changes in the incidental attributes of this nature, which is always preserved (*Metaphysics*, 983b5–18). Aristotle adds, however, that it was eventually seen to be necessary to seek another kind of cause as well, since even on the assumption that there are one or more permanent natures underlying all coming into being and perishing, there remains the question of what is responsible for these changes in attributes. And he goes on to say that some of those who spoke of only one underlying being, "as if defeated by this inquiry," came to the position that this one, or nature as a whole, is unchanging, not merely with respect to coming into being and perishing—the denial of which had been agreed to by all the philosophers—but with respect to every other kind of change as well (*Metaphysics* 984a16–b1; cf. 986b10–17). Aristotle does not explain here why the question of what is responsible for changes in the attributes of the underlying being or beings should be so difficult as to lead to such a paradoxical response. But the reason would appear to be this. If the allegedly permanent being or beings can change in at least some of their attributes without our adequately understanding why, as in fact we do not, this shows our ignorance regarding the beings themselves as well. Can we say, then, that we know the limits of what they can do and what they can suffer? Do we truly know that they are necessary beings, or even that they could not have arisen from nothing, as Hesiod suggests that the first beings did? And if we do not know this, as we seem not to, the attempt by the earliest philosophers to rule out the Hesiodic alternative, or to secure the intelligibility of the world by showing it to be grounded in some permanent and necessary substrate, is unsuccessful. Accordingly, Parmenides and the Eleatic school tried to buttress their other—not wholly conclusive—arguments against the alternative of coming into being from nothing with the claim that change itself is illusory.

As for the denial of multiplicity, to the extent that this is not simply a consequence of the denial of change and therefore of the evidence of our senses, one of Aristotle's main criticisms of this position in the *Physics* suggests that here too Parmenides was led to his claim by a concern to secure the intelligibility of being. Aristotle presents Parmenides as arguing that since there is nothing other than being or that which is, and since the term "being" has a single meaning, then that which is must be one. But in addition to denying at least the latter of these two premises, Aristotle objects to the argument itself that even if we consider only the white things, and even if white has only one meaning, the white things (and, indeed, even a single white thing) would still be many, since to be white is different from that which receives whiteness. This is the case even if that which receives whiteness is inseparable from its being white, for there is still a distinction here, one that according to Aristotle Parmenides did not yet comprehend (*Physics* 186a22–32; cf. *Metaphysics* 986b27–31). It seems impossible, however, that Parmenides could have simply failed to understand such a commonly acknowledged distinction as that between a characteristic and that which possesses it. And so let me suggest, rather, that his denial of multiplicity was an attempt to reject this distinction in the case of being itself, and with the aim of overcoming doubts as to its intelligibility. For no matter how intelligible a characteristic, including the characteristic "being," may be, the distinction between it and that which possesses it—at least if we apply this distinction, as is reasonable, to all characteristics—implies that this possessor, and thus the being as a whole, is not simply intelligible. Just as the fact that white things can change color reveals that there is something about them other than their being white, and indeed something that we do not adequately understand, so the very distinction between characteristics and that which possesses characteristics implies that we do not fully understand any particular being as a whole. We do not, therefore, know the limits to what it can do and what it can suffer, and we cannot even wholly rule out the alternative that it may have come into being from nothing. And it was in an attempt to escape this difficulty, with its threat to the possibility of philosophy, that Parmenides denied the particularity of being by making the paradoxical suggestion that being is only one.

But let us return to the Eleatic stranger, for it was in an effort to understand his reasons for trying, at first, to support Parmenides' claims that we were led to this consideration of Parmenides' reasons for making them. Now the stranger clearly shares his teacher's concern to secure the possibility of philosophy, as can be seen most simply perhaps from the central argument of the dialogue as a whole, which seeks to defend the view of the sophist as a deceiver and a producer of falsehood by refuting the sophist's argument that there is no falsehood (240c8–241b3; 260b7–d3). Like Socrates in the *Theaetetus,* the stranger is well aware that the possibility of knowledge or science (ἐπιστήμη), and hence of philosophy, is incompatible with the sophistic claim that all opinion is true in the sense of being true for the one who holds it. But unlike Socrates, his explicit statements about philosophy and its presuppositions do not set them against the alternative of sophistic relativism. Rather, he presents philosophy as following from the assumption that some kinds of things, but only some, can mix with or share in one another, in the sense, for instance, that motion and rest can be said to share in being, since they both are. For since, he says, only some kinds of things can mix with one another, there is a need for a science, which he calls dialectics and which he assigns to the philosopher, to determine which can mix with which and which cannot (252e9–253e5). The alternative presuppositions, which the stranger rejects, are that nothing or no kind of thing can mix with anything else, or that everything can mix with everything. Now the stranger explicitly characterizes the former of these views, since it implies that nothing can be said of anything else, as being destructive of all speeches, and hence of philosophy (259d9–260a7). And though he doesn't say so explicitly, the view that everything can mix with everything else is also destructive of philosophy, for if it were true, then horses might talk, humans might grow wings, and so on: the beings would have no fixed natures or limits to what they can do and what they can suffer, and on these grounds, as I have argued earlier, philosophy would be impossible.

The stranger's argument, then, that some, but only some, kinds of things can mix with one another is designed to show the possibility, as well as the necessity, of philosophy. And it thus stands to reason that his earlier arguments in support of Parmenides' denial of non-being, with its implicit denial of coming into being from nothing (and of all that would follow from it), were also motivated by the concern to confirm this possibility. Now of course those arguments in support of Parmenides proved to be unsuccessful. But since this later argument appears to succeed in ruling out the two alternatives incompatible with philosophy, the failure of those earlier arguments might no longer seem to be so important. For if it has been shown that there is mixing of kinds, but only within definite and stable limits, there may be less of a need for a further argument against non-being. It turns out, however, that the argument for accepting the conclusion that only some of the kinds can mix with one another is far less adequate than it first appears.

Initially, it was Theaetetus who had claimed to be able to settle this question about the mixing of kinds, and he tried to do so by arguing that motion and rest cannot mix with or share in one another, on the grounds that such mixing would require motion itself to be altogether at rest and rest itself to be in motion (252d2–11). But why couldn't motion be at rest or unchanging[2] in some respects without being "altogether" at rest? In the light of this possibility, it is noteworthy that the stranger expresses only tentative agreement, if any at all, that it is impossible for motion to be at rest and for rest to be in motion. Later, moreover, he reconsiders the alternative that motion might indeed have a share in rest—on the grounds, perhaps, as he had earlier suggested, that motion, insofar as it is intelligible, must have a fixed or unchanging character (256b6–8). And at this point, Theaetetus suggests that he could perhaps admit that there is such mixing, in which case motion would be spoken of as stationary, as long as they will agree that while some of the kinds are willing to mix with one another, some are not. Theaetetus seems more concerned, then, that there be *some* kinds that cannot mix with one another than with persisting in his earlier claim that motion and rest are among these kinds. The stranger replies that they have already demonstrated that some and only some of the kinds can mix with one another, by proving through refutation that this way is in accord with nature (256b9–c2). But in fact the only "proof" they have offered that there are some kinds that cannot mix with one another was based entirely on Theaetetus' earlier argument that motion and rest were such kinds. If this claim is abandoned, there is no longer even the appearance of a proof. And to speak of what is "in accord with nature" hardly seems sufficient in this context, since the very possibility of nature, or of fixed limits to what the beings can do and what they can suffer, is precisely what is in doubt. Now it seems to me that by his manifestly false claim to have given a proof regarding this matter, the stranger indicates that he is aware that there has been no adequate argument against the alternative that all of the kinds, or at least all those that can be imagined to do so without evident contradiction, might be able to mix with one another. And though he chooses to conceal this difficulty from Theaetetus, who is too easily discouraged as it is (cf. 261a5–c4), this challenge to the possibility of philosophy remains unresolved.

Not only, then, has the stranger failed in his attempted refutation of non-being, but also the argument that he seems to endorse against an unlimited mixing of kinds is not really an argument. He is too sober, moreover, to try to secure the intelligibility of being that philosophy requires by following Parmenides in his denial of multiplicity and change. He argues explicitly against the Platonist "friends of the forms," but also against Parmenides and his school, that if there is to be knowledge of even the truest and most unchanging being or beings, there must necessarily be the motion or change involved in its becoming known—a change, as he even suggests, that must affect such being itself (248a4–249b6, especially 248d10–e5; 249c10–d4, 242d5–7). And as for multiplicity, he argues for it explicitly as well, starting with the suggestion that those who try to speak of being as one (or, as he puts it, of the one as being) are by that very fact compelled to acknowledge manyness, since the terms "one" and "being" do not mean the same thing (244b6–c2 ff.). It is true that the manyness on which he most focuses is the manyness of kinds (γένη or εἴδη), especially those that are called the "greatest" kinds, such as being, motion, and rest, rather than the manyness of particulars, which I have argued presents the greatest challenge to philosophy (cf. 254c1–4). But what he means by kinds is in fact classes, that is, classes of particular beings or attributes, and so he thus acknowledges that there are also many particular beings.[3] Indeed, it is most likely because of his thinking of the beings as particular beings primarily that he has suggested that being must be changeable if it is to be known; for if the kinds are classes, they cannot be known without having come into being as the kinds they are through acts of a mind that first surveys the given particulars. And it is the limitedness of our knowledge of these particular and changeable beings that is at the root of the challenge to philosophy that we have been dwelling on.

It now appears that the failure of the stranger's arguments in support of Parmenides' denial that non-being can be is part of a more general failure to show that being is intelligible, or to secure the possibility of philosophy by refuting Hesiod's suggestion that there can be coming into being from nothing. And if the stranger indeed fails to show this, it would follow that when he speaks about philosophy and its lofty task he is speaking with less than certain knowledge. Or is there a way in which he can respond successfully to the challenge that Hesiod's suggestion poses to the possibility of philosophy? Now unfortunately, I am unable to give an adequate answer to this question. But I think I can show that the stranger's argument *against* Parmenides, in which he shows that that which is not is, contains an element that at least makes intelligible a basis on which he might begin to respond to Hesiod's challenge. In order to show this, let me first remind us of my earlier suggestion that his assertion of coming into being from nothing makes sense, to the extent it does, as a necessary consequence of belief in the Olympian gods as beings who come into being but never perish. For what if there are no such gods? These non-beings would still have to be in some sense, since after all we are able to speak of them; but they would have no being apart from human opinions and human speech (cf. 234c2–e2, 240d9–e4, 241a8–b1). And if this is true of the Olympian gods, the evidence that they seemed to provide would prove to be no real basis for the claim that there is coming into being from nothing. To be sure, this would not prove that the assertion of coming into being from nothing is false. But to the extent that genuine evidence is lacking for what is—if I may be allowed the liberty of saying so—an unsayable and unthinkable notion, awareness of this lack of evidence would certainly strengthen the case for its being impossible. And so let me now suggest that the stranger's argument for the being of that which is not is the first step in an attempt to show that there is a kind of being which is only in speech, for if this is indeed the kind of being that belongs to the Olympian gods, there might be a basis for an adequate response to Hesiod's challenge to the possibility of philosophy.

An immediate difficulty with this last suggestion arises from its implication that there are degrees of being, or that there is a kind of being, which we can also call non-being, that is in a lesser sense than the genuine beings. For in his argument that non-being is, the stranger explicitly claims not only that it is, but that it is in no lesser a sense than being itself, as that which is not big and that which is not beautiful belong among the beings just as much as the big and the beautiful do (257e9–258c4). It seems to me, however, that this explicit claim[4] does not correspond to the stranger's true opinion, as we can begin to see, I think, by reflecting on the following difficulty in his account of non-being. The stranger concludes his refutation of Parmenides by saying that not only have they shown that the things that are not are, thus successfully disobeying Parmenides' prohibition against trying to think this thought, but that they have even identified the species of non-being (258d5–7). This species, he goes on to say, is the part of the nature of "the other" opposed to each being or thing that is. That which is other than beautiful, then, or other than big, i.e., not beautiful or not big, is not merely analogous to the species non-being, but an instance of it. The stranger, however, is also well aware that we sometimes say, not that something is not beautiful or not big, but that it is simply not or, to use his expression, that it is not (a) being. And his account of non-being includes an attempt to explain what we mean by this. For his discussion of the interrelations among the five most comprehensive classes culminates in the assertion that that which is not necessarily is in the case of motion and all the classes, on the grounds that motion, which is his example, both is and is not (a) being, since it shares in being while itself being other than being (256c10–e2). Apparently, then, whereas to say that something is not beautiful means that it has no share in the class beauty, to say that it is not (a) being does not mean that it has no share in the class being, but rather that it is itself other than that class. But to leave aside for the moment any other questions as to the adequacy of this account, is the class motion really other than the class being? To be sure, what we mean by the term "motion" is not what we mean by the term "being," so that to say that something is, is not the same as to say that it moves. But does not the class of that which is comprise all that moves as well as all that does not, so that the class motion would be a part of, and not other than, the class being (see *Statesman* 262c10–263b11, especially b2–6)? The stranger had seemed to suggest as much for a moment, only to reject this alternative by speaking of being as a third class, which is other than the classes motion and rest together (250b8–11, c1–d3, 254d4–15; cf. 243d8–244a3). But in speaking in this way has he not substituted otherness in the meaning of the terms "motion," "rest" and "being," or in the defining character of these classes, for otherness of the classes themselves? This dubious understanding of the class being reappears on two other occasions, where the stranger claims that it is other than, not only motion and rest, but all the other classes, either singly or taken together (257a1–6, 259b1–5). On these occasions, however, the stranger invites anyone who is not persuaded by him to disagree or to say something better, an invitation that he makes nowhere else in the dialogue.[5] And so let me suggest that he means these invitations seriously, and that he thus acknowledges that the class being is not, as he appears to believe, one among a number of distinct classes, but rather consists of all the other classes taken together. Indeed, his concluding statement about non-being, namely, that it is the part of the nature of the other opposed to *each* being or thing that is, implies that the class being is nothing else than the totality of different kinds of beings. And if this is true, to say that something is not, or that it is not (a) being, could not mean that it is some particular class other than the particular class being.

But what else could it mean to say that something is not (a) being? I have already suggested that according to the stranger it can mean that it has no being apart from our opinions and our speech, as opposed to the genuine beings, which invite speech on the basis of an antecedently given character. And in order to see how the stranger directs us toward this view, let us consider the immediate sequel to his argument for the being of non-being. Having succeeded in making this case against Parmenides, he tells Theaetetus that they must next consider what speech is, and whether non-being mixes with opinion and speech (260a7–b11). His stated reason for these further questions is that in order to show that the sophist is a deceiver or a producer of falsehood, they must show that there is falsehood, which there cannot be, he argues, unless non-being is capable of mixing with opinion and speech. But from this perspective their discussion is of questionable value, since it never seriously confronts, as Socrates had done in the *Theaetetus*, the sophist's claim that there is no false opinion, or that all opinion is true for the one who holds it (260c1–2, d6–e3; cf. *Theaetetus* 167a6–8). Instead, they simply take for granted the falsity of the stranger's sentence, "Theaetetus, with whom I am now conversing, flies," which falsity they then interpret as the attribution to Theaetetus of things that are not [the case] concerning him. No wonder, then, that the stranger tells Theaetetus, who had expressed discouragement at having to face these additional questions, that false opinion and speech have been discovered more quickly than they had feared (264b6–9). Since this part of their discussion achieves so little with a view to its stated purpose, let me suggest that this was never its only aim. To see what other aim it might also have, it is worth noting that opinion and speech are not the only subjects that are here at issue. For when introducing his account of falsehood, the stranger had presented its existence in opinion and speech as a premise for there being deceit, from which it would follow, as he claims, that all things are necessarily full of images, likenesses, and appearance (260c1–9). Accordingly, when he follows up on their account by claiming that since false speech and false opinion have shown themselves to be, there is room for there to be imitations of the beings, it seems that what he has in mind by imitations of the beings are not merely false opinions and speeches about them, but also images and appearances more generally (264d4–7; cf. 260e3–5, 264a4–b4, c10–d2).

Now the dialogue has already characterized an image as a kind of non-being, a non-being that is, in a sense, but that is not genuinely or really, since it is not the genuine being that it resembles (240a4–c5). Moreover, the stranger's account of opinion and speech acknowledges that we do sometimes speak of the being (οὐσίαν) of (a) non-being (262c2–5), by which he implies that false opinion is not limited to attributing to a being something that is not [the case] concerning it, but also includes attributing genuine being to something that lacks it, e.g., an image.[6] He gives a further indication in the immediate sequel of how there can be speech about a non-being by reminding us that we sometimes speak of what are no longer or not yet beings (262d2–3). And in these cases, what we speak about is even less of a being than a portrait or other such image, for though a portrait is not truly what it resembles, it is at least truly a kind of body, as opposed to these beings that are only in memory or anticipation. And so I suggest that what the stranger means by images includes beings that are only in speech, or more generally in the human mind, and that his account of false opinion and speech is intended at least in part to show the possibility of such beings.

Now the simplest instances of beings that are only in the human mind are those that the stranger has referred to explicitly, in the first place, former beings that are remembered as they once were. Similarly, there can be future beings that are anticipated as they will later become, to the extent at least that they will be similar to beings we know. But the most important instance, for my present purposes, is that of beings, or non-beings, such as I have suggested that the stranger held the Olympian gods to be, beings that neither were nor will ever be apart from human opinion and human speech. And though the stranger never speaks directly of any beings of this sort, his account helps us to understand how they might be possible. To see how this is so, let us consider the stranger's sentence that I cited earlier, namely, "Theaetetus, with whom I am now conversing, flies." For this is a statement not simply about Theaetetus, but about the Theaetetus with whom the stranger is conversing.[7] But what if the stranger had not been conversing with Theaetetus, but with someone else? In that case, the sentence, "Theaetetus is the one with whom the stranger is now conversing," would have been false in the ordinary sense of attributing to a being something that is not [the case] concerning it. But the falsity of the stranger's actual sentence would not have consisted merely in this, but also in its attributing something, i.e., flying, to what is not truly a being at all. Moreover, this subject, the so-called "Theaetetus, with whom I am now speaking," might have been given a name of its own as if it were just like any other being. More generally, every statement that attributes to a being something that is not the case concerning it, or that denies to it something that is the case, can serve as the basis for a new, composite, subject with a name of its own even though it is not truly a being at all. And in this way we can begin to see how there can be statements about the Olympian gods even if they are not genuine beings, since we can attribute deathlessness, that is, we can deny mortality, to beings that otherwise resemble humans and then assign names to the so-called beings we have thus imagined (cf. *Phaedrus* 246c6–d2). These beings in speech would be a kind of image of the genuine beings we know from experience, not only by their pretence to be such beings themselves, but also by their deriving such intelligibility as they do in fact possess from their resemblance, or alleged lack of it, to these beings. And it seems to me that the stranger's discussion of the false sentence about Theaetetus is intended to help us to see the possibility of such images.

From the perspective we have now reached, it appears that the stranger's claim that non-being is in no lesser a sense than being itself, along with his corresponding claim that the class being is merely one among a number of distinct classes and his interpretation of what is not (a) being as whatever is other than that class, serves the purpose of avoiding thematic discussion of the kind of non-being that is only in speech (cf. again, however, 234c2–e2, 240d9–e4, 241a8–b1). And it makes sense that he should seek to avoid that discussion, since the acknowledgement of such non-being is, as I have suggested, meant as the basis for the claim that the Olympian gods are only in speech. More specifically, I think that the stranger's view of the Olympians is that they are only "by convention," meaning that unlike manifestly fictional beings, they are regarded by some community or communities as truly being, whereas in fact they have being only by virtue of this belief (cf. *Laws* 885c7 with 889e3–890a2). That this is indeed his view of them is suggested most visibly by the myth he tells in the *Statesman*, where he says that the present age, the so-called age of Zeus, in which living beings grow older rather than younger, is as it is in this and other ways because the greatest divinity gave up his piloting of the cosmos, after which all the other gods who had been ruling with him also abandoned the parts of the cosmos that had been in their care (*Statesman* 272e3–273a1; cf. 271d3–e2). This explicit denial of providential care, at least for ourselves and the other living beings as we know them now, is as close to a denial of the Olympians as one could openly go in a mythical framework. And the stranger goes no further, either here or in the *Sophist* itself. For to deny openly that there are these gods could well have been dangerous for him and those around him, since he was a foreigner visiting in Athens, and in a political climate that was soon to lead to the trial and death of Socrates on the charge of not believing in the gods in whom the city believed (cf. *Theaetetus* 210d2–4). But I do think that he did deny them, and that his account of the being of non-being, and in particular of its presence in opinion and speech, is meant in large part to show that this denial is at least intelligible.

But to show that this denial is intelligible, or even that it is plausible, in the light of the stranger's experience of the world, is of course not to show that there are no Olympians, nor even that they could not have made themselves known in the experience of others. And thus it is also not to show that there is no genuine basis for the belief in coming into being from nothing. Indeed, the difficulty of resolving the question of whether there are truly gods such as the Olympians can help to explain the connection between the most manifest teaching of the dialogue, namely, that there is non-being, including falsehood, and the argument I have tried to uncover about being in speech. For the sophist's denial that there is falsehood, or his assertion that all opinion is true for the one who holds it, may well have emerged as a response to the apparent insolubility of the conflict between the presuppositions of philosophy and the traditional claims regarding the Olympians. The sophist Protagoras in particular, who is famous for having refused to say or write anything about the gods, either that they are or that they are not, may have been trying above all to escape this conflict in abandoning the commonsense view of truth as being true for everyone and opposed to falsehood.[8] At all events, it is clear that his doctrine of the relativity of truth allows each side in this conflict, and thus in particular the nonbelieving side to which he seems to have belonged, to have its own truth without fear of being contradicted. And it seems to me that an adequate refutation of this sophistic doctrine of relativism, or an adequate completion of the dialogue's argument that there is falsehood, would have to resolve the impasse about the Olympians, which means for a philosopher that he would have to show the truth of the stranger's view that they are only in speech. Now whether the stranger thinks he can do this, i.e., whether he thinks his denial of the Olympians has an adequate basis in knowledge, is a question I cannot resolve. But the fact that he has devoted this effort to making intelligible the manner of being of fictitious beings suggests that at least he is well aware of the important role that such knowledge could play in making up for the deficiencies in his earlier arguments in support of Parmenides and of the possibility of philosophy.

NOTES

1   The words that I have here translated as "non-being" (237a3)—the singular definite article together with the negative particle and the participial form of the verb "to be"—will sometimes be translated instead as "that which is not." There is an ambiguity here that arises because this definite article together with any adjectival form means primarily "that which has the designated characteris-

tic," but it can also mean "that which has this characteristic, insofar as it has it," i.e., the class-character of the class in question. In the case of the verb "to be," then, the definite article together with the participle means primarily "that which is," but it can also mean "that which is, insofar as it is," i.e., "the being of that which is," or simply "being." In my translations and paraphrases, I will use the expression "that which is" or "being," or in the negative "that which is not" or "non-being," as seems appropriate in the context. But the reader should always keep the alternative sense in mind. If the definite article is plural, I will translate the words either as "the beings" or "the things that are," or in the negative "the non-beings" or "the things that are not." If there is no definite article, the participial form might mean "a thing that is" or "a being," as well as (the generic) "that which is" or "being," and I will sometimes translate it as "(a) being," or in the negative "(a) non-being," in order to remind the reader of this possible ambiguity. If there is no definite article in the plural, as in the citation from Parmenides' poem that I refer to in my first sentence, I have used the translation "(the) things that are not" for the same reason. The word "being" can also be used as a translation for a different Greek word (ἡ οὐσία), which might in some cases be translated as "beingness" if that were English. Whenever I use "being" for this Greek word, I will include the Greek οὐσία in parentheses.

References to Stephanus pages, such as the ones here, are to the *Sophist*, unless otherwise noted. All references to the *Sophist* are to the more recent Oxford Classical Text *Platonis Opera*, I, Duke, Hicken, Nicoll, Robinson, Strachan, eds. (Oxford, 1995). Line numbers do not correspond exactly to those of the older Burnet edition *Platonis Opera*, I, John Burnet, ed. (Oxford, 1900).

2   The Greek word κίνησις means not only motion, i.e., change of place, but also change in the widest sense of the term, and its contrary, στάσις, or rest, is thus opposed not only to motion in particular but also to change in general. I will use the word "motion" rather than "change," for the most part, because it is the more usual English expression for what is opposed to rest. But the reader should keep in mind that by "motion," as well as "change," I mean the Greek κίνησις.

3   That the stranger thinks of the kinds as classes of particulars is evident from a number of textual details, including the fact that he speaks of non-being, since it is a characteristic of each of the kinds in its being other than, i.e. its not being (identical with), being, as infinite in multitude (256d11–e6; cf. 257a5–6). For the infinity that he has in mind must be the infinity of particular beings, each of which is other than each of the (finitely many) kinds. Indeed, the stranger's reference to particular beings explains why he says in this context that "all" of the kinds, and not merely all of them other than the kind being itself, are other than being, since even the kind being, understood as a class, is (in a sense) other than each of its members, which are primarily the particular beings or things that are. The stranger's understanding of the kinds as classes of particulars is also clearly indicated in the *Statesman*, where he goes so far as to speak of the kind "herd animals characterized by walking" as itself a herd, which he proceeds to divide into its horned and hornless parts (*Statesman* 265c6–8, in relation to 266a2, b1, b5, c4–5, e5; cf. 266e6).

4 More precisely, the stranger explicitly claims that it is "the opposition" (ἡ . . . ἀντίθεσις) between non-being and being that is no less being (οὐσία) than being itself (258a11–b1, and contrast 258e2). The construction with the noun ἀντίθεσις at 257e6, which might seem to suggest that by "the opposition [between non-being and being]" he means "non-being, in its opposition to being," is not quite parallel to the one at 258a11–b1.

5 I read the passage from 259a2–b5 as a single statement.

6 It is true that the stranger also says in this context that a speech, whenever it is, must be a speech of (or about) something, and that he had argued earlier that to speak of something is to speak of (a) being (262e6–7; 237c10–d4). But it does not follow that every speech must be about a genuine being, or something that is in the full sense of the word "is." Indeed, this very claim that a speech must be a speech of (or about) something could be translated instead that it must be a speech of someone, i.e., that a speech, whenever it is, must have a speaker. As the discussion proceeds, moreover, the stranger couples this phrase, "of (or about) something (or someone)," with a different phrase that unambiguously means "about something" (262e13–263a11; consider the emphatic ἐγώ at 263a9). By thus using the two different phrases, he calls attention to the ambiguity of his original claim about every speech, and he invites the interpretation of it that though every speech must have a speaker, a speech is not necessarily about something, at least not about a genuine being.

7 The stranger calls attention to the composite character of the subject of this sentence at 263c1–3, where he makes the odd claim that the sentence is necessarily one of the shortest, a claim belied by his previous two examples, "a human being learns" and "Theaetetus sits."

8 Cf. *Theaetetus* 162d5–e2. Consider the difference indicated in the *Theaetetus* between Protagoras himself and those unnamed others who "do not altogether speak the speech of Protagoras," i.e., the conventionalists who assert the relativity of the noble, the just, and the holy, but who allow that judgments about what will be beneficial in the future are not merely matters of opinion (*Theaetetus* 172a1–c1). Protagoras' awareness of his lack of knowledge that there are no Olympian gods could well have made him dubious about all claims, including his own, to be able to promote the human good on the basis of merely human expertise (cf. also *Theaetetus* 178d10–179a3).

A RECOLLECTION OF EVA

Chester Burke

AS FATE WOULD HAVE IT, nearly thirty-six years ago I walked into a room on the second floor of McDowell Hall at St. John's College in Annapolis to discover that one of my two freshman seminar leaders was Eva Brann. Let me mention that the other leader, young, enthusiastic, and as new to the College as I, would be there only for a semester. Perhaps the fact that many of his opening questions took the form of "How would you imagine X (for instance, Oedipus) if he were in a movie?" had something to do with his brief stay. His second-semester replacement plays a large role in this story, which weaves together much of my life with that of Miss Brann.

Miss Brann's questions easily penetrated the atmosphere of our room, filled with the smoke from cheap tobacco clumsily though proudly rolled into cigarettes by students trying to wrestle with adult ideas by assuming the trappings of adults. I don't remember her telling us too many things, though I felt her strong preference for Odysseus over Achilles and watched her eyes sparkle when we talked about Nausikaa's remarkable encounter with Odysseus. I wondered whether, if given the choice for some future life, Miss Brann would have selected Nausikaa or Athena. The delight she took in Odysseus' lies made me suspect that it would be the latter, though this may have been because I was gradually elevating my teacher to the Olympian realm.

The arrival of Plato coincided with a dim realization that the seminar readings contained the deep and difficult truths of life. About this time, a stranger began visiting our seminar. Miss Brann, her voice full of excitement and admiration, introduced us to Mr. Jacob Klein. He didn't come often—I remember him for Plato's *Theaetetus, Sophist, Parmenides,* and *Timaeus,* and Aristotle's *Metaphysics.* Unlike his introducer, Mr. Klein did deliver speeches. They were short and scintillating. He always ended a speech by catching some student's look and then asking a question. I am eternally grateful that I was not the recipient of the question why being had to be *both* motion and rest. I could not have answered, as I was terrified by the way he said "being" and "both." We students could sense some strong connection between Mr. Klein and Miss Brann. I remember seeing Miss

Brann's face light up every time Mr. Klein began to speak. Often she would break out into soft laughter. Naturally we fantasized about secret conversations between the two of them, conversations where the high points of our own seminars served as mere stepping stones to the pure regions of being and thought. As a junior I was delighted to find out that they often watched the television show "Perry Mason" for entertainment.

It was difficult being a freshman at St. John's College. Though I knew I had made the right choice when I first gazed at the thin volume of Euclid's *Elements* ("Purchase the one without the notes," we were told by our mathematics tutor), I had absolutely no idea what I was choosing. Two stunningly different tutors guided me through that first year, Eva Brann and Alfred Mollin. Unfortunately, I was able to show my gratitude to the latter only at a memorial service. Fortunately, Eva has many good years left, more if indeed she is Athena in disguise.

The oral examination early in the freshman year put me on a path from which I have not strayed too far. I groaned in my inner heart when Miss Brann asked me to talk about the noble lie in Plato's *Republic*. To my utter amazement, we stayed with a few of Plato's sentences for the entire exam. As I was leaving the room, Miss Brann told me that I should talk more often in seminar. I felt as if a gigantic stone had been removed from my soul.

About that time I became friends with another student in the seminar, Jonathan Diggory. We were both young (Jonathan was fifteen when he entered the College) and both determined to understand what a Platonic form is. We suspected that Miss Brann knew everything we needed to know, and it was only shyness that prevented us from accosting her in the way Polemarchus ordered Socrates to "go back down" at the beginning of the *Republic*. We finally worked up the courage to question her one day on the steps of Mellon. I remember her saying many fine things, suggesting that we begin with a sensuous object and then one by one take away its particular qualities.

From then on, Jonathan and I would meet before seminar to discuss the reading and try to guess what Miss Brann would ask on the nights when it was her question. By then our seminar had been moved to the second floor of Mellon, and Beate Von Oppen had become the other leader. We wondered whether there was no end to the number of magnificent people with whom Miss Brann was connected. Miss Von Oppen immediately showed herself to be different from her co-leader. She seemed more formal, much more attached to the Europe from which we knew Miss Brann to have sprung, spoke less frequently, but with a gravity and intensity that made you wish you were far more mature than you were.

In love with Plato's dialogues, I would have been completely deaf to Aristotle had it not been for Miss Brann's opening questions and skillful guidance. The seminar on time was amazing. I remember running into countless classmates on the afternoon of the seminar, all of them trying to say what time is. I felt as baffled with respect to the notion of time as I had been months earlier with respect to the notion of love in Plato's *Symposium*. My memory of the seminar itself is one of Jonathan and Miss Brann engaged in a very beautiful dance around the mysteries of time. I would like to believe that our seminar provided the spark for Miss Brann's two lectures on time and eventually her book.

In the following years, new teachers and new friends filled my life. Where was Miss Brann? There were of course her lectures: one on the *Odyssey* and the other on Kant's *Critique of Pure Reason*. Jonathan and I attended these lectures, listening admiringly like proud children to our teacher's golden words. They seemed to flow so naturally; they cast light on the most obscure nooks, allowing our minds to bathe in clarity. I remember a fellow student commenting on the Kant lecture minutes after it had been delivered: "But she didn't say anything that wasn't right there in the text." My response was "Yes, but you didn't see it right there in the text before she said it."

I don't remember visiting Miss Brann at her house on Wagner Street until the end of our senior year. She invited Jonathan and me over one morning for coffee, tea, and treats. We sat around a very small table in her kitchen, a room where I immediately suspected Miss Brann spent a good part of her life. In later years I learned that the bathtub is another favorite place for her. On that hot, sunny morning, I felt for the first time that Jonathan and I had a special place in her heart and that she hoped we would keep in touch with her. Earlier in the year we had taken up the offer of a neighbor of mine on Prince George Street to help him sail a rather large boat from Norfolk, Virginia, to Florida. Neither of us knew the first thing about sailing (Jonathan at least knew how to swim), and this plan involved disappearing from school for several weeks. Needless to say, when we asked the permission of our tutors, none of them were very enthusiastic. One was openly hostile. In desperation we called Miss Brann (who was not one of our tutors at the time), and found her excited about the voyage. "You will take your readings on the boat, of course," she said. I remember her referring generously to our audacity in her commencement address to our class.

At the end of my senior year I had decided not to go to graduate school. Instead I went off to France with another tutor, Brother Robert, having some vague idea of becoming a professional flutist. Tutors such as Robert Bart (with whom I would later become very close) offered somber warnings: "It's all very well to study music. You know, of course, that after the age of thirty the mind becomes inflexible and you will be incapable of any serious learning." In some odd way Robert Bart always spoke the truth, especially when he warned me that Paris is a lonely and damp city. Eva, however, appeared to approve of my folly wholeheartedly. I felt the lifting of another stone.

Eva Brann is and always will be a mystery to me. While I've known her for thirty-six years, I sometimes feel that I do not know her at all. It was very important to me, however, that during my eight years in France she remained on Wagner Street, in the country she had made her own with a passion that would have astonished even Tocqueville. (In the years when she was driving enormous distances, I once went with her to have "cruise control" installed in her car. The crown of our outing was a stop for chicken nuggets at MacDonald's.) Even though I know she loves to travel, see and experience new things, visit vast numbers of friends, teach in other cities with fanciful names such as Walla Walla, I feel that she and her glorious work remain continually at rest in that small, dark, and peaceful house on Wagner Street. Now this is not by any means the "rest" of Newtonian physics. No, it is the rest that is most alive, a rest where books are read and written, where thoughts percolate in bathtubs and at kitchen tables, and then sparkle as they come into the light. How can it be that in a world of computers, cell phones, answering machines, one can almost always find Eva herself on the other end of an unadorned telephone, answering "Eva Brann"?

When I had learned to play the flute at a respectable level, I returned to America and began cobbling together a living in the music world. Eva and her friend Beate were my faithful concert attenders. Often after a concert I would introduce them to fellow musicians as one would introduce one's parents to a new set of friends. Eva and Beate were like perfect dinner guests, appreciative of every detail and the hard work involved in the achievement of the meal. Their comments on the various performances often rivaled the performances themselves. Eva was able to describe with deadly precision the character of a particular conductor after a single concert.

A year after returning from France, I nearly took a job at Kentucky State University in a program developed by a St. John's tutor, Tom Slakey. The morning after returning from the interview in Frankfort, I received a phone call from Eva informing me about a laboratory director job at St. John's. I felt machinations at work, but doubted that a musician would be allowed to run a laboratory. It's called "injustice" in the *Republic*. I had always dreamed about teaching at St. John's, but only after I had acquired a smattering of wisdom. Though wisdom was the last thing I could put on an all too degreeless resume, Eva, with the help of tutors Brother Robert and Michael Comenetz, was able to persuade the powers that be to give me a chance.

Not long after I moved to Annapolis, I became Eva's teacher, that is, her flute teacher. She had played flute and recorder for years and was the possessor of a wonderful Louis Lotte flute, which had previously been her brother's. I have certainly never had a flute student like Eva Brann. Let me explain.

Eva's appetite for the flute literature was voracious. I had spent the past nine years studying most if not all of the major classical works written for the flute. Eva wanted to learn them all. Were I to give her a don rag on her flute preparation, it would be long and glowing. She is probably the only student I've ever taught who took delight in practicing long tones, scales, and études. My pedagogical sense often told me to make her wait before attacking such monsters of the flute literature as the Prokofiev flute sonata. But Eva's *daimon* always insisted "yes." There was nothing that she was not willing to take on.

I think that Eva's moments of flute playing provided pleasurable interludes between long stretches of work on her book, *The World of the Imagination*. She seemed grateful whenever I asked her about her work or commented on one of her lectures I'd read in order to become clear about something I was teaching at the College. I sensed how lonely it is for a colleague who has temporarily removed herself from the bustle of College life in order to pursue a project toward which her whole life has been aiming. I sometimes imagined Eva as her hero Odysseus, at sea in the Protean world of the imagination, struggling to capture it in all of its splendor and intricacy.

Then all of a sudden Eva became Dean of St. John's College in Annapolis. I was a member of the committee who interviewed the College community. Though the interviews took weeks to complete, it was clear from the beginning that Eva would become our Dean. The time was right. I smiled when people, full of praise for her knowledge of the College, wondered whether she could handle the administrative part of the job. Those who know Eva know that she is nearly able to answer a phone call or a letter before it has been made or sent. I even suspected that she would enjoy the public life required of a Dean. The saddest part of her becoming Dean was her realization that she would no longer have the time to keep up the flute.

I tried to persuade her otherwise, but eventually saw that she was right. Then to my astonishment Eva gave me the precious Louis Lotte flute. I play it whenever I want to hear a beautifully clear and pure sound; and also when I want to think about Eva Brann.

Though Eva didn't teach in the classroom during her years as Dean, she certainly taught in her office. It seemed to me as if she was always meeting with students, discussing the small and large parts of their lives, helping them write papers. I was involved in one of the lesser known parts of her Deanship. A group of tutors, Anita Kronsberg, Stewart Umphrey, Eva, and myself, decided to read and discuss Hegel's *Science of Logic*. Eva thought that we should pursue this task in her office. So once a week we would shut out the life of the College and read a few pages of Hegel out loud. We'd stop whenever any one had a question or a comment. After a year, Anita's schedule prevented her from coming and Peter Kalkavage took her place. Three years later we reached the Absolute Idea and dispersed.

I often spent time with Eva in her office, which she had decorated with her favorite paintings, many done by friends. On one occasion she helped me with a translation of a paper by Heisenberg. I suspect that at the end of our work she understood the uncertainty principle better than I did. I remember her calling me into her office soon after I had received an NEH grant to study Leibniz. Her advice was short and stern: "Stop feeling responsible for the numerous activities of the College and get to work on your project."

After a short time, Eva's office felt like an extension of her house on Wagner Street; only the tea and cookies were missing. Lest this latter sound like a criticism, let me point out that Eva was sometimes known as "the food Dean," because she would supply the financial means by which members of the College community could eat together. Many a long Instruction Committee meeting was made bearable for me only because Eva had furnished a plate of treats.

The last story I will tell is of our year in seminar together, this time as co-leaders. It's something I had imagined happening ever since I returned to St. John's. The two of us plotted how best to pull off a pairing that would probably not be the first thing to occur to a Dean and Instruction Committee. Eva, no longer Dean, said, "I'll take care of it," and several months later we were sitting on opposite sides of the table in a room in Mellon Hall where I had had freshman laboratory with one of Eva's old sailing companions, Bert Thoms.

Nothing in life repeats itself. Neither Eva nor I were the same as we had been in that freshman seminar thirty years before. I was no substitute for Beate Von Oppen or Jacob Klein. Nevertheless, I felt an excitement in the room which lasted throughout the year. Eva now seemed less interested in pointing to important passages; that became my role. She was fascinated by the students as human beings, striving in their sometimes blunt and awkward ways toward ideas at the moment only faintly glimpsed. She was charmed, sometimes amused, sometimes deeply impressed, and rarely annoyed by their conversations. Though Eva had been in countless seminars and tutorials that no doubt had stumbled over the same arguments again and again, I had the impression that everything was new for her. I could sense the students feeling her delight, feeling her pleasure in their encounters with those beautiful Greek words with which she had spent her life. They knew they were in the presence of someone special, someone who took them seriously and delighted in their youth.

I too feel that I have been in the presence of someone special. The day I began writing this small piece, I was reading her translation of Heidegger's "What is that—Philosophy?" As has been the case so many times, both in her presence and through her writings, I felt swept up and sustained in a realm both playful and serious. Eva Brann's words can open up the insides of almost anything worth engaging in. As for her own insides, I've already said that of them I am entirely ignorant. But as it is not proper to end with a claim of ignorance, I will speculate by brazenly stealing a line from Alcibiades in Plato's *Symposium*:

"The way I shall take, gentlemen, in my praise of Eva Brann, is by similitudes. I choose my similitude for the sake of truth. For I say she is likest to the Silenus-figures that sit in the statuaries' shops; those, I mean, which our craftsmen make with pipes or flutes in their hands: when their two halves are pulled open, they are found to contain images of gods."

THE THEORETICAL PRESUPPOSITIONS OF LIBERAL EDUCATION

James Carey

THE COMING INTO BEING of liberal education presupposes certain political, social, and economic conditions, among which are leisure, the existence of letters, and enough political freedom for reason to be granted a voice, if only a muted one, in discourse on the things that matter most to human beings. These conditions are the practical presuppositions of liberal education, and a consideration of them is of great pertinence to the theme of liberal education and the conditions of its possibility. But they are not the concern of this essay. Instead of the practical presuppositions of liberal education, I shall be concentrating on presuppositions of a different kind. To articulate these presuppositions, which are theoretical rather than practical, we need to get clarity about what liberal education is and what it is not. It cannot be adequately grasped as an assemblage of related disciplines going by the name of the "humanities," nor can it be adequately grasped even as the seven liberal arts, at least not without getting clear in advance what "liberal" means in relation to education and arts.

The word "liberal" obviously refers to liberty and to liberation. Liberal education aims at liberating the mind from domination by unexamined or inadequately examined opinions whatever their source. If it takes its bearings by certain books that were written long ago, it does so only because these books are classics. They are not so much old as timeless, that is, written for the ages. Liberal education does not entail the veneration of ancestral authority *per se*. To be sure, it is open to the possibility that some of those who lived long before us may have seen certain important things more clearly than we see them now, if we see them any longer at all, and that we moderns may have forgotten more of what is most worth knowing than we have learned. But liberal education has no use for the concept of sacred tradition or even for the concept of a canon, which emerged out of the theological problem of determining which scriptures were divinely inspired and which were not.

In saying that liberal education aims at liberating the mind from thoughtless acquiescence in unexamined opinions, including current opinion, regarding the most important things, we understand its aim only negatively. Implicit in the negative aim, however, is the positive aim, and this is knowledge. Liberal education consists in the leading of the mind out of the dark night of mere opinion and into the bright daylight of knowledge. It can be objected, of course, that we are defining liberal education too narrowly. By putting so much emphasis on knowledge, we have virtually identified liberal education with philosophy itself, and we have said nothing about the liberal arts, which cannot be simply identified with philosophy.

The seven traditional liberal arts are divided into a group of four and a group of three, the quadrivium and the trivium. They could be said to encompass the elementary mathematical arts and the elementary verbal arts respectively. Concerning the former, it is worth noting that Socrates treats mathematics as a propaedeutic to what he calls "dialectic," which is the investigation of the fundamental principles of reality. Dialectic as Socrates describes it, and practices it, is philosophical inquiry. To be sure, the mathematical arts disclose all kinds of relationships that are intriguing, even sources of wonder. Moreover, in studying mathematics one becomes vividly aware of the distinction between opining something and knowing it. Even when knowledge about a certain mathematical relationship is only something longed for, we recognize a distinction between the knowledge we don't possess and the opinion we do possess. And yet mathematical knowledge, because of its hypothetical foundations, cannot, in the opinion of Socrates, serve as a paradigm for the kind of knowledge to which philosophy aspires.[1]

The relationship of the trivium—grammar, rhetoric, and logic—to philosophy is less obvious. No one will deny that logic has a relationship to the pursuit of knowledge. Grammar, which is the study of the elements of rational discourse, can be understood to be in the service of this pursuit as well. Rhetoric, however, seems to have little at all to do with the quest for knowledge. It may even seem to be an impediment to authentic learning, given that its intent is primarily persuasion and not demonstration. But not all who possess the ability to philosophize are initially inclined to do so, and rhetoric does have the power of making something that should be attractive also appear to be so. And yet if rhetoric is understood not superficially as persuasive speech merely, but as poetry, it cannot be demoted to the status of a mere *ancilla* to philosophy. Rather than philosophy, and perhaps even in opposition to philosophy, poetry might be understood as the right way toward knowledge, toward knowledge even and especially of the most important things.[2] If poetry is a liberal art then it, too, liberates from ignorance. The very concept of liberal art presupposes the possibility of knowledge, whether it has hitherto been actually attained or not.

That knowledge is at least possible might not seem like much of a presupposition. In fact, this presupposition has been seriously called into question, particularly by those who think that man is trapped within his opinions and, in principle, can never get beyond them other than by being exposed to more opinions. Knowledge is often likened to sight.[3] Like mere opinion, seeing is essentially perspectival. To the extent that knowing is like seeing, it might seem to be essentially perspectival too. But the perspectival character of seeing is precisely its limitation, and the point at which the comparison with knowledge breaks down. Knowledge is an awareness that transcends mere perception. Indeed, knowledge is what perception is held to aim at, if not always, at least often enough. It is that in which perception can be understood as finding its fulfillment.[4]

There is at present a broadly held opinion to the effect that knowledge is not even a possibility because, it is maintained, there is no absolute truth, which is to say, there is no truth. This view goes popularly by the name of "relativism." There are sophisticated and unsophisticated versions of relativism, and the proponents of the sophisticated version abjure the name. I shall use the term "relativism" for the opinion that what *is* is only a matter of personal and private perspective, and that no perspective is closer to the objective truth than another, because there is no objective truth.[5]

Relativism is attacked by Socrates in the *Theaetetus*. What is under consideration is the thesis of the famous sophist Protagoras, who taught that "man is the measure of all things, of the things that are, that they are, and of the things that are not, that they are not." This thesis is taken to be equivalent to the claim that things have no existence independently of how they are perceived, or opined to be, by man: there is no truth that is independent of human perspectives, and human perspectives differ. Socrates shows that, if Protagoras is right on this point, then the very claim that man is the measure of all things is no closer to the truth than the claim that man is *not* the measure of all things.[6] If the relativist is right, relativism is no more true than its opposite.

Aristotle continues this line of attack. He argues in the *Metaphysics* that only someone who says something can be refuted. "It is ridiculous to seek an argument (*logon*) against someone who does not say anything . . . for such a man is like a plant." In speaking, man "has to *mean* (*sēmainein*) something, both to himself and to another; and this is necessary if he is to say anything (*eiper legoi ti*)." By acting like a human being, that is, by saying something and meaning it, even the relativist speaks as though things are one way rather than another. He thus allows an exception to the exceptionless thesis of relativism.[7] Moreover, as Aristotle argues a bit later on in the *Metaphysics,* no one who understands himself to be a relativist acts in accordance with relativism.[8] In medical matters, for example, the relativist hardly acts on what should be his claim, namely, that a physician's diagnosis is no closer to the objective truth regarding an illness than the diagnosis of someone who knows nothing at all about medicine. Similar examples of discrepancy between the relativist's assertions and how he acts can be easily multiplied. The relativist advances, as an absolute even, the claim that all claims are relative and that none are absolute. He holds it to be true that there is no truth. He makes a claim that is an exception to the verdict he renders on all claims without exception. And he cannot make a case for this claim, indeed he cannot even make the claim, which purports to be self-identical and distinct from its contradictory, without refuting himself. One wonders, then, how relativism ever came to be taken seriously at all, given how remote it is from logic, common sense, and the conduct of everyday life.

The relativist will respond that the above criticisms do not trouble him, for they add up to nothing more than a charge of inconsistency. They presuppose the authority of reason and the consistent relativist does not acknowledge this authority. Let us step back, then, from our critique and consider briefly how liberal education would have to be transformed to become compatible with relativism. If a vertical progression from mere opinion to knowledge, or at least toward knowledge, is not possible, there is still room for a horizontal progression from opinion to opinion. A purely aesthetic appreciation of otherness, of diversity as we now say, disburdened of any tendency to evaluate, might well be of more than marginal educational benefit. For simply by becoming exposed to the traditions, outlooks, lifestyles, and preferences of others one might become less inclined to feel the kind of dogged allegiance to one's own that is the source of conflict, even of wars and persecution. The goal of liberal education, so revised, might still be understood as liberation: one is liberated from the opinion that one can get beyond opinion. But here again we encounter an objection to relativism, an objection that the relativist is apt to dismiss as a "semantic" trick: how do we *know* that it is not just an opinion, a prejudice even, that we cannot get beyond opinion?

The relativist uses logic when it suits his purpose and dispenses with it when it does not. For he is not content to be a silent relativist. He wants to make something of a case for relativism. Accordingly, he is forced to make use of language, and language is saturated with logic. He claims, however, that he enters into the realm of language and logic only to disclose the intrinsic limitations of language and logic. He is engaged in a kind of *reductio ad absurdum*. He uses rational discourse only to reveal the absurdity of rational discourse. In doing so, he gives credence to the principle that what is absurd, supposedly rational discourse itself, is false. And yet this principle is a logical principle, and the relativist is supposed to have disburdened himself of such principles. The case for relativism begins to look like an exercise in either stupidity or bad faith. The relativist, however, can deny that he is engaged in an exercise of bad faith. For relativism is conducive to something good. If relativism is not conducive to respect for diversity—for it is hard to know what the relativist could mean by "respect"—it is at least conducive to tolerance, and thereby to overcoming the divisions that threaten peace and comity.

We have caught sight of one of three independent developments that have contributed to the current appeal of relativism. Relativism seems to be both an extension of and a support for the egalitarian premises of liberal democracy. If knowledge is impossible, then not only are all human beings equal, but all opinions, including opinions about the human good, are equal as well, at least with respect to their "truth value." All human beings are equal in the sense most relevant to politics: they are all equally wise, because no one is wiser than anyone else. Political life, however, requires that certain decisions be made that do not accord with the opinions, desires, and wills of everyone affected. It has always been the hope, at least, that such decisions would be wise. The overarching practical task of politics is to secure the rule of reason, that is, to unite wisdom and political power. All other things being equal, the best regime would seem to be some kind of aristocracy of wisdom. But the great difficulty of making those who happen to be wise politically powerful and the even greater difficulty of making those who happen to be politically powerful wise lead quite understandably to abandoning as unrealistic the ideal of an aristocracy of wisdom and opting instead for some form of democracy as the best or, as is said, most "decent" practicable alternative. There is no good reason to expect that the majority will always, or even usually, be wiser than the minority. Wisdom, after all, has generally been recognized as something uncommon. Democracy, in which political power is ultimately vested in the many, in the common rather than the uncommon, seems to be, in the last analysis, the rule of those who are unwise. Since it is disconcerting to believe that one is living in a regime in which political power is ultimately vested in those who are unwise, there is something alluring about the assertion that no one is really wiser than anyone else. Those who are committed to liberal democracy are particularly susceptible to this allure. For, to repeat, relativism seems to be conducive to breadth of mind and appreciation of diversity. But it is not. Narrowness of mind and contempt for diversity are, on the thesis of relativism itself, neither more nor less warranted than their opposites.

The second development that has contributed to the rise of relativism is the increasing awareness of the wide range of opinion that has existed and continues to exist in the world regarding important matters, especially matters of religion, morality, and politics. It is, however, hard to see how this awareness by itself could be thought to justify the inference that no opinion concerning these matters can be the true opinion. Even on the questionable assumption that human reason has not yet had anything definitive to say about first principles and the human good, it would not follow that human reason could never have anything definitive to say about them. And regarding the assumption that reason has not yet had anything definitive to say about the things that are of the deepest interest to human beings, the only way one can find out if this is true is by considering what the greatest minds are recorded as having said about them, that is, by patiently and attentively reading the finest books that are available to us. To undertake this task is to subject oneself to the process of liberal education itself, with an open mind and no axes to grind, in the realization that cherished opinions will have to be called into question, and may have to be abandoned across the board. The magnitude of this difficulty should not be underestimated. Still, the inference from the *difficulty* of getting clear and compelling answers to the most important questions to the *impossibility* of getting such answers is manifestly invalid. It is motivated less by rational necessity than by indolence and prejudice. After all, the awareness that there are differences of opinion on matters of religion, morality, and politics has not always led, in the past at least, to the conviction that there is no truth concerning these matters, or even that there is truth but that it is inaccessible. Quite the contrary. As has been well noted, the awareness of such differences originally served as the impetus for trying to achieve clarity about the truth, and it continues to motivate the ongoing conversation between diverse voices that makes our intellectual tradition, the intellectual tradition of the West, a living tradition.[9] Liberal education has been the center of this tradition. Some types of education are compatible with relativism, but liberal education is not. For on the premise of relativism there is no genuine liberation, from anything or for anything.

We have thus far been belaboring the obvious. There is, however, a third development, both more complex and much more interesting, that has lent credence to relativism, at least to a certain kind of relativism. This development has occurred within philosophy itself, which has a way of calling the obvious into question. As is well known, modern philosophy from the time of Descartes on has taken as its primary theme the knowing subject, or, more precisely, the human mind. It is not the existence of the world, and certainly not the existence of nature, that is indubitable. What man finds indubitable is the existence of his own consciousness. The object of consciousness, as such, is dependent on consciousness. Thinking through the meaning and implications of the discovery that the human mind enjoys a privilege relative to all the other things of which it can be aware came to be regarded as the first task of philosophy. An implication of this discovery seemed to be that the objective world is constituted by human consciousness. Since consciousness can hardly be a product or part of something it has itself constituted, it is said to transcend all its objects, actual and possible, itself excluded of course. However, it is not human consciousness in its particular, private, and variable manifestations, i.e., *empirical* consciousness, that constitutes the objective world. It is, rather, *transcendental* consciousness, human consciousness in its universal, common, and invariable character, that does this. Because the mind has such a character, the world that it constitutes has invariant structures that can be determined with greater and greater precision, and intersubjective agreement, including scientific knowledge, can be secured by reason and recourse to common, verifiable experience. Human consciousness functioning at this higher level is not personal or empirical subjectivity, but transcendental subjectivity. It looks as though man is, after all, the measure of all things, though not by virtue of his particular, individual subjectivity, as Protagoras seems to have taught. All things, the world, or even the way of the world that is virtually consecrated by philosophy and endowed with the name "nature," are measured by—because constituted by—transcendental subjectivity.[10] It is the conviction that there is such a thing as transcendental subjectivity that prevents modern subjectivist philosophy from collapsing into relativism.[11]

The insistence on the primacy of the subject relative to the object is thought to be a unique feature of modern philosophy. But this primacy, or something approaching it, was at least intimated in antiquity. Aristotle, whose sobriety as a philosopher is unsurpassed and arguably unparalleled, says in the *De Anima* that colors, sounds, smells, tastes and tactile qualities have no actual, but only a potential, existence when they are not in the process of being actually perceived. In the *Physics* he says that time might not exist apart from the soul, which engages in the intellectual act of counting that constitutes time. And, in virtually the same breath, he wonders if even motion can exist without a soul. In the *Metaphysics,* he goes so far as to say that it is uncertain whether composite perceptible and intelligible objects—his examples are a bronze or wooden circle and a mathematical circle—exist apart from actual perception or intellectual apprehension.[12] Even Plato, by suggesting that the *eidos* is both the being of a thing and its intelligible "looks," implies an intrinsic relation of being to an intellect that at least *could,* at some point, *look* at it. For what would the "looks" of something be, were there no one *to* whom it could "look," sooner or later, like what it is? But to return to the more explicit and much more sustained elaboration of this theme in modern philosophy, we note that the subject was understood to be first of all the thinking subject, where thinking was understood primarily as a disinterested activity, as cogitation.[13] The subject originally relates to its object as though it were observing it, detached and from a certain distance, as it were. In the philosophy of Kant, where the subject synthetically constitutes objectivity, constitution is consummated in a theoretical *Begreifen,* that is to say, a grasping, comprehending, or conceptualizing of its object.[14]

Without abandoning the view of subjectivity as constitutive of objectivity, though scrupulously avoiding the language of subject and object, the twentieth-century philosopher Martin Heidegger attempted to show that the subject is not primarily, much less exclusively, cogitative. It does not exist first of all, much less most of the time, in an attitude of *theōrein,* of beholding its object. The subject, or rather human existence ("being there" —*Dasein*), is primarily *care.* The relationship of human existence to its object, to its world, is not primarily one of dispassionate looking *at* it, but of being *in* it. And human existence is not in the world as a mere piece of it. It is in the world originally and primarily by way of absorption with it. Care, then, is not a subsequent attitude that attaches itself to the world previously constituted as a merely perceived object. It has furthermore a structure, just as transcendental subjectivity was said to have. And so, the world invested with care throughout and from the beginning is not merely a private one. Indeed, in working through Heidegger's early magnum opus, *Being and Time,* the reader, whatever his reservations on this or that point, cannot help but

recognize the world that is familiar to all of us. The attitude of detached observation, of cogitation and theoretical understanding, which we assume
only from time to time, turns out to be derivative. The world construed as
a totality of things that are just, so to speak, "out there" in space and time,
which is to say, the world that science takes to be the real world, is a world
that is so far from being real, in the sense intended, as to be an abstraction.
Science itself, or rather theoretical understanding in general, can never give
a just account of the more concrete mode of being-in from which it has
abstracted itself. The world on Heidegger's analysis, though still constituted
by the subject, does not present itself first of all, or for the most part, as an
order in which man finds the projections of his reason, hypostasized as
immutable laws of logical, mathematical, and physical relationships, i.e., as
eternal truths.[15] To repeat, it can certainly come to have this appearance for
us. But, again, the world appearing this way has, according to Heidegger, undergone a modification.

A single example is sufficient to support these claims. A central issue in
every philosophically developed account of the subjective constitution of
objectivity is the constitution of time itself. In temporal awareness we *hold
on* to a past no longer present as we *reach out* to a future not yet present. It
is through this incontestably synthetic awareness that objects in general
present themselves to us, and it is here that we seem to find compelling evidence for our constitution of the world that we experience.[16] The synthetic
nature of temporal awareness was explored by Heidegger's teacher, Edmund
Husserl. In *The Phenomenology of Internal Time Consciousness,* Husserl describes how, in any single moment of time, we anticipate, or rather protend,
the immediate future while at the same time retaining the immediate past,
and how a progressively decreasing vividness characterizes the correlates
of these protentions and retentions the more remotely they are situated
from the moving present.[17] Time consciousness, it turns out, not only makes
possible our awareness of what comes to be and passes away in time; it even
makes possible our awareness of what is, or is believed to be, timeless or
eternal. For something altogether atemporal, for example, a law of logic,
can be apprehended as atemporal only insofar as it persists in its identity
against a backdrop of temporal flow. We say that something is timeless only
because we construe it as being right now, and into the future as well, just
as it always was.

Now, Heidegger is, to say the very least, just as convinced as Husserl of
the essential temporality of consciousness. But he realizes that Husserl's
analysis has assumed that the attitude of disinterested looking is conscious-

ness at its most elemental. If, however, care is more elemental, foundational, and pervasive, then an adequate description of time consciousness has to take this fact into account. As has been rightly pointed out, Heidegger's own description takes note of something central to the consciousness of time that went unnoticed in Husserl's description, namely, that time is experienced by us as finite, that is, as running out.[18] As we frequently say, we do not have enough time for this or that. We realize that we shall never have as much time as we would like, that sooner or later we shall no longer be able to pick and choose, and that we shall die. According to Heidegger, the real world, the world as originally constituted, presents itself as the field within which man as an essentially finite being, and one whose being is an issue for him, projects his concerns, the deepest of which is not the desire to know but the fear of death. Love of knowledge, indeed, the whole theoretical enterprise of man, is derivative from the consciousness of being-towards-death. If, however, consciousness is essentially temporal, and if time is essentially finite, then both the subject and its temporally constituted objects, that is, its whole world, are finite. Consciousness, including self-consciousness, is at bottom consciousness of finitude, and the theoretical life, in its search for an immutable order of truth, is a flight from finitude.

Heidegger includes in his account of the finitude of consciousness a remarkable analysis of the act of understanding. Understanding, he argues, is interpretation. To understand something is to interpret it in terms of something else. That is, to understand x is to interpret it *as* y, where y is thought to be something better understood, that is, more familiar, than x. But then to understand y is to interpret it, in turn, *as* z, and so on. This account, which denies that we have access to an unmediated act of understanding, or intellectual intuition, is not necessarily incompatible with the possibility of achieving genuine, objective knowledge in the traditional sense. The concepts we employ in our judgments may ultimately refer back, as Kant argued, to empirical intuitions and even to pure intuitions of space and time, and thereby yield objective, albeit limited, knowledge.[19] And even if concepts refer chiefly to one another, analogous to what happens with words in a dictionary, some sort of mutual co-founding is still thinkable. Co-intelligibility of concepts might well be compatible with knowledge, even with absolute knowledge, for the concepts themselves might form a systematic whole that comes into view only by way of the necessary progression from concept to concept, culminating in an overcoming of the distinction between concept and object. Such, in fact, was the teaching of Hegel, the philosopher who made the strongest claims yet for the scope of human knowing.

But for Heidegger, the context from which interpretative understanding originates and refers back is not a system of interrelated concepts, nor an assemblage of intuitions disinterestedly synthesized by the imagination. Rather, because the act of understanding and its correlative theoretical constructs are derived from a more primordial way of being in the world, interpretation refers back ultimately to this ground.[20] Understanding as interpretation is grounded in an ultimately unintelligible context that is the allotment of an unintelligent fate (*Schicksal*), of which human history (*Geschichte*) is, contrary to what Hegel thought, the essentially mysterious and, indeed, irrational dispensation. All understanding is conditioned by history. The deepest root of the rational is the irrational. Thought is incapable of entirely shedding the prejudices that shape, and are shaped by, the essentially particular historical context out of which it emerges. And so, it is prejudiced in the most precise sense of the word. For, prior to all judgments and cognition, there is an orientation determining these judgments, an orientation that cannot itself be simply left behind. Of course, the claim that all thought is prejudiced in this way does not necessarily lead to vulgar relativism, to the proclamation that all claims are "equally valid." Among other things, some prejudices may be more life-enhancing and conducive to the discharge of "creative" energy than others.[21] But the claim that thought is essentially prejudiced is indispensable to relativism, and the account that we have been considering, that is, Heidegger's, is responsible for the only respectability that relativism enjoys. When relativism is buttressed by this argument and motivated, as it was certainly not motivated in the case of Heidegger himself, by egalitarian political commitments, it becomes a formidable obstacle to taking seriously even the possibility of liberal education, which is, as we noted, precisely the attempt to replace prejudiced opinion about the most important things with unprejudiced knowledge.

Husserl had prided himself on the radical character of his enterprise. Rather than presuppose the authority of the positive sciences he wanted to ground their authority. He even expressed some disappointment that the term "archeology," literally an account of beginnings, had been appropriated by another discipline. By calling his enterprise "phenomenology" he understood it to be an account of things just as they show themselves to us, prior to any theorizing about them. He wished to give a description of the phenomena that are first for us, rather than a causal explanation of where they came from, for he was wary, just as Aristotle was, of accounting for the evident in terms of the non-evident. After all, explanation, which is the procedure of science, is premature if the phenomena as they originally present themselves to us are not first brought into focus and accurately described. Now, Heidegger, just like his teacher, wanted to start with what is first for us. But he radicalized Husserl's radical project further, disagreeing with Husserl, as we noted, about what is truly first for us. The philosopher Leo Strauss, who fully appreciated Heidegger's radicalization of Husserl's project, could be said to have undertaken a still further radicalization in light of what he had learned from Plato in particular, namely, that what is first for us is not so much the world, even as Heidegger compellingly describes it, but the political community.

Political communities, like the families and tribes that they comprehend, are particular. They vary from regime to regime, and they vary historically. They have, however, a common character. Among other things, in every political community there are a small number of people who are opinion makers and a large number of people who are opinion receivers. The received opinions constitutive of any given regime are opinions about the human good, and these are bound up with the religion or ideology that characterizes the regime. Every political community demands small sacrifices of personal happiness from day to day. On occasion it may demand enormous sacrifices of personal happiness, even of life itself. These sacrifices are accepted as obligatory in light of received opinions about the human good. It is through such opinions that members of political communities look beyond themselves, setting their sights on something they believe to be greater and even higher than themselves.

We human beings, as originally and by nature political beings, are oriented out beyond the here and now, beyond the merely historical and toward the transhistorical and permanent. This orientation, which is moral and intimately bound up with religion or with some secularized variant of religion, is, contrary to what Heidegger taught, not a flight from finitude subsequent to a more original care. The moral concern that characterizes political life is as much a part of what is first for us as is the fear of death, which moral concern tempers, though, to be sure, without eradicating once and for all. Our finitude is manifested not only in our awareness that we shall die but also in our awareness that we lack knowledge regarding the things we want to know most. However, our finitude is further manifested in our readiness to be content with inherited opinions regarding these things, in spite of an uneasy realization, which is particularly conspicuous in children and which continues into adolescence, that these opinions are not really knowledge. The young, at least, realize that they have not seen for themselves but are placing their trust in the authority of their elders. But inherited opinions, because they speak to our hopes, are reassuring, if only up to a point. We grow attached to them. As we grow older we can manage to convince ourselves that what we have inherited is not opinion after all, but knowledge.[22]

Now Strauss, like Plato and Aristotle before him, subjects political life not just to phenomenological description but to critical scrutiny. On examination it looks as though the moral convictions that are indispensable to political life might not be altogether coherent. If the religious opinions of the political community derive their credibility, at least in part, from moral convictions that are indispensable to political life, then religion would be rendered less than fully credible by a critique of these convictions. And rendering religion less than fully credible would be a great gain for philosophy. For according to religion, at least Biblical religion, the truths that matter most are not grasped by the unassisted human mind but are revealed by God, and they are no more likely to be revealed to philosophers than to non-philosophers, to shepherds, fishermen, and tent makers, for example. In fact, the philosopher's very commitment to human reason and to the ordinary experiences that are accessible to "man as man," as the sole authorities he is willing to acknowledge, could make him particularly unreceptive to mysterious disclosures held to be initiated from beyond in a suprarational and extraordinary manner. If such disclosures are actually salvific, as the Bible teaches, then the philosopher might be living a life that is not so choiceworthy after all. Moreover, if the philosopher cannot know that the way of philosophy is superior to the way of faith, then his siding with philosophy has something arbitrary, something willful, about it. It is not based exclusively on evidence.[23] It is a kind of faith. The philosopher has to wonder whether he might be only taking it on faith that the way of faith is not the right way. This state of affairs would not trouble everyone who calls himself a philosopher, but it could prove to be intolerable to a genuine philosopher. For the genuine philosopher knows that philosophy as classically conceived, that is, as a way of life and not just an academic discipline of analyzing concepts and arguments, stands or falls with self-grounding and self-justification, of which the critique of morality and revelation is an indispensable constituent. The genuine philosopher is induced by these considerations to undertake a demonstration of the impossibility of revelation or, failing that, at least of the incoherence of the moral convictions that motivate taking the possibility of revelation seriously and hearkening to what the believer himself holds to be announced in a still, small voice only.

But this theological-political critique is not the whole of philosophy. It is not even the sole indispensable constituent of the self-grounding and self-justification of the philosophic way of life. For this critique depends on the authority of reason, the very authority that Heideggerian historicism calls most seriously into question.[24] In fighting a battle on two fronts, that is, in contesting both the claims of Biblical religion and the claims of Heideggerian historicism, Strauss and his students must have recourse to the concept of nature as an immanent and a permanent first principle of things. They must presuppose, in particular, that there is a transhistorical human nature and that there are transhistorical truths regarding this nature that are accessible to thoughtful human beings at all times.[25] But without the assistance of metaphysics, which many Straussians distrust,[26] and epistemology, which they ignore or contemn, it is hard to say what is meant by the transhistorical, much less how we can be sure we have proper access to it.

Straussian criticisms of Heidegger and other modern philosophers for having abandoned the concept of nature, a concept that guided classical political philosophy, ring hollow in a world dominated by post-Aristotelian, nonteleological natural science. The nature that Heidegger is faulted for ignoring is not nature as modern science understands it, that is, inertial mechanics, fields of force, relativity, and quantum mechanics. It seems to be, rather, nature as Aristotle understood it. Now, one can certainly deny that post-Aristotelian natural science has made a significant advance beyond Aristotle. But to support this denial requires either re-asserting Aristotle's teleological nature or reinterpreting his account of it in such as way as to dispense with the comprehensive teleology he argues for. Strauss himself seems to have had doubts about the former.[27] And the latter does not solve but only aggravates the problem we have been considering. For if the cosmic order known as nature has slid out of chaos by chance and is fated to slide back into chaos, to be nature *only for the time being,* then its present, apparently stable character may well be an illusion. At least, it cannot be known not to be an illusion. For it is likely that nature undergoes modifications over time, most or all of which are barely noticeable, if noticeable at all, to us. And there is no compelling reason to think that human nature itself is exempt from this process of slight but ongoing alteration, if human nature is a part of nature, so considered. Man would then be historical in his very being, just as historicism contends.

One might respond that it is not man that is comprehended by teleological nature. Rather it is nature that is comprehended by teleological man. That is to say, nature, indeed the whole objective order, is constituted by, or at least is no more than a correlate of, transcendental subjectivity. But, as we have seen, the concept of transcendental subjectivity is vulnerable to historicist appropriation and disfiguring, except when—as is most conspicuous in Kant—it is understood to function in terms of *a priori* principles, which are the modern analogues of Plato's timeless *eidē*.[28] In any case, Aristotle's statement that man is by nature political means, at first glance, that man and his ends fit within a larger teleological whole, which is exactly what Aristotle argues nature to be and of which he argues formal principles, that is, *eidē* and not matter, to be the prime constituent.[29] If nature is not really teleological after all, then, to repeat, how can it comprehend human nature, which is incontestably teleological? What exactly is gained by speaking today of man as *by nature* political, as *by nature* possessing reason, and as *by nature* desiring to know?

What is gained, one might respond, is the notion of something essential and permanent in the makeup of man. But the status and even the meaning of essence and of the permanent, which used to be called "the eternal," is precisely the concern of metaphysics, which used to be called "first philosophy." The essences of things were held to form the content of eternal truth. It can be countered, of course, and it has been countered, that truth, though certainly non-spatial, is nonetheless temporal. It is just the changing "way" of things. But truth so understood is precisely the historicist's concept of truth and can hardly be deployed against historicism.

From the perspective of philosophy as classically conceived, a declared "draw" with Heideggerian historicism begins to suggest itself as a tolerable substitute for an outright refutation of it, a refutation that does not simply beg the question. After all, that the philosophic way of life is the most choiceworthy way of life might not appear to be radically undermined by an unresolved, or even irresolvable, intra-philosophical disagreement about whether human reason and the truth accessible to "man as man" are transhistorical or whether they are historically conditioned. But what is the religious believer to make of this intra-philosophical standoff?[30] Will he not point out that philosophy as classically conceived cannot so much as attempt to refute the possibility of revelation, or even the moral presuppositions of belief in revelation, if neither the concept of human nature nor even the authority of transhistorical reason, i.e., logic, to which all refutations appeal but which Heidegger calls into question, can be validated but must be asserted by an act of will, which, however resolute, is not *fully* determined by evidence?

In the analogy that Socrates presents at the beginning of the seventh book of the *Republic,* the cave has an opening to the outside. This opening can be discerned only because it is illuminated by a light that is shining outside the cave, a light that is not a product of human artifice. If there were no illuminated opening to the outside, one could at most tunnel horizontally through the walls of the cave, enter other caves, and celebrate the surprisingly diverse ways in which communities exist. According to the analogy, however, a vertical ascent out of the cave is indeed possible, and this possibility rests on a dialectical examination of opinions. The examination is said to culminate in catching sight not only of what *is* without qualification, as opposed to mere images, but of the *archē,* the chief source, both of what *is* and of truth.[31] The analogy of the cave, which invites and even requires a political interpretation, is nonetheless not fully intelligible without a consideration of the preceding analogies of the sun and the divided line, which resist political interpretation.[32] The attempt to detach political philosophy from metaphysics and epistemology, and to treat it as an entirely self-contained field of inquiry, marks a significant departure from the political philosophy of Plato and Aristotle. They were not content merely to point out the inconsistencies of Protagorian relativism, which is but the prototype of historicism, for they realized that there could not be "eidetic analyses" of anything in this world, including human morality, except in the light of *eidē,* that is, permanent principles that endow temporal things with whatever being and intelligibility they possess. And so they undertook metaphysical inquiries into being and truth that, though leading them far beyond the political, ended up shedding much-needed light back on the political.[33] Their inquiries enabled them to catch sight of an atemporal order in light of which they could understand the temporal realm of the human, independently of the claims of revelation. On the assumption that the philosopher aims at contemplating something other than his own autonomy and ability to live without hope, the possibility of the timeless, so far from being a threat to philosophy, is actually a presupposition of philosophy, at least of any philosophy that does not reduce to historicism or to some cruder form of relativism.[34]

Socrates says that as a young man he wanted to know the causes of things, not only why things come to be and why they pass away, but why they *are.* That Socrates regarded the last question as distinct from the first signals the interest he had, even in his "pre-Socratic" period, in the ultimate principles of being and not just becoming.[35] He does not describe his turn from sensory inspection of the visible world as a turn to the political but, more generally, to *logoi*, that is, accounts of things in human discourse. It is in *logoi* rather than sensory perception that permanent and universal principles seem to emerge. Socrates' turn to *logoi* entailed, to be sure, an examination of accounts of justice, if only because justice is commonly supposed to have some relation to the good, and the good seemed to him, even prior to his turn, to be closely connected with ultimate principles, perhaps even to be an ultimate supra-moral principle itself.[36] But human discourse, in articulating the "riddle of being," can and must consider not only political matters but other important matters as well, such as the nature of discourse itself, the foundations of mathematics, the character of the beautiful and its relationship to moral nobility, the distinction between knowledge and both perception and opinion, and even the architectonic principles of "the whole" to the extent that they can be caught sight of, if only dimly. Socrates, as Plato presents him,[37] and Plato himself took great interest in these matters, as did Aristotle.[38]

It is a presupposition of all philosophical inquiry, at least as classically conceived, and therefore a presupposition of liberal education itself, that there is such a thing as truth, incorporeal and atemporal. And it is a further presupposition that this truth is not divinely revealed but is accessible to human reason on the basis of ordinary human experience. These presuppositions are not only theoretical. They are metaphysical as well, for they cannot be reduced to statements about physical matter merely.[39] The concept of truth, as permanent and rationally accessible, a concept indispensable to the philosophical critique of both Heideggerian historicism and Biblical religion, can be validated only through metaphysical and epistemological inquiries. If a genuine validation cannot be achieved, then an account— even if nothing more than a likely story—must be given of truth that is at least as plausible as those advanced by the alternatives of historicism and Biblical religion.

Truth is often taken to refer to the agreement of a certain state of affairs with the mind, that is, to be a feature of propositions and not of things. It is surely not a spatial, corporeal thing, like a chunk of dirt or a stone. And it is neither an incorporeal quality of corporeal things like color and size nor an incorporeal relationship between them like distance. For truth has according to its very meaning an essential, however poorly understood, relationship to the mind, and the mind cannot be asserted without contradiction to be a corporeal thing or even an epiphenomenon of corporeal things.[40] It is often said that only a sentence or proposition can be true or false. Aristotle advances this conception,[41] but he also holds that being and truth are correlative, if not ultimately equivalent. In the *Metaphysics* he at one point says that the expression "is" means "is true." His example is "Socrates is musical."[42] Aristotle thinks that this sentence is equivalent to the sentence, "It is true that Socrates is musical." Accordingly, he says that the most proper sense of being is the true and the false. When one thinks what is combined *as* combined, one thinks truly; but when one thinks what is *separated* as combined, then one thinks falsely; and so forth.[43] Regarding things that cannot be otherwise than as they are, that is, things that are necessarily one way rather than another, statements about them are not sometimes true and at other times false, but are "always either true or false."[44] The "always" implies eternal truth. An eternal truth is one that transcends all context, history, and particular perspectives.

We typically speak of discovering a truth. The discovery of something, as opposed to the making or invention of it, presupposes the prior existence of the thing discovered. This is what is meant by discovery. For example, when one says that Galileo discovered craters on the surface of the moon one means, among other things, that the craters existed before he discovered them. Similarly, when one says that Galileo discovered the law of physics according to which bodies of different weights fall with equal speeds in a vacuum, one means that this law of physics existed before he discovered it. Galileo did not invent craters on the moon, and he did not invent the law of physics. He is said to have discovered both the craters and the law, and both are thereby implied to have existed prior to and independently of his discovery. Our discovery of a truth, of any truth, is the disclosing of something that was previously hidden from our view. But if that is so, then truth can hardly be just the agreement of some state of affairs with our mind, for it is not this agreement that is discovered. On the contrary, the agreement comes into being concurrently with the discovery and does not exist prior to it. Truth conceived as the agreement of our mind with the object it is considering turns out to be a secondary and derivative concept. The primary concept of truth is that of things *in their intelligibility*—of being *as intelligible*—for this is what we *discover,* in the strict sense of this word.

Of course, if our mind's original relationship to truth occurs not in a discovery, but in an act whereby it constitutes truth, however one might understand this to happen, then the discovery is a subsequent event in which the mind only becomes explicitly conscious of the antecedently constituted product of its own activity. But, *if* one breaks with this tendency, explicit in modern philosophy, to understand truth as originally constituted by the human mind, and commits oneself, instead, to the Platonic view that our original relation to truth is one of discovery rather than constitution,[45] and *if* one at the same time holds to the non-Platonic view that truth is essentially correlated with a mind that doesn't just discover truth but already knows it, then one cannot avoid the conclusion that, when we discover truth, what we are discovering is a relationship that already exists between it and a mind that already knows it, prior to and independently of our act of discovery. And *if* one holds, moreover, that the truth we discover is an eternal truth, such as a logical principle or a theorem of geometry, or even a law of physics, then there must be an eternal mind that is already, and always, knowing it. This conclusion follows of necessity if one accepts all three of these premises, namely, that the original relation of the human mind to the truth is one of discovery rather than of constitution, that the locus of truth is the mind, and that there are eternal truths. One or more of these premises can be called into question. But it seems that they are most frequently called into question not because taken individually they are implausible in their own right, but because taken together, along with the *further* premise that the human mind is not itself eternal, they imply a theology of some kind, and modern philosophy is resistant to theology of any kind. Nonetheless, it is precisely the conception of truth as the correlate or content of an eternal mind, in whose act of knowing we humans can from time to time participate, that is most resistant to historicist reduction.[46]

The possibility of eternal truth or even the possibility of a divine intellect should not be worrisome to philosophy.[47] What should be worrisome, as Strauss points out, is the possibility of revelation, which, like creation *ex nihilo,* is the act not of a divine intellect merely but of a divine *will.*[48] The possibility that a divine intellect, or God, could freely reveal something of decisive significance to human beings of his own choosing and at his own chosen time and place would be the undoing of philosophy, at least of philosophy classically understood as a way of life that can *definitively* justify its claim to preeminent choiceworthiness for those who are able to live it.[49]

These considerations lead us back to the issue of authority that we brushed up against earlier. It is incorrect to say that liberal education has no use for the concept of authority. In order to escape from being dominated by mere opinions, including inadequately examined personal convictions,[50] some authority must be invoked, and this authority is said to be reason itself. But there is an ambiguity in the use of the word "reason" here, as it can mean everything from logic to plain old common sense. Given that "common sense" is itself ambiguous, I shall use "reason" in the relatively narrow sense of logic, that is, deductive reasoning and the indemonstrable but self-evident principles, such as the law of noncontradiction, on which deductive reasoning depends. Reason takes it as axiomatic, as self-evident, that there is no contradiction between itself and truth, which is to say that truth is not self-contradictory and that from true premises only true conclusions can be validly inferred. Reason, understood as logic, concerns the form of thought. Reason does not, of itself, supply thought with any real content. The content with which thought busies itself has to come from outside of reason, and it comes from experience. But experiences vary. The experiences that liberal education takes as authoritative are experiences that are verifiable and available to "man as man."

The authority of ordinary verifiable experiences is not universally accepted, at least not as a final authority. It is not accepted as a final authority by Biblical religion, in particular. Biblical religion appeals to certain experiences, for example, the consciousness—which the critic can of course convince himself is deluded consciousness—that guilt is real, that charity is unqualifiedly good, and that the meaning of our lives consists of more than pleasure attained, more even than the pleasure of self-admiration attendant upon progress toward wisdom. This consciousness accounts for what receptivity there is to prophetic, scriptural, or ecclesiastical proclamations. The receptivity and the proclamation are the essential "moments," so to speak, in what is held to be revelation. This kind of experience is hardly the verifiable experience that natural science, which grows out of liberal education, takes as authoritative. According to uncompromising natural science, everything occurring in this world of ours must have a worldly cause exclusively. That is to say, there can be no miracles, neither free creation of the world *ex nihilo* at one extreme, nor radically free moral choice at the other, nor any miracles in between.

Natural science, however, lacks the wherewithal to rigorously demonstrate its architectonic principle that every event must have a cause distinct from itself but homogenous with it. Instead, it can only assume this principle.[51] Natural science is constituted and even defined by this assumption. It is reassured that this grounding, but ungrounded, assumption is justified because it never comes across any particular phenomenon that undermines it. The phenomena that would appear to undermine it, for example, the conviction that we possess an inscrutable, even supernatural, faculty of freedom whereby we are radically responsible for at least some of our actions, science says it can account for in its own terms. The conviction that we are morally free can be accounted for, so it is said, as successfully by psychology as by theology, and without the complications of the latter. But, for the religious believer, psychology is at most only an alternative account, the plausibility of which depends at least in part on the orientation, ultimately voluntary, of the one who hears it.

The real difference between Biblical religion and liberal education at its acme, that is, philosophy, does not consist, as is commonly alleged, in their different estimations of reason, or logic, but in their different estimations of common verifiable experience. Biblical religion does not understand itself to be irrational, and believers try to defend themselves against the charge of irrationality, that is, against the charge of believing something self-contradictory. Of course, logic does not supply belief with its content any more than it supplies natural science with its content. Rather, the content that reason works with is supplied, it is said, by God himself. In a crucial respect, then, the believer and the unbelieving scientific empiricist are in the same position, logically speaking. For both base their convictions on something that goes beyond the laws of logic. To give the claims of such common verifiable experience precedence over the claims of revelation is not more rational, i.e., it is not more logical, than the reverse. For logic is, to repeat, formal and indifferent to the source of the content to which it is applied. The so-called "conflict between reason and revelation" is tendentiously labeled, and would not be recognized as such by any theologian worthy of the name.

On the other hand, it can be countered that the deepest critique of Biblical religion does not consist solely in the assertion that what it purports to reveal is not borne out by common verifiable experience. After all, so far from denying the disparity between the findings of common verifiable experience and the claims of revelation, Biblical religion actually insists on this disparity. Rather than begging the question, as natural science does in its critique, philosophy tries to show that Biblical religion is in conflict with reason itself, in the worst possible way. It tries to show that the fundamental claims of Biblical religion, or their presuppositions, are either logically self-contradictory or contradict what is self-evident. Does Biblical religion not rest on an uncritical conception of justice and the human good, and overlook the fact that man's boundless longing for happiness is ingrained in human nature itself? Does it not pertain to the very meaning of the good that it is always one's *own* good? Is it not of the nature of law, whether of human or of allegedly divine origin, that it has to admit of exceptions in extreme circumstances and as dictated by prudence? Is the concept of a free will—whether of the creator or of the creature said to be created in his image and likeness—that is, a will neither determined by another nor altogether indeterminate and random, anything other than a logical absurdity? Can the believer make even elementary sense to himself and his fellow believers, to say nothing of his critics, of what he means by revelation? The question is whether Biblical theology is fully able to meet, on the common field of rational discourse, these and similar challenges posed by philosophical critique. Surely, if it is constitutionally unable to meet these challenges it reduces to an obscurantism that has no legitimate hold on the allegiance of a rational being.

Any theologian worthy of the name will try to rise to these challenges, and in response to the above questions he will ask questions of his own. Does the question of whether it is morality *or* happiness that is the human good overlook the possibility that it might be both together, not regarded as a mere sum but synthetically related as ground and consequence respectively? Is the pronouncement that the good is always one's *own* good intended to rule out the possibility that one's own good might include one's own moral *integrity,* the only good that nothing can take away without one's *own* consent? Could any circumstances, no matter how extreme, exempt one from obedience to the commandment to love God with the whole of one's being, or even from the command to love one's neighbor—that is, to will his good, his moral and intellectual flourishing—just as one loves oneself? Is the concept of self-determination, that is, of freedom of the will, any more self-contradictory than that of self-consciousness, or for that matter, self-knowledge? Might not revelation be precisely the supernatural penetration of an otherwise hopelessly self-deceived and wounded human nature by a call from beyond commanding us to return to what we were originally made and meant to be?[52]

The philosophical critique of Biblical religion, the critique that would go deeper than the question-begging empiricism of naive natural science, presupposes, in addition to a metaphysically and epistemologically *developed* conception of transhistorical truth that withstands the assault of historicism, a profound understanding of Biblical religion. Philosophy presupposes, to the extent possible, an understanding of Biblical religion as it understands itself, lest its critique be directed to a caricature only or deteriorate into mockery. A profound understanding of Biblical religion, however, cannot be achieved without a measure of sympathetic, however cautious, openness. And it is a question whether the philosopher can allow himself this openness while still being true to the ideal of autonomy to which he has committed himself. Oddly enough, it might be easier for the ostensibly closed-minded believer, assuming he realizes that he is only a believer and not a knower,[53] to engage with the ostensibly open-minded philosopher on the philosopher's own turf than the other way around.

The presuppositions that there is transhistorical truth and that the truth most worthy of being known is accessible to man without the assistance of supernatural revelation are equivalent to the presupposition that human reason and common verifiable experience alone are the final authorities for man. Philosophy, which is arguably liberal education at its foundation and at its peak, would like to ground this presupposition. The grounding that is called for is nothing less ambitious than self-grounding, guided by the lofty aspiration of autonomous, or radically free, humanity. Liberal education is ultimately a serious undertaking. It stands or falls with the critical examination of the presuppositions that animate it. And so the proponents of liberal education must listen to and learn what they can from the critics of liberal education, not simply because of the loftiness of their aspirations, but because of the gravity of what is at stake.

NOTES

1 *Republic* 510b–511c2; 533b6–c5. Compare Hegel, *Phänomenologie des Geistes,* edited by J. Hoffmeister (Hamburg: Felix Meiner Verlag, 1952), 35–39 (English translation of an earlier edition by J. B. Baillie, *Phenomenology of Spirit* [London: George Allen & Unwin, 1910], 100–05).

2 See *Republic* 515a1: "*kai andriantas kai alla zōia lithina te kai xulina.*" On the assumption that the artisans who make the artifacts, the shadows of which are cast on the wall of the cave, represent poets or the pupils of poets (377d2–5; 378d5), it follows that at least one of them has been outside the cave—apparently even before the prospective philosopher manages to leave it—and that, once out, he beheld the natural originals (*Odyssey* X, 303), which he subsequently imitated. Even if the animals he imitated were indigenous to the cave, like bats, or just wandered temporarily into it, the artisan could have procured the *wood* out of which he fashioned wooden (*xulina*) artifacts only from the region outside the cave. It is, however, not clear that he had to look at the sun to engage in his mimetic *poiēsis.*

3 See Augustine, *Confessions* X, ch. 35, and Martin Heidegger, *Sein und Zeit* (Tübingen: Max Niemeyer Verlag, 1927), 171 (English translation by John Macquarrie and Edward Robinson, *Being and Time* [New York: Harper and Row, 1962], 215); also Hans Jonas, "The Nobility of Sight," in *The Phenomenon of Life* (New York: Harper and Row, 1966), 135–52.

4 Edmund Husserl, *Erfahrung und Urteil* (Hamburg: Felix Meiner Verlag, 1972), 235–39 (English translation by James Churchill and Karl Ameriks, *Experience and Judgment* [Evanston: Northwestern University Press, 1973], 200–03).

5 The contradictory claim to the effect that not everything is a matter of perspective merely, that not everything is relative, but that there are at least some objective, even absolute truths, could be called "absolutism." But this word is as uncongenial to contemporary sensibilities, as "relativism" is the opposite. Moreover, it could be mistaken for the absurd claim that every opinion is absolute knowledge, a claim that would in fact be indistinguishable from relativism. The contradictory of relativism is not that *nothing* is relative but only that *not everything* is relative, that at least some claims or propositions are true and that their denials are false, without qualification.

6 *Theaetetus* 170e5–171c1; *Euthydemus* 286c2–4.

7 *Metaphysics* 1006a11–22; *Phänomenologie des Geistes*, 88–89 (English translation, 159–60).

8 *Metaphysics* 1008b12–31.

9 Leo Strauss, *Natural Right and History* (Chicago: University of Chicago Press, 1953), 10, 97–101; "Progress or Return," in *The Rebirth of Classical Political Rationalism* (Chicago: University of Chicago Press, 1989), 270.

10 Kant, *Critique of Pure Reason,* B 163–165, 263.

11 It is also what prevents modern subjectivist philosophy from collapsing into solipsism.

12 *De Anima* 426a20 (cf. 429a27–30); *Physics* 223a23–29; *Metaphysics* 1036a5–10; cf. 1040a3. Cf. *De Anima* 430a15.

13 Descartes, *Meditations* II: *Sed quid igitur sum? res cogitans; quid est hoc? nempe dubitans, intelligens, affirmans, negans, volens, nolens, imaginans, quoque et sentiens.* Although willing and willing-not-to are included in this list, Descartes still construes *cogitans* as primarily theoretical. *Volens* and *nolens* have an important role to play in the theoretical activity of the mind, quite apart from the sphere of the practical. Ibid., IV.

14 "An object . . . is that in the concept (*Begriff*) of which the manifold of a given intuition is united" (*Critique of Pure Reason* B 137). That for Kant synthesis is consummated in a theoretical grasping is only partially true. For the moral law is a synthetic proposition *a priori* (*Critique of Practical Reason* A 55–56). Nonetheless, as an imperative it is related back to a world that is already constituted as an object of perceptual experience (ibid., A 74).

15 *Being and Time*, Sections 13 and 44; also Heidegger, *Metaphysical Foundations of Logic,* translated by Michael Heim (Bloomington: Indiana University Press, 1984), 103–07, and *Einführung in die Metaphysik* (Tübingen: Max Niemeyer Verlag, 1953), 19, 92–94 (English translation by Ralph Manheim, *Introduction to Metaphysics* [New Haven, Conn.: Yale University Press, 1959], 25, 120–23).

16 That we constitute our *experience* of the world is indisputable. That we also constitute the *world,* even the world *that we experience,* is disputable.

17 Edmund Husserl, *Zur Phänomenologie des Inneren Zeitbewusstseins,* 1893–1917 (Husserliana, Band X, The Hague: Martinus Nijhoff, 1966), 19–72 (English translation by James Churchill of an earlier edition, *The Phenomenology of Internal Time Consciousness* [Bloomington: Indiana University Press, 1964], 40–97). Cf. Augustine, *Confessions* IX, 28.

18 *Sein und Zeit,* 420–28 (English translation, 472–80); Strauss, "An Introduction to Heideggerian Existentialism," in *The Rebirth of Classical Political Rationalism,* 29.

19 *Critique of Pure Reason* B 93: "[A] concept is never related to an object immediately, but rather to some other representation of it (be the latter an intuition or itself a concept). Judgment is therefore the mediate cognition of an object, and consequently the representation of a representation of it." On the implications of this statement see Gerhard Krüger, *Philosophie und Moral in der Kantischen Critique* (Tübingen: J.C.B. Mohr, 1931), 18–21.

20 Consider Heidegger's *aperçu* regarding Hegel in *What is a Thing?* (translated by W. B. Barton and Vera Deutsch [Chicago: University of Chicago Press, 1967], 150–51).

21 Still other criteria for the worth of opinions might be invoked, in lieu of freedom from prejudice, among them internal consistency, formal elegance, pragmatic utility, and conformity to current ideology.

22 Plato, *Lysis* 218a7.

23 Strauss, *Natural Right and History,* 75; Preface to *Spinoza's Critique of Religion* (New York: Schocken Books, 1965), 29–30; "Progress and Return," in *The Rebirth of Classical Political Rationalism,* 264–70.

24 *Einführung in die Metaphysik,* 18; *Wegmarken,* "Was ist Metaphysik?" (Frankfurt: Victorio Klosterman, 1967), 5 (English translation by David Farrell Krell, "What is Metaphysics?" in *Basic Writings* [New York: Harper and Row, 1977], 99).

25 Strauss, *On Tyranny* (Chicago: University of Chicago Press, 2000), 212. "Philosophy in the strict and classical sense is quest for the eternal order or for the eternal cause or causes of all things. It *presupposes* then that there is an eternal and unchangeable order within which History takes place and which is not in any way affected by History" (emphasis added).

26 I use the term "Straussian" with respect.

27 *Natural Right and History,* 7–8.

28 Note Kant's remark on "prejudice" in the *Critique of Pure Reason* B 77.

29 *Physics,* 193b8; compare *Metaphysics* 1037a18.

30 See Galatians 4:4; John 14:6.

31 *Republic* 508d2–509b7; 517c1; 532a1–534d1.

32 Allan Bloom, in his interpretation of the analogy of the cave, rightly insists, "Only by constant reference back to the divided line can one understand the

cave" (*The Republic of Plato* [New York: Basic Books, 1968], 403). However, Bloom's interpretation of the divided line, which he takes primarily as an illustration of what Strauss calls "noetic heterogeneity" (see note 38 below), is sketchy. Bloom focuses almost exclusively on the subjective modes of awareness that the four segments of the line represent and virtually ignores their objective correlates, perhaps because he is convinced that the analogy is intended less to instruct than "to dazzle the mind's eye as the sun dazzles the body's eye" (402). His most intriguing remarks concern the middle two segments, but he seems not to have appreciated—at least he does not address—Jacob Klein's argument that *eikasia* is in fact a more privileged mode of awareness than *pistis*, although he explicitly praises Klein's treatment of *eikasia* and recommends it for consideration (464; cf. Klein, *A Commentary on Plato's Meno* [Chapel Hill: University of North Carolina Press, 1965], 112–25). Bloom says little about *noēsis* in his interpretation of the divided line, and he is interested in dialectic primarily as a "combination of daring and moderation" (406; cf. Strauss, *What is Political Philosophy?* [Glencoe, Ill.: The Free Press, 1959], 40). Bloom offers not so much an interpretation of the analogy of the sun as a restatement of it (402), and he obscures the analogy of the cave, and thereby that of the sun as well, with the observation that "openness to philosophy is the light in the cave which Socrates and those near him fought to preserve when its infancy was so severely threatened" (411). But the light in which philosophy takes an interest is not simply the openness to *itself*. That light is the truth. Cf. Eva Brann, *The Music of the Republic* (Philadelphia: Paul Dry Books, 2004), 170–216.

33 Aristotle raises the question of whether the investigation of first principles, including the so-called principle of non-contradiction, is part of first philosophy, the enquiry into being qua being (*Metaphysics* 996b26–997a17). His answer is that it is (ibid. 1005a19 ff; 1005b20; see 1007a 22–b19).

34 Strauss realized that Heideggerian historicism could not be reduced to vulgar relativism. See his letter of February 26, 1961, to Hans-Georg Gadamer, "Correspondence Concerning *Wahrheit und Methode*," *The Independent Journal of Philosophy*, 2 (1978): 7, first full paragraph. Compare *Natural Right and History*, 26–29; and "Philosophy as Rigorous Science and Political Philosophy," in *Studies in Platonic Political Philosophy*, 31–33. Note also the following remark in "An Introduction to Heideggerian Existentialism," *The Rebirth of Classical Political Rationalism*, 30: "The more I understand what Heidegger is aiming at, the more I see how much still escapes me. The most stupid thing I could do would be to close my eyes or to reject his work."

35 *Phaedo* 96a9; 97b5; 97c8.

36 Ibid., 97c3–98a6; 99c1–6.

37 *Epistle II* 314c4. Aristotle, *Metaphysics*, 987b1–9; 1078b19–1079a4.

38 *Physics* 192b35–193a13 and 203a15; *Metaphysics* 987b1–988a17; 1028b190. In the *Metaphysics*—the principal theme of which is about as far removed from the political as is that of the *Organon*, which is single-mindedly preoccupied

with *logoi*—Aristotle distinguishes the inquiry in which he is engaged from that of the physicists (ibid., 1005a35 and context especially; *Physics* 192a35). First philosophy, every bit as much as political philosophy, orients itself by *logoi* (e.g., 1003a33, 1028a10, 1029b13, 1034b20, 1038b1, to cite just a few illustrative passages). See, in this connection, Strauss's letter of May 28, 1957, to Alexandre Kojève (included in *On Tyranny* [Chicago: University of Chicago Press, 2000], 277–79), and his further remarks on "noetic heterogeneity" in *What is Political Philosophy?* 39–40.

39   Cf. Edmund Husserl, *Ideas Pertaining to a Pure Phenomenology,* Book I, §30–§32.

40   Husserl, *Logical Investigations,* Volume I, Prolegomena, Chapters Three through Nine. For a brief but vivid exposé of this contradiction, see Hans Jonas, "Materialism, Determinism, and the Mind," in *The Phenomenon of Life,* 127–34.

41   *Metaphysics* 1011a25.

42   Ibid., 1017a31–35. By implication, then, "It is true that Socrates is musical" means that Socrates is, *really is,* musical. This necessary relation between truth and being is the basis for equating the true with the real or genuine. True friendship is real friendship, for example.

43   Ibid., 1051b2–5.

44   Ibid., 1051b16.

45   *Republic* 508 D.

46   The account of truth as unhiddenness and of beings as emerging, or having emerged, out of a hiddenness in which they were previously shut off from our view, does some justice to how truth is encountered by *us.* Cf. *Sein und Zeit,* 218 ff. (English translation, 261 ff.). Needless to say, if there is a perfect, i.e., divine, intellect, then there never was an original hiddenness out of which things subsequently emerged for *it.* From the perspective of a divine intellect, things were always unhidden. More precisely, they were always *present.*

47   *Metaphysics* 982b29–3a12; *Nicomachean Ethics* 1178b8–24; consider the conditional at 1099b11.

48   See note 23 above.

49   According to the terms of Plato's analogy of the cave, not only is it impossible, as has been recognized, for someone who has left the cave to bring the light of the sun back down into it, the sunlight (not to mention the sun itself) does not choose to come down into the cave, and according to the terms of the analogy could not do so in any case. The initiative for an encounter with this *archē* lies exclusively with man. (See *Republic* 381a6–c7, and compare 382e8.) It should be remembered that, according to Aristotle, God not only does not create the world, which is eternal, he cannot know or even think of its existence (*Metaphysics* 1074b20–35). He cannot know, then, that he is the prime mover. Even less can he know of, or take an interest, in man's moral strivings and religious observances. Nor can he reveal anything to man. After all, if he is known to be *noēsis noēseōs* solely, what's left to reveal? Not only the metaphysical inquiries

of Plato and Aristotle, but even their express theological teachings, so far from being mere pretences—forced upon them by political or pedagogical exigencies—of openness to the possibility of revelation properly so called, plainly and forcefully call this possibility into question.

50 "To follow one's conviction is certainly more than surrendering oneself to authority; but in the conversion from holding something as true on the basis of authority to holding something as true on the basis of one's own conviction, the content of what is held is not necessarily altered, and truth has not thereby taken the place of error. Sticking to a system of opinion and prejudice based on the authority of others and doing so on the basis of one's own conviction differ from one another only by virtue of the conceit that animates the latter" (Hegel, *Phenomenology of Spirit*, "Introduction").

51 Strauss, "Progress or Return," 266.

52 *Spinoza's Critique of Religion,* bottom of 8 to top of 9; cf. "Note on the Plan of Nietzsche's *Beyond Good and Evil,*" in *Studies in Platonic Political Philosophy* (Chicago: University of Chicago Press, 1983), 182, top.

53 I Corinthians 13:12; John 20:29.

COLLOQUIAL HERMENEUTICS:
EVA BRANN'S *ODYSSEY*

Mera J. Flaumenhaft

EVA BRANN HAS WRITTEN a most unusual book, one that will make its readers think both about Homer and about the meaning of "interpretation." Deceptively simple, *Homeric Moments: Clues to Delight in Reading the Odyssey and the Iliad* ignores all the conventions of contemporary scholarly books. It has forty-eight little chapters, the shortest only two pages long. Readers will be intrigued to find that several chapters have the same names; several bear names of characters, with the author's epithets substituted for Homer's. Phrases and sentences are repeated at different places, sometimes with slight variations. The first thirty-four pages are spent "Accounting for the Title." The author is learned about Greek mythology, religion, philosophy, syntax, diction, and metrics. But there are no footnotes, index, bibliography, or untransliterated Greek quotations. Ancient commentators are mentioned, but the vast secondary literature on Homer is not, although Brann obviously has read it too in the fifty years during which she has been poring over Homer's stories, "both by myself and with students" (xiii). Only poets are present as helpful fellow readers of Homer. For the most part, they are quoted anonymously, although identified in endnotes that also provide the locations of most of the Homeric passages discussed. Famous passages are not usually referred to by the names the scholars use—the "Teichoscopia" and various "aristeias," for example. The book contains no references to Brann's own scholarly tomes, *Greek Geometric Pottery, The World of the Imagination, What, Then, Is Time?,* and *The Ways of Nay-saying,* although *Homeric Moments* frequently explores these same questions. What Eva Brann is up to in her latest offering remains to be seen; it is obviously a labor of love.

Brann believes that Homer's poems are for everyone, that they are about recognizable human beings and the things they think about, and that those who delight in them should not turn them into alien artifacts accessible only to a few: "If you're human, Homer is home territory" (20). Thus, she

This review first appeared in *Interpretation,* Volume 31, Issue 1 (Fall, 2003), 93–102.

offers a "way of reading" the epics which she distinguishes from "what critics call a 'reading,' that is, a total interpretive hypothesis" (19). In the introductory chapter, she briefly acknowledges the recent academic debate about "criticism," making it clear that she thinks that *authors* write *books,* that they *intend* to convey ideas and to teach their readers, and that they give "clues" to help these readers see what they *mean.* She rejects the notion that "an ingenious professional reader . . . may play any half-plausible riff off the text" (12), as well as the postmodern denial of a poet behind the poem. Rather, in a spirit of "reverent faith" (13) that the poet knows what he is doing, the interpreter can help others read receptively and attentively by encouraging them to rely on their own lives and learning. The imaginative interpretation does not "deconstruct" the poet, legitimating any and all interpretations. Nor does it mine Homer for "philosophemes and political prototheory" (23). Brann does not doubt that the "poems contain them"—but "embodied and contingent, as life contains them," and not as "covert systematic lessons" (23). She does not discuss The Beautiful or Being or Becoming, although she does suggest that the "single-minded Parmenides . . . is in almost every way the intended opposite of Odysseus" (22). She does not provide a long theoretical discussion of the oft-noted first appearance in Greek literature of the word "nature." But references like those to "elemental nature" (191) and the "natural marriage bed" (299), as well as a pervasive concern with Homer's thinking about *human* nature, *will* guide the reader, in a tone appropriate to the story, to think about "nature" as an idea in Homer. Finally, she describes a monster, the three-headed Cerberus of misguided readings of Homer (24 ff.): "mentality," the error of reading the poems as records of alien or primitive thought; "formulaicism," the error of thinking that the formulas are *merely* instruments to help the oral poet remember; and "intratextuality," a "denatured" (30) way of reading Homer's stories as merely self-referential words cut off from a coherent "extratextual" world. Homer's world is a web, but it is not self-contained; we readers are meant to "round out the text" with our own "auditory and visual imaginations" (30). Except for an occasional remark, this is the last we hear of the critics. This clear and sensible explanation of matters of momentous importance to contemporary professional interpreters of literature now gives way to Homeric "moments" and "clues to delight."

Before we return to the title, a word should be said about Brann's distinctive style. It will come as no surprise that she speaks in ordinary conversational English, avoiding technical jargon and stuffy abstractions, and does not hesitate to use a modern colloquialism to catch the meaning of the original. Thus, Odysseus "snowed his audience" (47); he is aided by "a swine-herd and a ranch hand" (25). She speaks in the first person, and permits her-self exclamations (273), "oracular assertions" (175), rhetorical questions (180), and lists of "comments" (169, 228). The withholding of citations until the very end is intended to help the reader concentrate, without inter-ruptions, on Homer's text. But for some readers this might result in *more* flipping away from the story Brann is recounting. Perhaps brief locations of quotes and the identification of poets *within* the text might have made the book even more comfortable to read. Several pictures are included, and there are references to other stories, and observations about animals, chil-dren, shared human predicaments, and much more, in the coherent "extra-textual world" she defends at the beginning.

CLUES

Brann cautions against the elaborate verbal webs that some literary "the-orists" weave in their interpretations, yet she herself reads with sharp atten-tion to the "clues" in Homer's elaborate weaving of words. Technically, a "clew" is a ball of yarn or a thread, like the one that guided Theseus out of the Cretan labyrinth. In the preliminary chapter and the forty-eight chap-ters that follow, there are clues and cues, signs and keys, veiled facts and hid-den treasures. She says that the *Odyssey*, "the most complexly told tale I know," is "clear and decodable" (120), and she offers clues to the interpre-tation of allegories, verbal images, and whole stretches of the story. A brief allusion to a myth may reveal the deeper meaning of an episode. So, too, do Greek etymologies, especially of names, in which Homer often points to the character of a person or place.

A chapter about the gods begins the book. "The Homeric gods are not 'believed in'" (36)—this is not theology—but, carefully observed, they are an important clue to understanding the life of us mortals. Their levity points to our gravity, their freedom to our limitations. Like the divinities on the Parthenon frieze, they appear large and detached, yet they are present; they observe and they take us seriously. Paradoxically, these less serious "beings of the imagination" (45) show sharply how mortality itself is a clue to every-thing seriously human.

Similes are also clues with which the attentive reader can tease out the full meaning of Homer's "word texture" (83). Chapter 20, "Simile: the Dou-ble Vision," and many discussions of particular similes throughout the book show how these "brief raptures" (138) transport the reader from the present moment to the extended meaning of what they describe: to the peaceful background of the warring foreground of the *Iliad,* or to echoes of other characters and incidents. Brann will make the "poetic devices" come alive for both freshmen who don't yet know that they might matter to them, and for experienced readers who will find much that they have not noticed before. In the penultimate chapter, she offers a metaphor for the famous Homeric flashbacks. They are "time chasms," Homeric moments that allow the reader to travel long and far, while no time at all passes in the narrative. The embedded stories "*deepen* the human situation by opening up its foundations in the past beneath it" just as the extended similes project "harsh human events onto a distant horizon of art and nature" (292).

In the preliminary chapter, Brann cautions against the distractions of the "Homeric question" concerning the author of the epics, and of historical discussions about itinerant singers, oral verse, Yugoslavian bards, and other admittedly interesting topics. Such information must be obtained by reading secondary works that attempt to show how inherited, traditional formulas and epithets provide clues to the working mode of the "singer of tales." But Brann rightly insists that anyone, even a newcomer to the world of Homer, will soon see that the finished product as we have it is a thoroughly artful weaving together of these raw materials, wherever they came from, with an eye to the stories and thought of the poems. Following Brann's example, the reader will find clues for thought in Homer's selection of epithets and formulas, in his exact repetitions, variations, and changes in word order and rhythm. Unraveling this kind of clue will surely make the reader appreciate and delight in the "tight knit of Homer's tale" (38), even if we notice, as she does—with apparent delight—that Homer does occasionally nod.

Brann declares at the beginning her "agenda . . . to snaffle at least a few readers into learning Greek" (11). On nearly every page she shows how Homer's vocabulary, word order, and metrics are also clues to the meaning of his stories. She rightly assures us that even *some* access to the original Greek will enable a reader to understand *much* more while reading a good translation of Homer. But she is determined that even her Greekless readers will not remain clueless. With her transliterations, translations, and lucid explanations they too will be able to appreciate Homer's puns, and to begin to hear his pops and crackles, slips and slides, dactyls, spondees, and caesuras.

In addition to the many "small discoveries" that provide clues of the sort discussed so far, Brann shares several "large conjectures" (Preface). These more extended interpretations take shape in the course of the book and are stated in several extended passages. The first is that the *Iliad* and the *Odyssey* are continuous, the former is the background: harsh, austere, and admirable; the latter complements and contains it, is softer, multifaceted, and delightful. Achilles and Odysseus are best understood in each other's light: *minunthadios* ("brief-lived") and *tlaôn* ("enduring") are mutually revealing, as are *mênis* ("wrath") and *mêtis* ("guile"). Odysseus is the same man in both books. It takes a second epic to reveal that Ajax has a tragic as well as political dimension, and that Helen is capable of doing some good in the world she once shattered. Thus, although Brann remains an agnostic about the Homeric question, in her "way of reading" she is an unabashed "Aggregationist." She does not look to philological evidence or the shapes of shields, but focuses steadily on the plot, characters, and thought of the poems. Quite sensibly, she thinks that the night raid of Book Ten of the *Iliad*, whenever and however it got there, is undeniably "Homeric" (63). Perhaps this is why she weaves together the twenty-four books of the *Iliad* and the twenty-four books of the *Odyssey* into forty-eight continuous interpretive chapters.

A second larger conjecture in Brann's reading is that the *Odyssey* is not the other half of the *Iliad*, but is double in itself. Here she "clues out" (a quaint verb that she seems to like) a plausible reading that shows that there are two "odysseys." One is the *Odyssey* told by Homer, about a man who returns from a distant war after ten years of delays, detours, lost companions, and adventures in the "real" world. The other is the "odyssey" told by that man himself. Peopled by nymphs, monsters, and extra-human helpers, it has a fairy-tale quality. But these adventures are "truths told in figures" (247), and are thus rich in observations about real opportunities, desires, and dangers in Homer's real human beings, ones that every reader of Homer will recognize as his own. Odysseus tells this "odyssey" to the Phaeacians, and, again, at home, in bed, to his wife after they are reunited. Brann also carefully examines the "lying tales" Odysseus tells before he reveals his true identity in Ithaka; they are a "tissue of fact" (246) spun from scrambled versions of the "real" voyage home after the fall of Troy.

The discussion of Penelope's immediate recognition and delayed acknowledgment of her long-wandering husband is one of the most satisfying sections of Brann's book of clues. Here the delight is partly that she is pointing her fellow readers to Homeric clues about *clues*—the "signs" (*sêmata*) that these two astonishingly well-matched people are sending to each other as they come together after twenty years. Homer becomes more and more complex even as we see more deeply into the web.

MOMENTS

An extended discussion of time as a philosophical question is not to be found in this book. Instead, one encounters dozens of pregnant and provocative observations—momentary comments on the lives of beings that, while ephemeral, are nonetheless capable of transcending time: in memory, anticipation, and imagination. Some, like Achilles, glow intensely, but briefly, and go out, leaving behind them an eternal memory of their moment of glory in the world. Others, like Odysseus, live long, patient, calculating lives; they build and acquire, travel and govern, explore and inquire, and come home to wives and to children who will live after them. Rather than extending the discussion of these great Homeric alternatives, Brann illustrates them, not with purple passages yanked out like raisins from a cake (10), but offered as "moments . . . that are artfully enmeshed in the surrounding narrative" (11). She focuses the reader's attention on moments when time stops (98), or is at a standstill (155), when someone marks time (259), keeps time from running out (265), or kills time (265). There are moments that seem to last forever, and years that go by faster than it takes to chant a few lines of dactylic hexameter. In epic there is no single "Moment of Recognition as there is in tragedy" (284), but multiple recognitions that unfold in stages. Learning differs from development. Odysseus can be stable in character yet *polutropos*, different at different moments. Brann reminds us how, at different moments, we all "can be beautiful: we glow and crumble" (49–50). At the end of the *Odyssey,* "even the palace glows" (50). Such changes are a great wonder in Homer and in our own lives, familiar, yet so strange that we too might almost say a god is behind them.

Some of Brann's "oracular assertions" are explained, others are offered momentarily for the reader to live with and ponder for as long as he likes. The book seems to attempt in writing something like the experience of a stimulating seminar, a "seeding" ground for further thought. Brann points to some clues, explains and develops others, and keeps sending the reader back to the text to see how to respond to her suggestions. Some will find the book choppy and wish she'd say more, comment more thoroughly on everything in a Homeric moment, conclude a fully developed argument about the whole epic. But this is clearly not her aim. For example, she touches briefly, though repeatedly, on the question of verbal and visual description. Homeric moments are vignettes, snapshots, points in pointillist paintings, and fragments of a mosaic. Depictions in words, however, unlike pictures, take time; their parts are not simultaneous and they can never be instantaneous moments. But painters like Breughel the Elder and de Clerk show details that Homer's words can only "intimate" (125). To supplement her own words, Brann includes some pictures: a detail from a Greek potsherd and the old shoes from Van Gogh's painting. The carefully selected nine blocks of the mosaic-like cover depict—in the glowing red and black of painted pots—epic moments in the lives of the people Homer makes us see. This "mystery of cognitive mysteries" (130)—"how words can bring about images" (130)—is not pursued here, but she says that the "visibility" of blind Homer's poems requires of his readers "visuality . . . the readiness to form mental images . . . that are independently revelatory" (130) from moment to moment as the story unfolds. The discussion then moves on from what the reader sees to what Achilles sees as he faces Hector.

ONE "HOMERIC MOMENT": AN EXAMPLE

A brief account of one of Brann's interesting explorations will demonstrate the "way of reading" that she offers. Following her example, readers will take note of the beginnings, middles, and ends of the poems. She notes Odysseus's central adventure, and at one point even calculates the middle line of the *Odyssey*. Spartan Helen is, by any account, one beginning of the stories of both Achilles and Odysseus. When she is present, she is usually the center of attention. She appears three times in the *Iliad* (Books III, XXII, XXIV) and is mentioned frequently elsewhere. In the *Odyssey* she appears, ten years later (Books iv, xv) in what appears to be a stable and decorous restoration of her position as queen of Sparta. In *Homeric Moments*, she takes center stage at the virtual center of Brann's forty-eight chapters. (Chapter 24 is the second longest in the book.) Her first observation is that Helen, whose irresponsible self-indulgence has been the source of terrible suffering and destruction, is nevertheless capable of sensitivity and generosity that help prepare an unformed and apprehensive youth for manhood. She recognizes Telemachus and acknowledges him as his father's son, and she treats him as worthy to be that son. Brann "clues out" remarks and gestures that make all the difference to Telemachus. I won't repeat them here; the reading makes sense, and, as she says, "the delight is in the details" (107).

A second clue in this middle chapter suggests something about the man of many turns that may not have occurred to many readers before: that in addition to his liaisons with island nymphs and goddesses, and his flirtation with a nubile princess who would marry him in a moment, our hero Odysseus has also had more to do with Helen of Troy than is explicitly reported by Homer or by himself. We know that although he is not a handsome playboy like Paris or a rich king like her husband, he has, at various moments in the decade it took to destroy Troy, caught the attention of Helen. Brann points to Helen's reports of him in the *Iliad* (Book II) and the *Odyssey* (Book iv) and even to the custom of bathing strangers, as evidence that "much-daring" (another meaning of *tlaôn*) Odysseus and the most beautiful woman in the world have, at some moment, fully known each other. This conjecture, perhaps the sort of "wild surmise" (4) she hopes her readers will make, is surely worth more than a moment's thought. Brann does not extend the discussion, presumably because she reserves this "delight" for her readers who should head straight back to the text—preferably having learned some Greek on the side—to see if they agree. Those who end up rejecting her conjecture will think hard about both Odysseus and Helen on the way to that rejection.

In this spirit, let us return to Book Four of the *Odyssey*. The reader who appreciates Brann's observations about Helen and Telemachus and about Helen and Odysseus may, nevertheless, have reservations about the picture she paints. Helen and Menelaus are living a decorous life at Sparta, but surely a sorry one. The whole story, as well as Homer's details, point to this conclusion. Brann suggests that the weddings at the beginning of Book Four conjure up an incongruity: the thought of Helen as a grandmother. Her readers might also note that Menelaus seems to have doubts that his line will be perpetuated. They might "clue out" that the daughter Helen abandoned when she ran off with Paris (and who, by one of Brann's calculations, might be thirty years old) is to marry Neoptolemus, the one whose picture Brann found on the potsherd in the agora and has included in this book. This son of Achilles is shown hurling Priam's young grandchild to his death from the wall of Troy. Further sleuthing about Neoptolemus will reveal his subsequent murder of Priam himself—on an altar. The other wedding is of Menelaus's son Megapenthês ("great sorrow"), born to a slave woman after the legitimate mother of his children took off with her guest. The hospitable weddings and feastings that Telemachus finds on his arrival are proceeding with all due decorum, but if the reader attends to the details, he may find that the scene that Menelaus and Helen have stitched together is a brittle cover-up, even if it can yet do some good in the world. Menelaus is a sad and aging man who says that his treasures mean little to him. He seems to be waiting, as his Greek name suggests, to be released from the pains of life to the Elysian immortality that is due to him because he is Helen's husband.

Who can imagine, after all that passed, that he ever really wanted her back? In an unfinished story, "After Ten Years," C. S. Lewis (though not a poet) captures what it must have felt like when they were reunited. Years later, in the *Odyssey,* they have, as people do, patched up a life. The Egyptian tranquilizer *nêpenthês* ("banish sorrows," cf. Megapenthês) that Helen adds to the wine must be considered together with what Brann herself says about the dehumanizing forgetfulness offered by the Lotus Eaters, Circe, and Calypso. No doubt she has considered these details and hopes the reader will too. But, although she recognizes the deep melancholy of Sparta, to this reader, her delight in some of her discoveries makes her account seem—in that word that she often uses so effectively—too "glowing." At the end, she speaks of Helen's gift of a bridal gown for the future wife of the grateful, even worshipful, Telemachus as "the most apt one possible" (166). But I think Homer means for us to wince—or at least smile—at this wedding gift from Helen of Troy. When Telemachus is more mature and after he comes to understand a genuine marriage, like the one that produced him, surely he will put Helen's gift in a far corner of his Ithacan storeroom—and leave it there.

INTERPRETATION AND POETRY

Homeric Moments presents itself as an open and a simple book, a generous offering of advice, examples, and cues to further discussion. It promises "delight" of the highest sort, the pleasure that comes from learning. But, as Brann says about Homer, do not be deceived. Although she urges us to start anywhere and "poke around" (4), this is an artfully constructed book, and the more one thinks about it, the more one wonders about its own echoes of the poet she explicates. We read Homer with "an acute sense of homecoming" (14); the interpreter, like Hermes, guides our Return. This most colloquial of hermeneutics has forty-eight parts, a highly charged midpoint, new, interpretive epithets ("Ajax the Silent," "Patroklus the Friend," "Hektor the Holder"), an allegorical monster of misreading, phrases that, like epic formulas, repeat exactly or with slight variations at distant moments in the discussion ("poor stupid kid" [198], "poor, hopeless boy" [198]; hair "silver and sparse" [46, 244], and fabulous tales "hermetically sealed" [174, 248]). Are these the usual devices and reprises of literary interpretations? Or do they place Brann herself somewhere between the poet she explicates and the poets who are the only commentators she cites? Do some of her "conjectures"—perhaps the one about Helen and Odysseus, or what she "imagines" (290) about Laertes and the conditions of Penelope's marriage to Odysseus—resemble those of Tennyson, Auden, Muir, and the other poets who have also "clued out" the *Odyssey*? Are some of her clues imaginative, though plausible, additions to Homer, like those of the poets? She does not mean to offer revisions ("oppositional" readings) as some poets do, and she certainly hopes to avoid the irresponsible "riffs" of the "ingenious" theorists.

Finally, does Brann ever "nod" in her own reportage of what's in Homer? Readers will have to return to the text to see whether the embassy in Book Nine of the *Iliad* is a daytime event (61). Are ten days lost at the beginning of her *Iliad* calendar (61, 98), or is Zeus on "non-linear divine time" (111) here as well as, as she conjectures, in the *Odyssey*? Should we (246) or should we not (226) consider the Odyssean adventures a "fairy tale"? Does *Polyphemus* "grow" the grapes that grow in his land, or are they part of "elemental nature" in the land of the Cyclops? Is Helen forty (156) or fifty (161)? Is it really so unusual for her, and not a handmaid, to have bathed Odysseus, since in the previous book, Nestor's daughter, the princess of Pylos, bathes and oils Telemachus? Brann calls attention to a nice detail: Penelope orders a bed to be made up for the beggar Odysseus "inside the house" (xix.598). But isn't it confusing to call this the "fore-hall" of the palace? That is where Eurykleia says the beggar actually *did* sleep that night (xx.143), just as Telemachus sleeps in the "fore-hall" in Sparta (iv.302). The difference here is crucial because, of course, it points to the climactic question of the location of the bed Odysseus made for Penelope.

Brann's last chapter, "Twice Told, Thrice Dead," returns to her "main notion" (4) that Odysseus's story is told twice. At his demise, he will make a third return to Hades, where he will have been twice before, once literally (Book Eleven) and once figuratively after he has returned to Ithaka. Here, the interpreter of Brann's interpretation may add two last observations. The first is this: It is good in these times of prolific professional literary scholarship that there is still room for a learned, intelligent popularization accessible to all readers of Homer. This kind of interpretation is sometimes so revealing precisely because it *retells* the story, calling the reader's attention to as yet unremarked details—momentous clues and clarifying moments—that send him right back to the first telling and then to further discussions with other readers. In this sense, by the end of Brann's book, the "odyssey" has been *thrice* told. The second observation is this: Although Odysseus will be "thrice dead" at the end of his story, imaginative interpreters like Eva Brann—and her companion poets—will keep him alive—and "glowing"—forever.

WHAT ALEXANDER BAUMGARTEN DID TO HORACE'S *ARS POETICA:* THE CONSTRUCTION OF AESTHETICS

Richard Freis

Aesthetics (the theory of the liberal arts, the epistemology of the lower faculties of knowing, the art of thinking in the medium of the beautiful, the art of the analogue of reason) is the science of sensory cognition.[1,2]

—*Baumgarten,* Aesthetica

INTRODUCTION

THIS ESSAY IS an account of one thread in the complex transition from premodern to modern understandings of the right way to reflect on poetry, and the "fine arts" in general—a kind of reflection which Alexander Baumgarten claimed to raise to the level of science and for which he coined the telling name "aesthetics." As I begin, I keep in mind the warning against just my sort of project by Christian Wolff, a follower of Leibniz, who also influenced Baumgarten. "He is much less able," Wolff writes, "to pass judgment on philosophical controversy who has only *historical* knowledge of the *philosophical* knowledge of another" (Wolff #53). I intend the historical analysis to be also what Eva Brann calls an "incitement" to deeper reflection (Brann, 1999 xi-xii). The first part of the essay traces aspects of the transformation of traditional poetics in the work of Alexander Baumgarten; the second part is a case study of the anachronistic interpretations that occur when presuppositions derived from modern poetics are applied to premodern poetry.

This essay is based on an extended monograph in which the understandings of Horace, Leibniz, and Baumgarten and their interrelationships are presented with more rigor and fullness. The monograph belongs to a larger project of examining the transition from premodern to modern and postmodern poetics.

I. THE TWO POETICS

In Baumgarten's first publication, his master's dissertation, which he published in 1735 at twenty or twenty-one, appears a nascent unfolding of the thinking which forms the foundation of his aesthetics. Upon this foundation over the next fifteen years he elaborated the 624 pages of his unfinished *Aesthetics* (1750). He named his first work *Meditationes philosophicae de nonnullis ad poema pertinentibus (Philosophical Meditations about some things pertaining to the poem)*. The word "Meditations" places Baumgarten's work in the lineage flowing from Descartes through Leibniz and Baumgarten's teacher, Christian Wolff.

Baumgarten is aware that by juxtaposing Rational Philosophy and poetry he is taking on—and offering—a challenge. He magnifies it by quoting from Horace's verse epistle, the *Ars Poetica*, apparently from memory, thirty-eight times.[3] His direct and unidentified quotes and references to the *Ars Poetica* all appeal to Horace as the authoritative teacher of rules for writing perfected poems. Yet this raises a question: Why, if Horace's teaching about the nature of poetry and how to write it is authoritative, does Baumgarten feel compelled to write his own poetics, which he understands as "aesthetics"?

Let me quote some words from his preface, which have the particular iridescence that often marks the words of the ambitious young, in which pride and humility succeed each other as bewilderingly as colors in a peacock's tail:

> [I] have selected a matter which by many, indeed, is held [to be] slight and from the acuteness of philosophers most removed, [yet] to me seems, in proportion to the slightness of my powers, sufficiently weighty and in proportion to its dignity, suitable to exercising minds occupied in searching out the reasons of all things. *I would demonstrate that from one idea of a poem, which has long now clung to the mind, many things can be proven, [things] said a hundred times, but scarcely once proven,* and I would place before the eyes philosophy and the science of composing a poem, often held for the most disparate things, joined in the most loving marriage. (Italics added)

For Baumgarten, where Horace falls short is that his poetics, while true, are ill-founded. Horace cannot justify his teaching nor demonstrate the excellence of his poetry and the poetry of the other poets Baumgarten loves before the bar of Rational Philosophy. This is the service Baumgarten has to offer. He can found "the art of thinking in the medium of the beautiful," as he will call it in his later *Aesthetics,* within the terms of the rationalist system of sciences.

In accordance with this, Baumgarten, like Spinoza, Leibniz, Wolff and others in the lineage of Rational Philosophy, chooses as his literary form one which, imitating the manner of geometry, exhibits the rational structure of his argument by shaping it as a set of numbered sections which contain definitions and axioms and deductions drawn from them as well as appended scholia which justify or extend matters related to the argument.

Baumgarten constructs aesthetics on the foundation of Leibniz's framework of the grades or levels of being and knowing.

The *distinct, intensively clear, adequate, abstract* representations governed by the Principle of Contradiction embody the truths of science or philosophy.

Baumgarten looks at what one might call the negative space remaining after one has carved out the distinct, intensively clear, abstract representations of the higher cognitive faculty. He recognizes in that space the basis for a philosophical account of poetry.

Baumgarten sees that the very fact of our being able to make a philosophical distinction between two realms, the realm of necessary, philosophical or scientific truth, governed by the principle of contradiction, and the realm of concrete, sensory representations, governed by the principle of sufficient reason, means that philosophy can state truths about the sensory representations. Baumgarten sets out to construct a new science about the realm of sensory representations, which will be the basis of a method that enables those who use it to maximize the kind of power intrinsic to sensory representations in poetry and by implication other fine arts.[4]

To form his new scientific poetics he stays within the framework of Leibniz and assigns to sensory representations qualities the reverse of those which Leibniz assigns to the discourse of philosophy or science. This procedure already determines the conceptual foundations of his new poetics.

Hence the representations of poetry are not *distinct* but *fused-together* (*confusus*). Moreover, the clarity of sensory discourse is not *intensive* but *extensive;* or, to paraphrase the terms, clarity can exist in two directions, deep and broad.

Depth of clarity combines clarity with distinctness. "Distinct representations, complete, adequate, deep through every gradation" (§14), "which penetrate through every distinction of identifying characteristics to the depth of cognition, cause one representation to be *intensively clearer* than another" (scholium to §16; italics added).

Breadth of clarity combines clarity with fused-together and multiple individuating details, and is therefore *extensively clearer* (§16).

This distinction determines at the level of definition what kinds of poetry are to be sought and what are to be excluded. Prized as extensively clear are representations that are more determinate (§18), hence of individual things (*individua*), which, because they are determined in every respect (*omnimode determinata*), are "wholly poetic" (*admodum poeticae*) (§19). This means that writers who represent the typical aspects of things rather than seeking the maximum individuation—which would embrace most ancient, medieval, and neoclassical writers (and include Tolstoy[5])—are less perfect poets.

Finally, the distinction between typical and individuated overlaps the distinction of universal and particular representations and their respective value for poetry. A universal representation is intensively clear, simple and abstract; a particular representation is extensively clear, complex, and sensorily determinate.

It will clarify the transformation from premodern to modern poetics, and thus the character of the poetry each poetics fosters, to compare briefly Horace's and Baumgarten's starting points.

Horace, like the philosopher Aristotle, begins his consideration of poetry with the *endoxa*, the opinions about and phenomena of poetry as they present themselves in ordinary life. Horace writes from the perspective of a poet-citizen, informed by his reading in a tradition shaped by Aristotle's *Poetics* and *Rhetoric*, the classifying activity of the Hellenistic *rhetorici* and *grammatici*, and the history of poetry in Rome.

The poems Horace writes, including the *Ars Poetica*, like most premodern poems in any genre, are organized either as narrative structures, including dramatic speech by a character, or as persuasive speeches, utilizing rhetorical versions of rational argument and patterns of generic classification of human characters, roles, settings. They are intimately connected with typical situations in life, the beseeching or celebration of the divine, lamentation of funerary or erotic loss, praise of victors in war or other contests and more generally of exemplary figures, amatory or symposiastic lyrics, civic exhortation, satiric exposure of folly, didactic instruction. The forms that are narrative may be small or they may be large-scale as in epic and drama, which themselves are intimately connected with the life of a community.

Horace does share with Baumgarten the commitment to a kind of perfection in a poem. It is not the perfection of sensory discourse but of art.

What is the meaning and value for Horace of that art which tradition placed first in the poem's title? Horace appeals to the distinction between inborn genius or inspiration and art throughout his poetry. Genius and inspiration are given, art has to be learned through persistent and laborious effort, and its effects are in some degree deliberate. Art, conscious skill, is what allows its possessor, when fleeing one fault, to avoid falling into the opposite (*A.P.* 31). Study and practice would have given the early epic poet Ennius the art of writing metrical lines (*A.P.* 262). Mastering the art is what improves an untrained performance, however brilliant, into a trained one. The right use of art is geared to particular contexts of genre, subject, character and others, even if it aims at universal standards of achievement, so the right practice of an art is not the application of a universal method.

Such poems reveal a consistent allegiance to two ends. The first is fidelity to the *materia,* the *res,* the thing being represented. The second is the rhetorical purpose of achieving desired responses in an audience. As Horace writes, for poets and poet-playwrights these desired responses are two:

> Poets aim to profit or to please
> Or speak alike delight and use for life . . .
> The elder order snubs shows with no fruit,
> the young-and-in pass over the austere.
> He wins all votes who blends the good with sweet,
> alike to guide the reader and delight.
> This book earns sellers cash, fares overseas,
> and brings the writer longer life in fame. (*A.P.* 333–4, 341–6)

For Horace the profit the poet aims for is not only to the individual but to the city, whose wellbeing the poet helps form as a moral teacher.

Baumgarten, on the contrary, begins with a formal system of sciences, within whose structures and methods the classification of the object of inquiry must be treated (Klein 117–25). Baumgarten's primary perspective on poetry is its epistemological character, which he defines by contrast with the epistemological character of scientific and philosophical discourse. The very name of his poetics, which at the close he designates *aesthetics,* focuses on the epistemological issue as *"the science in its general aspects of putting forth sensory representations [derived from sensory cognition] in a perfected way"* (§117). Everything else is either treated in this perspective or does not come to view.

It will help us grasp the shape of Baumgarten's poetics to notice what he omits. In traditional poetics the classification of fictions is the normal place for the treatment of genres. Yet Baumgarten leaves the division of poetry "into epic, dramatic, lyric with the various species and analogues" to the rhetoricians, "who introduce historical and experiential knowledge [of these forms] into minds." (§117)

Similarly, in his relatively extended treatment of language as sound, which includes metrics, Baumgarten discusses matters parallel to Horace's formal treatment of metrics (*A.P.* 251–274) but has no section parallel to questions of the appropriateness of different meters to different kinds of poetry, character, and circumstances (*A.P.* 73–98). He also leaves out questions about the appropriate literary treatment of characters. Thus Baumgarten excludes topics that traditional poetics considers crucial.

In order to make poetics methodical in the sense of Rational Philosophy, and thus more certain in its control of the poetic outcome, Baumgarten must take a perspective which gives major importance to that which is reducible to his method—the quality of the representation—and less importance to that which is not so reducible, genres, the representation of character, the appropriateness of different meters to different genres, and (with only one briefly stated exception) the nature of the audience and the ways to move and form it.

The revolutionary changes initiated by Baumgarten are veiled by his immense piety toward Horace and his own unawareness of their implications, which unfolded in the poems of subsequent generations. Where the sensory is detached from its determining situatedness in typical life situations, where the typical and universal are secondary to the individuated and particular, where the essence of poetry is found in the purity of the sensory representation and genre, character, and the appropriateness of metrical form to these and to life setting are demoted to rhetoric, the poetry fostered by such critical and methodical imperatives will differ from the premodern.

The rationalist non-rational system of aesthetics that flowed in part from Baumgarten's work came to sponsor art increasingly *sensory or formal.* The middle range of ordinary experience, in which formal and sensory, universal and particular, come to us as intrinsically present aspects of the objects we come upon and think about, was correspondingly excluded. Wesley Trimpi speaks to this circumstance:

> Were a literary theory to suggest how one might represent such unique particulars as objects, it could only recommend trying to isolate independent impressions of them in images, which, however sharply imagined individually, could have little or no connection with each other or with human experience as a whole. (Trimpi 96)

Trimpi later remarks on a factor which I believe is one link between a poetry of perfected sensory representation and formalism, the concept of *purity:*

> Although this ultimate purity [he is speaking here of Plotinus] admits no formal predication, its very formlessness is formalistic in that it expresses a negation of all specific content. Purity is the only form, that is, sufficiently undetermined to express a reality whose power to determine itself is infinite. . . .
>
> From the eighteenth century on, for instance, literary symbols have been increasingly associated with the expression of purity . . . which could be achieved through the elimination of denotative reference and of the coherent structure of logical propositions. The stylistic attempts to obscure or conceal completely the external comprehensibility of the object through enigmatic juxtaposition in order to release and represent an inner, intuited source of informing energy have been particularly prevalent in twentieth-century aesthetic attitudes. (Trimpi 189)

A radicalized Baumgartean poetic discourse, stripped down to its poetic essence, will be a sensory image, an image faithful to an empirical original, or an enigmatic symbol of the realm beyond form, or bare letters on a page or paint on a canvas sufficient in themselves.

It was predictable that many of those involved with poetry as critics and poets would decontextualize the preference for sensory or formal aspects of poetry from the epistemological and methodical purposes which privileged them and come to view them as superior absolutely. It was equally predictable that other critics and poets would take up the standard of that which the method could not handle, leading to the dialectic between such oppositions as those named "Realism" and "Symbolism," positions increasingly distant from ordinary experience and founded in sedimentation and forgetfulness.

In the closing three sections of his *Meditations* Baumgarten steps back and looks at his "poetic philosophy" in larger perspective. Let me summarize and comment on these sections under three heads.

A Science Which Directs Sensory Discourse to Perfection. Baumgarten devotes §115 to defining and arguing for the good of a science which directs *sensory* discourse to perfection. Such a science presupposes that sensory knowing is a cognitive faculty, even if a lower one than the clear and distinct intellectual cognition whose results are vouched for by the principle of contradiction. This new science might be classified, Baumgarten proposes, as belonging to the province of an *extended* (*sensu generali*) logic, supplementing the role of logic in the strict sense as the science which directs the higher cognitive faculty to philosophic truth. Even if it is not classified as a supplemental form of logic, it might benefit philosophers "to inquire even into these devices, by which they are able to refine the lower faculty of cognition, and apply them with a more abundant fruitfulness (*felicius*) for the advantage of the world (*orbis*)."

The Name of This New Science: Aesthetics. In §116, with his new field defined, Baumgarten sets out to find a technical name (*terminus*) for it. He chooses one that has the authority of tradition. (The Greek in the following passage lacks breathing marks and accents following the convention of the original edition.)

> Now the Greek philosophers and the [F]athers always carefully distinguished between νοητα [things known] and αισθητα [things perceived] and it is clear enough that they did not equate αισθητα [things perceived] with sense impressions alone, since even things with sense absent [*absentia etiam sensa*] ([and] therefore [being] images) were honored by this name. Therefore νοητα [things known] are to be known by the higher cognitive faculty as object of logic, [and] αισθητα [things perceived] [are to be known by the lower cognitive faculty] επιστημης αισθητικης [of knowledge related to perception] or AESTHETIC [AESTHETICAE].

This name is a seal on the special association of poetry with the sensory.

The Species of This Science: General Rhetoric and General Poetics. In §117 Baumgarten concludes his thesis. Here he considers more carefully the place and divisions of aesthetics and the duty of the philosopher toward the field. In doing so he speaks emphatically as a philosopher in distinction from the poet or rhetorician, itself a piece of rhetoric which credentials the aesthetic as a proper concern for philosophy.

Baumgarten begins by presenting the writing philosopher as a foil to those who write as practitioners of the αισθητα: "As the philosopher thinks [*meditatur*], so he puts forth [his thoughts], hence in the putting forth no —or very few—particular rules must be observed." (This from a man who shaped the presentation of his philosophy after the conventions of geometry!) After brief further development, and without relinquishing the forceful differentiation of the philosopher from those practitioners in the aesthetic realm, Baumgarten turns to a fuller conspectus of the fields of sensory discourse:

> Now since [the putting forth] can be done in a perfected or unperfected way, the latter treats GENERAL RHETORIC, *the science in its general aspects*

> *of putting forth sensory representations in an unperfected way,* the former
> [treats] GENERAL POETICS, *the science in its general aspects of putting forth*
> *sensory representations in a perfected way.* As of the former into sacred and
> profane, forensic [*judicialam*], epideictic [*demonstrativam*], and deliberative
> [*deliberativam*], etc., so of the latter into epic, dramatic, lyric with the var-
> ious species and analogues, philosophers relinquish the definitions of
> these arts to rhetoricians, who introduce historical and experiential [*exper-*
> *imentalem*] knowledge of these [forms] into minds. Let the philosophers
> [*ipsi*] be occupied in demonstrating general aspects and especially defin-
> ing accurate boundaries of poetry and prose eloquence, which, indeed, dif-
> fer only by degree [*gradu . . . solo*]. (Italics in the first sentence added.)

At this point Baumgarten has defined within the system of the sciences the
new science of sensory discourse, has named it from the philosophical tradition, and differentiated its species in terms of their common genus and
specific differentiae.

Ernst Cassirer sums up the meaning of Baumgarten's establishment of
aesthetics within the philosophic context he embraced. Cassirer begins by
noting Baumgarten's widely recognized greatness as a student of logic, even
though *Baumgarten finds a place for aesthetics by recognizing reason's limits.*
And he acutely adds:

> Baumgarten does not remain a mere "artist of reason"; in him that ideal of
> philosophy is realized which Kant called the ideal of the "self-knowledge
> of reason." (339)

II. MODERNS READING ANCIENTS: A CASE STUDY

In this section I will offer an example of one kind of distortion that may arise
when presuppositions acquired from reading the symbolists, impressionists,
imagists, and similar schools of poetry downstream from Baumgarten's poetics are applied as a framework to understanding premodern writers. This
kind of distortion most readily arises in bringing modern lenses to premodern writers, such as Pindar, Aeschylus, Vergil, and Shakespeare, whose
image-making faculty is naturally fertile and whose work, therefore, appears
to be an early example of associative, image-based writing.

Fidelity to the *res*, the experienced world of apparently independent
persons and things, which marks the premodern poets I name above, has
dropped out of the interest of many nineteenth, twentieth, and twenty-first
century poets and fiction writers. Relationships within a work are indicated

by such devices as image-networks and *leitmotifs,* either exclusively or as a supplement to traditional narrative or argument. A *leitmotif* is a symbolic reference designed to create an association and response without requiring of reader or auditor full realization of an intended thing. As an instrument of impressionism the repeated word or phrase, which provides a cluster of connotative, indeterminate associations as a way to unify the work, is a check intentionally drawn on a largely unfunded account, which the reader is invited to fund from her or his own imagination. Or, in more fully symbolist uses, the taste of the indeterminate non-rational connotations for their own sake becomes the sufficient reason for other elements of the poem.

There is a suggestive parallel here to Leibniz's distinction between speech which is like the indeterminate representations of algebra and speech which is like the concretely realized representations of geometry:

> That the truest good is so little sought after is mainly due to this, that in matters and on occasions in which the senses have very little influence, most of our thoughts are, so to speak, insensible [*sourdes*] (I call them in Latin, *cogitationes caecae* [blind thoughts]), that is to say, they are void of perception and feeling and consist in the bare use of symbols, like the work of those who make calculations in algebra, without looking from time to time at the geometrical figures. *In this respect words usually have the same effect as arithmetical or algebraic symbols. We often reason in words, hardly having the object in mind at all.* (*Nouveaux Essais,* bk.ii. ch 21, Para 35 [E257 a; G. v. 171], cit. Latta 147, italics in last two sentences added.)

For Leibniz, who wants to have the words determinately conceived as vehicles of an important rational understanding, the possibility of using words disembodied from a clearly realized understanding of real objects is a weakness (although from other perspectives it is a capital strength for modern mathematics and poetry).

By the time of Mallarmé this possibility of indeterminacy becomes a vehicle of pleasure for its own sake:

> Exclude if you begin
> the real which is cheap.
>
> Its too sharp sense rubs thin
> your vague literature. (89–90)

The use of such tonal or image clusters can magnify the power of a determinate narration or argument, but in the symbolists and imagists *it replaces such narration or argument as a principle of such paradoxical wholeness as speech can have.* For this reason modern or postmodern readers often seek such image clusters in pre-modern poetry, looking to them as a primary vehicle for the coherence of a work, and at the same time ignore such other factors as the premodern writer's contemporary critics, the comprehensive practice of the writer and his or her contemporaries, and the multiple internal features of the work as clues to the work's primary organizing principles.

It is evident that I cannot fully articulate and argue in an essay for the proposition that such interpretations are as anachronistic as the moralized Ovid of the Latin Middle Ages. I can, however, give an example of the way modern or postmodern readings based on these interpretive principles can make us miss the perspective and intention of the premodern poet.

Let me begin by quoting an account of the Horatian ode by J. V. Cunningham, a poet and critic to whose great talent and understanding I am deeply indebted, but whose understanding of the Horatian ode I believe to be wrong. In presenting his position, I will begin with his characterization of the Horatian ode as a genre. Then I will introduce his translation of *Odes* 1.9, the Soracte ode, which is informed by his analysis of the genre characteristics of a Horatian ode. And third, I will cite part of his analysis of the Soracte ode itself.

Cunningham defines the form of a Horatian ode by distinguishing it from Medieval Latin lyric:

> The latter [the Medieval Latin lyric] he [Cunningham is speaking in the third person about himself] found uncompromisingly rational and logical in structure. In the former [the Horatian ode] he discerned a unity of sensibility which exhibited the vagaries and unpredictability of experience and resisted an abstract, logical, or classificatory form. (Cunningham, *Essays* 419)

Here is his very beautiful translation of Ode 1.9, a near miracle in its ability to capture Horace's powerful plainness and to convey the metrical feel of Horace's Alcaic stanza in English:

Horace, *Odes* 1.9

See how resplendent in deep snow
Soracte stands, how straining trees
   Scarce can sustain their burden
      Now that the rivers congeal and freeze.

Thaw out the chill, still heaping more
Wood on the fire; ungrudgingly
   Pour forth from Sabine flagons,
      O Thaliarchus, the ripened wine.

Leave all else to the gods. They soon
Will level on the yeasty deep
   Th' embattled tempests, stirring
      Cypress no more, nor agèd ash.

Tomorrow may no man divine.
This day that Fortune gives set down
   As profit, nor while young still
      Scorn the rewards of sweet dancing love,

So long as from your flowering days
Crabbed age delays. Now through the parks
   Soft whisperings toward nightfall
      Visit again at the trysting hour;

Now from her bower comes the charmed laugh,
Betrayer of the hiding girl;
   Now from her arm the forfeit
      Plundered, her fingers resisting not.

Cunningham offers his analysis of the ode:

> He [again, Cunningham speaks in the third person of himself] analyzed the famous Soracte ode (1.9) which begins with an extended description of a midwinter scene and closes with an extended, but in no way parallel, description of a summer love scene. By a relative clause, and in an unemphatic manner, a description of the equinoctial storms is worked in. The sequence of images gives by implication, but by implication only, the theme: that season follows season, and that time is fleeting. . . . [T]he point of the poem is qualified by images, whole and concrete in themselves, which cannot be said to illustrate the point. They are not subsumed under it as examples . . . (Cunningham, *Essays* 420).

Sentence by sentence I believe this analysis falsifies Horace's text. In reading Horace Cunningham foregrounds the images and backgrounds the rhetorical-logical structures of discourse as secondary and ministerial to the effect of the images which appear in them. He sees the Horatian ode as having the structure of a typical "modern" poem.

In reading Medieval Latin poems, by contrast, he foregrounds the "rational and logical in [their] structure," and evidently backgrounds images as secondary and ministerial to the effect of the rational and logical structures. I believe this description is true and it can be shown that the Medieval Latin lyric has these qualities because of its continuities with classical western lyric, including the lyrics of Horace.

In order to adjudicate this disagreement, it will be helpful to examine what the rhetorical-logical sequence of structures of discourse is in Horace's poem and how the poem's images relate to it.

Here is the rhetorical-logical anatomy of the ode:

Stanza one is a narrative description of the outdoor setting, a winter scene in which everything is burdened and paralyzed by snow and cold. The speaker begins by inviting "Thaliarchus," whose name means "Master of the Revels," to look out on this scene.

This is followed in stanza two by the speaker's dramatized exhortation to Thaliarchus to turn from the scene of distress outside by giving lavishly of the available indoor pleasures of fire and wine.

Stanza three contains a second image of a storm outdoors. Now, however, the troubled weather the poet describes is not the snow and cold that paralyze the mountain of stanza one but a tempest roiling the sea as well as the trees of the land.

Cunningham feels the incongruity between the two descriptions of troubled weather. He reads the second image as a continued reference to the narrative setting outside the place of revel, but set at the spring equinox, when such storms might occur. In accordance with this, he assigns the time of the second storm to the future: "They [the gods] soon *will* level."

Here Cunningham makes a significant mistranslation. The verb he translates as a future is in the perfect tense. What, then, is the relation of the two incongruous images of weather, the winter stillness in the first stanza, the tempestuous disorder in the third stanza? The clue is to recognize that the structure of discourse that contains the elaborated image of tempestuous storm in the third stanza is not narrative as in the first and second stanzas.

In stanza two the speaker has made a particular exhortation to Thaliarchus to turn to the available pleasures. In stanza three the speaker makes the correlative exhortation to let go of what is not in Thaliarchus' control, and he justifies the exhortation by stating a universal condition of human life.

A literal translation reads: "Leave the rest to the gods, who as soon as/ *they have dispersed* the winds on the boiling sea/ wrestling together, neither cypresses/ nor aged ash trees *are [anymore] agitated.*"

This is a universal statement or *sententia* which employs a frequent figure of thought in Horace, a doublet in which the second element stands in polar contrast to the first, thus defining the limits of a range within which the statement applies. In his work on Pindar Bundy named these after their function "universalizing doublets" (Bundy, 1962a 24, 24n 56).

In this stanza Horace uses a land and sea (= everywhere) doublet to convey the universal reach of disorder in the world and the gods' power. The description of the trees in turn is worked out as a subordinate universalizing doublet, the pliant cypresses contrasted with the aged and stable ash trees. This image of weather is not framed as a piece of *narrative discourse* as was the scene in stanza one but as *metaphors in a sententia*. The exhortation embodies the common Horatian wisdom, which I have described elsewhere in this way:

> Just as the root of evil in human actions and experience is concern with that which overreaches the given limit, with *quod ultra est* (2.16.25), so the root of good in human action and experience is attention to what is present, to *quod adest* (3.29.32). Even so, "attention" is too cold a word; rather let us say that the wise learn to find in *quod adest* the fullness of what is sufficient, *quod satis est* (3.1.25). In the words of Horace's poet's prayer, whose formulation links the notions of *quod adest* and *quod satis est:* Grant me to enjoy what is prepared, *frui paratis . . . dones* (1.31.17–18). (Freis, 2005a 65)

The fourth stanza remains on the level of universal statement that was introduced in stanza three. The stanza begins with two more *sententiae*. The first gives a reason that justifies the exhortation of stanza three to leave in the gods' hands the things beyond our immediate situation. The reason we should not allow ourselves to become preoccupied with the future is because we cannot foresee it, and therefore cannot control it and make it the scene of our satisfactions from life. The second *sententia* is a general exhortation, based on the preceding truth, to turn from preoccupation with the future and focus on the pleasures available today, accounting them as profit gained. The temporal scope of this exhortation is more embracing than but does not exclude the narrative present established in the first two stanzas. This span is the whole span of youth: Do not, Thaliarchus, "*while young still/* scorn the rewards of sweet dancing love."

Horace completes stanza five and opens stanza six with images correlated with this enlarged "now," the season of Thaliarchus' youth. Stanza five introduces a third image of weather, which begins with an emphatic appeal to this enlarged "now," an urban, summer evening, where lovers tryst in parks with soft whisperings. Stanza six begins with a second emphatic appeal to the "now" and offers a further image of lovers' play.

Cunningham seems to understand the image of stanza six as a continuation of the outdoor scene in the stanza before it. This appears to be his rationale for the unlikely translation which makes the laugh betraying the hidden girl come from her "bower." [6] Further, to make the second image a continuation of the first does not accord with the typical conceptual structure of Horace's doublets, which I described above: In contrast with Catullus, who typically writes doublets in which the second element repeats and reinforces the meaning of the first, Horace radically prefers doublets in which the second element stands in polar contrast with the first, thus universalizing the range of a statement's application. [7] I therefore read the two descriptions of the play of lovers as universalizing the occasions offering "the rewards of sweet dancing love." They embrace "outdoor" and "indoor" occasions and therefore refer to any season within the scope of the designated "now" of Thaliarchus' youth.

The images of stanzas five and six do not enter the discourse structures of the poem as narrative descriptions of a present place (as in stanzas one and two) nor as metaphors expressing a universal *sententia* through a pattern of universalizing doublets (as in stanza three), but as particularizations of the domain of application of a parainesis or exhortation, which is characteristically ramified into a universalizing doublet.

To be able to foreground the images as Cunningham does in this case one must read the images as appearing in a neutral medium that does not distinguish the differences in function of the structures of discourse in which they occur. One has to experience as in some degree aesthetically inert and conceptually formless the logical and rhetorical structures of the discourse and therefore to look to the images, decontextualized from their narrative and rhetorical functions, as the only source of the (in some trans- or subrational sense) meaning and connection.

Horace, like the Medieval Latin poets who learned from him, was so deeply sensitive to the different logical-rhetorical structures of discourse that he spontaneously foregrounded them and backgrounded the images as subordinate to the logical-rational structures of discourse. Context at many levels would have made it almost impossible for him to focus on the "images" in relation to each other independent of the discourse structures which contain them with their different functions in his lyric. And if he could have broken free to do so, who would have been able to read the lyric with those eyes?

If my analysis is correct, *Odes* 1.9 could be assigned to a logic class as a sequence of rhetorical syllogisms or enthymemes to be expanded into a sequence of fully explicit syllogisms. The images are governed by and are ministerial to the logical-rhetorical structures and their functions.

Even if Horace in an ode should intentionally make two images echo each other, the primary structure of the ode will be narrative and logical-rhetorical. I believe this is equally true of Pindar, Aeschylus, Vergil, and Shakespeare. These differences in the practice of poets are related to differences in the matrix of understanding regarding metaphysics, epistemology, psychology, and language in which the positions of poetics are more or less integrally embedded. These understandings in modernity—we find them nascently in Baumgarten—support the primacy of the sensory, individual, intentionally indeterminate, connotative, associative, non- or anti-rational possibilities of poetry. The parallel understandings in premodernity limit or exclude, intentionally or through unawareness, such modern possibilities of poetry. For this reason, if we propose an image-centered, associative, connotative analysis of a Pindaric ode, Aeschylus' *Oresteia*, Book II of Vergil's *Aeneid,* or Shakespeare's *King Lear,* we are introducing something the poet did not intend and in almost every case concomitantly excluding something the poet did intend. What we exclude is what falls outside our ordinary horizon of thinking; what we add is the familiar, which enables and limits our understanding.

NOTES

1 Among the writers whose heterogeneous views have contributed to my thinking about the continuities and differences between the premodern and modern/postmodern, let me name Jacob Klein, Leo Strauss, Hans Blumenberg, Eva Brann, Louis Dupré, David Lachterman, and Stanley Rosen.

2 *AESTHETICA (theoria liberalium artium, gnoseologia inferior, ars pulcre cogitandi, ars analogi rationis) est scientia cognitionis sensitivae* (Baumgarten, 1750, §1).
   I have translated from the Latin all passages from Horace and Baumgarten. A real desideratum for wider study of this transition is the publication of a translation of the *Aesthetica* into a modern language.

3 The *Ars Poetica* was part of the education of most educated men in England and Western Europe in the eighteenth century. It is often quoted without line references as Baumgarten quotes it. Baumgarten seems both unintentionally to err and intentionally to adapt quotations to his immediate context: he reverses lines (*A.P.* 307–8 in §56); makes conditional recommendations unconditionally prescriptive (*A.P.* 19–20 in §56); runs together in a montage lines from various parts of the poem on similar topics (*A.P.* 151–2, 339–40, 118, 341 in §57); changes a first person to a third person statement (*A.P.* 25–6 in §74). The most reasonable explanation of these divergences from Horace's text in this context seems to me to be that Baumgarten did not consult Horace's text when writing. Precision in such quotations was not required by his readers.

4 Out of different reasons, in their focus on the sensuous particular as definitive of poetry, rationalist and empiricist poetics often worked toward similar views.

5 "[Isaiah] Berlin praises Tolstoy for perceiving and representing each thing he writes of 'in its absolute uniqueness' (51). However, Tolstoy understood himself as capturing *the typical*. This is indicated by a characteristic mode of phrase, some examples of which I will quote almost arbitrarily from the first chapter of *War and Peace*. 'He spoke *in that* refined French *in which our grandfathers not only spoke but thought,* and with the gentle, patronizing intonation *natural to* a man of importance who had grown old in society and at the court' (3). 'Prince Vasili did not reply though, with the quickness of memory and perception *befitting a man of the world . . .*' (7). '*As is always the case with a thoroughly attractive woman,* her defect—the shortness of her upper lip and her half-open mouth— seemed to be her own special and peculiar form of beauty' (8). 'Here the conversation seemed interesting and he stood waiting for an opportunity to express his own views, *as young people are fond of doing*' (8). The 'fullest individual essence' (51) of each thing, in Berlin's phrase, is in large part conveyed rhetorically by appealing to the reader's recognition of its truth to a common type. This repeated rhetorical gesture also presumes that the reader is as knowledgeable and discriminating as Tolstoy about the typical features of a vast variety of human characters and situations; in this respect, it is part of the working alliance Tolstoy sets up with his readers" (Freis, 1998, 23, references in the original).

6 "Angulum" refers to any corner—of a room, a triangle, a retired spot—but does not connote "bower."

7 The distinction between typical Catullan and Horatian doublets is from an unpublished study (Freis, 2005b).

8 Such application of modern presuppositions to premodern discourse extends into many areas beyond literature in the narrow sense. For example, many contemporary analyses of structure in the gospels or Pauline letters are framed in terms of complex "thematic" rings, whose identification depends on a modern understanding of the elements of such themes, in which a proposed connotative implication can correspond to an earlier element, even if there is no similarity of denotative meaning (Freis, 2005b).

9 I want to express my grateful indebtedness to St. John's College, which first engaged me with the sort of question I address here, and to Eva Brann, Jacob Klein, and all my teachers at St. John's College in Annapolis, including my fellow students. My debt continues to Harrison Sheppard for a friendship of almost fifty years.

WORKS CITED

Baumgarten, A.G. *Aesthetica.* 1750. Reprint in photocopy, Hildesheim: Georg Ohms, 1961.

―――. *Meditationes philosophicae de nonnullis ad poema pertinentibus.* 1735. Translated by Karl Aschenbrenner and William B. Holter. Berkeley and Los Angeles: University of California Press, 1954.

Brann, Eva. *What, Then, Is Time?* Lanham, Md.: Rowman & Littlefield, 1998.

Bundy, Elroy L. "Studia Pindarica. I: The Eleventh Olympian Ode." *University of California Publications in Classical Philology* 18 (1962): 1–34.

Cassirer, Ernst. *The Philosophy of the Enlightenment.* Translated by Fritz A. Koelln and James P. Pettegrove. Princeton: Princeton University Press, 1951.

Cunningham, J.V. "The Quest of the Opal: A Commentary on *The Helmsman.*" In *The Collected Essays of J.V. Cunningham,* 405–24. Chicago: The Swallow Press, 1976.

———. "Odes I.9 and a Note from the Quest of the Opal." *Arion* 9 (1970): 175–77.

Freis, Richard. *Patrick O'Brian and the Art of Fiction.* Signed and numbered limited edition. Jackson, Miss., 1998.

———. *"Amor and Pietas:* The Catullan Revolution and the Horatian Counter-Revolution." In *Defining Genre and Gender in Latin Literature,* edited by William W. Batstone and Garth Tissol, 61–78. New York: Peter Lang, 2005.

———. "The Structure of Mark 8.27–9.1." In manuscript. (2005b): 1–26.

Klein, Jacob. *Greek Mathematical Thought and the Origin of Algebra.* 1934–36. Translated by Eva Brann. New York: Dover, 1992.

Leibniz. *The Monadology and Other Philosophical Writings.* Translated with introduction and notes by Robert Latta. London: Oxford University Press, 1898.

Mallarmé, Stéphane. "Toute L'âme Résumée. . . ." In *Selected Poems,* translated by C.F. MacIntyre, 98–99. Berkeley and Los Angeles: University of California Press, 1971.

Trimpi, Wesley. *Muses of One Mind: The Literary Analysis of Experience and Its Continuity.* Princeton: Princeton University Press, 1982.

Wolff, Christian. *Preliminary Discourse on Philosophy in General.* 1728. Translated with introduction and notes by Richard J. Blackwell. Indianapolis and New York: Bobbs-Merrill, 1963.

Eva Brann and the Philosophical Achievement of Jacob Klein

Burt C. Hopkins

PART OF THE unique philosophical achievement of Jacob Klein is to have surpassed the understanding of his famous teachers Martin Heidegger and Edmund Husserl on important matters while remaining as unknown in the world of the academy and beyond as his teachers are, to this day, known. Accounts by those who knew Klein attest that his lack of fame is not an accident. In a letter to Stanley Rosen written in 1959, Klein replied to Rosen's invitation to be considered as a candidate for a senior professorship at the Pennsylvania State University:

> I do appreciate the intention that is back of your proposal. But you do not seem to realize that my relation to St. John's is not simply that of holding a teaching position at this institution. Some of my life blood went into the building and consolidating of this fantastic little college. What the future may bring (apart from death) is, of course, uncertain, but right now and in the foreseeable future I could not possibly leave St. John's.[1]

Leo Strauss, a year later, writes about "Mr. Klein's idiosyncratic abhorrence of publicity—of anything which remotely reminds of the limelight," and relates how, when they were students together talking for hours in a coffeehouse near the Prussian State Library in Berlin where they had just spent long hours "cultivating their minds," [I] "derived enjoyment from suddenly exclaiming as loudly as I could, say, 'Nietzsche!' and from watching the anticipated wincing of Mr. Klein."[2] After his death, Klein's wife reported that "[h]e had no interest in academic fame, nor did he want disciples,"[3] and at his memorial service Robert S. Bart observed, "He could be almost cruel to anyone who would be a disciple."[4] For most who knew Klein, the explanation for what Strauss characterizes as Klein's "idiosyncrasy" is as obvious as it is profoundly principled: What Jacob Klein was about is learning; anything that would stand in the way of "the spontaneity of thought in those who would learn from him"[5] is something he had a natural aversion against. Since the "authority" typically associated with being a "professor" is inimical to the sine qua non of learning, namely, to the dialogical interrogation of the unknown, it follows that Klein would be interested in neither fame nor epigones.

Klein was also a man of immense formal learning, however, who at one time had prepared himself to become qualified to teach in the German university system. He was educated in Russia (Lipetsk, 1908–1912),[6] Belgium (Brussels, 1912–1914), and Germany (Berlin, 1914–1917, and Marburg, 1920–1922).[7] For a time after the outbreak of the First World War, when he was prevented from attending the gymnasium because of his status in Germany as a foreign national,[8] he was privately tutored in Latin, French, German, history, and mathematics by a gymnasium professor.[9] On Passover in 1917 he entered the University of Berlin, where he studied mathematics and physics for six semesters.[10] In 1919 Klein visited Edmund Husserl in Freiburg with the intention of studying with him, but was unable to find lodging.[11] Husserl sent him to the University of Marburg, to study with Paul Natorp. According to Klein's wife, however, "that was dry, dry, advice. Then there was Nicolai Hartmann, who was not dry, but not anything great."[12] Klein received his Ph.D. in 1922 (at the age of 23!), after three semesters at Marburg, with a dissertation directed by Hartmann, titled "The Logical and Historical Element in Hegel's Philosophy" ("Das logische und geschichtliche Element in Hegels Philosophie").[13] From 1924 until 1928 Klein attended off and on Heidegger's lectures in Marburg,[14] and from 1928 to 1929 he studied with Professors Max Planck and Erwin Schrödinger at the Institute for Theoretical Physics in Berlin.[15] By 1933, he had completed his Habilitationschrift,[16] but he was prevented from habilitating by the Nazi Law for the Restitution of the Professional Civil Service (*Gesetz zur Wiederherstellung des Berufsbeamtentums*), which was passed April 7, 1933, and which banned Jews from the civil service.

The Nazi laws, however, did not prevent Klein from tutoring. From 1932 until 1938,[17] when he immigrated to the United States, he supported himself tutoring and giving seminars on Plato.[18] During this time he also published a very long, two-part article in *Quellen und Studien zur Geschichte der Mathematik, Astronomie und Physik*, a prestigious journal edited by Otto Neugebauer. The title, while undoubtedly an accurate description of its content, gives no real indication of this article's truly groundbreaking nature: "Die griechische Logistik und die Entstehung der Algebra"[19] ("Greek Logistics and the Genesis of Algebra,"[20] in Strauss's literal rendering). Strauss remarked in 1959 that Klein's work is

much more than a historical study. But even if we take it as purely a historical work, there is not, in my opinion, a contemporary work in the history of philosophy or science or in "the history of ideas" generally speaking which in intrinsic worth comes within hailing distance of it. Not indeed a proof but a sign of this is the fact that less than half a dozen people seem to have read it, if the inference from the number of references to it is valid.[21]

This remark is even more relevant today. Eva Brann's studious and readable translation made Klein's study available to the English-speaking world in 1968, but if there have been since then a few additional references to those Strauss noted, there has been nothing even remotely resembling the kind of scholarly recognition that its groundbreaking content warrants. Like Klein's lack of fame, this too is not an accident. Eva's translation rescued from oblivion[22] what (following her translation) is commonly called Klein's *Math Book*. Her remarkable achievement of rendering Klein's scholarly German into as plain an English as possible, however, has not been able to prevent the book from acquiring the reputation of being "too scholarly." For some, this is above all a defect of the book's vocabulary and composition, which—especially in comparison with Klein's later writings—are thought to manifest a style characterized by "pomposity, stuffiness, and turgidity."[23] For others, "the overpowering scholarship of [Klein's] argument," together with Klein's "erudition . . . [being] so great and thorough," produces the consequence "that there are few men living who can move familiarly on his terrain."[24]

Klein himself contributed to the *Math Book*'s reputation as "too scholarly." In the "Author's Note" to Eva's translation, he writes:

> This study was originally written and published in Germany during rather turbulent times. Were I writing it today, the vocabulary would be less "scholarly," and the change from the ancient to the modern mode of thinking would be viewed in a larger perspective.[25]

Moreover, not once does Klein refer to his *Math Book* in any of his American lectures or articles,[26] a fact that has no doubt contributed to its invisibility. That the content of his book is available at all today is something that Klein not only did not contribute to, but from all accounts, something that he actually worked against. Strauss remarked that were it not for Klein's "idiosyncrasy," it would be impossible to excuse Klein from being "justly . . . blamed for misanthropy," because "he did not take care that such a contribution does not remain inaccessible to everyone who does not happen to come across volume III of section B of '*Quellen und Studien zur Geschichte der Mathematik, Astronomie und Physik*'."[27] Klein's wife recalls, "There was always the controversy" between Klein and Strauss, "that Strauss said well you have your little boys and girls, and you tuck them into bed, instead of doing something really important. And Jasha really thought that teaching was more important; when Strauss used to tease him about not writing books, he always answered that the spoken word is more important than the written word."[28] Eva has confirmed this; she traces Klein's distancing himself from the activity of a scholar as he came to place greater value in the eliciting of thought from the young.[29] Indeed, she relates, "he had a positive aversion to publishing."[30]

Whatever the ultimate source of Klein's reluctance to have his first major study disseminated in English, the source of its overcoming is clear: Eva Brann. Her proposal to translate the work received so little encouragement from Klein that she had to "set about the task surreptitiously, over the course of a year."[31] Eva's "unauthorized activity" was quickly forgiven by Klein, however, when he was presented with its fruit, and he became very interested in the publication of the *Math Book*.[32] Eva reports that "only one change of interest"[33] made its way into the English version, the rendering of Klein's German phrase "symbolische Abstraktion" ("symbolic abstraction") as "symbol-generating abstraction." The issue behind this term is the crucial transformation of the ancient Greek *arithmos*, a determinate assemblage of definite objects, into the modern number, a general concept whose meaning is inseparable from the sign through which it is represented. It is the main aim of Klein's study to show that the significance of this transformation is lost when the difference between *arithmos* and number is interpreted in terms of a difference in their respective degrees of "abstractness." Such an interpretation cannot get at the difference in question, because it presupposes that an *arithmos* and a number have a common mode of being, namely, their "abstractness." Klein's study demonstrates the falsity of this presupposition, and in the process coins the term in question to characterize—in contrast to Aristotelian *aphairesis*—the novel kind of "abstraction" productive of the symbolic numbers employed by modern mathematics. Eva pointed out to Klein that the phrase "symbolic abstraction" is at best ambiguous, because as a mode of conceptualization the "abstraction" involved is productive of a new conceptual object, the symbol, but it is not itself symbolic. Klein welcomed her suggestion.[34]

Eva's translation introduced another innovation in terminology that needs to be remarked upon, because it concerns her involvement in the philosophical achievement of Jacob Klein in a manner that transcends her role as his translator. The term in question is "Begrifflichkeit." Klein uses this key philosophical term in two senses: One refers to the characteristic "mode of being" or nature of a concept, as when Klein is comparing and contrasting the Greek *arithmos* "concept" and the modern symbolic number "concept"; the other refers to the manner of concept formation itself, as when he points to the irreducibly different manners in which concepts are formed in ancient Greek and modern European science. The literal English rendering of this term in either sense is "conceptuality," which most scholars would say captures perfectly the meaning of Klein's use of the German term. Why, then, does Eva not so translate it, but instead use a word whose choice is not at all linguistically obvious, to wit, "intentionality"? The answer, I would suggest, is found in Klein's attitude toward the reification of abstract, second-order concepts, which relate not to first-order beings or objects but to other concepts, albeit to other concepts that are mistakenly interpreted as having the same mode of being as first-order beings or objects. In the *Math Book* Klein identifies the invention of modern algebra as the historical locus proper to this reification of abstract concepts, and he credits the mistaken interpretation of the mode of being of these concepts to the early modern philosophers, above all, to Descartes. This misinterpretation, notes Klein, characterizes to this day the self-understanding of the discipline made possible by both of these developments—mathematical physics. Eva relates, "It was the personal consequence of his studies" that such reified and mistakenly interpreted second-order concepts were "deeply, even passionately repugnant to Klein."[35] This leaves me with little wonder not only why she would avoid translating "Begrifflichkeit" with any English word that would even hint in the direction of such concepts, but also why she did not discuss with Klein the word she employed to avoid any suggestion of them.[36] Quite simply, given Klein's attitude on this matter as well as his unwillingness to sanction the proposal to translate the study that was the source of his attitude, both of Eva's decisions make perfect sense to me. Moreover, the word she chooses instead of "conceptuality," "intentionality," is employed in the *Math Book* by Klein in accordance with its medieval meaning, which distinguishes "first" and "second" intentions and, therefore, first and second intentional objects, and is employed thus to express the difference in the manner in which concepts are conceived in ancient and modern science. And Klein himself, just three years after the second part of his study had been published, did not hesitate to articulate both the rationale and methodology of his investigation in the *Math Book* in terms of Husserl's last writings on "intentional history."[37]

Viewed within the contemporary "scholarly" context of Klein's philosophical achievement, however, the question has to be asked whether something that made perfect sense over three decades ago continues to do so today. What is it exactly that the *Math Book* demonstrates? Strauss's remark that this book is "much more than a historical study" is as accurate as it is incomplete. That the "much more" left unsaid has to be addressed from the perspective of the thought of Klein's teachers, Heidegger and Husserl, will be seen immediately by anyone who considers that each of these thinkers, in his own fashion, defined his philosophy in relation to the very problem that Klein investigates in his *Math Book,* the problem of the "formalization" of concepts. This is a problem for both Heidegger and Husserl because when a concept is formalized, on their understanding,[38] it is left undetermined whether it refers to particular objects (or beings) or to their being as such (or essential structure). Husserl's thought (from its beginning to its end) was driven by the conviction that only "phenomenology" is able to provide a proper evidential foundation for the *mathesis universalis,* the formalized science of being that modern mathematics and logic have bequeathed to us and that contemporary formal logic and formal mathematics mistakenly (in his view) attempt to investigate using the purely mechanical apparatus of the symbolic calculus. Heidegger's magnum opus, *Being and Time,* is directed to but one aim: to "deformalize" [*Entformalisieren*] the "formal concept of phenomenon" and therewith to disclose the true phenomena that otherwise remain concealed with the formalization of concepts.

What makes Klein's investigation of ancient Greek mathematics and the origin of algebra much more than an historical study is its concern to answer the respective questions that underlie his teachers' responses to the problem that formalization poses to *philosophy,* questions about how to restore the integrity of knowledge in the wake of its formalization (Husserl's question) and about the most original meaning of being (Heidegger's question). Klein's "answer" to these questions surpasses in an important respect the understanding of formalization exhibited in both of his teachers' thought. The formalization that presents itself as a problem to Husserl's and Heidegger's philosophies is shown by Klein to be exemplified by the formalization of ancient Greek mathematics accomplished by the innovators of modern mathematics. He also shows that the essential structure of this historically located formalization is paradigmatic for the formalization of non-mathematical concepts, the latter being a tendency that on Klein's view is the most salient characteristic of the "modern consciousness." The respect in which Klein's *Math Book* surpasses Husserl's and Heidegger's understanding of formalization is perhaps most aptly characterized by its demonstration of the derivative nature of the questions that inform Husserl's and Heidegger's responses to the problem of formalization. Klein's study quite literally shows that the process of formalization and the formality of the concepts that it generates cannot be grasped so long as thinking approaches them as something that is always known. Another angle has to be found in order to manifest and grasp them, one that does not presuppose that the accomplishment of the formalization and conceptual formality in question is something that is already known. Husserl's thought presupposes just this by understanding the unity characteristic of the general concept that comprises the object of formal logic and formal mathematics, which he calls the empty formal concept of the "anything whatever," to have its basis in the "intentionality"[39] of individual objects, in the intentional relation that characterizes the experience of individual things.[40] The intentionality of individual objects, which for Husserl is a mode of perception and therefore something that is always known, is supposed to account for the unity of the conceptual formality that is in question. Heidegger's thought likewise presupposes that the conceptual formality in question is something that is always—and, therefore, already—known, by posing its most basic question about being, the question about the meaning of the being of beings, in terms of the question about the meaning of being as such. Such a question supposes that it is already known that the being of beings is something that has a "meaning," that is, a "significance," that is distinct from the "beingness" of beings.

The angle that Klein's *Math Book* comes up with in order to investigate the formalization and formality of concepts as something that is not always known is found in the lowly—and decidedly non-formal—arts of counting and relating numbers (calculation). Both the objects and practice of these arts exhibit an understanding that is related to an aspect of the world that is transparent in a manner that refutes for all time the attribution of relativity to *all* aspects of human understanding. These arts comprise the guiding clue for Klein's systematic study in the *Math Book* of the relationship between mathematics and philosophy, first in ancient Greek knowledge, then in early modern knowledge, and, finally, in the comparison of ancient Greek and early modern knowledge. Klein's study demonstrates—from precisely the ground of the non-relativity of the understanding and objects that comprise its guiding clue—the mathematical and philosophical stakes involved in the transformation of the basic characteristic of conceptual formation that occurs when the paradigmatic concepts proper to ancient Greek science are refashioned into the paradigmatic concepts of modern European science. The occurrence of this very transformation itself, and, therefore, the difference in the manner in which concepts are formed in ancient Greek and modern science, remain inaccessible to Husserl's and Heidegger's thought, and do so for the simple reason that their respective engagements with formalization occur at a conceptual level that is incapable of encountering formalized concepts in relation to their "other," that is, to the non-formalized ideal concepts (*eidê*) of pre-modern philosophy.

Because Klein mentions neither Husserl nor Heidegger in the *Math Book*,[41] the contemporary scholarly context of its philosophical achievement is not easy to discern. Once it is discerned, however, the association to Husserl's phenomenology invoked by the term "intentionality" becomes problematic. The angle employed by Klein to grasp formalized concepts and the process of formalization that yields them allows both to be encountered in terms of their proper cognitive priority over all ancient and modern theories of mind. This is to say, the exemplary object of Klein's study, "number," enjoys a priority over the intellect in both ancient and modern theories of knowledge, and Klein capitalizes on this by focusing on both the different statuses of number and the difference in how these statuses are characterized in ancient and early modern philosophy. Klein's invocation of the medieval distinction between first and second intentional objects exercises extreme care to attend only to the "objective" distinctions between ancient and modern numbers, namely, the status of the former as the unity of a multitude of beings and the status of the latter as the unity of the apprehension of such a multitude. This distinction is employed by Klein exclusively to express a distinction in the "mode of being" of two different types of number, a distinction that is equally inaccessible to ancient Greek, medieval, and modern theories of knowledge, albeit for different reasons.[42] Klein's appeal to the medieval distinction between first and second intentions is therefore anything but Scholastic, because the use to which he puts it is designed to show that what is distinctive about modern numbers is *not* simply their status as objects of "second intentions," but, quite properly, the unconscious *interpretation* of them by their inventors (Descartes above all) as nevertheless having the same mode of being as objects of "first intentions." This is what Klein shows makes possible—at once—both the mathematical symbol and the defining tendency of modern thought to understand the "true" being of the nature of all things to be of one substance with the concepts that "define" them. That "intentionality"—whether Scholastic or Husserlian—cannot properly capture what is at issue in the transformation of the ancient numbers into the modern ones, because what is really at stake is the transformation of something that properly has priority over the activity of the mind, no less an interested party than Eva Brann has recently affirmed.

Thus, some forty years after completing her translation of the *Math Book*, she writes:

> It seems to me now a major finding that the revolution in the conceptuality of "number" both marked and characterized the inception of modernity. I say "conceptuality"—as opposed to "concept"—advisedly: Such abstract "second intentional" terminology . . . was deeply, even passionately repugnant to Klein; it was the personal consequence of his studies. Yet the revolution in question was not about this or that individual notion, but about the mode of concept-formation itself, which is properly called "conceptuality."[43]

That Klein's philosophical achievement is exhausted neither by the finding mentioned here by Eva nor by the ingenious angle of the orientation that guides his discovery of it, is something that I think must be mentioned, because the very incompleteness of the *Math Book*'s treatment of what Eva calls its major finding raises a fundamental question about a matter of unparalleled importance—and raises it from a perspective unique to anyone who has followed the book's argument and gotten its point. The point is twofold: (1) From the standpoint of the history of ideas, the thesis that there is a conceptual continuity in the conceptuality of scientific knowledge is mistaken; (2) from the standpoint of philosophy, the incommensurability of the original significance of its basic concepts with their contemporary significance brings with it the truly *fundamental* question of whether the philosopher should serve his or her ancient or modern masters (serving both, at the same time, being out of the question). Despite the "abstract" (in the colloquial sense) nature of the considerations that give rise to this question, I think nothing can be more personal than the answer that one gives to it. The best account of Klein's answer to this question that I have found is contained in a letter to an unnamed woman written in 1943, during the height of the Second World War:

> The College [i.e., St. John's] does not believe that what in institutions of higher learning is taught and sold as scientific knowledge offers a foundation for educating a human being. This is true both of the content of knowledge and the manner in which it is presented, whether by knowledge is meant natural science or the humanities. There is the suspicion —maybe presumptuous but definitely revolutionary—that there is something wrong with science and I don't mean some caricatures of scientists or the empty business of science. The fundamentals are buried; the meanings of scientific values are distorted. A great effort is necessary to rectify these things. One cannot rely on authorities for this task.[44]

I believe it is self-evident from what is written here that in speaking for the College, Klein is also speaking for himself. I also believe that it is appropriate to end my reflections in honor of Eva Brann by noting that her half-century involvement in the "great effort" Klein speaks of here can leave no doubt about her personal answer to the fundamental question that is inseparable from the unique philosophical achievement of Jacob Klein.

NOTES

1 Jacob Klein to Stanley Rosen, letter dated October 15, 1959. Copies of Rosen's (September 1, 1959) and Klein's letters may be found among Klein's papers, which are housed in the St. John's College Library in Annapolis, Maryland. (Hereafter referred to as "Klein's Papers.") A letter dated April 20, 1959, from Hans Jonas also invites Klein to have his name considered for a professorship at the New School for Social Research. While no written reply to Jonas from Klein has apparently survived, according to Klein's wife, "Jasha [the name by which Klein was universally known to friends and intimates] wrote to him, 'No, this is my place'." (The quote is from p. 14 of a typed transcript of the tape-recorded interview of Else [Dodo] Klein by Wendy Allanbrook and Beate Ruhm von Oppen. The transcript [the tape recording is apparently lost] of the interview is among Klein's Papers. Hereafter cited as "Interview.") Both offers were made shortly after Klein relinquished his long deanship of St. John's College, a fact to which both letter writers report Leo Strauss had drawn their attention.

2 Leo Strauss, "An Unspoken Prologue to a Public Lecture at St. John's [In Honor of Jacob Klein, 1899–1978]," *Interpretation* 7 (1978), 1–3, here 3. These remarks were written in 1959, on the occasion of Klein's sixtieth birthday. Hereafter cited as "Prologue."

3 Interview, 14.

4 "Memorial Service for Jacob Klein," in *The College* [published by the Dean, St. John's College] 30, no. 2 (January 1979): 25.

5 Ibid.

6 Klein was born (in 1899) in Libau, which was then in Courland and is now a part of Latvia. Because his father divorced his mother shortly after Klein was born, he lived in the house of his grandparents until 1908, when he moved with his mother to Lipetsk, where they lived with her second husband until 1912. According to Klein's wife, "that was a very strict Jewish household," and Klein had "as a tutor . . . a rabbi, who instructed him and he liked it very much" (Interview, 4). In 1912, Klein's father took Klein to live with him in Brussels, where he was "put into a boarding school" (ibid.). The dates of Klein's studies are recorded in two documents written by him dated April 22 and 23, 1917, which appear to be drafts of a letter addressed to "the Commander of German Administration in Courland," requesting permission to enter the University of Berlin (Klein's Papers).

7 Seth Benardete recalled that Klein "once talked about the fact he had experienced Russian education, Belgian education, which was French, and German education, and he thought the Russian education was best" (*Encounters & Reflections: Conversations with Seth Benardete,* edited by Ronna Burger [Chicago: University of Chicago Press, 2002], 77).

8 According to Klein's wife, "At first he had to go every day to the police station to present himself, then after a while he only had to go once a week, and then not at all, because the Germans had occupied the Baltic Provinces. Since that was his birth land—his fatherland—he could enter the university" (Interview, 3).

9 Interview, 3, 25. The professor's name was "Pahl." Professor Pahl's sons had left his home to fight in the war, and Klein was taken on as boarder for the duration of the war (Interview, 3).

10 Undated document titled "Lebenslauf" (Curriculum Vitae), written sometime after February 2, 1922 (Klein's Papers).

11 Returning war veterans had priority for rooms (Interview, 14).

12 Ibid.

13 Klein's famous opinion of his dissertation was that it "is not worth the paper on which it is written" (Jacob Klein and Leo Strauss, "A Giving of Accounts: Jacob Klein and Leo Strauss," *The College* [April 1970]: 1–5, here 1). (Hereafter referred to as "Accounts.") Klein's Papers contain a copy of the dissertation.

14 Klein's Papers include his Seminar notebooks from the following lecture courses of Heidegger:

1924 Summer Semester lecture course:

Grundbegriffe der aristotelischen Philosophie (Basic Concepts of Aristotelian Philosophy)

1928 Summer Semester lecture courses:

Logik: Metaphysische Anfangsgründe der Logik (The Metaphysical Foundations of Logic)
Phänomenologische Übungen zu Aristoteles, Physik III (Phenomenological Practicum to Aristotle, Physics III).

There is also a Winter Semester 1924/25 registration form that records Klein's payment to attend the following lectures:

Heidegger, Plato (Kratylus, Philebus)
Heidegger, Übungen zur Ontologie des Mittelalters (Practicum to the Ontology of the Middle Ages)
Hartmann, Übungen über Spinoza (Practicum on Spinoza)

It is worth mentioning that the description of Heidegger's Plato course on Klein's registration form does not accurately reflect the content of the course Heidegger actually delivered, a third of which was on Aristotle and the rest on the *Sophist.* A transcript of the course based on Heidegger's and some of his students' notes is available as *Plato's Sophist* (Indiana University Press, 1997), and it is now recognized as one of Heidegger's most groundbreaking works. It is no doubt to Heidegger's lecture courses that Klein refers in 1970, when he credits Heidegger as being "the first man who made me understand something written by another man, namely Aristotle" (Accounts, 1).

15 This information is found in Klein's September 21, 1929, application for a research stipend, addressed to "the Emergency Association of German Science" (Klein's Papers).

16 Which was the first part of his "Die griechische Logistik und die Entstehung der Algebra," see note 21 below. Nicolai Hartmann was going to be his sponsor.

17 Between 1933 and 1937, Klein mostly lived in Berlin. He went to Copenhagen (May–June 1934), hoping that Otto Neugebauer would give him a job (letter to Leo Strauss dated April 17, 1934, in Leo Strauss, *Gesammelte Schriften,* vol. 3: *Hobbes' politische Wissenschaft un zugehörige Schriften—Briefe,* edited by Heinrich Meier [Stuttgart: J.B. Metzler, 2003], 499; hereafter cited as "*GS*")—but this failed (letter to Strauss dated June 11, 1934, *GS,* 508). He had career plans regarding Prague (letter to Strauss, March 22, 1933, *GS,* 459) and hoped to receive some help from political connections (letter to Strauss, March 27, 1933, 462). He considered obtaining his habilitation in the Natural Sciences Faculty of the German University in Prague, under Philipp Frank, a neo-positivist with whom Klein could not agree (cf. letters to Strauss, July 6, 1933, *GS,* 464; April 17, 1934, 499; September 9, 1934, 520–21). He was in Prague in October, to give a lecture about the historical foundations of modern algebra and axiomatics (letter to Strauss, September 20, 1933, *GS,* 470); he mentions planned lectures in November and December 1933 (letter to Strauss, October 21, 1933, *GS,* 481), and again in November–December 1934 (letter to Strauss, *GS,* September 9, 1934, 521)—he had still hoped to be habilitated there at that time. Because of problems in the University, it was closed in November 1934, and Klein could not give the planned lectures (letter to Strauss, November 28, 1934, *GS,* 530). They were delayed to January 1935. The lectures are not mentioned again, and it is not clear whether Klein eventually gave them. There is a library card in Klein's papers from the Universitätsbibliothek in Prague, dated 1934/35, and a certificate of registration from the University of London, University College session 1936–1937, 3rd term, May 6, 1937, for a course titled "Phonetics." There is also a statement of fees for the 3rd term dated April 29, 1937, and a library card from the University of Columbia Library dated June 13, 1938, in the name of Dr. Jacob Klein, University of Prague.

18 One of Klein's students in a 1933 Plato seminar was Ellie Rosenberg, daughter of Edmund Husserl, who invited him to visit her brother Gerhart in Kiel. Klein accepted the invitation, and soon became friends with the extended Husserl family and Gerhart's wife, Else (Dodo) (Interview, 17). (Gerhart Husserl divorced Else in 1948; she and Klein were married in 1950 [Interview, 9].)

19 Jacob Klein, "Die griechische Logistik und die Entstehung der Algebra," in *Quellen und Studien zur Geschichte der Mathematik, Astronomie und Physik,* Abteilung B: *Studien,* vol. 3, no. 1 (Berlin, 1934): 18–105 (Part I); no. 2 (1936):

122–235 (Part II). English translation: *Greek Mathematical Thought and the Origin of Algebra*, translated by Eva Brann (Cambridge, Mass.: M.I.T. Press, 1969; reprint: New York: Dover, 1992). Hereafter referred to as "*Math Book*."

20 Prologue, 2.

21 Ibid.

22 The volumes of the German original are extremely rare today.

23 Sabetai Unguru, "On the Need to Rewrite the History of Greek Mathematics," *Archive for History of Exact Sciences*, vol. 15 (1975): 67–114, here 109. Unguru is referring here to the German original. NB: Unguru has recently characterized this remark as "nasty and uncalled for," and attributed it to his "hubris" (Sabetai Unguru, "Words, Diagrams, and Symbols: Greek and Modern Mathematics or 'On the Need to Rewrite the History of Greek Mathematics' Revisited," *St. John's Review*, vol. 48, 1 [2004]: 71–90, here 88).

24 Hiram Caton, "Review of Jacob Klein's *Greek Mathematical Thought and the Origin of Algebra*," *Studi Internazionali di Filosofia* 3 (1971): 222–26, here 226.

25 *Math Book*, v.

26 The only English writing of Klein to refer to the *Math Book* is his *A Commentary on Plato's Meno* (Chapel Hill: University of North Carolina Press, 1965), where six references to it can be found in its footnotes (83, n. 25, 117, n. 24, 124, n. 45, 139, n. 98, 142, n. 106, and 207, n. 15). Especially noteworthy is the absence of any reference to the *Math Book* in his 1940 essay written in memory of Edmund Husserl, "Phenomenology and the History of Science" (in *Philosophical Essays in Memory of Edmund Husserl*, edited by Marvin Farber [Cambridge, Mass.: Harvard University Press, 1940], 143–63; reprinted in Jacob Klein, *Lectures and Essays*, edited by Robert B. Williamson and Elliott Zuckerman [Annapolis: St. John's Press, 1985], 65–84; hereafter cited as "*PHS*"), because what he there describes as a "task" (84) for phenomenological research, "the reactivation of symbolic abstraction and, by implication, the rediscovery of the original [Greek] arithmetical evidences," is something that the two long articles that are the basis for his *Math Book* had already accomplished four years prior to this article.

27 Prologue, 3.

28 Interview, 13.

29 Eva Brann, "Preface to Burt C. Hopkins, *Edmund Husserl and Jacob Klein on the Origination of the Logic of Symbolic Mathematics*" (the "Preface," like this book, is currently unpublished). Hereafter cited as "Preface."

30 Ibid.

31 Ibid.

32 Ibid. Klein's wife remembers that he always had a copy of the German original, and that "he looked at it, and I remember that he once or twice said, 'Well, it's pretty good'"(Interview, 14).

33 Preface.

34 Ibid.

35 Ibid.

36 Personal communication with Eva Brann, 1995.

37 Although Klein did distance himself from Husserl's presentation of the "actual" history behind the "intentional" one (See *PHS*, Part IV) and, as I mentioned in note 27 above, he failed to mention his *Math Book* in connection with any of this.

38 But not, as I will make clear, on Klein's understanding.

39 "Intentionality" is the key term in Husserl's phenomenology. It refers to the a priori correlation between consciousness and the object to which all consciousness is related. Husserl's account of the exact nature of the intentional correlation is much closer to Descartes' "cogito" than to the medieval distinction between first and second intentions. The latter relate exclusively to the intellect, understood as a capacity of the soul that is distinct from the soul's other capacities, i.e., perception and imagination, while the former, in addition to the intellect, is inseparable from perception and imagination.

40 Edmund Husserl, *Formal and Transcendental Logic*, translated by Dorian Cairns (The Hague: Nijhoff, 1969), 210.

41 Paul Natorp is the only teacher of Klein that he mentions, and he does so just once (*Math Book*, 76).

42 In the case of ancient Greek and medieval knowledge, their temporal priority to the invention of modern numbers prevents this. In the case of modern knowledge, this is prevented by both the innovators of modern mathematics and their progeny interpreting as identical the mode of being of ancient *arithmoi* and numbers in the modern sense.

43 Preface.

44 Letter (written in German) to an unnamed woman, dated October 26, 1943. The original and the (excellent) English translation I quote from here can be found among Klein's Papers.

HEGEL'S LOGIC OF DESIRE

Peter Kalkavage

> There is such divine harmony in the realm of lifeless nature, why this
> discord within the rational?
>
> —*Schiller,* The Robbers

To OPEN THE PAGES of Hegel's *Phenomenology of Spirit* is to enter a labyrinth. The Minotaur of these regions, the Demon of Difficulty, haunts every chamber. The difficulty of Hegel is both legend and cliché. It tends to be so great and so persistent, so much a part of how Hegel thinks and speaks, that we risk losing our way at every turn. Early on, Hegel tells us that the *Phenomenology* chronicles no mere path of Cartesian doubt but a Way of Despair (49).* And yet, how little he seems to realize that his book, intended as a ladder to the absolute (14), is a way of despair for the would-be reader.

This essay is an introduction to the *Phenomenology of Spirit*. I shall try to provide a thread to guide us through Hegel's labyrinth. The center of this labyrinth is the self. This is the point around which everything else in the *Phenomenology* turns. The word "spirit" or *Geist* that appears in the title, a word that also means "mind," refers to selfhood in its fully developed form. Hegel's book tells us how this condition is achieved. In his famous commentary on Hegel, Alexandre Kojève offers the following definition: "Man is self-consciousness." My efforts take their cue from this definition and are devoted to an exploration of what Hegel means by the self.

The *Phenomenology* belongs to a quartet of greatest works on the theme of education. The other three members of the quartet are Plato's *Republic*, Dante's *Divine Comedy* and Rousseau's *Emile*. Despite their profound differences, these works have important similarities. For one thing, each reflects on education through some overarching story or *mythos*. In the *Republic* this *mythos* is the founding of the best city in speech; in the *Divine Comedy* it is Dante's journey to God; in *Emile* it is Rousseau's fiction of playing governor

---

This essay is based on a lecture delivered at St. John's College on the Annapolis campus in March, 1995. An earlier version appeared in the *St. John's Review*, Vol. 43, Number 2, 1996, pp. 1–19.

*Numbers in parentheses refer to page numbers in *Phenomenology of Spirit*, translated by A. V. Miller (Oxford: Clarendon Press, 1977).

to a child not his own by nature. In the *Phenomenology,* too, education is not simply talked about but presented as a drama or story. It is the story of how spirit, which for Hegel is somehow both human and divine, struggles for self-knowledge. Another similarity is that each story is a tale of liberation. Each tells of how man is freed from some enslaving condition: from a cave, or a dark wood, or the corrupting influence of society or, in the *Phenomenology,* from what Hegel calls "natural consciousness."

Hegel educates his reader by initiating him into the minds of others. In the final chapter, he calls the *Phenomenology* a picture gallery (492). The gallery is a colorful array of human types—"shapes of consciousness," as Hegel calls them. These shapes are the phenomena or appearances, of which the *Phenomenology* is the logos or reasoned account. They include the modern scientist and the ancient warrior, the Stoic and the Skeptic, the Unhappy Consciousness and the Beautiful Soul. Some are lifted from the realm of fiction: Faust, Karl Moor from Schiller's early play, *The Robbers,* Antigone, and Rameau's nephew from the novel by Diderot. All have their place within Hegel's picture gallery. All are stages on the way to the fully developed selfhood of spirit.

The defining feature of these human types is that each embodies a specific *claim to know.* This claim is put forth as unquestioned and unqualified, in other words, as absolute. Absolute knowing, the top of Hegel's ladder to the absolute, is not confined to the final chapter but permeates the whole. It is present in all the preceding chapters, not as genuine absolute knowing, but as the claim to such knowing. Hegel calls this claim "certainty." To grasp the various modes of certainty, the reader must play the role of impersonator and spy. He must infiltrate the appearances of absolute knowing and enter into the spirit of their characteristic certainties. In a sense, he must become Hegel's characters if he is to see them for what they are: mortal shapes or *moments* within a greater whole. These shapes undercut themselves in the negative process Hegel calls "experience." The most amazing thing about this process is that it is also positive. As a shape dies, it gives birth to the next and higher shape. Sense-Certainty, for example, in dying gives birth to Perception. In this way, the character types in Hegel's picture gallery generate the greater whole of which they are passing moments. In their logical death, these types constitute the path that leads from mortal thought to divine knowing.

One of the greatest difficulties for a first-time reader of the *Phenomenology* is that the education Hegel depicts is not that of a single human individual. A Stoic, for example, does not convert to skepticism and then to

Christian faith. What makes the transition from stage to stage is mind or spirit in its universality. It is what Hegel calls "the universal individual" (16). Spirit as the universal individual manifests itself in the various epochs of world history. Many of Hegel's character types are crystallizations of these epochs. Antigone, for example, sums up the family aspect of Greek ethical life; the Unhappy Consciousness sums up medieval Christianity; and Rameau's nephew sums up the perverse world of culture. To be sure, Hegel's reader goes through all these stages too. But he does so as someone who is "in the know." He enters the labyrinth of each mode of certainty vicariously, playfully. He does not lose his way—at least, he is not expected to. Nor does he share the self-ignorance and self-deception of the characters he is analyzing. In following the logical thread that connects the shapes of consciousness, the reader thus comes to experience the systematic unity of what in some sense he already knows rather than learns what he did not know.

I have spoken of shapes of consciousness. What, then, is consciousness? Clearly, we must ask this question if we are to understand *self*-consciousness. Consciousness for Hegel is that mode and aspect of thinking in which thinking stands opposed by an object external to, and other than, thinking. Consciousness is the subject-object opposition. It is inwardness that is outer-oriented, outer-directed. Ordinary sense experience offers a simple instance of consciousness. I see an apple before me. It is one thing; I am another. My gaze is directed, vector-like, away from myself and toward the apple. This is the attitude of consciousness. Consciousness does not give subject and object equal weight. The apple is there. It exists. It would be there if I weren't looking at it. The apple is assumed by the attitude of consciousness to be real, substantial, and true, while the light of consciousness that falls on the apple is assumed to have nothing to do with the apple. What we must note here is that consciousness does not merely perceive the object. It also values or esteems it insofar as it is an object. Moreover, consciousness values or esteems the object as higher and more real than the thinking subject.

To educate natural consciousness is to lead it out of this attitude that values objects over and above thinking subjects. Natural consciousness is man in an intellectual state of nature. In this state man identifies the true with the natural. Natural here means more than the apples that exist outside me. It is anything that is assumed to have immediate existence or immediate truth. Natural means logically undeveloped—not thought through or, to use Hegel's word, *mediated*. The natural is anything that is assumed to be true simply because it is *given*. This realm of the natural includes more than sensuous givens like the apple. It also includes intellectual and spiritual givens like innate ideas, intellectual intuition, the categorical imperative, faith, and conscience.

Consciousness for Hegel is the human condition from a certain point of view. It is also a divine condition, a mode in which God as universal mind appears on earth in and through human history. For now, however, I want to focus on the human side of Hegel's man-God identity. In our condition of natural consciousness, we find ourselves thrown into a world of external objects. This world includes laws, customs, and institutions, as well as apples. In this condition of naturalness, we regard all these things not only as over and against us but also as over and *above* us. With all its apparent solidity, the world rises up before us like an irresistible authority figure.

These observations reveal the moral dimension of the *Phenomenology*. Natural consciousness is man's cave and dark wood, his condition of bondage. The education of consciousness is the path by which consciousness becomes fully itself or *free*, free of the tyranny of nature as the realm of external givens. Dialectic for Hegel is the process of mediation by which this givenness and immediacy are destroyed. Dialectic is not only the path to the True. It is also the path to our highest Good in the form of freedom. Man for Hegel is not free so long as the external world is alien to him, so long as it is not the embodiment of thinking. To know the world dialectically, to think it through, is to make it our own. In this sense, Hegel's *Phenomenology* traces the path by which the external world ceases to be the place of exile and estrangement, and comes to be the place where we are fully at home.

Hegel's chapter on self-consciousness is the centerpiece of the whole *Phenomenology*. It is also the point at which the book finds its true beginning. The stages that come before self-consciousness, although important and necessary, form the prologue to Hegel's imperial theme of the self. Now, all the characters in the *Phenomenology* are shapes of consciousness in the sense I mentioned earlier: they all embody spirit or mind caught up in the subject-object opposition. The three opening stages of Sense-Certainty, Perception, and Understanding, however, represent consciousness in its narrower sense. Here the thinking subject places the truth in a non-thinking object: Sense-Certainty in the sensuous This, Perception in the thing and its properties, and Understanding in force. These stages are objective in two senses of the term: they locate truth in an object, and they are detached or uninvolved. The subject here merely "takes" its object and is neither practical nor productive. It does not act, make, or feel. Nor is the object a reflection or embodiment of the thinking subject. The sensuous This, the thing, force— these neither live nor think. The "cool" detachment of consciousness thus stands in sharp contrast with the "heat" of self-consciousness.

The key to the self-consciousness chapter, and to Hegel's book as a whole, is the violence with which self-consciousness first appears. This violence exerts its influence over all the characters we meet in the chapter, not only the warrior and the master, but also the Stoic, Skeptic, and Unhappy Consciousness. Hegel's technical word for this violence is *negativity*. The experiential word for it is *desire*. In the introductory section entitled "The Truth of Self-Certainty," Hegel tells us: "Self-consciousness is desire" (105, 109). The remainder of my essay is an effort to understand this sentence.

In order to get at why self-consciousness is violent, let us ask a more basic question: What does Hegel mean by the self? Toward the end of the *Phenomenology*, Hegel offers a helpful answer to this question. He says: "The 'I' is not merely the self but the *identity of the self with itself*" (489). The self, in other words, is not a thing but a relation, the relation of self-identity. More precisely, it is the *act* of self-relating. One is tempted to coin the verb "selfing." The self, for Hegel, is not something I have but something I do, and this doing is what I most deeply am. Ordinarily, when I refer to my self, I refer either to my body or to something mysteriously lodged in or attached to my body. I treat the self as though it were an object that is simply there, like the apple. For Hegel this way of thinking about the self belongs to natural consciousness, the condition of bondage from which man as self-consciousness must be delivered.

Self-consciousness is the spelling out of selfhood as the act of self-relating. It is the experience of what it means to say, not just "I" but "I am myself." Self-consciousness is the Law of Identity, A = A, that has bubbled up to the surface of human experience in the form of I = I. My selfhood, my act of relating myself to myself, is this law brought to life and awareness. For Hegel, this act of self-relating is negative or self-contradictory. The reason is that in being aware of myself, I hold myself before myself: I am both subject and object. To pursue the spatial metaphor, I generate an inner distance between myself and myself. In logical terms, I generate the condition of *self-otherness*. Were it not for this self-otherness, I would not be self-aware. But clearly I cannot stop at this moment of distance or self-otherness, for then I would not be aware that what I hold before me as somehow external to myself is *myself*. In order to be aware of myself as self-identical, I must generate a distance *and overcome that distance* in one and the same act. This single act is self-consciousness. It is my awareness of being at once self-same and self-other.

Self-consciousness is thus the paradigm of what Hegel calls "determinate negation." This is negation that preserves what it negates. In being self-conscious, I negate my simple or immediate self-identity, my naturalness, and simultaneously negate the negating. Determinate negation is negation with a positive result. In this case the result is—*me* as a self-conscious individual. This explains why the Law of Identity, I = I, is an incomplete, or what Hegel calls abstract, truth. It is incomplete because it conceals and even seems to deny the self-otherness, without which my selfhood is impossible. To be grasped in its wholeness and truth, self-consciousness must be grasped as the unity of the Self-Same and the Self-Other. If the logical dissonance within this unity were resolved in the sense of being obliterated, I would cease to be self-aware. *I* would cease to be.

Earlier I said that self-consciousness was the spelling out of what it means to say, "I am myself." What are the moral consequences of defining man as self-consciousness, as the being who says, "I am myself"? To address this question, we must bring in one of the most important terms in Hegel's book: individuality. The chapter on self-consciousness is Hegel's exploration of what it means to be an individual. "I am myself" is the maxim of individuality. It is the claim that captures my certainty of myself as an inward or self-relating being. No one who utters this sentence, or hears it uttered, can fail to note its assertive, militant tone: "I AM MYSELF." This is not a mere statement of fact, the "cool" observation that I happen to be identical with myself. On the contrary, it is an affirmation, an act of will. In saying, "I am myself," I stand up for myself. I affirm the value and dignity of my being not just human but *this* human, my value and dignity as an individual. Moreover, I assert that this value and dignity derive from my ability to say, "I am myself," that is, from my inwardness or self-consciousness. In saying, "I am myself," in affirming my individuality, I am saying: "I am an end and not a means, a whole and not a part—and must be respected as such." This self-affirmation, this battle cry of individuality, is man's Declaration of Independence. It is man's affirmation of his individuality as absolute.

The militant tone of "I am myself" brings us back to the violence that defines self-consciousness. This violence derives from the identity of self-consciousness with *desire*. What, then, does Hegel mean by desire?

Like every other character in the *Phenomenology*, self-consciousness starts out in the condition of mere certainty, as an unsubstantiated claim to absolute knowing. Here the self is certain not of external objects but of itself.

The most immediate, natural form of this self-certainty is egotism or, as the French authors call it, amour-propre. Hegel's technical term for this egotism is "simple being-for-self" (113). At this primitive level of selfhood, the individual is imprisoned in his utterly private perspective on the world. He is, in the colloquial sense of the word, subjective. In this subjective, self-centered condition, the individual is at war with the external world, at war with *otherness*. As consciousness, the self was mesmerized by the apparent solidity of external objects. This worship of objects vanishes with the individual's certainty of himself. To be sure, the external world is still there. But it has been demoted. No longer a realm of independent substantial beings, it is now no more than fuel for the engine of self-love.

This negative attitude toward externality or otherness is what Hegel means by desire. Self-consciousness is desire, because, in the condition of radical egotism, the individual asserts himself at the expense of the world. To illustrate this, I return to the apple from my earlier discussion. As a self-conscious individual, I no longer want to look at the apple. Nor do I want to understand the natural laws by which the apple grows or falls to the ground. I want to eat the apple. For Hegel, human desire does not derive ultimately from my hunger for apples but rather from my belief, my certainty, that I am substantial while the apple is not. I eat the apple in order to prove that this is the case, to affirm my being and its nothingness. In the Sense-Certainty chapter, Hegel praises the animals for their negative attitude toward the external world: "They do not just stand idly in front of sensuous things as if these possessed intrinsic being but, despairing of their reality, and in complete certainty of their nothingness, they fall to without ceremony and eat them up" (65). Self-consciousness is higher than consciousness because it knows the wisdom of the animals. It knows that objects exist only to be destroyed.

Hegel's logic of desire is a radical departure from how we ordinarily think about desire. Desire in its ordinary sense is positive and other-directed. It is the desire *for* something other than myself. For Hegel, however, desire is negative and self-directed. It is negative because it is the impulse to destroy rather than to acquire. It is more like hatred than love. And it is self-directed because the whole point of this negativity is the self's affirmation of itself. Man, for Hegel, is not evoked, called forth, by some being outside him, neither by the Platonic forms nor an unmoved mover nor the grace-bearing Beatrice. He is driven from within, impelled by his self-certainty to prove the truth of that certainty through antagonism toward the external world. What man strives for, desires in the broad sense of the term, is not an object other than himself, nor a divine condition he longs for without ever attaining, but his own full self-expression. Man, in other words, is his own end. This autonomy is apparent in self-consciousness as it first appears: in man's simple being-for-self.

Desire as the drive to negate is clearly present in the fight to the death, with which the drama of self-consciousness begins. The individual at this primitive stage finds himself in a world that includes both external objects and other self-conscious individuals, other beings that say, "I am myself." And even if they do not say it, one can see the pride of self-certainty in the look in their eyes and in their bearing. From the individual's perspective, these others are thieves and usurpers of the sacred pronoun "I." Only I can say I. But although certain of himself, the individual is also aware that that is all he has—mere certainty, the untested opinion that he is the legitimate bearer of the proud name "I." Out of this awareness is born the individual's need to prove himself in order to achieve recognition. In Hegel's language, he is driven to raise his certainty to truth. Positively, he must prove himself to himself, prove that his value as an inwardly turned, self-conscious being is more important than his life. Negatively, he must destroy the merely apparent selfhood of his opponent, who is also driven to prove *his* self-worth.

In its state of desire, the self wishes to destroy its object. But it also thrives on this object. If the object were consumed once and for all like an apple that is eaten, the self would have nothing to "feed off." Since self-consciousness derives its sense of self from the negation of an other, this other must somehow be preserved. In the fight to the death, the warrior individual realizes that killing his opponent is unsatisfying, and that what he really wants from his opponent is recognition or honor. The individual who fights for recognition wants to deprive the other self-consciousness not of his life but of his selfhood, his right to say "I am myself." He does so by getting the other individual, who is terrified at the prospect of violent death, to negate himself, that is, to prefer life to honor. At this point in the drama, the warrior becomes a *master,* and his terrified adversary a *slave.*

Having won the battle for recognition, the master is now free to indulge his lower desires. He can eat the apple pie that the slave has made. But the slave, precisely through his subservience to his master in the form of *work,* rises above his master. He does so because his servitude, together with the fear of death that made him a slave in the first place, has stifled his former will to destroy, his former desire. The apple pie may be food to the master. But to the slave it is a work of art, an independent thing that the slave makes but is not permitted to consume. In the independence of the thing made the slave beholds the embodiment of his independence as a maker. The pie is not just the product of his work. It is also the objectification of the slave's act of working, his investment of himself in an external object. The master, by contrast, remains in the condition of desire. Partly, this is because desire, once gratified, only repeats itself. I eat the pie, and an hour later I am hungry again. The result of giving in to desire is the reappearance of the desire. But what is more important, the master, as Hegel observes, cannot be satisfied by recognition that comes from his slave, for the slave is a debased human being, who lacks independence. The mastery of other selves is thus self-defeating. Recognition is satisfying and genuine only when it comes from an equal.

The initial war of the proud selves reminds us of Hobbes's state of nature. Hegel appropriates Hobbes's view that man is by nature proud and competitive or warlike. But he also gives this view a logical grounding in the dialectical structure of the self. What for Hobbes was a fact is for Hegel the manifestation of the self's dialectical identity, its logical dissonance of Same and Other. The individual is by nature at war with other individuals because, as a self-consciousness, he is at war with himself. Earlier we saw how selfhood for Hegel was the unity of the self-same and the self-other. The clearest indication that I am a divided being is that I am alive. I am a self-consciousness sustained by and rooted in an organic body. This body is an "other" that is also myself. My body shadows and obscures my inwardness. It detracts from my dignity and worth. At its most immediate and therefore most violent level, self-consciousness is at war with its body and its life. It feels its dignity and worth undercut and rendered questionable by the animality that clings to it. That is why the warring individual risks his own life in seeking to destroy the life of his opponent, why the fight to the death is combat rather than murder.

For Hegel, the violent desire for recognition is the first manifestation of my desire to complete my vision of myself in another individual, to reconcile the two warring aspects of my own selfhood through a reconciliation with this externally existing, actual other. The desire to be recognized or known by another is in fact my desire to *know myself* in the context of a real human community. This community is what Hegel calls the "I that is We and the We that is I" (177). Hegel's prime example of such a community is the ancient Greek polis, which appears at the beginning of the chapter entitled Spirit. The combatants do not know that genuine recognition comes about only if it is reciprocal or shared, only if the one who recognizes me is not a slave but my equal. This later stage of mutual recognition cannot be reached without the original violence. Progress for Hegel is made not through smooth degrees, nor by tempering extremes, but by pushing extremes to their logical, self-defeating conclusions.

The negative spirit of desire continues into the second section of Hegel's chapter, the section entitled "Freedom of Self-Consciousness." The Stoic, Skeptic and Unhappy Consciousness are all instances of the will to negate the world in order to affirm the self. On the surface, the Stoic seems to be above desire. He affirms himself. He does so not through action in the external world, which is the place of turmoil, but in the unperturbed realm of *thought*. The stubborn inwardness of the Stoic, his will to be himself regardless of what happens to his life in the external world, makes the Stoic implicitly violent or, in Hegel's technical meaning of the term, desirous. Skepticism is the truth of Stoicism because it unleashes this violence. The Skeptic here is Sextus Empiricus. The Roman Skeptic, like his Stoic counterpart, aims at mental tranquillity as the true form of freedom. He cultivates this tranquillity by demonstrating that all things are logically unstable or self-refuting, and that consequently we should suspend our judgment, not cling to anything as though it were absolute truth. The Skeptic in this way brings about the intellectual destruction of the world that the Stoic implies but is too noble to carry out.

We now come to the crowning moment of Hegel's chapter on self-consciousness. Here we meet the character type Hegel calls the Unhappy Consciousness. Like every other shape in the *Phenomenology,* self-consciousness starts out in certainty and ends up in truth. The truth always contradicts and undermines the original certainty. The Unhappy Consciousness is the negative truth of self-consciousness *as a whole,* the truth that undermines the original effort at self-affirmation in the fight to the death. The individual started out as a proud warrior. He wanted to prove that he was simply *for himself.* Having passed through the stages of Slave, Stoic, and Skeptic, consciousness now reaches the opposite extreme. It becomes the medieval Christian, who lives only *for Another,* that is, for a transcendent God. Egotism has been transformed into the obsession with *annihilating* egotism. The violence of desire, formerly directed toward the external world, is turned back on the self. Negativity is now self-sacrifice, and self-certainty self-condemnation.

The Unhappy Consciousness emerges from the dialectic of Skepticism. The Skeptic says, "All things are self-contradictory or self-other." But he puts forth this teaching as an absolute truth that is self-same. This contradiction reveals that there are in fact two minds, two *selves,* within the Skeptic. One experiences unchanging truth. The other experiences its thoughts as constantly contradicting one another. The Skeptic, says Hegel, keeps going back and forth between these two minds or selves. He is a unity of opposites but does not know that he is a unity of opposites. The Unhappy Consciousness is the explicit awareness of this unstable union of a changeable and an unchangeable self. It is, to quote Hegel, "the consciousness of oneself as a doubled, merely contradictory being" (126). Contradiction has been at work in every shape of consciousness that has emerged so far. But only now is there the actual experience of contradiction as such.

Hegel's account of the Unhappy Consciousness is logically complex. It also contains many allusions to medieval Christianity. I will confine myself to showing how Hegel's sentence, "Self-consciousness is desire," continues to be operative. For the Unhappy Consciousness desire appears in three guises. The first I have already mentioned. Painfully aware of his egotism and carnality, the individual penitent seeks to negate his individuality. He desires to be rid of his self-love, which he identifies with the unessential and changeable aspect of his being. Second, there are all those desires he seeks to negate, bodily desires that separate him from God. The third instance of desire is what Hegel calls the *infinite yearning* for God as the one true Self. This is the first time that God appears in the *Phenomenology*. To emphasize God's logical function in the argument, however, Hegel prefers to call him the Unchangeable Consciousness.

From the perspective of the Unhappy Consciousness, infinite yearning is directed toward God as the sacred Other. The individual is the tragic lover and God the beloved. As Hegel regularly reminds us, however, we must distinguish the perspective that is *for us* from that of the consciousness under investigation. In this case, what the Unhappy Consciousness regards as an infinitely remote Other is, from our more knowing perspective, the divine or unchangeable aspect of *itself*. This follows from the definition of the Unhappy Consciousness. The Unhappy Consciousness is the experience of a mortal self and a divine self *in one and the same consciousness*. Or, as Hegel puts it, it is "the unity of pure thinking and individuality" (130), where thinking is my self-sameness or divinity, and individuality is my otherness and mortality.

What, then, is the true nature of the infinite yearning for God? It is what Hegel regards as the abiding goal of human striving: man's inner compulsion to be fully himself. What the Unhappy Consciousness interprets as the desire to be *with* God is in reality man's desire to *be* God. At the end of Hegel's chapter, the unhappy individual, having failed repeatedly to be worthy in the sight of God, hands himself over to the Church and its priesthood in a final gesture of despair. But out of this despair there arises, amazingly, a new and positive version of self-consciousness. Hegel calls this reborn self-consciousness *Reason*. Instead of trying to negate the world, or itself, instead of being desirous, the rational individual now strides confidently through the world, certain that he will find himself embodied there. Whereas the Unhappy Consciousness belonged to the medieval world, Reason is a *modern*. Among the fascinating character types we meet here are the observational biologist, the phrenologist (who can read your spirit in the bumps on your head), Romantic "bad boy" heroes like Faust and Karl Moor, and achievement-animals who use their talent in society to prey on the accomplishments of other achievement-animals. Such is the vast range of Hegel's picture gallery.

In spite of its many subdivisions, the *Phenomenology* is composed of only three main parts: Consciousness, Self-Consciousness, and a third part that Hegel leaves untitled. In this third part of the *Phenomenology*, the longest by far, man's quest for selfhood is completed. Man becomes complete when the logical implications of his self-identity rise to the level of conscious experience, when man is explicitly what he is implicitly or in his concept. But what is man implicitly? What is man's *concept*? This we have already seen in the earlier account of self-identity. Man as self-consciousness is the unity of the self-same and the self-other. Man is the being who beholds himself and can say "I AM MYSELF." How, then, is man to experience himself for what he is? What can it possibly mean to *experience* the determinate negation that is logically inscribed in man's self-awareness, in man's concept?

With these questions, I reach the last leg of my journey through Hegel's labyrinth. Consider the title of Hegel's book: *Phenomenology of Spirit*. Phenomena or appearances, whatever else they may be, are outward or showy, while spirit is inward and deep. To give a phenomenology of spirit, then, is to give a reasoned account, a *logos*, of what it means for spirit to appear, what it means for the inner to make itself outer, for the deep to be showy while still remaining deep. For Hegel, the inner and the outer, self and world, are both necessary to the full expression of selfhood. That is why desire failed. It failed because the individual wanted to affirm himself at the expense of the world. If there is no world, or if the world is just a vale of tears, then there is nothing solid, nothing objective, in which I might contemplate my worth, in which I might behold myself. Just as consciousness, in its idolatry of objects, lost sight of the true goal, so too does self-consciousness in its effort to destroy objects. Complete selfhood demands that the purity of thinking and the solidity of the world somehow come together in a way that is not a mere contradiction or dissonance, as it was for the Unhappy Consciousness. In my earlier account of natural consciousness, I stressed the tyranny of the external world. But that is not the only tyranny that besets man in his quest for complete selfhood. There is a worse monster than the external world. This monster is man's fascination with his own spirituality or inwardness, his tendency to become—a *Beautiful Soul*.

The Beautiful Soul is a character type made famous by Goethe and Schiller. This type or figure appears in the *Phenomenology* at the end of Hegel's account of Morality and Conscience. In what follows I shall discuss the human aspect of the Beautiful Soul. We must remember, however, that all the human types we meet in Hegel's book are also manifestations of the divine—efforts by which God struggles to know himself in time. The Beautiful Soul is an episode in the life of God on earth. As Hegel tells us in the final chapter, the Beautiful Soul "is not only the intuition of the Divine but also the Divine's intuition of itself" (483).

The Beautiful Soul is a more tragic version of the Unhappy Consciousness. The Unhappy Consciousness was a lover. It longed for union with an infinitely remote God. The Beautiful Soul, too, is in love—but not with an object. It is in love with its own inner purity, in love with *itself* as the moral genius whose absolute knowing rises above and negates all specific moral duties. Whereas the Unhappy Consciousness distanced itself infinitely from the one true Self, the Beautiful Soul identifies with this Self, with God in his purity. The Unhappy Consciousness found itself hopelessly worldly and carnal. The Beautiful Soul, by contrast, acts as though it did not even have a body, let alone bodily desires. In Hegel's characterization, the Beautiful Soul "lives in dread of besmirching the splendor of its inner being through action and existence" (400). Having turned its back on the world of action, this pure soul dies for want of a life. It vanishes, Hegel says, "like a shapeless vapor into thin air" (400).

The Beautiful Soul dies because it denies the self-otherness that is necessary to man's self-identity. Man cannot be fully himself, cannot behold himself, unless he somehow preserves the world as his objective Other. To fulfill the destiny of his self-otherness, man must become reconciled to the world's externality. Man's inwardness must somehow come to terms with the outward realm of action and existence.

Reconciliation is the climax and "happy ending" of Hegel's story of consciousness. It is the moment in which the Way of Despair becomes divine comedy. In reconciliation, God comes on the scene, not as a Beyond, but as a living presence within a community of selves, God as the spirit and self-knowledge of that community. The last two chapters of the *Phenomenology*, Religion and Absolute Knowing, are further developments of what reconciliation has accomplished. In Religion, God is grasped through stories and pictures; in Absolute Knowing, he is grasped through concepts.

In the moment leading up to reconciliation, two individuals confront one another, just as they did in the earlier fight to the death. One judges; the other is judged. The judge is the Beautiful Soul who has not succumbed to death. As a devotee of Conscience, he posits his own pure inwardness as the absolute. He condemns others who are not pure like him, the Napoleons of the world, who have traded in their purity of soul for worldly preoccupation and fame. The self-righteous individual judges the other to be immoral. He does so not because that other has done something wrong, but simply because he has done something, because he has allowed himself to have an outward existence and a concern for action. To the judgmental individual, this worldliness is the greatest betrayal of which a human being is capable. It betrays the sacred inwardness, the true spirituality of Conscience, which alone makes us worthy of respect. The judge judges the other to be a hypocrite, someone who claims to be spiritual or inward but in fact prostitutes this inwardness by action in the real world. The judge sets himself up as the Emperor of Inwardness. In doing so, he is an even bigger hypocrite than the individual he judges. The reason is that judgment for Hegel must take the form of outward speech. But speech is a kind of deed or act, with which the self sets foot onto the world-stage. The judge cannot pass judgment on the other individual without becoming like him. He cannot denounce hypocrisy and also remain pure or inward.

Reconciliation occurs when both individuals admit to being the betrayers of spirit as pure inwardness. Each must confess his worldliness to the other. This is clearly more difficult for the judge, since he must sacrifice his purism, abdicate as the Emperor of Inwardness. As the judge confesses his own hypocrisy and forgives the hypocrisy of the other, he gives his blessing to the secular world he once had cursed. In this moment of reconciliation, the most sublime metamorphosis in the *Phenomenology*, each self sees itself in the other and admits to this seeing. At last, there is mutual recognition.

In logical terms, hypocrisy is self-otherness that pretends to be self-sameness. When each self in Hegel's drama admits to seeing itself in the other, self-otherness, the moment of self-identity that had been denied for the whole course of the journey up to this point, at last receives its due. The long-suppressed self-otherness rises to the surface of human experience. The most important feature of reconciliation is the change that takes place in the relation between self and world. With the confession of self-otherness, the external world ceases to be the inimical Other over and against the self. It is now the home of spiritual manifestation, the place of God.

Reconciliation for Hegel is a human experience with a conceptual or philosophic meaning. Much more is going on in this phenomenon than the individuals involved realize. In the act of forgiveness, the hard heart melts. This softening of the hard heart is in truth a dialectical or logical accomplishment. The softening of the heart, the melting of hard being-for-self, is the feeling of dialectical fluidity and motion. It is the feeling of *thinking*. Now, it is the peculiar power and sublimity of reconciliation to retain past enmity as something that has been overcome. Reconciliation is thus the human experience of determinate negation, negation that preserves what it destroys. In this feeling of determinate negation, man at last experiences the complete unity of his self-identity, the being-together of the self-same and the self-other.

In the section on Revealed Religion, Hegel gives us a definition of spirit. "Spirit," he says, "is the knowledge of oneself in the externalization of oneself; the being that is the movement of retaining its self-identity in its otherness" (459). This is precisely the condition that has been dialectically generated in the phenomenon of reconciliation. In the confession of hypocrisy, the two selves flow beyond the limits of their private selves. They become external to themselves while remaining inward or spiritual beings. There is now mutual recognition, unlike the one-sided kind we had earlier in the master-slave relation. The individuals here experience the divine in time. In being reconciled to one another, they generate *universal* self-consciousness. This is the I that is We and the We that is I—the ultimate goal of the desire for recognition. Hegel describes this communal selfhood in an utterly remarkable way: "[I]t is God manifested in the midst of those who know themselves in the form of pure knowledge" (409).

All this, we must note, takes place through the power of language. For Hegel, the inner must become outer. The inner is by definition the drive or compulsion to be an externalized or expressed inner. That is why the self-righteous judge must not simply think his condemnation of the other. He must utter it—indeed, throw it in the face of the individual who has dared to act. So too, in the moment of reconciliation, the two hypocrites must confess their hypocrisy openly to one another. Language is in this way the outpouring and manifestation of spirit.

Language plays a central role in the *Phenomenology*. For Hegel, language is not mere communication. It is rather spiritual or intellectual *presence*. In

Hegel's words, it is "the being-there or existence of spirit" (395). Language is the outward expression of inward thought. When I speak, I translate my inwardness or self-consciousness into something outer and real. I make my thought present for my listener and also for myself. Language is thought standing in its own presence, thought that beholds itself as thought. But this outward expression is not a direct and smooth translation of the inner into the outer: it is not without its moment of conflict. To speak is to betray a thought. In uttering a thought, I betray it in the negative sense that I turn against my inwardness and hand it over to its enemy—the external world. To speak is to act. But now comes the magic of language, the magic that distinguishes language from every other human action. Even as I betray my inward thought by making it outer, I turn against this very betrayal and defeat the bad effects of externality. That is, I betray my thought in the positive sense that I express or reveal it *as thought*. In other words, language, the defining act of man, is the prime instance of spirit as Hegel defines it. It is the retaining of inwardness in the very act of externalization. Like forgiveness, language is the overcoming of betrayal in its negative sense. Reconciliation, for this reason, is not just an instance of speech but the logic of the very act of speaking brought to the level of experience.

In the phenomenon of reconciliation man experiences himself as the dialectical unity of Same and Other. He grows beyond his private selfhood and, as I noted earlier, becomes an "I that is We and We that is I." But man is not fully himself for Hegel until he thinks the reconciliation of all opposites at the level of pure conceptuality—thought without pictures. This ultimate reconciliation is Absolute Knowing. At this level, mind, now purged of all naturalness or anti-mind, wins the condition of complete self-identity and freedom. Mind, the true self of man for Hegel, is now free to be itself: to develop spontaneously into a coherent system, and to lead the life that is completely its own.

In the *Phenomenology* man does not simply come to know the truth: he comes to know that he *is* the truth. He learns that his concept as a self-conscious individual is identical with *the* Concept. This is the divine intelligibility, the *logos* that steers its way through all things. This divine logos, the life of pure thinking, is embodied in Hegel's *Science of Logic*. By entering into this life of the mind, man enjoys the divinity that is inscribed in his self-consciousness. In the spontaneous unfolding of what Hegel calls the Concept or Notion—Hegel's analogue to the Platonic Good—man enjoys the very principle of his cherished freedom and the pure play of his self-identity. No longer an Unhappy Consciousness, he is transported to the true heaven.

As I now take my leave of Hegel's labyrinth, I bid farewell to all its monsters and heroes. Hegel ends on a grand theological note. He speaks of world-history as the Place of Skulls, the Calvary where spirit suffers and reveals its glory (493). My closing note will be much simpler. Hegel cautions us in the Preface against becoming enchanted with things uplifted and remote. He warns philosophy, which aspires to divine knowing, not to forget its worldly origins and home. We hear this warning in the words of Zarathustra, whose plea captures the spirit of Hegel's *Phenomenology:* "I beseech you, my brothers, *remain faithful to the earth.*"

Zion Light

Susu Knight

Zion Light
pastel, 19" × 8"

FAVORITE ANALOGIES

Sam Kutler

I AM EXHIBITING HERE my favorite proportions—*analogia* in the Greek—and I am attempting to make clear why they are my favorites. This scheme is an imitation of a summer lecture that I gave to the freshmen and graduate students at St. John's College in Annapolis called *Four Favorite Irrational Numbers*. These irrationals, which I include below, should be everyone's favorites, but I do not claim that my favorite analogies should be so for everyone.

A proportion proposes two relationships together with the assertion that, at least in some respect, the relationships are the same. I use a Leibniz symbolism from 1684 that consists of a single colon in each relationship and a double colon between the relationships to express my assertion that they are the same. After a glance at identity as a relationship,

$$A:A::A:A \quad \text{or} \quad A:B::A:B \quad \text{or} \quad A:A::B:B,$$

let me ignore identity to claim that in mathematics, at least, the simplest of relationships occurs when the antecedent is double the consequent. My first example is with whole numbers. Ten has to five the very same relationship that six has to three:

$$10:5::6:3.$$

However, when the antecedent is incommensurable with its consequent, the sameness might not be so apparent. I enjoy the following proportion with irrational numbers:

$$1:\sqrt{2}::\sqrt{2}:2.$$

To see that this is so, multiply the antecedent and consequent of the first ratio by $\sqrt{2}$, or instead notice that the product of the extremes equals the product of the means. Thus $\sqrt{2}$ is the mean proportional between one and two.

If I extend the proportion to read

$$1:\sqrt{2}::\sqrt{2}:2::2:\sqrt{8},$$

then I arrive *in modern terms* at the *Meno* problem of finding the side of the eight-foot square. Of course, for Plato $\sqrt{8}$ would not be a number; instead it would suggest a restatement of the question: How long is the side whose square is eight?

Let me introduce one of my favorite proportions—an area theorem—that I find in XII.2 of Euclid's *Elements:*

> circles are to each other as the squares on their diameters.

This proportion is used by Hippocrates of Chios, who wrote a book called *Elements,* now lost, that appears in a commentary on Aristotle's *Physics* by Simplicius. This treatise precedes Euclid by at least 125 years. Hippocrates uses the proportion between circles and squares to square a lune. The proof is so simple and clear that I'll present it here:

> In a circle AGBCD with O as center inscribe the square ABCD. On side AB of the square as diameter, construct the circle AHBO. Construct perpendiculars OE and OF from O to sides AB and AD. I say that the lune AHBG is equal to the square AEOF (Figure 1).

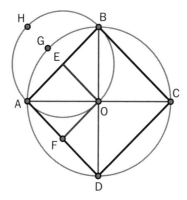

FIGURE 1. Squaring lune AHBG

Demonstration: From my proportion between circles and squares, I have

Circle AGBCD : Circle AHBO :: Square AC : Square AB
Semicircle ABCO : Semicircle AHBE :: 2 :1
2 Semicircle AHBE = Semicircle ABCO
Semicircle AHBE = Quadrant AGBO; subtract common area AGBE
Lune AHBG = Triangle ABO = Square AEOF

In his *Elements,* Euclid busied himself in the first two books with squaring any polygonal figure; that is, he showed how to find a square equal to any polygon. Euclid would have liked to square the circle, but the closest he is able to come to this is the proportionality between circles and the squares on their diameters. Hippocrates managed to square three different lunes, and in the nineteenth century Thomas Clausen squared two other lunes. If every lune could be squared, then, contrary to fact, the circle could be squared by Euclidean means: with straightedge and compass.

Because of the diagram in Figure 2, it might have seemed evident to Hippocrates that circles are to each other as the squares on their diameters.

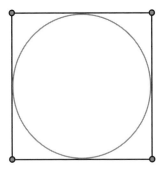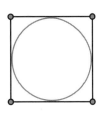

FIGURE 2. Circles inscribed in squares that are proportional to the squares on their diameters

Euclid, however, does not merely accept the theorem; instead he provides a complete proof that the proportion holds. Euclid's proof is by *reductio ad absurdum*. If the proportion does not hold, then for some area S different from that of the second circle,

Square D : Square d : : Circle C : S

Euclid finds his *reductio* to the above proportion by "exhausting that circle." First he inscribes a square inside Circle C, then a regular octagon, etc. He keeps doubling the sides of the regular polygons until the difference between the area of the circle and its inscribed polygon is less than the difference between the circle and the supposed area S. To be assured that there is such an exhaustion, he has as a basis the first theorem of Book X, which shows that given two magnitudes, a greater and a lesser, and if I continually subtract from the greater its half or more, eventually, after a finite number of trials, I have reduced the area of the greater magnitude until what is left is less than the smaller one. Euclid X.1 is a calculus-like statement. But what is the basis of X.1 itself? It is the fourth definition of Book V:

> Magnitudes are said to have a ratio to one another which are capable, when multiplied, of exceeding one another.

This statement is sometimes called a postulate and is attributed to either Eudoxus or Archimedes. It rules out both infinites and infinitesimals.

Finally, let me lay out a short road from my proportion to the irrational number π. Let me begin again from this proportion:

circle C : circle c :: square D : square d

and write it as a variation:

the areas of circles vary as the squares on their diameters, or its equivalent, with the squares on their radii

$c \propto r^2$.

With the advent of real numbers, there is a constant, call it π, such that

$c = \pi r^2$.

This concludes my discussion of the proportionality between circles and the squares on either their radii or their diameters.

To lead to the second of my favorite proportions, let me turn to proportions in only three terms, that is, proportions with a middle term M between A and B.

A : M :: M : B

Outside of mathematics, let my paradigm be

Grandmother is to Mother as Mother is to Daughter.

The relationship is **gives birth to a daughter.** Let us dare to give a particular proportion in three terms:

Socrates is to Plato as Plato is to Aristotle,

where the relationship is **gives birth to a desire to lead a philosophic life.**
Now let us formulate the golden ratio, which Kepler calls the divine proportion. Given a line AB cut at C so that

the whole : larger part :: larger part : smaller part, or
AB : AC :: AC : CB.

The point C provides the golden cut (Figure 3).

FIGURE 3. The line divided into the golden ratio

In algebraic language, if the whole is x + 1 and the parts x and 1, then

$$(x + 1)/x = x/1$$

and there are two solutions for x, call them τ and σ:

$$\tau = (1 + \sqrt{5})/2 \quad \text{and} \quad \sigma = (1 - \sqrt{5})/2.$$

τ is called the golden number and σ, which is negative, shares with τ the property of being one less than its square:

$$\tau + 1 = \tau^2 \qquad \sigma + 1 = \sigma^2$$

also

$$\tau + \sigma = 1.$$

Thus I have arrived at the irrationals π and τ via proportionality.

Now let me complete the introduction of my four favorite irrationals, this time without proportions.

First of all,

τ lies between 1 and 2, and
π lies between 3 and 4.

For my other two favorite irrational numbers

e lies between 2 and 3, and
γ lies between 0 and 1.

Fortunately, there are accessible books, one devoted to e, and another, amazingly enough, to gamma. Each contains an elementary account: *e: The Story of a Number* by Eli Maor, and *Gamma: Exploring Euler's Constant* by Julian Havil.

Before I return to the theme of proportionality, let me plot each of the four irrationals on the number line. To do so, I'll use one-place accuracy after the decimal point so that

$$\gamma \sim .6, \quad \tau \sim 1.6, \quad e \sim 2.7, \quad \pi \sim 3.1$$

(See Figure 4.)

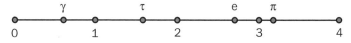

FIGURE 4. Four favorite irrational numbers

When I add together these approximations for the four constants, the sum is exactly 8. Alas, that result fails to hold when I use greater precision. However, there is a constant "near" gamma, which, if I sum it with the other three irrationals, makes exactly eight, and I may wonder whether this "near" gamma has any other properties of interest.

Let me mention how Euclid enters the geometrical realm and then try to imitate that beginning in arithmetic. In Euclid's *Elements* I find points and lines, and to guide me, five postulates that allow me to connect points with straight lines, extend straight lines continuously, construct circles with any center and radius, and assert the equality of any two right angles. The fifth postulate, however, is the one that makes the geometry Euclidean. It states that if two straight lines make the interior angles on one side of a transversal less than two right angles, then when these two lines are sufficiently extended, they form with the transversal a triangle. In other words, the two lines are not parallel. With this postulate of non-parallelism, but not without it, or something equivalent to it, it is possible to show that the angles of every triangle sum to two right angles, from which, for example, the theorem of Pythagoras follows. The fifth postulate, then, is responsible for making the geometry Euclidean.

Was it to be hoped that Euclid would also supply for us five arithmetic postulates, which similarly might provide a basis for arithmetic?

Do Euclid's geometric postulates have the same relationship to Euclid's geometry as Euclid's arithmetic postulates have to Euclid's number theory?

Such a hope is dashed when in Book VII of the *Elements,* where Euclid does turn his attention to arithmetic, there are definitions, but there are no special postulates for numbers at all. To find such postulates, let me turn to the writings of Peano, who is writing on the heels of Dedekind's treatise, *Was sind und was sollen die Zahlen?* (*The Nature and Meaning of Numbers*).

The most significant undefined terms in Euclid's beginning are **part** and **whole**. In the Peano approach the most significant undefined term is **successor.**

Here is a version of the Peano postulates:

A. 1 is a number.

If I consider A to be an "existence postulate," then Peano is claiming here that there *is* at least one number. In the language of set theory, the set of [natural] numbers is not empty. In geometry, on the contrary, Euclid does not claim that there are points. However, *if* there are points, then there are straight lines, for the very first postulate claims that a straight line may be drawn to connect any two points. Thus, if I wish, I may consider Euclid's geometry to be conditional: If there are points, then such and such theorems and constructions follow. This account seems to fit into the divided line section of Plato's *Republic,* where mathematicals are on the third part of the divided line, and the faculty on that part of the line is mathematical thought, which depends on hypotheses or suppositions.

 B. Every number has a unique successor.

The uniqueness of the successor relationship assures me that the numbers do not have a structure like this, in which f has two successors, p and k:

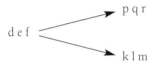

 C. 1 is not the successor of any number.

Thus 1 is the very first number. Since the successor relationship is unique, the successor of 1, s(1), differs from 1, and I define s(1) = 2; s(2) = 3, and s(3) = 4.

 D. If two successors are equal, their predecessors are equal.
  [s(x) = s(y) implies x = y.]

This avoids a structure like this, in which r and m have the same successor, d:

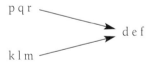

Finally, the fifth arithmetic postulate sets up a schema that will allow mathematicians to prove that a proposition holds for all numbers:

 E. If a proposition P(k) is true for k = 1,
  and if **for every k,**
  P(k) implies P(k + 1), then proposition P is true for every
  number.

The procedure, which is called mathematical induction but is in fact a form of deduction, was first enunciated and employed by Francesco Maurolycus in 1575 to prove theorems. It became known after it was employed by Blaise Pascal in his work on the arithmetical triangle to show that his observations on that triangle held true for every number.

In addition to these five arithmetic postulates, I need definitions for addition and multiplication. The following are recursive definitions:

Addition	Multiplication
n + 1 means s(n)	n • 1 means n
s(n + m) means n + s(m)	n • s(m) means (n • m) + n

Now I can verify, for example, that $2 + 2 = 4$ and $2 \times 2 = 4$.

$$2 + 2 = 2 + s(1) = s(2 + 1) = s(s(2)) = s(3) = 4,$$
$$2 • 2 = 2 • s(1) = 2 • 1 + 2 = 2 + 2 = 4.$$

The analogy between geometry and arithmetic, where each is based on five postulates, seems to break down because beginning in the nineteenth century with Gauss, Lobachevsky, and Bolyai, I have another geometry to set beside Euclid's. In the world of numbers, however, how could there be a non-Euclidean arithmetic? Perhaps only in this way: With the Peano postulates, there are other "unintended models" that satisfy them. For instance, Thoralf Skolem found an example in which the elements are functions rather than numbers. If you try to add a postulate to rule out an unintended model, there will still be other unintended models.

For my next favorite analogy, let me ask, Is one a number? To begin to answer this question, let me propose an antinomy about numbers, which consists of a thesis and an antithesis:

Thesis: One is a number.   **Antithesis:** One is not a number.

Perhaps the best beginning here is with my ability to count. At first this seems universal, but let me compare it with the ability to recognize color or musical tones. The color-blind person might be unable, say, to tell red from green, the tone-deaf person to hear an interval of a third. Is there number blindness? Even if a person can mechanically count off one through eight people in a room, what if that person doesn't realize that that is just how many proficient people are needed to perform an octet? In other words, saying the number is not enough, instead it is necessary to know what the number means.

Shall I follow Tobias Dantzig in his claim that normal people possess a **number sense**? He believes that certain birds, for example, do so too.

A source for the thesis can be found in the first of the Peano postulates, for it states that one is a number.

Furthermore, just about everyone considers one to be a number, and when number is mentioned, I have to wonder not whether one is a number, but instead what kind of number I am discussing, for in all of the following, one is a number:

1.   Whole numbers
2.   Fractions (without negatives)
3.   Rational numbers (with negatives)
4.   Real numbers
5.   Complex numbers

Furthermore, consider **the number line.** It is perhaps the most persuasive of mathematical images, and, of course, one is on that line.

Finally, the numbers are now taught as belonging to a set by means of one-to-one correspondences. The notion of a correspondence is taken as more primitive than the notion of a number, and hence correspondences can be used to define number. Then in a version of founding arithmetic, the empty set is a given, and the set containing nothing but the empty set is used as an exemplar for the sets that contain one and only one item.

Now for the antithesis:

One is **not** a number.

First of all, with finite collections, perhaps the reason that there is that one-to-one correspondence is because those collections have the same number of elements, rather than the other way round.

Secondly, not everyone considers one to be a number:

Husserl doesn't. He understands that the modern notion of number is necessary for the purpose of natural science, but he considers that the authentic notion of number does not include one.

The simplest way to understand the antithesis is by means of this proportion:

One is to number as point is to line.

One is at the beginning of every number count, just as a point A is at the beginning of the line AB, but one is not a number, just as a point is not a line.

Synthesis. The best solution is to let one be a number but not an *arithmos.* Then while the whole numbers are

1, 2, 3, . . .

the *arithmoi* are

2, 3, 4, . . .

and *arithmoi* are just what Euclid calls them: **multitudes of units.**

For the next in my list of favorite proportions, let me turn to the *Republic* of Plato. At the point in the dialogue, or monologue, where the divided line occurs, the text itself, but not necessarily the line, is cut in a golden section. Call the straight line AB and divide it unequally at the point C, where AC is the larger part and CB is then the smaller part.

For reasons that will soon become clear, I form this scheme:

$$1$$
$$1 \qquad 1$$

which means that at first there is a line, and then there is one larger part and one smaller part.

AB is intended to represent the universe,
AC the intelligible realm, CB the visible realm.

Now cut AC at D and CB at E, such that

AC : CB :: AD : DC :: CE : EB

Necessarily, the middle parts

DC and CE

are equal.

EB is intended to represent images: shadows, paintings
EC the originals of those images: tabletops, people
CD the meanings in thought of those originals
DA what is simply intelligible, *noeta*

The faculties that go with these four parts are

EB is intended to represent imagination
EC trust in what appears
CD thinking through or step-by-step reason
DA intellectual insight

In my scheme:

$$1$$
$$1 \qquad 1$$
$$1 \qquad 2 \qquad 1$$

The third row means a larger part, two equal middle parts and a smaller part.

If I cut the line again, I can demonstrate that the arithmetical triangle of Pascal will continue:

These additional sections can serve as a reminder that each of the divisions can in turn be subdivided.

The major purpose of the image of the divided line, in my opinion, is to serve as a claim for what has the greatest actuality, the greatest being in the cosmos: Mere images are the least actual; intellectual insight is the most actual. As an example, a photograph of a president can serve to remind us of a particular president. More actual is the president whom we might see in the flesh. However, that is not yet the president. There are the meanings of his speeches and his decisions. They are more the very being of the president than what we can sense. Finally, there are some insights, intellectual insights, upon which whatever truths there are in those meanings of his speeches and decisions are truly founded.

These are, at least for now, my favorite proportions. But as a finale, I set up a grand analogy between a mathematical and a physical system:

Einstein's Special Relativity is to the Minkowski diagram
as The Complex Number System is to its diagram:
The Complex Plane.

A complex number might arise when I solve a quadratic equation:

$$x^2 + 4 = 0.$$

There is no root for this equation among the real numbers, for the first term being a square is greater than zero. Yet, if I let i equal the square root of negative 1, then both 2i and −2i are roots of that equation. In general, polynomials of any degree have roots among the complex numbers, which have the form a + bi, where a and b are real numbers. The number $i = 0 + 1 \cdot i$. Mathematicians nowadays routinely use a plane for the geometric representation of complex numbers, just as they use a line to represent the real numbers. In Figure 5, I have placed enough complex numbers to give the general notion of points lying in the complex plane.

To add together two complex numbers, consider the numbers to be at the head of a vector, where the origin is its tail. Complete the parallelogram, as in Figure 6, and the sum is at the head of the diagonal.

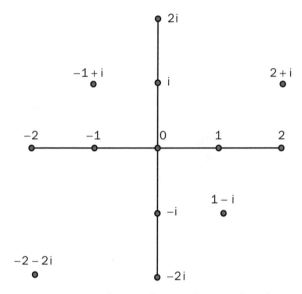

FIGURE 5. Complex numbers in the complex plane

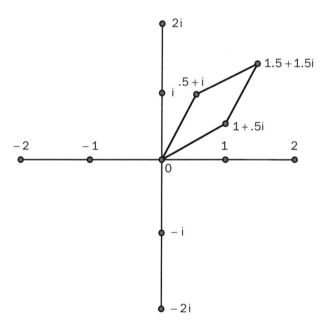

FIGURE 6. Adding two numbers in the complex plane

But the magic of the complex plane is the way it exhibits multiplication. To multiply two numbers together, again imagine each complex number as the head of a vector, and to find the vector that represents the product, simply multiply their distances from the origin and **add their angles.**

In Figure 7 are not only the fourth roots of unity: 1, i, −1, and −i, but also the third roots of unity 1, ω_1, and ω_2. Each is seen to be so, on the diagram, by multiplication. For example i • i = −1 works out on the diagram because a 90° rotation from the first i leads to 180°, where I find −1. Similarly ω_1 cubed is equal to one, as is ω_2 cubed. Then 1, ω_1, and ω_2 are the three third roots of unity, just as 1, i, −1, and −i are the four fourth roots of unity.

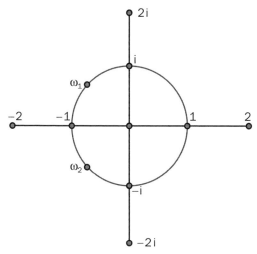

FIGURE 7. Cube roots and fourth roots of unity

In this way, the geometric representation helps make the science of complex variables come alive.

Now, let us hint at the other half of the analogy between the representations for complex numbers and special relativity. Minkowski found a representation that similarly helps to make special relativity come alive. Unfortunately, I need four dimensions: three for space and one for time, but I'll settle for a projection onto two dimensions: one for space and one for time. As Minkowski pointed out, the notions of separated space and time are doomed to fade away, and instead I have space-time. What I seek, then, is a visualization of the relativity of time: How can we imagine pictorially an event that is in the past for one observer and in the future for another? What works is to use t and x axes that are not orthogonal. The situation is two rocket ships that pass at time zero and when both observers are at the origin. Try to interpret the event E that is in the past for observer K′ and the future for K″. In Figure 8 I draw my time lines parallel to each observer's x-axis until it meets that observer's t-axis.

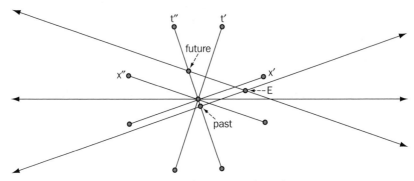

FIGURE 8. Passing spaceships in Minkowski space-time

I close by recapitulating my favorite proportions in reverse order:

6. The complex plane is the perfect image for the complex numbers, just as Minkowski space-time is the perfect image for events in special relativity.

5. Point is at the beginning of line, but points are not lines, just as one is the beginning of number, but one is not a number, that is, an *arithmos*.

4. The intelligible realm is to the visible realm as originals are to images and as intellectual insight is to step-by-step reason.

3. Euclid's postulates support his geometry as Peano's postulates support number theory.

2. For a straight line, cut it so that the whole is to the larger part, as that larger part is to the smaller.

1. Circles are to each other as the squares on their diameters.

A WORLD OF WORLDLESS TRUTHS, AN INVITATION TO PHILOSOPHY

David Lawrence Levine

Nature likes to hide.

—*Heracleitus*

Not only the reason of millennia but their madness too breaks out in us. It is dangerous to be an heir.

—*Zarathustra*

People should not have points of view but thoughts.

—*The Future of Our Educational Institutions*

I

IT IS A GOOD THING that you are sitting down, for I am about to hit you over the head with a hammer,[1] or at least the philosopher about whom I will say a few words intends to hit you over the head with one. Friedrich Nietzsche begins one of his earliest works with what might at first look like a fairy-tale opening. It is a very modern tale and thus not a happy one:

> "Once upon a time . . . ,"[2] in some sloughed off corner of the universe, poured out in innumerable glittering solar systems, there was a heavenly body, on which clever animals discovered knowing. It was the haughtiest and most mendacious minute of "world history," but it was only a minute. After nature had drawn a few breaths, the heavenly body grew cold and congealed, and the clever animals had to die.

This essay is based on a convocation address given on June 20th, 1999, to open the summer session of the Graduate Institute in Liberal Education, St. John's College, Santa Fe. This address will consider an early essay by Friedrich Nietzsche, "*On Truth and Lies in a Nonmoral Sense* (1873)" (*Philosophy and Truth: Selections from Nietzsche's Notebooks of the Early 1870s,* translated by Breazeale, 1990, pp. 79–97; the editor allows that a more literal translation of *aussermoralischen* would be "extramoral"). Nietzsche's brief essay is one of those gems the author prided himself on containing whole books in a few sentences (*Twilight of the Idols,* # 51).

Shocking! Indeed. But this is the picture of the universe given to us by modern natural science.[3] There's a wonderful T-shirt in the St. John's bookstore in Santa Fe depicting the vast swirl of the Milky Way. An arrow points to some seemingly indifferent place within, with the words "You are here!" Our question is, Where is here?

Shocking! Nietzsche felt he could not quietly, in scholarly fashion, draw our attention to this question but had to dramatize it, had to "philosophize with a hammer" or bring about a personal "earthquake" in the outlook of his readers. Writing in the late nineteenth century, he sought to capture the attention of an audience that was becoming increasingly unreflective about the character of their lives or, as he would revealingly illustrate, would begin their day by reading the morning newspaper instead of meditating on a devotional reading as had previously been customary. So he had to shock us, and this in an age not yet formed and therefore desensitized by television, web surfing and other contemporary forms of diversion.

The character of our lives: transient, yes; exceptional, yes; but problematic too. Modern philosophy, following what it took to be the deepest implications of modern science, had informed us that the truth of our lives was even more curious than previously credited.[4] This needed to be thought through. Indeed, deep reflection on the presuppositions of modern science would reveal for Nietzsche two very different implications: on the one hand, it would reveal what he feared were "the nihilistic consequences of natural science,"[5] on the other, it would allow "completely different kinds of 'truths'" to come to light (88). And Nietzsche—only 29 years old at the time he wrote this essay—took it upon himself to commence his lifelong task to reassess and come to terms with modern learning.

II

It is not that we are lost in the infinity of space (nowadays, 81 billion light years) that is most earthshaking for Nietzsche, however, nor even that we are lost in the vastness of time (nowadays, 12 billion years since the Big Bang). To be sure, this is discouraging enough. What is still more consequential for us in his view is the radical revaluation of ourselves and our faculties of knowledge that the standpoint of modern science requires.

Let us take an example, a noun, for instance, such as "wood." A noun intends to name a thing. Are such designations, however, congruent with the things they seek to name? Is language therefore, as once thought, the "adequate expression" of a "reality"? We are told by the new sciences that a word is something like "a copy in sound of a nerve stimulus" (81). But from a nerve stimulus can "a cause outside of us" be inferred? We say, for example, that this wood lectern is hard (82)—[Knock, knock]—and by hard we mean that the material is solid. Yet particle physics tells us that wood is not continuous, indeed is composed mostly of empty space. By hard, then, we can only mean our response to the fact that our knuckles hurt when we hit it ("a totally subjective stimulation"). When we speak otherwise, Nietzsche concludes, "we overstep the canons of certainty" (82).[6]

What follows from this is earthshaking, for this is so not only in the case of nouns. "With words [generally]," he infers, "it is never a question of truth, never a question of adequate expression. . . ." "The 'thing in itself' (which is precisely what the pure truth . . . would be)," he says, "is likewise something quite incomprehensible. . . . The creator [of language] only designates the relation of things to man and for expressing these relations, he lays hold—[and here Nietzsche surprises us]—of the boldest metaphors."

What, then, is a word? A word is a metaphor.[7] This conclusion is far-reaching. Nothing short of the traditional understanding of the truthfulness of perception as "adequate" or "corresponding" to (if not actually "identical" with) its object is herewith rejected as untenable.[8]

Perhaps a repetition of this earthquake is in order. He says, "To begin with, a nerve stimulus is transferred into an image: first metaphor. The image, in turn, is imitated in a sound [as a word]: second metaphor. And each time there is a complete overleaping of one sphere right into the middle of an entirely new and different one." What first is presumed to begin in the realm of physics is then "transferred" into the realm of neurophysiology and then psychophysiology that, in turn, is then "imitated" in the realm of psychology and linguistics. From one sphere to another to another to another. Yet how is one to account for the fact that we say that the image of the lectern we have in our minds is the wood lectern outside of us, that is, for the presumed continuity between a subject and its object? According to Nietzsche there is no such accounting possible.

The problem of continuity here is far more difficult than any comparable one, for example, that of translation from one language to another. For there, at least, they are all of the same "sphere," all languages (however different). In the case of perception, however, we know no such common basis. It is like trying to determine the original language of a text on the basis of a translation alone. The image Nietzsche comes up with to help us picture this conundrum admittedly falls short of the full difficulty. He compares the great rift—the "complete overleaping"—to that of a deaf person who, failing to hear sound, might identify what other people speak of with the vibrations that he experiences.

"It is this way with all of us concerning language," Nietzsche reiterates, "we believe that we know something about the things themselves when we speak of trees, colors, snow and flowers, and yet we possess nothing but metaphors for things—metaphors which correspond in no way to the original entities" (82–83). "All the material . . . with which the man of truth, the scientist, and the philosopher later works and builds," he says, "if not simply derived from cloud cuckoo land (*Wolkenkuckucksheim*), is at least not derived from the essence of things." Nietzsche's metaphors, in short, are not metaphors in the traditional sense. They have lost all sense of "likeness" and intend a marked unconnectedness.

The immensity of the universe (the so-called infinity of space) is, in this view, but a vastness of our own making, of our own interior, as is the vastness of time (88). Perception, understood as of something genuinely other, is incomprehensible in this scientific perspective. Indeed, all we can ever see are our own "metaphors." Thus the world that was supposed to be rendered intelligible by modern science ends up being puzzling through and through, thinkable only as a product of our own making. The so-called "windows" of the senses have been transvalued and judged to be but self-reflecting "mirrors." Rather than opening us up to a world at large, they now close us off. Blind to any presumed nature of things as they are themselves, we are left deluded (and disoriented) by the closed movie set of subjectivity ("chamber," "prison," "shaft"). He here spells out with disconcerting clarity the implications of the closed sphere of subjectivity or "monadology" of modern philosophy. In the words of another of his works, "[T]here is absolutely no escape, no back way . . . into [some presumed] real world!"[9]

III

The route to the formation of concepts is no less mysterious, no less problematic, in the eyes of our author. A "word" becomes a general "concept" when it can "fit countless more or less similar cases" (83), but it can do this only by "the equation of unequal things" (reduction or abstraction). For example, the concept of "leaf" arises when we disregard all the differences among sumac, oak, aspen, mallow and mullen and disregard all the countless differences of the leaves themselves. This is the way we produce an "original model" or concept (form, universal). But "we obtain [this] concept, as we do the form, by overlooking what is individual and actual, whereas nature," he says, "is acquainted with no forms, and no concepts, and likewise with no species, but only with an 'X' that remains inaccessible and undefinable for us."

Given an unknowable nature, what then can "truth" ever mean? He concludes about thought what he was compelled to about perception: "Between two absolutely different spheres as between subject and object, there [can be] no causality, no correctness, and no expression; there is *at most* an aesthetic relation. . . ." Truth, then, can be nothing more than "a movable host of metaphors, metonymies, and anthropomorphisms . . . a sum of human relations which have been poetically and rhetorically intensified, transferred and embellished . . ." (84).

We are now ready for another of Nietzsche's famous earthquakes. "Truths," he now finds himself unable to avoid saying, "are [but] illusions that we have forgotten are illusions."[10] In contrast to us perhaps, rather than being filled with apprehension by such a disorienting claim, Nietzsche allows himself to be moved by admiration: "Here we may certainly admire man as a mighty genius of construction,[11] who succeeds in piling up an infinitely complicated dome of concepts . . . ," and this despite the destabilizing fact that all this is built on a most "unstable foundation . . . as it were, on running water" (85).

From the outset modern science and modern philosophy knew well this problem of correspondence.[12] Their attempts at a solution took various forms of idealism (problematic, subjective, critical, and transcendental). Yet, in the end they had to forgo any external, objective standard and content themselves with an internal one, consistency above all. Modern science had hoped—a hope devoutly to be wished—that it would "be able to dig successfully in this shaft [of laws of nature] forever, and [that] all things that [were] discovered [would] harmonize with and not contradict each other" (87). But this is only a comforting, if imperative (84), self-delusion. In the words of another of Nietzsche's works: "All our so-called consciousness is a more or less fantastic commentary on an unknown, perhaps unknowable but felt text. . . . To experience is to invent."[13]

Both his reflection on the truth of perception and on the truth of thought have led Nietzsche to the same ultimate insight: "The drive toward the formation of metaphors is *the* fundamental human drive, which one cannot for a single instant dispense with in thought, for one would thereby dispense with man himself" (88). That clever animal, once conceived as the "rational animal" with insight into nature, is now understood anew, as an artist,[14] a genius of construction, a maker of metaphors and thereby the maker of his own world.[15] We see here why this outcome is far more humanly consequential for Nietzsche than the specific developments of the modern sciences themselves. For it means that we are not so much "lost in space" as "lost in thought."

IV

Given these earthshaking "truths," where is here? Whatever tendency we might have had to seek refuge in some consoling notion of "phenomena" must now be distrusted,[16] according to Nietzsche (87). Indeed it is no longer even an option. If the "empirical world" is but the "anthropomorphic world" (88), all that is present to us, both what appears and what we think underlies what appears (whether objectively or subjectively), all of this is the work of our own genius.[17]

Yet our human drive to metaphor formation is hardly exhausted by the natural sciences. As alluded to earlier, there are other "completely different kinds of truths" (88). Indeed our drives can take other, more modern directions—directions that have come to define what we mean by the term "modern" (and post-modern).[18] We are here presented with another of Nietzsche's earthquakes, though this time with one that no longer throws us off balance, but with one by which we ourselves are now very much defined. He says: "[Our drive] seek[s] a new realm and another channel for its activity, and it finds this in myth and in art generally" (89).

We are herewith directed to a very different realm, one where "[our] drive continually confuses the conceptual [that is, scientific and rational] categories . . . by bringing forward new transferences, metaphors, and metonymies. [One where] it continually manifests an ardent desire to refashion the world which presents itself to waking man, so that it will be as colorful, irregular, lacking in results and coherence, charming, and eternally new as the world of dreams" (89).[19] What is this other dimension of human experience that now intrudes, that impresses itself on us most distinctively when asleep, when caught in a web of imaginings, when spiritually intoxicated? What is this that manifests itself in such different forms of expression as myth, epic, lyric poetry, tragedy, dance, song, and the plastic arts? And above all, what is this language that isn't literal but finds its expression only in symbolic representations? Has it a rhyme (since nothing has a reason as such any more) of its own? Nietzsche describes it here only tantalizingly: it is the world and language of intuition (90).

For Nietzsche the recovery of the full range of our human experiences requires that we look elsewhere for that depth and significance that had been lost sight of by "scientifically disenchanted thinkers." For a glimpse, he asks us to look anew at the life of pre-modern peoples, at "mythically inspired peoples," and especially at the culture and literature of the ancient Greeks. It is there that we see life in its manifoldness, where "intuitive man" takes his rightful place alongside "rational man."[20]

But what kind of truth is this "completely different kind of 'truth'"? Nietzsche describes it in this way: "By shattering and mocking the old conceptual barriers, [one] may at least correspond creatively to the impression of the powerful present intuition" (90). Here Nietzsche gives a new (very modern) answer to the old problem of "correspondence." We are to "correspond creatively." Since there is no longer available to us any objective correspondence, we have but this one, that of an internal correspondence, a "creative" response to our own intuitions. The "liberated intellect" (90), as Nietzsche now calls it, is opened at least to creativity, if not to insight.

We are here witness to (one account of) that great revolution in our sense of ourselves and our being in the world that came to fruition at the end of the nineteenth century (although the outcome of centuries of philosophical discourse). Here is the metaphysical revision that returns to prominence such fundamental human[21] experiences as intuition, dreams, myths, symbolism, morphology on the one hand, and imagination, spontaneity, creativity and aesthetics on the other. Dignity (and equi-primordiality) is thus restored, it was thought, to that realm of human experience that modern rationalism has disparaged as but the work of "subjectivity."

But the "arts," as newly understood here, are viewed in a "completely different" way. This metaphysical revision requires that we see them no longer simply as the products of culture but as themselves formative of culture, as one of its originative sources. And with this, a new understanding of the "liberal arts" follows. This new philosophical take on the arts has changed the way we think about these liberal disciplines. There is consequent a revitalized interest in the humanities (*trivium*), a new way of "reading" all human products as expressions of these "completely different 'truths,'" and a new model of significance, the text. Hence these are the "modern liberal arts."[22] Let us not forget, however, that this new way of reading the world was adopted because it was thought that the mode of insight represented by the modern sciences did not provide the exhaustive archetype of intellectual discovery, and this because the traditional understanding of "objective correspondence" was thought forever foreclosed.

V

So where are we? Where is here? In some remote corner of the universe or in some far off corner of the vast, nay infinite reaches of the human mind, that is some metaphorical world of our own making? These two questions, as we have seen, emerge from the same problem, a problem that we too inherit.

What Nietzsche feared is now plainer. "The nihilistic consequences of natural science"[23] seem to stem from at least two sources: 1) modern science's inability to adequately address the problem of correspondence and subsequent alienation of subject and object, and 2) its correlative failure to understand subjectivity and consequent depreciation thereof. Nietzsche confronted these questions boldly. He found the underlying unity in the very same place as did modern idealism (Kant!), namely in "subjectivity," if in this case a much richer one. Thereby he thought he saw a way to restore the full breadth and depth of human experience.

Nietzsche's attempted responses to these problems are not without their own difficulties, however.[24] He is not any more successful than his predecessors in peering through a crack in "the chamber of consciousness." All of human experience remains "subjective in the highest degree."[25] The result: a world of worldless truths, truths without objective reference, without universality, and accompanied by an exaggerated suspicion of our own faculties of discovery (an overreaction to our earlier inflated expectations). This too is our inheritance.[26]

Nietzsche sought to find the common source out of which all human experience emerges. Yet, though attempting to overcome the scientific-romantic polarities he inherited—subject and object, reason and intuition, science and art—he ends up perpetuating them in turn (though subjectivized). He thus ends up in some sense where he began, thereby highlighting for us the very great importance of making the right beginning.

VI. Afterword: Goethe and Nietzsche

I once saw a storm raging over the sea
and a clear blue sky above it; it was then that
I came to dislike all sunless, cloudy passions
which know no light, except the lightning.[27]

As conceived by Nietzsche, the fate of modern philosophy (if not also of modern man)—to be sealed in a windowless "chamber of consciousness" (80)—was not one with which he could easily live. He would have preferred a very different "tale," one where we were "lost in space" perhaps—for at least then we would be open to a world—but not "lost in thought." Still, this is the world that modern philosophy bequeathed to him, and to us, and from which he feared one could find "no escape or back way."

This led to his own titanic efforts to peer through "a crack in the chamber of consciousness," to push the complements of modern materialism and idealism to their logical end. He says: "To have paced out the whole circumference of modern consciousness, to have explored every one of its recesses—this is my ambition, my torture, and my bliss. . . ."[28] Yet failing to pull reality out of the hat of metaphor, he had to content himself with worldless truths, with an immediacy without objectivity, an exaggerated phenomenalism, and to remain—horrible to say—an idealist, if a resistant one, one who sought to think through to its bitter end the significance of our not ever being able to peer through to some "real world." The result was, as he wrote, that "my life is now comprised in the wish that the truth about things be different from my way of seeing it: if only someone would convince me of the improbability of my truths."[29]

There was someone who, if he did not "convince [him] of the improbability of [his worldless] truths," at least held out the prospect of a different way of being in the world and dealing with the fundamental challenge of modern philosophy: Goethe. What he sought most deeply, Nietzsche said, was "really to overcome [modern] pessimism—and as a result [to reach] a Goethean vision full of love and good will (*ein Goethischer Blick voll Liebe und guten Willens*)." Despite being attracted to such an alternative, Nietzsche was never "convinced" that such a way was possible anymore.

We see this later (1881–6) when he reconsiders the "indecency" of his earlier philosophical voyeurism:

No, this bad taste, this will to truth, to "truth at any price," this youthful madness in the love of truth has lost its charm for us: for that we are too experienced, too serious, too merry, too burned, too profound. We no longer believe that truth remains truth when the veils are withdrawn: we have lived too much to believe this. Today we consider it a matter of decency not to wish to see everything naked, or to be present at everything, or to understand and know everything. . . . One should have more respect for the bashfulness with which nature has hidden riddles and iridescent uncertainties. . . . Oh, those Greeks! They knew how to live. What is required for that is to stop courageously at the surface . . . to adore appearances, to believe in forms, tones, words, in the whole Olympus of appearances. Those Greeks were superficial—*out of profundity*. And is not this precisely what we are again coming back to, we daredevils of the spirit who have climbed the highest and the most dangerous peak of present thought and looked around from up there—we who have looked down from there?[30]

Here Nietzsche says he would be content "to stop courageously at the surface." Yet as such, he remains caught in the traditional polarity of "appearance and reality," "surface and depth," "superficiality and profundity," "veil and nakedness" (radicalized in modern times as "text and subtext") that he sought so desperately to overcome. A return to a world of primary experience, of "forms" and "words," seemed lost forever. He found no "escape or back way." Indeed our very efforts to think our way "out or back" appear only to have put it that much more out of reach.

This is the closest Nietzsche himself could come to Goethe's wisdom,[31] a wisdom he characterized in a still later work (1888) as "a grand attempt to overcome the eighteenth century and modern philosophy." Unlike himself, Goethe was able to "surround himself with nothing but closed horizons." "He did not sever himself from life, he placed himself within it." "Goethe conceived of a strong, highly cultured human being . . . [who] dares to allow himself the whole compass and wealth of naturalness, who is strong enough for this freedom. . . ." And his final judgment: "A spirit thus *emancipated* stands in the midst of the universe with a joyful and trusting fatalism, in the *faith* that only what is separate and individual may be rejected—*he no longer denies*. . . . But such a faith is the highest of all possible faiths: I have baptized it with the name *Dionysus*." Dionysus!

But Nietzsche feared such a paradigm was "a beautiful 'in vain'."[32] He was a man of the nineteenth century, unable himself to take such a regulative leap, to share in such a "high faith." Though seeking what Goethe sought, the outcome was the opposite of what was intended. "How does it happen," he asks, "that the total result is not a Goethe but a chaos, a nihilistic sigh, a not knowing which way to turn . . . [a] brutalized eighteenth century, that is to say a *decadence*?" In short, Nietzsche was not himself able to break with his beginnings. As he said in his early essay (1873): "Only by forgetting this primitive world of metaphor can one live with any repose, security, and consistency; only by means of the petrifaction and coagulation of a mass of images which originally streamed from the primal faculty of the imagination like a fiery liquid . . . only by forgetting that he is himself an artistically creating subject does man live in repose. . . . If but for an instant he could escape from the prison wall of this faith [in a 'real world'], his 'self-consciousness' would be destroyed" (86; see also 81, 84).[33] Nietzsche's "forgetting," Nietzsche's "faith," thus remains a denial. It is not Goethe's "high faith," not an affirmation. "Truths," after all, "are illusions we have forgotten are illusions," ones that he could not bring himself to forget.

Despite his early distrust of such consoling notions of phenomena (87), there is here a "coming back," a resurfacing, but only by keeping the "veils" in place. Thus there is no simple return. Goethe's alternative is not retrievable for him. By contrast, Goethe would have us think and live very differently: If there is truth in the "surface," we have to find a mode of being and access (not "point of view") that can touch such "profundity" without devaluing it as "superficial." Indeed, that the process of the "artistically creating subject" is ultimately unaccountable or mysterious—that all we can say (with Kant) is that it is the result of the "spontaneous employment of the faculties"—opens up, in turn, the old question: whence the ground of its possibility? Therewith the character of "subjectivity" has once more to become a question for us.[34]

NOTES

1   *Ecce Homo,* translated by R. J. Hollingdale (London, 1979), 37; the prospect by itself should be enough to drive us to thought. But it does not. People have often wondered about Nietzsche's exaggerated, not to mention hysterical, presentations. But he would ask that we think about ourselves and our insensitivity to the simple, direct, and gentler mode of speech.

2   Nietzsche says, "one might invent such a fable" (79), and thus Breazeale translates it.

3   At the onset of the modern age, Pascal gave poignant expression to our metaphysical gasp in the face of the new universe: "The silence of these infinite spaces frightens me" (*Pensées,* # 206; contrast Goethe, *Conversations with Eckermann,* April 11, 1827).

4   "Natural science is in the process of becoming self-conscious . . ." (#179 / p. 95).

5   Erich Heller remarks that this was a frequent jotting of Nietzsche at this time (*The Importance of Nietzsche: Ten Essays* [Chicago, 1988], 7).

6   Paul de Man cites Nietzsche (1956 Schlecta edition [III 804–5]): ". . . We have seen that the perceptions which one naively considers as determined by the outside world are much rather determined from the inside; that the actual impact of the outside world is never a conscious one. . . . The fragment of the outside world of which we are conscious is a correlative of the effect that has reached us from the outside and that is then projected, *a posteriori*, as a 'cause'" ("The Rhetoric of Tropes," in *Allegories of Reading* [New Haven, 1979], 107).

7   It is interesting at this point to remember an earlier use of "metaphor" when it designated a unique capacity for insight (requiring a rare natural endowment), one that allowed us to transcend particular differences and comprehend fundamental commonalities (Aristotle, *Poetics*, 59a; also cf. 51b). Here by contrast, metaphor marks our non-originality, our derivativeness, our inability to transcend the world of our own making. Cf. Aristotle, *De Anima*, I 409b26–410a13, II 417a1–418a6; *Nicomachean Ethics*, VI 1139a10.

8   "The adequate expression of an object in a subject is a contradictory impossibility [*Unding*]" (86).

9   *Daybreak [Dawn]: Thoughts on the Prejudices of Morality,* translated by R. J. Hollingdale [Cambridge, 1982], #117 / p. 73.

10 "Truths are illusions which we have forgotten are illusions . . . metaphors that have become worn out . . . drained of sensuous force, coins that have lost their embossing and are now considered as metal and no longer as coins" (84).

11 Comparable to spiders (though in contrast to bees): ". . . man builds with the far more delicate conceptual material which he first has to manufacture from himself" (85).

12 Cf. p. 86 and Descartes, *Meditations on First Philosophy*, III AT29: "The principal error and the commonest which we may meet within them [judgments], consists in my judging that the ideas which are in me are similar or conformable to the things which are outside me . . ." (in *The Philosophical Works of Descartes*, translated by Elizabeth Haldane and G. R. T. Ross [New York: Dover Publications, 1955], 160).

13 *Daybreak*, #119 / p. 76; also "Truth and Lie," p. 85; *Beyond Good and Evil*, #22.

14 It is perhaps surprising, indeed shocking, to hear people like Nietzsche use the word "artistic" in this context. Did not people once think that "the artistic constitution of experience" was a recipe for fantasy? But even his predecessor, the sober "Mandarin of Königsberg," intent as he was to penetrate the hiddenmost workings of consciousness and in spite of the fact that he had gone far to articulate the deepest rational principles that make experience intelligible, even Kant could in the end come up with no better term to characterize what we

must be doing when we make our experience "whole" and give it the integrity that is implied by the word "world."

> The reflective judgment thus works with given appearances so as to bring them under empirical concepts of determinate natural things not schematically, but technically, not just mechanically, like a tool controlled by the understanding and the senses, but *artistically*, according to the universal but at the same time undefined principle of a purposive, systematically ordering of nature. Our judgment is favored . . . by nature in the conformity of the particular natural laws (about which the understanding is silent) to the possibility of experience as a system, which is a presupposition without which we have no hope of finding our way in the labyrinth of the multiplicity of possible special laws. Thus the judgment itself posits *a priori* the *technic of nature* as the principle of its reflection, without being able to explain it or to determine it more exactly or to have thereby an objective basis of determination for the universal concepts of nature from a knowledge of things in themselves, but only in order to facilitate its reflection in accordance with its own subjective laws and needs while also in harmony with laws of nature in general (Kant, "Of Reflective Judgement," in *First Introduction to the Critique of Judgment,* translated by James Haden [Indianapolis, 1965], 18–19).

This is not a flippant use of a term by Nietzsche (or Kant), giving license to our worst and most irresponsible tendencies. It is one that seeks to name our profoundest and most responsible activity as world makers, we who, as Nietzsche put it, "invented knowledge."

On Kant's legacy, see also S. Rosen, "Transcendental Ambiguity," in *Hermeneutics and Politics* (Oxford, 1987), 19–49.

15   "All that we actually know about the laws of nature is what we ourselves bring to them." "We produce these representations in and from ourselves with the same necessity with which the spider spins." See E. Blondel, "Nietzsche: Life as Metaphor," in *The New Nietzsche* (New York, 1977), 151.

16   Cf. Leo Strauss, *Thoughts on Machiavelli* (Glencoe, Ill., 1958), 297.

17   And "knowing" this doesn't get us out of the conundrum (Cf. de Man, "Rhetoric of Tropes," in *Allegories of Reading,* 112). Indeed, for Nietzsche there is no "second sailing" (Plato, *Phaedo,* 99), no "simple and artless speech" that will save us from the harsh realities, but only a "third sailing," a speech whose significance no longer refers to being, no longer strives for "adequacy." Hence Nietzsche's boldness: we have but this one choice, making a virtue of necessity, to relish the new possibilities for "meaning."

18   "This drive is not truly vanquished and scarcely subdued by the fact that a regular and rigid new world is constructed as its prison from its own ephemeral products, the concepts" (89).

19   Nietzsche is arguing for the equivalence of the world of dreams and the world of natural science. That there are sometimes linkages between dreams and wak-

ing experience doesn't here necessarily mean that dreams are the "truth" of waking experience. It is rather the presumed greater truthfulness of scientific constructions that he is at pains to dispute.

20 Here at least it is only a question of recovery. That both reason and intuition vie for preeminence—"they both desire to rule life" (90)—does not mean that one can do without the other. Cf. Nietzsche's great fear that he will be misunderstood (Letter to his sister, June 1884, cited by Heller, *The Importance of Nietzsche*, 2).

21 The root of the modern manifesto ("That which makes us human is something totally *subjective*" [#178 / p. 95]) and of the modern value trinity ("The truest things in the world are love, religion, and art. . . . These are the three illogical powers" [#177 / p. 95]).

22 We all become "psychologists" or "readers of signs" (*Human, All Too Human*, translated by R. J. Hollingdale [Cambridge, 1986], section 8, p. 10).

23 See *Twilight of the Idols*, #50, where he speaks of ". . . the reckless realism [of the 19th century] . . . whose result is a chaos, a nihilistic sigh, a not knowing which way to turn, an instinct of weariness." This he contrasts to Goethe's realism that had no such outcome. See VI. Afterword: Goethe and Nietzsche.

24 If the modern critique is credible, that there is no way that we can know "the secret springs of nature" (Hume), the "thing-in-itself" or *noumenon* (Kant), then this "truth" applies no less to the new realms of experience reopened for our discovery as well (not excluding the "drives," will, Dionysian spirit, *Geist*, history, and all those presumably equi-fundamental inexplicit, if not unconscious, principles that modern philosophers and psychologists have claimed work "cunningly" behind our backs [Hegel]). While perhaps not cognitive, categorical, or rational, they are no less the work of this "genius of construction" of ours (and constituted by the same categories [88]). In this respect, Nietzsche remains a Kantian.

25 There is thus *no* "crack in the chamber of consciousness:" ". . . Woe to that fatal curiosity which might one day . . . peer . . . through a crack in the chamber of consciousness . . . and suspect that man is sustained . . . by that which is pitiless, greedy, insatiable and murderous" (80). Is curiosity fatal here?

26 Revolutions have not always solved the problems they sought to address, nor always ended up ameliorating the failings they sought to correct. This is true both of modern science and Nietzsche.

27 Notes from the time of *Zarathustra* (cited in Heller, *The Importance of Nietzsche*, 16); see note 4 above.

28 *The Will to Power*, #1031 (Heller's translation).

29 Letter to Overbeck, July 2, 1885 (cited in Heller, *The Importance of Nietzsche*, 16).

30 *The Gay Science,* translated by Walter Kaufman (New York, 1974), Preface, #4 / p. 38; cf. also *The Future of Our Educational Institutions,* translated by J. M. Kennedy (New York, 1964), 23, and *Philosophy in the Tragic Age of the Greeks,* translated by Marianne Cowan (Chicago, 1964), 30–31.

31 *Twilight of the Idols,* #49; see also David Lawrence Levine, "The Political Philosophy of Nature: A Preface to Goethe's Human Sciences," *Graduate Faculty Philosophy Journal* 11, no. 2 (1986): 163–78.

32 *Twilight of the Idols,* #50.

33 From reflections of this sort, some in the nineteenth and twentieth centuries have drawn the conclusion that there must be a hierarchy of realms, that the "surface" has to be subordinated to some "depth," that "consciousness" is derivative of some "unconscious realm." In such a view, the up-thrust, the outcropping, or seepage is from something thought more fundamental and therefore the primary source of meaning. At least in this early work, Nietzsche is reluctant to take this characteristically postmodern step and claim that the one is the ground of the other. That something can be "traced back to a necessity" (#183 / p. 96) doesn't mean that one necessity is prior. In this sense, Nietzsche is not yet a depth-psychologist.

34 See David Lawrence Levine, "At the Very Center of the Platitude: Goethe's Grand Attempt to Overcome the Eighteenth Century," Dean's Lecture, St. John's College, Santa Fe, August 29, 2003.

THE POLITICAL IMAGINATION: EXISTENTIALISM IN THE *RAJ QUARTET*

Paul W. Ludwig

READING PAUL SCOTT'S *Raj* novels from the perspective of political theory may fairly be said to neglect the literary values that make these novels most worth reading—a mistake Eva Brann never made. My own political theory lens seems doubly distorting because the novels' philosophic contribution is primarily moral and social rather than political.[1] Certainly Scott's political thought is rarely statesmanlike. Nevertheless, Eva Brann has succeeded in distilling the political wisdom of the *Raj Quartet* in her contribution to a volume of essays on political theory, as well as making clear the world-class greatness of the work for its moral and writerly excellences in essays written for *The St. John's Review* and for the journal *Philosophy and Literature*.[2] She discovered—in passing and with typical deprecation of the significance of her discovery—the influence of Heideggerean existentialism on the novels. The philosophy of existentialism, taken together with Scott's unsurpassed power of imagining the inner life of characters, made it possible for his protagonists to philosophize with considerable depth about the extent to which historical communities constitute (and therefore determine) the selves that belong to them. Scott's English and Indian characters struggle against the sheer extent of moral determinism that comes of their involvement in a great historical process: the retreat from empire and the Indian Independence movement. They seek to exercise moral agency but discern no courses of action besides those predetermined for them by the absconding Raj community and the roles it supported.[3] Only in existentialism do they find a

Previous versions of this essay were delivered as a panel paper for the American Political Science Association in September 2003, and as a Friday Lecture at St. John's College, Annapolis, on November 5, 2004 (Parents' Weekend). I would like to thank the members of a 2003 faculty study group on the *Raj Quartet* at St. John's funded by Adolph Schmidt and, in particular, to remember Beate Ruhm Von Oppen and Kitty Kinzer, through whom the *Raj* novels were first introduced to the St. John's faculty.

philosophy that allows them to be moral agents despite the overwhelming evidence of historical and communal determinism. The imagined concrete working-out of philosophy in people's lives captures the perverse strength and beauty of existentialism in a way that an analytic approach never could. Scott's use of existentialism also lays bare an important strand in the development of the school of thought that would later be known as postcolonialism. In further elucidating what political theorists can learn from the *Raj* novels, I hope to compensate for the concomitant neglect of literary values by beginning with an account of the primary experience of reading these novels: wonder.

I

Consider three brief historical flashbacks in the first volume, *The Jewel in the Crown.*[4] One of Scott's techniques to create wonder is to involve the main story's present time (World War II India, 1942) with past and future Indias: the eighteenth-century India of princedoms, the nineteenth-century India of merchant-imperialists, and post-Independence India. What sends a shiver up the spine is that in three of the four time periods, the same sorts of occurrences are repeating themselves. An illicit, usually cross-racial, love affair is always veering toward tragedy. Like a telescope closing up, time past and time future are ever present—in the *Raj Quartet*—in time present. The wonderment created in his characters (and readers) by this possibility of cyclical, eternal recurrence[5] allows Scott to make his protagonists begin to philosophize explicitly about history and human agency.

The first flashback deals with native India, divided into many small princedoms. The British are already in the land, trading and defending their trade with armies, but there are many princedoms they have not taken over yet (many of which in fact they would never take over, the so-called Native States):

> The [MacGregor] house stands in the middle of the garden, protected from the outside world by close-formed battalions of trees: neem, pipul, gol mohur, tamarind, casuarina and banyan; it goes back to the late eighteenth century and was built by a prince who conceived a passion for a singer of classical music. To build a house and install a woman in it is an expensive way to beg her favours. It was said that he came to visit her morning and evening, and that she sang to him . . . and that he became enamoured finally only of her voice and was content to listen while she instructed the

pupils he permitted her to receive. Scheherezade told stories to postpone the hour of her execution. The singer sang to guard her honor. When the singer died the prince grieved. People said he died of a broken heart. The house was deserted, closed. Like the state it decayed, fell into ruin. The prince's son succeeded to the gaddi. He despised his father for his futile attachment to the singer. He would let no one live there. He built another house nearby, the Bibighar, where he kept his courtesans. He was a voluptuary. He emptied the treasury. His people starved. An Englishman at his court was poisoned and so the new prince was deposed, imprisoned, his state annexed, and his people were glad of it until time lay over the memory of the old bad but not the badness of the present. The decayed house of the singer was rebuilt by a red-faced Scottish nabob called MacGregor who feared God and favoured Muslims, and was afraid of temples. The story goes that he burned the Bibighar to the ground because he said it had been an abomination. (*Jewel*, pp. 67–68)

The British tell themselves that MacGregor destroyed the Bibighar—which literally means "house of women"—because keeping a house full of courtesans was immoral. But much later in the novel we learn a different version of the story. At least one hundred years separate the India of the princes—father, son, singer, and courtesans—from the India where MacGregor, a merchant and a "collector," is carving out a fortune and acting as the *de facto* ruler of the (fictional) town of Mayapore where the two houses stood:

[MacGregor] burned Bibighar, not, according to the Indian version, because it was an abomination in his eye and the eye of the Lord . . . but because he fell in love with an Indian girl and lost her to a boy whose skin was the same colour as her own. There are two versions of the Indian account of the burning of Bibighar. The first is that he discovered that the girl and her lover met in the Bibighar, and that he then destroyed it in a fit of jealous rage. The second is that he told the girl she would have to leave the MacGregor House and live in the Bibighar. He took her there and showed her the repairs he had made to it and the furnishings and clothes he had bought for her comfort and enjoyment. When she asked him why she must leave the MacGregor House, he said: Because I am going to Calcutta to bring back an English wife. So that night she stole away with her true lover. When he found that she had gone, he ordered the Bibighar to be burned to the ground, and then utterly obliterated.[6] (*Jewel*, pp. 140–41)

This perspectivism, or blending of rival perspectives, is Scott's second device to create wonder. Not only are there two versions of the story, British and Indian—there are two versions of the Indian version. What people say about an event comes to be as important as the event itself. Competing versions, later overlays, anachronistic reinterpretations populate the pages of the *Raj Quartet,* each time forcing the reader (and the protagonists) either to adopt an inquiring stance or to make a decision to close off inquiry. The narrator of *The Jewel in the Crown* initially appears to be an omniscient narrator: he seems like Paul Scott himself. But in fact this narrator is gradually revealed to be an unnamed historian (himself with a limited viewpoint) who has returned to India in 1963 to learn about what happened in those last years before Independence, specifically what happened on a night of civil unrest in 1942, when an Englishwoman was raped after another cross-racial love affair and the local Raj of Mayapore was able to close its ranks against liberalization and the Independence movement by using her as a rallying cry.

The third flashback returns to the India of the princedoms, when the voluptuary son gets the last word over his father. Recall that the singer's house fell into ruin, after her death, before MacGregor came along to rebuild it, but the Bibighar, the "house of women" or of prostitutes, flourished:

> In those days, when Mayapore was a kingdom, on that side of the river there were no other buildings, and so those two houses were marks on the landscape, monuments to love, the love of the father for the singer and the love of the son for the courtesans, the son who despised his father for an attachment which, so the story goes, was never consummated. Day by day I think the son climbed the tower of the palace or to the highest room in the Bibighar to survey that other house, the singer's house, to glory in its decay, and said to himself, *Such is the fate of love never made manifest.*[7] (*Jewel,* p. 139, emphasis in original)

The story of the last days of Britain's Indian empire will be the story of a love never made manifest, an erotic attraction to India that could only be consummated in a kind of rape but could never dare to admit to itself that it might be love, for that would have led to an open embrace or dalliance that would have put the English and the Indians on an equal footing, undermining the ethical pretext of the "civilizing mission" that had become the way the British justified their empire to themselves.[8] Paul Scott or his narrator is not on the side of the father who did not consummate his love, but, surprisingly, on the side of the voluptuary son, who at least made his love— such as it was—manifest.

Perspectivism and the telescoping of time make the protagonists and readers wonder about whether the past is really past at the same time as they wonder about the impossibility of retrieving or uncovering a definitive past. These questions gain urgency as the main story sharpens them into wonder about the moral determinism of history and about how selves cannot escape being constituted by their communities. To all these problems, existentialism will offer a solution. Let us look briefly at the story line proper.

II

1942. An English girl has come to live in the MacGregor House. Her name is Daphne Manners. She has lost her family in the Blitz, and has been driving an ambulance during the bombing of London. She comes to live in India with an aunt, Lady Manners, the only family she has left. The story of Daphne's initial revulsion with all things Indian is too detailed to go into, but it is beautifully told. She initially stays with her aunt, the widow of a governor, in the predominantly Muslim city of Rawalpindi. Just when she thinks she might be growing to like India a little bit, she journeys to predominantly Hindu Mayapore where her aunt's Indian friend Lady Chatterjee, widow of an Indian who was knighted for his service to the Raj, lives in the MacGregor House, one of the only Indian homes on the British side of the river. Mayapore is now split into the British town north of the river, and the Indian town south of the river. Daphne's descent into ever greater alienness, first into Islam and then into Hindu territory, is accompanied by extreme revulsion, not only or primarily with the poverty and living conditions, but with the utterly alien cultures, with what the locals consider edible, and with the ways of living and dying.

The MacGregor House is one of the few places in Mayapore where Indians and British mix socially, and then only at carefully contrived drinks parties. Daphne possesses progressive, liberal notions about the meaninglessness of racial distinctions as well as an unprejudiced heart that attempts to find the human in the other. But she finds her fellow Brits in India to be living in a land that time forgot; their attitudes toward race and their resistance to eventual self-rule for India are essentially nineteenth-century holdovers living on into the twentieth century. Daphne is determined to appreciate and eventually love every aspect of India that she possibly can, and we gradually realize that this girl who is too tall, clumsy, average-looking, nearsighted, and naive has capacities for cultural assimilation which give her what can only be called moral grandeur. If Daphne were ever to fall in love, she would make her love manifest.

She falls in love with a young Indian named Hari Kumar. And here is the first twist: Hari, too, has just come to India. He grew up in England, son of an Indian father who admired British ways, assimilated, made and lost a fortune, committed suicide, and left his eighteen-year-old son stranded at his elite English boarding school with no money. Hari, too, has just come to live with his Aunt, and Hari is, if anything, more revolted by India than Daphne was. This is because Hari is, essentially, the most English character in the book. In everything but skin color: in attitudes, outlook, character, he is utterly English and utterly at sea in India. Not only is he English, he is even upper class (thanks to his boarding-school education); he shares the hauteur of the ruling British, but in India he can never be one of them. Somewhere on the ship over to India, it happened. Although Hari had scarcely noticed he was brown-skinned before (he had white friends, he was accepted in his English school), at some point near the Gulf of Suez, his fellow British passengers began to exclude him and socialize only among themselves. People who would never have felt that way at home became, as India approached, frightened or racially conscious for the first time, and joined ranks against him, expecting that he too would now join his own kind. But Hari has no kind, unless it is the British themselves, for Hari is as far from an Indian as it is possible to be. And this is one of the historical and academic glints that decorate and inform the novels, because Hari Kumar (in England he was called Harry Coomer) is one of the "brown-skinned Englishmen" whom the historian and planner of empire Thomas Babington Macaulay envisioned in a famous speech before the British parliament on how Indians should be educated (the 1831 "Minute on Indian Education"): to create "a class of persons Indian in colour and blood, but English in tastes, in opinions, in morals, and in intellect . . . who may be interpreters between us and the millions we govern."[9] Paul Scott, who published over one hundred reviews of books about India before and during the time he was writing the *Raj Quartet*,[10] takes Macaulay at his word and shows us such a person. But what will happen to such a person if the British ever decide to leave India? Not British enough for the British, not Indian enough for "the millions we govern," Hari is destined to be forever a loose end in the incomplete project of empire.

When Hari finally scrapes up courage to cross the river into the British town, he feels as if he has come home: clean lines, uncluttered streets, ordered civic life. When he enters a pharmacy, his heart leaps up to discover brand-name items that he is used to. But when he attempts to purchase a bar of soap, he encounters only contempt and prejudice, particularly when the memsahibs (white ladies) hear him speaking (aping, as they see it) upper-class-accented English. An Indian does not belong in the British town, unless he is the servant of a white. Hari becomes a man without a country, or without a community. He concludes:

> his father had succeeded in making him nothing, nothing in the black town, nothing in the [British] cantonment, nothing even in England because in England he was now no more than a memory. . . . (*Jewel*, p. 242)

This language of nothingness will loom very large. For nothingness (as in Jean-Paul Sartre's title *Being and Nothingness*) is just what an existentialist thinks we ought to think about ourselves. That we are nothing, on our own, nothing but a web of influences, totally determined by our backgrounds: our genes, our race, our religion, our upbringing, even our sex and height. In short, history determines us. There is no escaping these determinants, or at least there is no way to be certain we have freedom to escape them. Every choice we make can be traced to these all-powerful factors. The perspectival lack of a definitive history strengthens rather than weakens this historicist claim: because we can never be *clear about* how much these factors determine us, we can never get *clear of* such determinants.[11] The constitutive power of community over the selves in it now takes center stage in the narrative.

Hari and Daphne will become secret lovers. They meet at a racially mixed party at the MacGregor House. They have trouble from the start—not because of the outward pressure from the different communities they belong to, the English and Indian communities, both of which consider interracial love to be taboo. That is the least of their problems. Their problems are internal: the communities they belong to predispose them (it is so unconscious that it is like a genetic predisposition) to accept the taboo. Theory alone, theory that racial distinctions are meaningless, is not enough. It is very hard to put the theory into practice. Part of Hari's situation is that "a dark-skinned man touching a white-skinned woman will always be conscious of the fact that he is—diminishing her" (*Scorpion,* p. 217).[12] When Hari begins to fall in love with Daphne, he deliberately attempts to put her off, warn her away from him, by behaving on one of their illicit dates the way he imagines a middle-class Indian male would behave. Since the English will not let Hari be English anymore, since he must be Indian, he will behave like the English stereotype of an Indian male: outwardly polite, but underneath selfish and aggressive, eating with his fingers, treating the servants like dirt, making the girl conform to his wishes, playing Indian music which he hated (and expected her to hate) on the gramophone. But he underestimates Daphne, who by this time has come to love many aspects of India. She particularly likes Indian music, which she says is the only music in the world that is conscious of breaking silence. Daphne does not mind Indianness if Hari wants to be Indian; she is only worried why he is acting so strangely.

But Daphne, too, feels the artificiality of their being together: "nothing came spontaneously, or easily or *happily*" (*Jewel*, p. 392).[13] Their dates become a tightrope walk: almost any spontaneous act throws her (and Hari) into prescripted roles and assumptions. When Hari has trouble giving instructions to the tonga-wallah (horse-drawn taxi man) because Hari speaks little Hindi, Daphne with her better Hindi fears to take charge lest she become the memsahib dominating both the tonga-wallah and Hari. If Daphne smiles and says "What a fuss they make," she falls into the role of the memsahib slumming (pp. 386–87). So much forethought is needed to avoid these roles that an ethically-lived-through experience is impossible for the couple. Crossing the color line necessitates that their relationship become theoretical. Daphne never anticipated that she might have to prove to herself (and to Hari) that she was not loving him merely to display her defiance of the surrounding mores (p. 397). She becomes introspective to ascertain that her motives are not those of a mere adventurer, nor those of a charitable person condescending to do Hari a favor that could as well be proffered to any Indian.

When the moment comes in their relationship when Hari should touch Daphne, she recalls:

> He was afraid to. He was too conscious of the weight that would have made touching a gesture of defiance of the rule . . . , and he didn't have that kind of courage, and so I was deprived of my own. The defiance had to come from him first, to make it human, to make it right. (*Jewel*, pp. 410–11)

Daphne's defiance of the taboo would further unsex Hari (p. 411): a ruling memsahib taking a hapless Indian by the hand.

The communities they currently inhabit (the Raj and the Indian town) lay a cold hand of influence upon the possible selves Daphne and Hari can become, though neither grew up in those communities. The surrounding mores have begun their work of constituting the selves which now belong to the communities. Daphne and Hari are stymied by their awareness that a brown man with a white woman must be "taking advantage of her" in some way or another. A general thesis put forward by less liberal-minded Brits is that "an Indian will always take advantage of an English person who is friendly." And there is some truth to the thesis, since indeed the ruling caste of whites always does hold the keys to all advancement for a ruled caste of browns. It follows that Indians always want something. It also follows that any union between the two of them must be exploitative.

One night—a dangerous night of civil unrest in Mayapore: the British have interned Gandhi and the Indian National Congress party leadership because they have a war to fight with the Japanese, and Gandhi's noncooperation movement is not helping—Hari and Daphne sit together in the deserted Bibighar garden. The ruined "house of women" where love was at least made manifest is gone, only a garden remains, which has become a kind of informal public park.

Daphne takes Hari's hand briefly to light her cigarette:

> After a while he said, "What were you trying to prove? That you don't mind our touching?"
> I said, "I thought we'd got beyond that."
> "No," he said, "we can never get beyond it." (*Jewel*, p. 416)

The "gesture of defiance" that needed to come from Hari finally materializes when he takes away her cigarette (an Indian-made cigarette that he considers disgusting). He grabs her wrist and throws the cigarette away. "That catching hold of my wrist was like the impatient gesture of a lover. For him it was like that too" (p. 417). Once the boundary is crossed, their desire overwhelms the dam.

Unbeknownst to the couple, a group of Indian men, rioters who have come in from the country during the political unrest, are watching them in the darkness of the garden. For these men, a taboo is broken when they see a brown man touching a white woman. Catching the couple unawares, they forcibly restrain Hari and rape Daphne. Hari himself becomes the prime suspect in the rape because no one will believe that an English girl was in the garden alone with an Indian, consensually. What will happen to Hari? His angst over his loss of Britishness and his despair over his inability to become Indian are about to meet with an explanation and a way out. That way out is existentialism.

III

Enter the philosopher. The British District Superintendent of Police, Ronald Merrick, who hauls Hari in for questioning and subjects him to brutal torture, attempting to extract a confession, proceeds to give a closely reasoned explanation to Hari of all the problems he has been experiencing and thinking about since he came back to India, and especially since he met Daphne. Merrick offers his philosophy in order to induce Hari to confess to the crime, a crime he knows Hari did not commit.

Contrary to the reader's expectation of ordinary police corruption or racism, Merrick's conflation of the innocent with the guilty stems from an idiosyncratic, existentialist definition of "guilt." His concept of guilt makes up part of a full-blown philosophy of history and human agency.[14] Hari recounts how Merrick began to talk about a philosophy of the so-called "situation." "He said history was a sum of situations whose significance was never seen until long afterwards because people had been afraid to act them out. . . . They preferred to think of the situations they found themselves in as part of a general drift of events they had no control over . . ." (*Scorpion*, p. 297). The Raj—British rule in India—has felt itself swept along by just such a current or drift since well before the onset of World War II: attitudes are changing and British power in India is unraveling. History itself seems to be drifting in the direction of liberation, and both the civil and military Raj functionaries passively assume there is nothing they can do to stem the tide. Tonight, a white and a brown, Merrick and Hari, find themselves in a position to reaffirm the Raj's power. To prevent their moment together from sinking into the general drift, Merrick believes both he and Hari must avoid the passivity of the aforesaid Raj whites, those who "couldn't face up to their responsibility" for their situations. Curiously, the passive majority are probably correct about the hopelessness of taking control of the moment, in Merrick's view: "He didn't think he could go so far as to say you could change the course of events by acting out situations you found yourself in. . . ." At most Merrick and Hari will have the satisfaction of knowing they did all they could to stem the tide of the liberalizing drift: "[Y]ou'd . . . take what steps you could to stop things drifting in the wrong direction, or an unreal direction" (*Scorpion*, p. 297).

Merrick insists Hari should take responsibility. "That's what you've got to admit . . . your responsibility for that girl getting [raped]. If you were a hundred miles away you'd still be responsible" (*Scorpion*, p. 298). In respect of this idiosyncratic notion of responsibility, Merrick practices what he preaches: he, too, is willing to take responsibility for something he did not commit. Merrick says he will take responsibility for the liberal whites' misrule, even though Merrick himself has obviously contributed nothing to the Raj's drift toward liberalization and eventual liberation. Precisely taking responsibility for situations that are *not* one's fault is what Merrick recommends. This notion of "responsibility" and of guilt goes back to Martin Heidegger's *Being and Time*.[15]

In the scholarly literature on the *Raj Quartet,* no one has made the Heidegger connection besides Eva Brann. One scholar noticed similarities with Jean-Paul Sartre, an epigone, in this regard, of Heidegger and the proximate source of existentialism's influence on Paul Scott.[16] Heidegger defines the term "Situation" as "definite factical possibilities" that are disclosed when a person becomes resolute. In the following passage, "Being-There" (*Dasein* in German) is Heidegger's special word for *human* being: the kind of beings that are "there" in a fuller, more fundamental way than animals or things are "there." Incidentally, the Peter Sellers movie *Being There,* and the novel of the same name by Jerzy Kozinski that the film was based on, were parodies of existentialism. Heidegger writes:

> In the term "Situation" ("situation"—'to be in a situation') there is an overtone of a signification that is spatial. . . . [S]uch an overtone is also implied in the 'there' of Dasein [Being-There]. Being-in-the-world has a spatiality of its own. . . . Dasein 'makes room' in so far as it factically exists. . . . Just as the spatiality of the "there" is grounded in disclosedness, the Situation has its foundations in resoluteness. The Situation is the "there" which is disclosed in resoluteness—the "there" as which the existent entity is there. It is not a framework present-at-hand in which Dasein occurs, or into which it might even just bring itself. Far removed from any present-athand mixture of circumstances and accidents which we encounter, the Situation *is* only through resoluteness and in it.[17] (Heidegger, p. 299)

The inauthentic grasp of a situation comprehends a situation as a "mixture of circumstances and accidents" that we encounter. When Merrick says that most people prefer to think of situations as part of a general drift of events they have no control over, he refers to this inauthentic grasp. Merrick's term "unreal," as in "drifting in . . . an unreal direction," corresponds to Heidegger's distinction between authentic and inauthentic (Heidegger, p. 297).

For Heidegger, our understanding of historical significance results from *resoluteness.* What does he mean by resolute? We resolve on a course of action, we make a decision, a resolution, and we stick to our decision, come what may. The existentially resolute individual has made an unalterable decision—oddly, for Heidegger, a decision without grounds. Ordinarily, we let the facts determine what we should resolve to do. We work within the framework of possibilities permitted us by facts. Heidegger reverses this: "Resoluteness does not first take cognizance of a Situation and put that Situation before itself; it has put itself into that Situation already. As resolute, Dasein is already *taking action*" (Heidegger, p. 300). Such taking action exposes for the first time the "facts," or as Heidegger would say, the "facticity" with which a person must work. *"The resolution is precisely the disclosive projection and determination of what is factically possible at the time"* (p. 298).

Analogously, Merrick emphasizes "enactment" as the only way of knowing the facts about what the historical situation is. Enacting this particular situation—Merrick means playing at dominance and submission—is the way to understand its significance. Ordinarily, we might want to examine the facts first: are brown people naturally the servants of whites? Is Merrick really Hari's master? But no, Merrick and Heidegger say, disclosing facts like those always presupposes a stance, a decision you have made, a resolution. This Heideggerean idea has trickled down into our ordinary speech and way of looking at things: we call it "commitment." How you view the facts depends on your prior commitment. Liberals commit themselves to finding the races equal; when they examine the evidence, they find it supports their commitment. Racists are committed to finding the races unequal; when they examine the evidence, they find it supports their commitment. In the existentialist philosophy, the prior decision lights up the world, reveals the facts for the first time. There are no pure or uncommitted facts. Ordinarily, Merrick says, the significance of situations is "never seen until long afterwards because people [have] been afraid to act them out." And later: "It wasn't enough to say he was English and I was Indian, that he was a ruler and I was one of the ruled. We had to find out what that meant" (*Scorpion,* p. 298).

Now we are in a position to think more about Merrick's radical new concept of guilt: that one should admit guilt precisely for those things one is *not* responsible for. For Merrick, accepting responsibility is the inner truth of taking action, or enactment, as opposed to remaining passive. Hari ought to take responsibility for the rape of Daphne, even though he did not commit it, because the rape of Daphne by some Indians somewhere is symbolic of the situation which all Independence-minded Indians and all liberal whites everywhere conspire to create. The liberal whites by their egalitarian behavior are practically assuming that Hari can have their womenfolk; and Hari, by acting in kind at their invitation, is practically assuming it too. The real situation (in Merrick's view—and we have already seen the evidence for his view) is that no brown man can touch a white woman without sensing that he is violating her. Their sexual union must always be a rape, even if neither party wills it to be such. It is simply part of the situation. The best Hari can do is face up to this situation.

The same sense of guilt or responsibility is the inner meaning of resoluteness for Heidegger. Resoluteness is defined as the *"self-projection upon one's ownmost Being-guilty . . ."* (Heidegger, p. 297). Guilty of what, for what? Merely guilty—primordially so, Heidegger says. "'Being-guilty' also has the signification of 'being responsible for' [*"schuld sein an"*]—that is, being the cause or author of something. . . . These ordinary significations of 'Being-guilty' . . . can go together and define a kind of behaviour which we call *'making oneself responsible' . . ."* (p. 282; emphasis in original). Conscience proclaims us guilty, and conscience is the manifestation of care or of solicitous, concernful being-in-the-world. Whenever we care for or feel solicitous toward other people or things, we feel a call of conscience which does not have a specific grounding in any act we may or may not have committed.

Heidegger's (and Merrick's) notion of guilt is actually quite plausible. Particularly when we suddenly realize that we have been carelessly accepting a situation made by others, and so not exercising our human freedom, we feel guilty. If we realize we have been drifting with the current (remember, the liberal members of the Raj were letting themselves drift), we suddenly feel guilty; if we then use that guilt to become resolute, to say, I'm not going to drift anymore, I'm going to be a free chooser, and make my own way in the world, then we are close to becoming resolute the way Heidegger wants us to. Close—but we are not quite there yet. For this is the truth about facticity, that is, the set of facts (sex, height, biographical givens, social roles, customs) that make us who we are: none of these facts were acts of our own free will. We made none of them but rather are stuck with them, and we are seemingly determined by them. We are "thrown" into them, to use Heidegger's language, and our natural mode is to get lost in them, not to exercise our determining freedom. But herein lies the rub: there is no evidence we can ever get free of them. The only way to get outside of the facts that determine us is to *make them our own*. Admit responsibility for them, admit guilt precisely for facts not of our own making. Step one: come to admit that you are totally indebted—to your sect, your nation, your genes— feel these facts as debts, things lacking. Realize you are a nullity, a nothing. Step two: take responsibility for these facts (even though they are not your fault), make them your own, make them your fault. Heidegger calls this "Being-the-basis of a nullity" (p. 283). "Being-a-basis" means *never* to have power over one's own being from the ground up (p. 284). In understanding the call of conscience, in taking responsibility, *Dasein* listens "*to its ownmost possibility of existence.* It has chosen itself" (p. 287).

A Heidegger scholar has ventured an example. Existential guilt is indebtedness to culture (among other factors); his example is being brought up feminine.[18] A woman may feel she has no possibilities she can truly call her own: every role is preordained for her by the culture. Reacting against them would be to let them determine her in an equal, but opposite, way. To have none of one's own possibilities is to be a *nullity*. However, she can take over these public, prescribed roles *in her own way,* making them her own. She achieves this by accepting responsibility for them, thereby becoming the basis for (i.e., the author of) her own nullity. Embrace your nothingness. This is the only way out. This is an exercise of freedom—the *only* freedom open to anyone. In much the same way, Merrick wants Hari to accept responsibility for the facts that make him what he is: brown, dependent, inferior, coddled by a white elite, attracted to a white girl—a rapist whether virtually or actually. This is the only freedom open to him. When Hari fails to live up to this freedom, Merrick claims he has more contempt for him than ever. Hari is merely pretending the world does not exist (*Scorpion,* p. 304).

Before getting back to the storyline, let us look briefly at Jean-Paul Sartre, whose more popular rendition of Heidegger's ideas helps make them easier to understand. There is in fact no evidence that Paul Scott had read (or read about) the philosophy of Heidegger. There is evidence that Paul Scott read and grappled with Jean-Paul Sartre: in an important nonfiction essay in which he explains why he writes, Scott refers to Sartre by name and devotes several pages to what he explicitly calls Sartrean "engagement" with the "historical situation" (*Muse,* pp. 131–49). Though it would have been anachronistic to mention Sartre in the *Raj Quartet* since *Being and Nothingness* first appeared in 1943, too late for the 1942 Indian milieu in which Merrick gives voice to its major tenets, Scott himself knew of Sartre's ideas in the 1960s and '70s when he was writing the *Raj Quartet,* and he made the ideas a part of his art. The same ideas were around in 1942, however, in a more thoroughgoing and rigorous form than Sartre's: Heidegger's *Being and Time* had been first published in 1927 and republished in 1935. Whether Heideggerean existentialism wielded any influence over the rise of Nazism and fascism in Europe is debatable. But Paul Scott, though Heideggerless and a self-described Bloomsbury liberal, was imaginative enough to see that the Left existentialism of Sartre could just as easily exist on the Right, as it had in Heidegger, and so he made Merrick into a kind of British fascist. To claim even more for Scott, his power of imagination was so great that he often extrapolated from Sartre, happening upon formulations that seem to owe more to their original, unread German source, in something like the way the Greekless Shakespeare is thought to have taken liberties with North's translation of Plutarch, making changes that happened to coincide better with the original.

Being and Nothingness provides concrete examples where Heidegger was studiously abstract. For both Heidegger and Sartre, human being has no fixed essence but only an existence: a "standing out" (Latin: *ex stare*), hence the term "existentialism." Humans "stand out" from the way things "are" in favor of the way things *might be*. Heidegger calls it "projecting possibilities." Sartre emphasizes the negative; he calls it "nihilation": annihilating the actual in favor of the possible. Both Sartre and Heidegger seek a way out of the determinism inherent in the assumption that man's nature is essentially fixed and that he is part of a causal chain. While Heidegger writes as if the resolute individual can add nothing but a style or manner to the role which history has prescribed for him or her (all you can do is "make it your own"), Sartre by contrast insists that man has "absolute freedom," albeit sometimes within very narrow bounds—precisely the bounds of the historical situation.[19] A master and a slave have very different facticities: one seems to have unlimited scope of freedom, while the other seems to have little scope at all. Sartre would not disagree; but within these vastly differing scopes, the freedom that both master and slave can exercise is absolute. No one forces the slave to continue being a slave: he can resolve to make a break for freedom, risking death, at any time he chooses. He may, of course, not succeed, but the choice will have been his own in a way precisely equivalent to the way his master's choices are his own. Even if escape turns out to be impossible, his freedom to make the attempt was absolute. And here is the crucial part: the slave can never *know* his escape attempt is doomed until he has made the attempt, for only resoluteness discloses facts. For example, a man wishes to climb a rock but says, "That rock is unclimbable." Now, the true fact about the rock's climbability can never be known until the man actually *resolves* or decides to attempt to climb the rock. Resolutely trying, he may fail, but whether he succeeds or fails, he will have exercised his human freedom. If he were to decline to climb the rock on the grounds that he somehow "knows" in advance that the rock is unclimbable, he would be in what Sartre calls "bad faith." Only in resoluteness can any such "fact" about the rock be disclosed (Sartre, pp. 482, 488–89).

Earlier I promised that Merrick's philosophy would have explanatory power: that it would give a reasonable (if existentialism can be called reasonable) accounting to Hari of the problems Hari has been experiencing and thinking about since he came to India, and especially since he fell in love with Daphne. And so it proves. Merrick claims that if Hari will only take responsibility for the rape, Hari's whole situation will be revealed to him, and he will at last understand it. In this Merrick turns out to be correct.

IV

Existential responsibility solves Hari's problem of being a man without a country. When asked in a later interview whether he might indeed have tried to take advantage of Daphne sexually, Hari confesses:

> I may have done for all I know. My behaviour at that time left a lot to be desired. . . .
> I'd forgotten how to act in that kind of company. Or if I'd not forgotten, trying to act as I remembered I should act seemed—artificial. (*Scorpion*, p. 250)

Hari's confession that he might indeed have tried to take advantage of Daphne sexually is corroborated by what actually occurs in their first and only sexual union, in the deserted Bibighar garden before the gang attacks them. As Daphne recounts, Hari, after violently seizing her wrist to throw away her cigarette, cannot initially act out or "enact" their union in any other way than the rape which the taboo says such unions must always be:

> There was nothing gentle about the way he took me. I felt myself lifted onto the mosaic. He tore at my underclothes and pressed down on me with all his strength. *But this was not me and Hari.* . . . [H]e made me cry out. And then it was us. (*Jewel*, p. 417, emphasis added)

"But this was not me and Hari"—the sentence is important, because it shows that Daphne does not wish to believe that Merrick's racial situation is in fact all-determinant here. But Scott is toying with just how close to being correct, if not entirely correct, Merrick is. Daphne's assertion that this was not the real Hari falls within a prescripted role—it is the characteristically pathetic rationalization of a white girl who has fallen in love with an Indian only to find herself taken advantage of. Scott now proceeds to turn the screw even tighter, showing how difficult it is to create a sense of self beyond the racial selves that their communities have constructed for them.

After the "real" rapists leave them, Daphne in her delirium thinks she is alone, having "this idea that Hari had gone off with them because he had been one of [the rapists]." The communal ideology is strong enough to make Daphne subconsciously adhere to the scenario for which Merrick asks Hari to take responsibility. Like Daphne, Hari initially accepts Merrick's version of the situation. Merrick pretends during the interrogation (a policeman's trick) that Daphne went ahead and incriminated Hari. Merrick offers to let Hari confess to a lesser charge and avoid punishment for rape, for surely he can prove that Daphne agreed to meet him, that she wanted him? Merrick is correct in his assessment of how Hari will feel at Daphne's betrayal. Hari later realizes to his humiliation that he actually believed Merrick was telling the truth and that Daphne had given evidence against him. But we readers know that Merrick's lie corresponds to a kind of reality. Daphne did betray Hari in her mind, however briefly. Just as Daphne had believed, briefly, that Hari was one of the rapists, so Hari, for a few hours, believed that Daphne, as an English girl, would consider him, an Indian, one of the rapists. And we know as well that their sexual union was a rape, if only for an instant. It all fits into a seamless "situation."

After more torture, Merrick offers Hari water and helps him drink it. Then Merrick tells Hari if he were honest he would admit he was grateful for the water and would thank Merrick for it. He gives Hari another drink. "'After a bit I heard myself say [thank you]'" (*Scorpion*, pp. 300–1). Merrick says they both "know" where things stand now. In other words, by enacting the situation of master and slave, Hari has learned something about himself, just as Merrick said he would. Enactment is disclosive. During the night, Hari wakes up and calls for help. "'The name I called was Merrick.'" Hari is helped to see himself as an Indian—a dependent Indian—for the first time.

But because Merrick is no longer in the cell with him, no longer there to help the dependent Indian, Hari now proceeds to a rather different enactment, one which makes a different disclosure. He becomes resolute himself, rather than depending on Merrick's resoluteness. Hari first decides to confess to the rape charge. That is the attractive course because he could add thereby something of *his own* to his enemies' attempt to destroy him. Destroying himself would be the only course left in which he could "exercise his own free will" (*Scorpion*, p. 302). Hari is now at the Heideggerean stage of admitting guilt and making it one's own, and at the Sartrean stage of absolute freedom within a narrow circumstance. At the same time, Hari comes once again to realize his own nothingness. "I thought, well anyway what's going to be destroyed? Nothing. An illusion of a human being. . . . [A] nonentity . . ." (p. 302). He now has the two essential elements of existentialism: nullity or nothingness and guilt.

As Hari now revolts against Merrick's situation, it could easily seem to the reader that Scott has taken pains to show the victory of liberalism or humanism over the existentialist philosophy of the situation. For example, Hari in his jail cell comes to a sudden realization:

> . . . no one had any rights in regard to me. I was the only one with rights. . . . I wasn't to be categorized or defined by type, colour, race, capacity, intellect, condition, beliefs, instincts, manner or behaviour. . . . So who had the right to destroy me? *Who had the right as well as the means?* The answer was nobody. I wasn't sure that they even had the means. (*Scorpion*, p. 302; emphasis in original)

This reads as a modern liberal vindication of the rights-bearing self. It would be easy to assume from this that a rights-based liberalism here wins out over Merrick's existentialism.

But it is only in and through an existentialist engagement with the situation that Hari achieves this vindication of his own rights and individuality. Resoluteness discloses a situation in which he has rights. Hari asserts: "[T]he situation about Hari Kumar was that there was no one anywhere exactly like him. So who had the right to destroy me?" Part of his reasoning is as follows: "I saw . . . something Merrick had overlooked. That the situation only existed on Merrick's terms if we both took part in it. The situation would cease to exist if I detached myself from it" (*Scorpion*, p. 303). Hari has realized that the master-slave dialectic needs a slave: he is like Sartre's slave who realizes he can still choose. But when Hari says Merrick's situation ceases to exist, he does not mean that no situation of any sort exists any longer. On the contrary, Hari refers to "the situation" many times throughout his later prison interview, endorsing the concept in his own right and without irony, sometimes infuriating his interviewers with his mystifying assertions about what "the situation" is and what it entails. When they try to prevent him from talking about the situation, Hari says that it is impossible for him to forget the situation (*Scorpion*, p. 283). He says:

> . . . you begin to see that I am the least important factor and that without intending to you're asking questions about what *I call the situation*. That's why you're annoyed and accuse me of lying, because the *situation* threat-

ens to be more than any conscience can cope with. (*Scorpion*, p. 292; emphases added)

Hari's silence, his refusal to participate in Merrick's version of the situation, not only incriminates him but also contributes to the prosecution of the five other prisoners innocent of the rape in the Bibighar garden. When this is pointed out to him, Hari replies: "Yes, I had to consider that. It was part of the situation." When Hari's testimony is finished, he notes with irony that the clerk had been sent out of the room during the part that incriminated Merrick. He suggests, "That's part of the situation too, isn't it?" (*Scorpion*, p. 305).

Hari has been converted to existentialism by Merrick lock, stock, and barrel. He merely disagrees with Merrick over what the situation is. Or rather, Hari's resoluteness discloses a situation different from the situation disclosed by Merrick's resoluteness. He finds the tin mug that Merrick gave him water out of. He puts a towel around his middle, covering his naked, lacerated body. He walks up and down his jail cell, holding the tin mug. He remembers his Hindu grandfather, who had become *sannyasi*—disavowing all responsibilities in his old age except the responsibility to take up a beggar's cup and go out into the world to acquire merit. Hari now reminds himself of the "good Indian" his relatives have been trying to make him become since his return to India. For Hari the idea of *sannyasa* is a way of being Indian that connects with the idea that he is not answerable to anyone but himself: no one has any claims over him. "[N]o one had any rights in regard to me" (*Scorpion*, p. 302). Enacting—literally play-acting at—this small piece of Indian culture enables him to come to a decision to be silent and confess nothing. Hari sees this as vindicating his existential freedom: "it seemed like a way of proving the *existence* of Hari Kumar . . ." (p. 303; emphasis added). The issue becomes whether Hari—constituted by a community (the English) that now rejects him—can through a groundless existential choice come to understand and embrace the Indian culture that was previously alien to him.

It is crucial that neither Scott nor his protagonist asserts that Hari here reconstitutes himself as part of a new community: "I don't know whether that made me a good Indian" (p. 303). He, a brown Englishman, does not appropriate Indian values such as *sannyasa* in the direct or simple way his Hindu grandfather might have done. Rather, he takes from *sannyasa* only what he needs. His appropriation of Indian cultural values is momentary, transient, and opportunistic, and is permitted only by his acquaintance with a liberal philosophy of rights that is not Hindu (at least, not for Hari) but comes from the tradition Hari learned in England. It would be tempting to think that Hari takes from Indian culture only what his historical situation permits, that is, that his is an English appropriation of India. Nevertheless, we would make a mistake if we succumbed to this temptation: from an existentialist point of view, we would have it all backward. The situation does not reveal to Hari the opportunity to appropriate Indian cultural values. Instead, through enacting a Hindu custom (a way of being resolute), Hari finds out about his situation; or facts are revealed to him for the first time.

Obviously, enacting a far different role with Merrick also disclosed a situation to him. Which situation is the real situation? The question is once again backward since it presupposes that the facts are epistemologically prior, forming a situation we somehow know about in advance, a situation into which "we might even just bring ourselves" (Heidegger, p. 299). Only the enactment or resolution discloses and explains those facts. Hari's dependent-Indian enactment with Merrick explained a lot, and Hari's silent-Indian enactment explains a lot too. The greater genuineness or authenticity of one situation over the other is perhaps ascertainable only by distinguishing different levels of commitment or resoluteness. In the end, Merrick does not have his way with Hari because Hari's commitment not to play along is firm, and Hari's situation wins out, although at the cost of imprisonment and of never again seeing Daphne, who dies giving birth to the child conceived that night in the Bibighar garden.

V

The *Raj Quartet* is important for political theorists because it highlights the intellectual triggers by which liberal thought about the colonial encounter transforms itself into that post-liberal thinking which today goes by the name "postcolonialism." By highlighting these triggers, the *Raj Quartet* also reveals the debts which postcolonial thought owes to existentialism. In his nonfiction, Paul Scott expresses distaste for Sartre's philosophy of the situation, but he also presents himself as a liberal and a humanist who wrestles with existentialism and who, in doing so, loses his way. The dilemma of "Liberal Humanism," Scott asserts, is that the very core of humanism—namely, the principle that humans should be accorded dignity on the basis of their humanity alone—is a notion that has faded. "We're no longer certain what a human being is" (*Muse*, pp. 48–49; cf. 142–43, 121–26). In part, the problem can be rephrased as: How can we be certain our idea of the human is not a culturally produced, particularistic view which we then foist onto other cultures that have produced different ideas? The protagonists of the *Raj* novels undergo an evolution illustrating dawning awareness of this weakness in humanism. Daphne loves India in an explicitly humanistic way—for example, in monuments such as the Taj Mahal she seeks out that "which is neither Indian nor un-Indian," looking for the "general human emotion" (*Jewel*, p. 398). By contrast, Sarah Layton, the heroine of the later novels, gives voice to Scott's own sentiment from his nonfiction: she perceives that her "world" only "thought it knew what human beings were" (*Scorpion*, p. 331; cf. pp. 164, 213). Paul Scott is thus an authorial case-study of a liberal humanist for whom the colonial encounter raised difficulties about the philosophical underpinnings of liberal humanism.

Existentialism, eschewing any fixed human essence, is free from this weakness of humanism. Sartre initially embraced humanism in "Existentialism is a Humanism" (whereas Heidegger's response, the "Letter on Humanism" was skeptical of the term).[20] Sartre's concern for Algerian national self-assertion ultimately led him to renounce humanism as an inadequate and in fact collaborationist response to colonialism in his preface to Frantz Fanon's *The Wretched of the Earth*.[21] This renunciation of humanism has since become routine in postcolonial theory. Humanism is thought to be naïve because it is "essentialist"—a term originally opposed to existentialist. Scott's struggle with existentialism led him to the above dilemma, which might be described as an ambiguous disavowal of liberal humanism.[22] Scott thus chose a path that was to become well traveled: his journey away from liberal humanism in the '60s and '70s is representative of philosophical debates through which liberal colonial thought was transformed into postcolonial thought. His case reveals to us the existentialist concerns that lie at the foundations of postcolonial thought.

At great political cost, existentialism brings together the separate realms of determinism and freedom, healing the Cartesian dualism of mind and matter. Historicism had treated human choice deterministically, emulating physical science's treatment of matter. In existentialism, by contrast, historical determinism becomes only one moment, while a second, separate, moment is comprised of radical freedom. The unified whole of the two moments reveals that both determinism and freedom were incomplete thoughts on their own. Instead of a world of brute facts upon which humans are somehow able to project values, Heideggerean existentialism lets the human projection of possibility disclose the facts for the first time. The costly political ramifications follow from the premise that the substitute for true humanity, authentic "Being-there," is a status accorded only to the resolute, who rise above the "They-self" (*das Man*). Only the resolute live up to the name Being-there: only they are "there" in the full sense. All bets are off about how the resolute ones should and will treat the irresolute, inauthentic, less-than-"there" members of the They-self. Political and ethical courses of action can be disclosed only in the moment of truth: becoming resolute.

Paul Scott saw the difficulty inherent in substituting existentialism in place of humanism as a grounding for his liberal morality. The fascistic potential of existentialism was clear, and he depicted it in Merrick. But Scott was also attracted to the freedom that existentialism could offer to persons like Hari upon whom empire had placed dire constraints. One of the perverse beauties of existentialism is that its rigorous pessimism nevertheless permits individuals to find—within selves constituted from without—a core of agency. This freedom ungrounded in essentialist humanity made existentialism crucial to the development of postcolonialism. Thus the same philosophy that provided a grounding for domination also provided a means of escape from domination. Despite his distaste for it, existentialism spoke deeply to Paul Scott when it came to the philosophic wonder implicit in the questions he posed.

NOTES

1 Scott saw the novel as a "moral dialogue" between writer and reader, and called himself a "social novelist rather than a philosophical novelist" in *My Appointment with the Muse: Essays 1961–75,* edited by Shelley C. Reese (London: Heinemann, 1986), 114, 127; cf. 122–23. Hereafter this volume will be referred to as *Muse.*

2 "Paul Scott's Raj Quintet: Real Politics in Imaginary Gardens," in Joseph M. Knippenberg and Peter Augustine Lawler, eds., *Poets, Princes, and Private Citizens: Literary Alternatives to Postmodern Politics* (Lanham, Md.: Rowman and Littlefield, 1996), 191–209; "The English *War and Peace*: Paul Scott's *Raj Quartet,*" in *The St. John's Review* 38.3 (1988-9): 75–87; "Tapestry with Images: Paul Scott's Raj Novels," in *Philosophy and Literature* 23 (1999): 181–96.

3 The word "Raj" in this context refers to British rule in India.

4 Paul Scott, *The Raj Quartet,* vol. 1, *The Jewel in the Crown* (Chicago: University of Chicago Press, [1966] 1998). The succeeding volumes, also published by the University of Chicago Press in 1998, with their original dates, are as follows: *The Day of the Scorpion* (1968), *The Towers of Silence* (1971), and *A Division of the Spoils* (1975). Henceforth the volumes will be referred to as *Jewel, Scorpion, Towers,* and *Division.*

5 For the "cycle of inevitability" see *Jewel,* 125, 129.

6 Spoken by the character known as Sister Ludmila.

7 Another of Sister Ludmila's musings.

8   Francine S. Weinbaum, *Paul Scott: A Critical Study* (Austin: University of Texas Press, 1992), 99, 105, 124–29, 162–65.

9   Compare *Jewel*, 248, with *Division*, 301. See also John Keay, *India: A History* (New York: Grove Press, 2002), 431.

10 Robin Moore, *Paul Scott's Raj* (London: Heinemann, 1990), 43.

11 The language is that of Hubert L. Dreyfus, *Being-In-The-World: A Commentary on Heidegger's Being and Time, Division I* (Cambridge, Mass.: The MIT Press, 1990), e.g., 307. In other words, one must assume the worst. The implicit premise is that despair is superior to hope (i.e., hoping one has free will), so long as hope bears a possibility of being deceptive.

12 Spoken by the villain Merrick.

13 Emphasis in original. Daphne here describes the difficulty Merrick faces in his project to remake himself but the thoughts apply equally well to her own struggle to assert values alien to the community around her.

14 Only in the second volume, *Scorpion*, do we find out what passed in their jail cell interrogation, when Hari is interviewed after eighteen months of imprisonment, during which he overlays the following meditation on the events of 1942.

15 Martin Heidegger, *Being and Time*, translated by J. Macquarrie and E. Robinson (New York: Harper and Row, [1927] 1962), Division Two, Chapter 2: "Dasein's Attestation of an Authentic Potentiality-For-Being, and Resoluteness," especially section 60.

16 Brann, "Tapestry with Images," 192; see also Peter Childs, *Paul Scott's Raj Quartet: History and Division* (Victoria, British Columbia: University of Victoria, 1998), 117–32.

17 Pages cited refer to the marginal pagination, i.e., to the German text. In the translated text the German for the capitalized English "Situation" is *Situation*, for small-case "situation," *Lage*. Emphases in this and the following passages are all in the Macquarrie and Robinson translation.

18 Dreyfus, 307.

19 Jean-Paul Sartre, *Being and Nothingness: An Essay on Phenomenological Ontology*, translated by Hazel Barnes (New York: Philosophical Library, 1956), especially 6–35.

20 Sartre, "Existentialism is a Humanism" (1946), translated by Philip Mairet, in *The Existentialist Tradition*, edited by Nino Langiulli (Garden City: Doubleday, 1971), 391–416, and Heidegger, "Letter on Humanism" (1947), translated by Edgar Lohner, also in Langiulli, ed., 204–44.

21 See Sartre's 1961 Preface in Frantz Fanon, *The Wretched of the Earth*, translated by Constance Farrington (New York: Grove Press, 1968), 7–31, especially 24–26. Cf. Childs, 118–19.

22 See Janis Haswell, *Paul Scott's Philosophy of Place(s): The Fiction of Relationality* (New York: Peter Lang, 2002), 109, 219; contrast Childs, 119.

ON TWO NOVELS RECALLING
WORLD WAR II

Chaninah Maschler

INTRODUCTION

TWO SHORT NOVELS came my way this past year, *The Assault* and *A Pale View of Hills*. The former was written by a Dutchman with a Hungarian name, Harry Mulisch; the latter by an Englishman with a Japanese name, Kazuo Ishiguro. The two books not only bear the same copyright year, 1982, their narratives span the same time interval—roughly from 1945 till the early 1980s. Displaying the presence of the World War II past in the lives of the war's survivors is a major objective of both books. Born in Holland in 1927, Mulisch lived through the war in Holland. For him, retrieval of the past takes the form of an unidentified undramatized narrator's account of the adventures of a fictional character. Ishiguro, a younger man born in Nagasaki nine years after the war's conclusion, was schooled in England (his family moved there when he was six years old). He chooses a first-person monologue as vehicle for recollection.

Given Eva Brann's love of novels and the prominence of time, memory, and recollection in her oeuvre and in *The Assault* and *A Pale View of Hills,* it is not unreasonable to call these two books to the attention of the readers of the Festschrift.

I

An omniscient narrator tells of a boy, Anton Steenwijk, who lives with his father, mother, and older brother, Peter, in a somewhat down-at-the-heels would-be villa on the outskirts of the Dutch town of Haarlem.

> It was January, nineteen forty-five. Almost all of Europe had been liberated and was once more rejoicing, eating, drinking, making love and beginning to forget the War. But every day Haarlem looked more like one of those spent gray clinkers that they used to take out of the stove, when there had still been coal to burn. . . .

In the silence that was Holland then, six shots suddenly rang out . . .
Anton froze and looked at his mother, his mother at his father, his father
at the sliding doors; but Peter picked up the cover of the carbon lamp and
put it over the flame. Suddenly all was dark. Peter stood up . . . "They
shot someone," he said. "Someone is lying there." (pp. 9–16)

The man who has been shot is Fake Ploeg, Chief Inspector of Police in
Haarlem, a Dutch Nazi. His body had fallen in front of the house next door,
but the neighbors reposition the corpse so that it lies in front of Anton's
house. Peter runs out, meaning to drag the body away. His efforts to do so
are interrupted by shouts of "Halt! Hands up!" Anton sees his brother
run away.

Shortly after Peter's disappearance, a gang of German soldiers invades
the Steenwijks' house and carts off Anton's parents. The house is torched.
Anton is dragged off separately. He ends up spending the night in a jail cell
meant for solitary confinement but already occupied by a woman. The two
of them—twelve-year-old Anton and the unnamed woman—are in total
darkness. She draws him out and comforts him. They converse:

"Those bastards . . . Believe me, the Russians and the Americans will make
short shrift of them. Let's think about something else . . . while we still
can."

"What do you mean?"

"Well, while they still leave us together in here . . . What shall we talk
about? Or are you tired? Do you want to sleep?"

"Not me."

"Good. We've been talking all the time about the dark; shall we talk
about light?"

"Fine."

"Just imagine, lots of light. Sun. Summer. What else?"

"The beach."

"Yes, before it was full of bunkers and barricades. The dunes." . . .
Suddenly, without transition, she began to talk as if to a third person in
the cell.

"Light, yes, but light is not always just light. I mean, a long time ago
I wanted to write a poem comparing light to love—no, I mean love to
light. Yes, that's another possibility of course. You could also compare light
to love. Maybe that's even more beautiful, for light is older than love. . . ."
(p. 37 f.)

Not until much later in the novel, when Anton visits the resistance
fighter who had been in love with his cellmate, the man who figured as the

"third person in the cell," will Anton feel as intense a fellowship as he experienced with the woman that night in jail. What she looked like, what name she bore, whether she was still alive or, if not, how she died, whether she had anything to do with the assault—all this Anton will find out eventually, but not as a result of his inquiry. By chance he will overhear someone at a funeral gathering say, "I shot him first in the back, then in the shoulder, and then in the stomach as I bicycled past him" (p. 108). That sentence prompts a vivid, quite involuntary reinstatement of the ring of shots in his memory and an almost equally involuntary outburst: "Wasn't there a fourth and a fifth shot? And then one more, a sixth?" (p. 109).

Mulisch's book is divided into chronological "Episodes" identified as First, 1945; Second, 1952; Third, 1956; Fourth, 1966; and Fifth, 1981. For those of us who were adults in 1981, the named years are associated with world historical events that I imagine Mulisch expects us to have stored at least in an abbreviated record in our memory: 1945 is the year of the defeat of the Nazis and the liberation of Europe; the Korean War is going on in 1952; 1956 is the year of anti-Communist unrest in Poland and Hungary; 1966 belongs to the Vietnam War; and in 1981 there were immense gatherings of crowds all over Europe to protest the building and stockpiling of nuclear arms. The remembered happenings of Anton's private life are inserted into the niches thus provided by Eurocentric current history. The Now from which this sequence of Thens—both of private and of public history—is considered is identified by the narrator on the book's last page. It coincides with the year in which Mulisch was granted a copyright for *The Assault*, 1982.

Precisely what is gained by telling Anton's story in this way is not obvious. Perhaps the fact that there is an odd number of five episodes matters? The biographical and historical events that belong to the Third Episode, 1956, are made central.

> [T]he rumble of the Russian tanks which had rolled into Budapest still echoed within Holland, and nowhere more audibly than around the corner from Anton's apartment. There, in a large eighteenth century building called Felix Meritis, were the headquarters of the Communist Party. Unruly mobs roamed the city, destroying everything that had anything to do with the communists, from their bookstore to the windows of their homes . . . Anton was totally uninterested in all this. He would never have taken part; he even avoided conversations about it. Somehow he couldn't help thinking that though it was all pretty terrible, it was only child's play really . . . The worst problem for him was the constant racket. (p. 82 f.)

Crushed by the mob, Anton is trying to figure out how to enter his apartment. Suddenly people run away from his doorway, except for one big fellow with a rock in his hand who stands there with his back toward Anton. The man turns around, looks at Anton, and greets him: "'Hello, Ton,' he said. Anton looked into the wide, coarse face. Suddenly he knew. 'Hello, Fake'" (p. 85). Fake is the son of the collaborationist policeman whose assassination opened the novel's course of events. Anton invites Fake in. The two men converse and learn what happened to each of them in the eleven years since the catastrophe.

> "Is your mother still alive?" Fake nodded. "Yes," he said after a silence. He made it sound like a kind of admission, as if Anton had asked, is *your* mother still alive? He had not meant it that way—but even as he said it he realized that perhaps it was what he had meant, after all. (p. 87)

In the course of the highly dramatic confrontation between the two men, Anton finds out that Fake refuses to grant that there is any important difference between his father's death and the death of Anton's family. His father was just as innocent as were Anton's parents, Fake claims: He simply carried out his duties as a policeman *during* as previously *before* the war. He had not known a thing about what the Germans did to the Jews. It was from conviction, not from base motives, that he was a fascist, as was shown by the fact that he became a member of the Dutch Nazi party very late, at a time when many who had profited from collaborating with the German invaders pretended that all along they had been in the Resistance. It was because he stood up and let himself be counted that they shot him! At least, this is what Fake's mother told her son and his siblings after their father was assassinated. Anton asks himself how Fake can possibly believe all this and concludes, "Love was what caused it all—love, through thick and thin" (p. 92).

Until the meeting with Fake, Anton had avoided encounters with everyone connected with life before the catastrophe. True, he had returned to Haarlem, but that was to look at the *place* of his childhood—the herringbone pattern of the brick pavement, the view of the farms, the cottages, the mill. Anton entirely abstains from gathering information about the War, or the death of his parents and brother. He chooses to become an anesthesiologist: "He had . . . the more or less mystical notion that the narcotics did not make the patient insensitive to pain so much as unable to express that pain, and that although drugs erased the memory of pain, the patient was nevertheless changed by it."

The active attitude required of someone who investigates, discriminates, appraises, and assigns or withholds blame is incompatible with the stance that had made life sustainable for Anton, the attitude that had shrunk his part in history to that of victim (p. 112). Like Joseph in the book of Genesis, he must remember to forget. But lacking a God who stands by him, is it any wonder that his memory plays him tricks? The Second Episode holds an apt description of this: Mrs. Beumer, the neighbor Anton encounters to his chagrin when he returns to the place where he once lived, informs him that nearby there stands a monument. Anton finds it. It records the names of his parents along with four others who "fell for queen and fatherland." When he gets back to his uncle and aunt's house in Amsterdam, he complains that he was never told "there's a monument standing on our quay" (p. 75). But his aunt and uncle remind him that three years back, when the monument was unveiled, he turned down the invitation to attend the ceremony.

> "I remember exactly what you said . . . You said they should go to hell with their monument, for all you cared . . . Don't you remember?" Anton shook his head and kept silent . . . For the first time he felt a kind of fear, something sucking him in, a deep hole into which things fell without reaching the bottom, as when someone throws a stone into a well and never hears it land. (p. 75)

The image of the fallen stone that fails to send the message of having reached bottom is followed by another, of his own falling into a tunnel he had drilled to the center of the earth. There he'd be weightless and immobile, fixed in eternal meditation on the course of things.

I stressed the accidental character of Anton's finding out the identity and fate of the young woman who had been his cellmate. Yet it was by choice that he attended the funeral where he overheard the sentence which prompted him to speak up and mention the three additional shots: Anton knew ahead of time that, as the narrator puts it, "it was not so much a funeral as a reunion [of members of the resistance]" (p. 102). He went there, clearly, because he *wanted* to be surrounded by people who had fought against the Germans. Perhaps he even hoped to find the woman of twenty-one years earlier there? (p. 109).

The moving tête-à-tête at the funeral between Anton and the resistance fighter, Takes—in the course of which Anton learns the details of both Takes's and his woman-friend's part in Fake Sr.'s assassination (pp. 108–120) —is sympathetically described by the omniscient narrator. Both men cried and for the same reason. As Anton realizes somewhat later, "It was the first time that he [Anton] had cried over what had happened, yet it wasn't because of his parents, or Peter, but because a girl had died" (p. 129).

Anton's encounter with Takes in the Fourth Episode continues what was begun in the Third Episode—an accidentally triggered but increasingly active and engaged retrieving of the past. Issues of blame and justification are again highlighted, this time not, as when Anton ran into Fake, from the perspective of the family of the Nazi assassinated, but from the perspective of the Communist lover of the woman who did the killing. An experienced man of the theater, Mulisch has designed his novel on the pattern of the traditional five-act drama, whose plot revolves around the events of Act III. Equally traditional is the device of isolating the hero or heroine from the group and arranging for sparring matches between the chief protagonist and a series of partners.

How about the ending, the Fifth Episode? Does the story simply stop, or does it reach a conclusion, some sort of satisfying resting place? Mulisch himself seems to be bringing up the question when he begins his Fifth Episode with the sentence "And then . . . and then . . . and then . . . Time passes" (p. 151).

The opening lines of Scene 2 of Act V link the narrative's beginning to its end as follows:

> The memory of that night during the War in nineteen forty-five plagued him one last time in his life. On a Saturday in the second half of November, nineteen eighty-one he woke up with such an unbearable toothache that something had to be done at once. At nine o'clock he called the dentist who had been treating him for over twenty years. . . . The dentist told him . . . he wasn't about to do any work that day, he was going to the demonstration. (p. 163)

Anton, the fastidious avoider of crowds, now gets blackmailed into becoming a participant in the anti-nuclear demonstration that his friend the dentist insists on attending. The toothache, which gets cured by the dentist with miraculous ease, looks like a comic counterpart to the migraines and nightmares that plagued him before. Will what is said of the toothache ever come to hold of Anton's other pains? "The miracle had happened. The pain receded behind the horizon and disappeared as if it had never existed. 'How is it possible?'" (p. 167).

In the final year of our novel, 1981, the second child, from a second marriage, the second Peter in Anton's life, is twelve years old, which was Anton's age at the beginning of the story. Peter and the girl child from the first marriage, Sandra, attend the peace demonstration and catch sight of their father in the crowd. Sandra, older than Peter, is amazed at seeing her father being a participant (p. 170). We readers too are astonished. There has been a change in Anton: "A curious euphoria pervaded Anton, a state not agitated or anxious, but dreamlike, connecting him with something far far back that had existed before the War. He was no longer alone but a part of all these people" (pp. 168–169).

What is it that cured Anton? It may have something to do with cross-word puzzles and poetry: In Episode Two we learn that Anton reads news-papers for their crossword puzzles. One such, a sort of pun-and-anagram puzzle, came his way in Episode Five, while he was suffering that dreadful toothache. The clue involved the sun god, lack of definition, and stones arranged helter-skelter (p. 165). When Anton experiences himself as a member of the crowd, three things happen simultaneously. He feels that "these hundreds of thousands of people, these endless streams of human lives, were helping him . . ."; he sees and touches his son Peter, smiling at him; and the solution of the riddle occurs to him. (p. 184) The delights of cross-word puzzles were earlier described as having something to do with the fact that "most letters had a double function, [serving] in both a horizontal and a vertical word. . . . That these words were paired in a mysterious way pleased him no end. It had something to do with poetry" (p. 81; cf. p. 5 in the Prologue, about "a man walking backwards to push something forward, while staying in the same place himself").

Do the five numerals that are used as headings for the five segments of the book serve as do a crossword puzzle's letters, which make one word when the reading is horizontal and another when the reading is vertical? Do the happenings of public and private history after all both belong to History, as both the horizontally and the vertically placed words of a crossword puzzle belong to one language? Mulisch's novel shows that for the constituting of a life, recognizing the intersection of private and public chronologies matters. How it matters is not said.

II

Niki, the name we finally gave my younger daughter, is not an abbreviation; it was a compromise I reached with her father. For paradoxically it was he who wanted to give her a Japanese name, and I—perhaps out of some selfish desire not to be reminded of the past—insisted on an English one. He finally agreed to Niki, thinking it had some vague echo of the East about it. (p. 9)

The economy of the opening paragraph of Kazuo Ishiguro's *A Pale View of Hills* is remarkable. From it we learn that the speaker has two daughters, that the father of the younger daughter is probably English, that the narrator's relation to this husband, as well as her relation to her past, is complicated. Further, we note that she is tough enough to insist on getting what she wants (or at least, to avoid what she doesn't), yet vulnerable and self-judging.

With "Niki," the name of her twenty-something daughter, the narrator's recollections begin. They end with her standing by the garden gate to watch Niki leave for London. In between are five days spent in her daughter's company—sharing meals, walking to the village, having tea in a tea shop, encountering neighbors; five days also of noting her daughter's way of walking, dressing, talking on the telephone, her impatience with the quiet of her mother's life, and her air of patronizing her mother.

Niki's visit is prompted by the recent suicide of her half-sister, Keiko. It is not that Niki has come to share her mother's mourning. She is quite frank about not having loved her sister. Niki is visiting to help free her mother from feeling to blame for her firstborn's death.

Keiko, unlike Niki, had been "pure Japanese." We never find out the precise circumstances of the narrator leaving her first husband and Japan, marrying a second time, and moving to England. Since our information is so inadequate, we are not able to gauge whether Niki's sizing up of her mother's past conduct is right. According to Niki, her mother showed admirable independence and courage in leaving her first marriage. She wants her mother to agree that this remains true even if Keiko's suicide might be regarded as an effect of her mother's breaking with Keiko's father.

Niki asks her mother what she is thinking about. In answer her mother reports that she is thinking of a woman she used to know when she was still living in Nagasaki, "long before I met your father" (p. 10). Niki does not persevere with questions and returns to the book she's been reading. We are the ones who hear about her mother's friendship with an impoverished widow, Sachiko. Not until Sachiko is on the scene do we learn our narrator's name, Etsuko (p. 14).

The recollections released by Niki's question occur in the course of five spring days that mother and daughter spend together at what used to be the family's house in the country. In the daytime, Etsuko's thought dwells on the hot summer months of early pregnancy that long ago she shared with Sachiko in Nagasaki. At night, she dreams of a little girl on a swing. At first she thinks the dream is provoked by her recently watching just such a girl playing in the park. The dream recurs. She becomes aware that though "it seemed to be that little girl . . . it wasn't" (p. 95). The little girl on the swing somewhere in England yesterday will turn out to be/have been a little girl on a cable car in Japan some thirty years earlier.

Evidently, it is the mind's work of remembering and misremembering rather than the clean-cut events that fed the mind that absorb Ishiguro. In retrospect, I see that this was announced from the beginning, when the narrator told us that it was her desire to avoid remembering the past that is "perhaps" responsible for her visiting daughter bearing the name "Niki."

The temporally and spatially distant three-month period when her first child was in prospect (the time of the Korean War as experienced in bombed but recovering Nagasaki) is brought emotionally close by Etsuko's conveying to us how strongly she was attached to three people who were then her intimates: Sachiko; another impoverished widow, Mrs. Fujiwara, who had been Etsuko's mother's best friend; and Ogata-San, Etsuko's father-in-law.

Etsuko's friend Sachiko, with whom the stream of recollection begins, is an educated upper-class woman who has fallen on very hard times. She could provide for herself and her daughter Mariko by returning to live with wealthy relatives, an aged uncle and a cousin. Or she might, though it would be humiliating, sustain herself by working for Mrs. Fujiwara, who runs a noodle restaurant in the Nakagawa District, an older section of Nagasaki.

Throughout the period of the two women's acquaintance, Sachiko is cultivating a chancy relation with an offstage American soldier, Frank. Neither Etsuko nor we ever meet this man. We only get to see the battered white car in which he drives up to visit Sachiko. At times Sachiko talks to Etsuko as though she really expects to marry Frank and go to America with him. At other times she writes him off as an irresponsible drunkard.

As Etsuko's memories continue to pour out, we readers become transported to post-World War II Japan. We become as empathetic, slow, and gentle as is the Etsuko whom Etsuko recalls. We hesitate to judge the people whom Etsuko loves.

The early weeks of Etsuko's friendship with Sachiko are also the period of her father-in-law's first visit: The father-in-law, Ogata-San, upon retiring from his post as headmaster of a school in Nagasaki, has returned to Fakuoka, the city of his birth. Ogata-San probably left Nagasaki because his son, Jiro, upon marrying Etsuko, refused to share the house with his widowed father. The departure of Ogata-San must have been felt as a grave loss by Etsuko: In 1945, when she was orphaned by the bomb, Ogata-San had taken her in. It was only later that she became acquainted with his son, Jiro.

Etsuko's loneliness is so palpable that we side with Ogata-San, who gives Etsuko the affection she needs, rather than with his son Jiro, who withholds affection. At least, we are gentle in our headshaking as we watch the old man foolishly insist on finishing the game of chess he has begun playing with his son. We may hesitate to condemn him when we catch him being, on the one hand, astounded and upset that a husband and a wife should be voting for different political parties and, on the other hand, entirely unruffled by the possible fact that the husband, to punish the wife for her independence of judgment, hit her with a golf club. We feel rather uneasy, however, when we hear Jiro, in response to his father's nostalgia for the Japan of before the American victory, remind his father that prior to the war's end, Jiro was taught in school that the Japanese nation is "divine and supreme" (p. 66).

Soon after arriving at his son's apartment, Ogata mentions that he has come upon an article in a recent issue of an educational journal according to which he and a certain Dr. Endo should have been dismissed from their posts as educators at the end of the war. It's a good thing, says the author of this article, that the two men decided to retire (p. 31).

Etsuko's reaction to the article is, "It seems very disloyal" (p. 31). The comment is not inappropriate, since Ogata had mentioned that, as a child, the article's young author, Shigeo Matsudo, used to come to his house, was spoiled by his wife, and owed his present position to Ogata having introduced him to the headmaster of the school where he still teaches. Jiro abstains from judgment and leaves for work.

Time and again Ogata tries but fails to persuade his son to either demand an apology from Matsudo or formally to disassociate himself from him. Finally the father decides that he will call on Matsudo, and they have their meeting. After polite opening exchanges, the older man insists on bringing up the offending article. The younger man tries hard to avoid a clash. But at last, according to Etsuko's report, "an air of authority seemed to enter his manner." He answers Ogata's question as to what made him write the article quite explicitly: "In your day, children in Japan were taught terrible things. They were taught lies of the most damaging kind. Worst of all, they were taught not to see, not to question. And that's why the country was plunged into the most evil disaster in her entire history" (p. 147). Ogata still does not abandon the project of receiving an apology from the younger man. But Matsudo, in reply to Ogata's chiding him for speaking in ignorance, reports that he happens to know for a fact that Ogata, in 1938, was responsible for the dismissal and incarceration of five teachers. Having said this, he excuses himself and leaves for school.

How ought we who read these recollections so many years after the occurrence of the words and deeds that are being called to mind by our narrator, how ought we to react or judge? Ishiguro makes things hard for us: We have come to love Etsuko. Etsuko is unreservedly her father-in-law's partisan. "What nonsense he was speaking, what vile nonsense. I don't think you should pay the slightest attention, Father," is what she says to Ogata-San about Matsudo's words. *That* can't be the right attitude for us. Indeed, when during conversation between Ogata and Mrs. Fujiwara the names of various teachers are brought up and Ogata claims not to know what became of them, I caught myself wondering whether they had been among the ones dismissed owing to Ogata's devotion to the ethos of pre-democratic Japan. On the other hand, when twice in Matsudo's speeches I caught the phrase "a new dawn," I wondered whether we were meant to think that there was also something canned in Matsudo's words. His having joined the Communist party was mentioned in an earlier conversation between Ogata and Jiro.

This feeling of not having the wherewithal to be fair in our appraisal of characters applies also to our take on Sachiko. Plainly, she often puts on uncalled-for superior airs when she is in Etsuko's company. Sometimes, as in her attitude to Mrs. Fujiwara and her noodle shop, she is rude. And there can be no doubt that she pays far too little attention to Mariko. Yet it is not until we reach the penultimate Chapter 10 that we roundly condemn her: We are horrified when we read that Sachiko, though she knows herself to be watched by her little daughter, tries to drown the pet kittens whose future life Mariko had been planning throughout the time of the two women's friendship.* We are outraged because we know from an earlier conversation between the women that Sachiko is well aware that the drowning of the kittens whom Mariko had been mothering *must* remind the child of the drowning of a human baby that she had witnessed while she was still in Tokyo (pp. 73 f.).

It is in anticipation of Frank's driving her and Mariko to Kobe the next day that Sachiko kills the kittens.

---

* Mariko is as persevering about finding homes for the kittens as Ogata is about receiving an apology from Matsudo. She and Ogata both fail.

Etsuko makes a lantern-illumined excursion into the darkness to try to find Mariko, who has stayed outside ever since watching her mother with the kittens. When she finds Mariko, Etsuko asks her why she is not coming in. The little girl answers repeatedly that she doesn't want to go away and that she doesn't like "him." "He's like a pig." Etsuko's prissy comeback, "You're not to speak like that," starts out being simply annoying. But when she adds, *"He's very fond of you, and he'll be just like a new father. Everything will turn out well, I promise,"* the feeling of collusion among untrustworthy adults turns annoyance into anger. Anger becomes bewilderment when we hear Etsuko say to the little girl, *"If you don't like it over there, we can always come back . . . But we have to try it and see if we like it there. I'm sure we will"* (p. 172 f.).

What is one to make of this "we"? After all, it is Sachiko, not Etsuko, our narrator, who is about to leave with Mariko for "over there."

My best guess is that the words which Etsuko in England imagines herself to have spoken to Mariko, the words I quoted, with emphasis added, were actually said to her own daughter Keiko when, something like seven years after her summer of pregnancy and the imagined conversation with Mariko, she decides to leave Japan for England with a new husband who is to serve as surrogate father to Keiko.

However slow Etsuko may have been to sit in judgment on her friend, must she not, in the end, like ourselves, have found her guilty of child neglect and mental cruelty? And is it not plausible that, now that Etsuko is grieving for the death of the child with whom she had been pregnant in the days of her friendship with Sachiko, the old feeling of deserving blame for taking Keiko away from Japan and from her father should return? It is true that Etsuko says to herself, "My motives for leaving Japan were justifiable, and I always kept Keiko's interests very much at heart" (p. 91). Both claims are probably warranted. So to us, the readers, the difference between Sachiko's and Etsuko's culpability may seem vast. But not perhaps to Etsuko: Though she has gone over "these matters" again and again, she is shown never to be done with them.

CONCLUSION

It was mere coincidence that the Dutch and the English novel summarized in the foregoing pages fell into my hands in the summer of 2005, a little more than sixty years after the Hunger Winter of 1945 in Holland, a little less than sixty years after the second use of the atomic bomb in Japan; and that this was also the time when the editors of this Festschrift invited me to write something in Eva's honor. It occurred to me that the children and children's children of Anton and Etsuko and their likes might still today be served by fiction that particularizes and universalizes the experience of those who underwent the war as children. I also thought that there might be a gain in clarity if one examined the two novels side by side.

I noticed, for instance, that structurally there is some resemblance: Both books are arranged around scenes of exceptional vividness that serve as the books' moral center. In *The Assault* Anton's encounter with Fake plays this role. Its description occurs at pretty nearly the exact middle of the book. As was said earlier, the meeting of the two former schoolmates had a psychologically freeing effect, making it possible for Anton eventually to shed his passivity. But in my earlier comments on the scene I focused too narrowly on Anton. Let me make amends. I reported that Anton was astounded to find out in the course of their meeting that as far as Fake was concerned, there was perfect moral equality between the two sets of parents—Anton's and Fake's—none of them deserving what they got. I neglected to mention that, to highlight the absurdity of this equality, Anton put it to Fake that he is claiming that his Nazi father's name ought to have been memorialized along with the names of Anton's parents and assorted resistance fighters, all of them indifferently having died "for queen and country." The narrator describes Fake's response to this bitter joke as having consisted of, first, a sob, then a question: "I've thought what you went through; did you ever do the same for me?" (p. 92).

Perhaps Mulisch is insinuating that recovery from "the inexhaustible bitterness" (p. 173) cannot occur apart from sympathy with the suffering of the descendants of the guilty? Yet, as if to prevent the reader from drawing this moral too easily, Mulisch adds a wonderfully apt incident of violence: Fake, cornered by Anton's question, hurls the rock, which he has been carrying for use in his participation in the assault on Communist headquarters, at something precious in Anton's room, an antique mirror. Anton is described as fearing for his life, first when Fake takes aim to throw the rock; later when Fake reenters Anton's apartment after his run down the stairs. I do not remember whether, on first reading, I started out sharing Anton's fear. By the end of the scene pity has replaced fear; in me at least, if not in Anton.

In Ishiguro's *A Pale View of Hills*, Chapter 7, devoted to describing a day trip to Mt. Inasa, has something like the function assigned to the Third Episode in Mulisch's book: It opens a future for the chief protagonist(s).

This first chapter of the novel's Part Two begins with Etsuko remembering the overwhelmingly depressing aspect of the summer landscape that surrounded her when she was pregnant with Keiko. Also recalled are the moments of vacantly gazing through the apartment's window at the trees and the yonder side of the river, and, on clear days, at the "pale outline of hills visible against the clouds" (p .99). This more distant prospect, which manifestly is the source of the novel's title, is remembered as occasionally having given her relief from bleakness. A little later in the chapter, Etsuko recalls how the three of them—Sachiko, Mariko, and Etsuko—took the ferry to spend a day touring "the hilly area of Nagasaki overlooking the harbor" (p. 103). The previously unidentified view from her apartment window then turns out to have been a view of these same hills of Inasa.

Chapter 7's most striking feature is the fact that the same Mariko who has been so exasperating, so much sinned against, so unhappy and even frightened in most of the book is now exuberantly on top of the world. While Etsuko feels uncertain whether Sachiko will really return to live with the uncle and cousin, Mariko banks on it (at least for a little while): "We're going to live with Yasuko-San again. Did mother tell you?" (p. 112). Both her immediate future and her present hold joy: She tests how the world looks through the toy binoculars Etsuko has given her. She draws with her new crayons. She climbs trees. She keeps her own counsel when talked about in simpering phrases like "little lady." She clearly outcharms the painfully overprotected little boy with whom she briefly shares the hills of Inasa.

Mariko is happy that day; Etsuko as well. Through Mariko, her previously gloom-infested pregnancy is given hope. Sachiko picks up on Etsuko's unwonted cheerfulness, and Etsuko confirms that there has been a change in her:

> "It's so good to come out here. Today I've decided I'm going to be optimistic . . . Mrs. Fujiwara always tells me how important it is to keep looking forward. And she is right. If people didn't do that, then all this"— I pointed again at the view—"all this would still be rubble." (p. 111)

A little later she reprises this forward-looking sentiment: "It's only in the last few days I've really thought about what it's going to be like. To have a child, I mean. I don't feel nearly so afraid now" (p. 111). For the time being Sachiko backs her up. Yet towards the end of the chapter (122), Sachiko turns against her; at least, she depreciates Mrs. Fujiwara's life to nullity. When Etsuko calmly opposes Sachiko, urging that the noodle shop and the one surviving child give Mrs. Fujiwara a stake in life, Sachiko responds with a tired smile and "I suppose she has her son." Clearly, she disbelieves what she said earlier to her pregnant friend: "[Y]ou'll discover soon enough, it's being a mother that makes life truly worthwhile" (p. 112. Cf. 170, 171). No reasons or causes for Sachiko's undermining of her young friend's new cheerfulness are given. And we are also left to our own speculations about what triggers Sachiko's final decision against staying in Nagasaki. Similarly, we are given hardly any assistance when we try to understand why a little more than seven years after the interlude of friendship with Sachiko, the outing to Inasa, and the birth of Keiko, Etsuko leaves her Japanese husband (p. 90): As she describes this husband to herself, he physically compared unfavorably with his father (p. 28 f.); he was, perhaps, a bit of a coward in that he tended to avoid "confronting" troublesome situations (p. 126); and when we readers of the novel are made to overhear how Jiro speaks to his wife and his father, we find him prickly and ungracious towards his wife though on the whole courteous to his father (p. 132 f., p. 154). However, this last observation is mine, not the narrator's.

Given the grave importance of family loyalty in Japanese culture, of which we were told at some length by Ogata-San (p. 65), and given Etsuko's emphatic self-identification as Japanese (p. 10, p. 90), it is rather surprising that the shortcomings of Jiro mentioned by Etsuko added up to a divorce. Etsuko rejects her English husband's damning picture of Jiro and thinks that Niki's notions about her mother's first marriage, wholly based on the English father's account, are "inaccurate" (p. 90): "Jiro worked hard to do his part for the family and he expected me to do mine; in his own terms, he was a dutiful husband. And indeed for the seven years that he knew his daughter, he was a good father to her" (p. 90).

Why does the novel arrange to leave us stymied? In life outside fiction we often fail to understand why people do what they do. Is it to make our experience of his fiction come closer to our experience of real life that causal connections and chronological sequencing are made so difficult to grasp in Ishiguro's novel? Is he trying to undo what seem to him illusions of comprehension that are the outcome of novelists' invention?

It is helpful to consider the titles of the two books. The title of *The Assault* announces an act of violence and the book's plot describes the deed, its causes, and its consequences. But what is the plot of Ishiguro's book? Its title forecasts a particular view—that of the Hills of Inasa—and, perhaps more generally, views or perspectives—on landscapes, on people, perhaps even on nations or cultures. There is, of course, an initial deed—Keiko's suicide. Yet what I said about the hiddenness of the reasons for Sachiko's and

Etsuko's choices to leave Japan holds at least as much for Keiko's choice of death. We only know that she isolated herself from her family, withdrawing into her room so long as she lived at home, and eventually leaving home for another city. We know that she has been unhappy for years. Is that sufficient explanation for her suicide? As for consequences, the book that we are reading, which sets out Etsuko's recollections, is probably the major consequence of Keiko's self-inflicted death. It is as though Ishiguro has taken on the task of writing the poem about Etsuko's difficult life that, according to Niki's report, one of her London friends is in the process of writing (p. 89, p. 177).

The grammatical subject of the first sentence in Mulisch's novel is third person singular, "a certain Anton Steenwijk." The grammatical subject in the corresponding sentence of Ishiguro's novel is first person plural, "we." The consistently maintained objectivity in Mulisch's story-telling accords with the clarity of its plot. Contrariwise, Ishiguro's choice of a restricted subjective point of view harmonizes with his decision to let us experience how little we know that would explain why people do what they do. The connectedness of the people whose voices we get to hear through Etsuko, the feelings that they and the landscapes in which they are imbedded evoke, the moods that overtake them—these are made vivid.

At the beginning of my remarks about *A Pale View of Hills,* I quoted its opening paragraph, which strikingly introduces the theme of "us and them" (p. 9). On the book's next page the theme is reiterated: "The English are fond of their idea that our [the Japanese] race has an instinct for suicide" (p. 10). In the last chapter of Part One, the contrast between us and them is again brought into play. Niki's journalist father is Etsuko's topic. Of him she says, "Despite all the impressive articles he wrote about Japan, my husband never understood the ways of our culture" (p. 90). Talk and thought about "us" and "them" runs through the novel; the "I" that enacts the role of speaker and rememberer stays the same while switching partners and contrasting third persons. On the shocking fusion or confusion of her friend Sachiko's child, Mariko, with her own child, Keiko, I commented earlier. This fusion of mutually assimilable "you's" is thematic to the book, as is the great puzzle of first person plural, "we." We see this on the second to last page of the book: Niki asks her mother what was so special about the excursion to Inasa that a photographic view of the harbor there is made to sum up her memory of Japan. Etsuko answers, "Oh, there was nothing special about it. I was just remembering it, that's all. *Keiko was happy that day. We rode on the cable cars.*" (p. 182) Keiko, of course, was still in the woman's belly that day. The

"We" *then* consisted of Etsuko and Mariko, though as felt *now* (at the time of her talking with Niki) that "We" and the one consisting of Etsuko and Keiko are indistinguishable.

When first I picked up on the third person singular/first person plural contrast between Mulisch's and Ishiguro's narratives I thought it had something to do with the choice of masculinity or femininity for the distinct tones of the two books. *A Pale View of Hills* is overwhelmingly peopled by females—female children, female neighbors, female tourists, female friends. And the narrator, at least as long as she dwells imaginatively on her life in Japan, is infectiously feminine. But I ended up believing that it was for the sake of directing attention away from meting out justice to others, focusing instead on the experience of self-blame that Ishiguro selected a largely female cast of characters and a far from omniscient, fallible female monologuist to tell their and the world's tale. If recovery from bitterness toward others who caused pain is what Anton's story is about, recovery from bitterness toward oneself for having been the cause of pain could be said to be Etsuko's story.

THE DYING VINE

Ronald Mawby

Ignorance may not be bliss, but it does seem to be a disease largely free
of painful symptoms, and so few are willing to undergo the radical and
frightening transformation that is the cure.

—*Grey McLachlan*

"RARE, UNPOPULAR, AND DESIRABLE"

"RARE, UNPOPULAR, AND DESIRABLE"—with these terms T. S. Eliot describes
poetic sensibility. The terms would serve as well to describe a rigorous liberal education. Liberal education I take to be a process that consists in part
in the acquisition of the arts of intentional inquiry, in part in the habit of
employing those arts, and in part in the transformations of the soul that
can result when inquiry is directed at significant questions.[1] The arts of
intentional inquiry I believe give a clear contemporary meaning to the liberal arts, which are the freeing arts of the intellect. An intellect that possesses
the knowledge, skills, and habits that enable it to guide its own inquiries and
learn quickly and well is free in a double sense: it is sovereign over its own
activities and it has the power to perform its proper functions of understanding, appreciating, and choosing. In a pluralistic society, in which a
multitude of traditions stand behind us and a plethora of life choices stand
before us, we need an intelligent way to choose the ends that guide our
lives. Reflective exploration of the desirable forms of human life is thus one
aspect of liberal education. When reflective inquiry seriously takes up large
questions of permanent human significance, such as who we are and what
we ought to do, inevitably our implicit and usually thoughtless opinions are
drawn into the light. The reverberations of such inquiry can transform the
whole tenor of the mind, and such transformation I include as part of liberal education.

My central question here is this: Why should liberal education be such
a long, slow, difficult, and painful process of uncertain outcome? The answer
I propose is threefold and locates the difficulties directly in the nature of
liberal education. First, students who undertake a liberal education must

acquire through intentional inquiry the arts of intentional inquiry; they thus face a cognitive bootstrapping problem. Second, students often misconstrue the character of liberal education, and though their misconstruction is remediable in some degree, it does not occur quickly. Third, since liberal education addresses itself to fundamental issues, it is inherently disorienting, and students, who darkly glimpse education's tendency to unsettle them, always will be ambivalent about facing the danger of learning. I am not saying that liberal education is hopeless or pointless, nor that it cannot be made easier. I am saying that we delude ourselves if we think it ever can be made short or fast or easy or painless, or that teachers can simply control or measure its outcome. Let us see why.

Liberal Arts: Developmental Spirals and Vicious Circles

Liberal education consists in part in the acquisition of the liberal arts of intentional inquiry. The liberal arts of inquiry involve both operational and propositional knowledge—both knowing-how and knowing-that—and the processes by which we acquire the liberal arts are the same as those by which any kind of knowledge is attained.

Now the processes by which we attain knowledge are not uniform. In certain cases it appears that knowledge acquisition is fundamentally maturational, in that experience of the environment triggers rather than shapes what is acquired.[2] Knowledge acquisition in such cases tends to be common across individuals, regular in sequence, largely effortless, and, in any but the most horrific environments, inevitable. First language acquisition is the paradigm instance. Put a normal pre-pubescent child in any linguistic environment in the world and very soon the child will acquire the language. "Normal child" here covers a wide range, for with the exception of the severely retarded, language growth is basically identical across all intelligence levels. And acquisition is essentially effortless. Developmental psycholinguists estimate that six-year-olds know about 13,000 distinct words, which means that since their first birthday they have acquired an average of one new word every two waking hours.[3] Children pick these words out of the air, without a systematic course of instruction and without the deliberate study that adults must use to learn a new language. If everything were as easy to learn as a first language, education would be a snap.

But not everything is so easy to learn. Knowledge acquisition in other cases results only from intentional inquiry. For instance, although no one need intend to acquire a first language, no one learns quantum mechanics without intending to. In this case art must complete nature. Without the competencies provided by maturational processes, intentional inquiry would not be possible. But without intentional inquiry, these underlying competencies would often remain merely potentials.[4] Mathematics above the elementary level, modern scientific and technical knowledge, and advanced levels of literacy all depend largely for their acquisition upon intentional learning.

In the domains of knowledge acquired through intentional inquiry we find wide individual differences, a notable influence of education, and differences in skill level due to differences in "artfulness" at inquiry (e.g., meta-cognitive strategies). This is to be expected, for in these domains the acquisition process is largely directed by deliberate, effortful, intentional means. It is not the all-but-inevitable outcome of normal transactions with the world. Arts of inquiry must be employed for this type of cognitive development to occur.

When we ask how one acquires artfulness at inquiry, we discover part of the difficulty of liberal education. The crux is this: the skills and habits by which one acquires the liberal arts of inquiry are themselves the liberal arts. We bootstrap ourselves from less developed to more developed forms of these arts. All teachers agree that the easiest students to teach are those who already know what we are teaching. Nature, the teacher of first languages, succeeds so well because her students are born knowing. If college freshman classes were filled with college graduates, teaching freshman might be a breeze; if all first-year graduate students were post-docs, graduate seminars would go better. But when the conditions for knowledge acquisition consist precisely in the knowledge that is to be acquired, we should expect acquisition to be long, slow, and difficult.

Liberal education consists not just in acquiring the liberal arts of inquiry, but in habitually employing them. The habit of employing the liberal arts is the habit of thinking, and like knowledge acquisition, thinking is not a uniform process. As the cognitive psychologists put it, cognition has distinct modes. Whereas in knowledge acquisition the relevant contrast is between intentional and maturational, in cognitive processing the relevant contrast is between intentional and automatic. The paradigm of automatic cognitive processing is perception. Perception is easy, fast, and mandatory. Whatever the computational or causal complexities in the sequences that link ambient objects to perceptual experience, perception is phenomenologically immediate. To look is to see, and while we are awake we can hardly avoid perceiving. Perception occurs automatically and effortlessly, and so if one has a perceptual capacity little deliberate choice or effort is required to employ it.

Contrast perception with intentional inquiry. While to look is to see, to inquire is not always to discover. A perceptual question, such as what is behind me, can be answered with a glance. A conceptual question that arises during inquiry, such as what is behind the difficulty of education, will in general never have such a direct, immediate, and effortless answer. Conceptual inquiry is neither easy nor fast nor mandatory. It must be sustained by deliberate intentional effort. Even if one has the ability to inquire, one must choose to do so. Whereas perceiving is easy, thinking is hard.

I mentioned that mathematical and scientific knowledge depend upon intentional inquiry. One difficulty with mathematical and scientific education is that in these domains learners must make conscious and explicit what is automatic in perception, namely, the inferential links between evidence and conclusion. A student may memorize a scientific fact, and such a fact as an isolated true proposition validated by an authority may be acquired by the learner with the same ease and immediacy as a perceptual fact. Indeed, in this form it just is a perceptual fact: it is the content of a linguistic perception—one knows what one has been told. But merely to have been told such a fact is not to know the fact scientifically. A scientific fact is a (perhaps defeasible) inference from an organized body of evidence. To know the fact scientifically is to know its place and standing in that evidentiary body, and such knowledge comes neither immediately nor easily. Of course as one becomes more expert in a domain, inferences therein become more automatic. The expert sees at a glance the import of a new piece of evidence. But the condition for such intellectual seeing is the prior acquisition of the knowledge that enables one to see, and acquiring that prior knowledge demands extensive hard thinking.

The knowledge acquisition and cognitive processing conclusions converge. Insofar as liberal education involves possessing the liberal arts of inquiry and habitually employing them, liberal education is difficult. The conditions for acquiring a liberal education are just the conditions that describe part of what is to be acquired: the abilities and habits that support fruitful inquiry. The best candidates for a liberal education thus fall into two classes: (a) those who have the ability but not the habit—the bright but lazy student who can become ignited with a passion that turns into a habit of reflection—and (b) those who lack some abilities but have habits that support their acquisition—the attentive and industrious student who will begin to grow by dint of effort, and whose growing efforts will snowball. These two groups are each halfway there, and the half they have can be used to acquire the half they lack. By engaging in and reflecting on intentional inquiry, i.e., by thinking and thinking about what they are doing, their skills may become their proper possessions: intellectual arts that are deployed consciously, freely, deliberately and generally. But a student with neither wit nor discipline has a much harder time. Whereas the able can bootstrap themselves up a developmental spiral, the less able seem trapped in a vicious circle.

MISCONSTRUING THE PROCESS: THREE IMAGES OF EDUCATION

Suppose all of our students had the ability to progress up the developmental spiral. What other obstacles might stand in the way of their advance? In my experience one of the greatest impediments to liberal education is an erroneous understanding of what that education is all about. Naturally a complete misunderstanding of what one is engaged in makes a significant obstacle to success. One is likely to do the wrong things, or fail to do the right things, and so any intellectual activity that occurs will likely be wasted. We can explore various understandings and misunderstandings of liberal education by looking at three images of teaching and learning, namely, filling an empty container, sowing seeds, and assisting in the birth of ideas.

Pouring

The first image is the most common, in that it underlies most educational practice, though it is rarely advocated in educational theory. The image posits the mind as a container and knowledge as a liquid that the mind contains. Containers are of various sizes, filled to different levels. The size of the container indicates intellectual capacity, the level of the container indicates level of knowledge. The teacher is understood to be filled more fully than the students. This is why elementary and secondary teachers are required to have college degrees, and college teachers are required to have graduate degrees.

Teaching on this model consists in pouring out knowledge; learning consists in catching and holding the knowledge poured out. What is required for the transfer of knowledge is that the student be still so the knowledge is not poured out wastefully. That is the first lesson children learn in grammar school. They must sit still, and pay attention. And that is all. The teacher must pour out knowledge. And that is all. The teacher actively pours, the student passively receives. The responsibility of the teacher is to keep order and pour accurately.

At the end of the pouring process the teacher tests reception and retention by tapping into the students' containers at various levels. The highest level at which knowledge pours back out indicates the appropriate grade assignment. For instance, if the hole bored at the 70% mark spews out liquid, but the hole at the 80% mark does not, then the student is assumed to possess only 70% of the knowledge. On this image to have knowledge is to be able to spout off on demand.

Just as liquids take the shape of their containers, the knowledge takes the form of the student, and does not change that form. The shape of the student's soul is not altered by the process of learning. Empty or full, the student is the same shape. And when the liquid leaks out or evaporates, the container is as it was before the liquid entered it. Forgotten knowledge leaves no trace. In this image knowledge and the mind are externally related.

The pouring model is charmingly simple. It would be very nice if it were true. It would simplify the problems of education enormously if it were true. But it is not true. That the pouring image is false can be seen by an example. Let me pour out some knowledge for you. "Any torsion module of finite type over a principal ideal domain is isomorphic to a biproduct of primary cyclic modules." For most of you, I trust, as for me, this sentence conveys nothing. I recognize that it is English, but I have no idea what it means. That is, I cannot construct a representation of its meaning. I can hear it, I can say it, I could memorize it for the test on Friday, but I cannot understand it. For what strikes my ear is an acoustic signal, not a meaning. The meaning must be apprehended by me, by my mind. The acoustic signal provides the occasion for an understanding, but it cannot compel its own understanding. Thus when teachers, either living teachers or books, pour out speech, it is not the case that learners can be still and passively be filled. For what is poured out must be grasped, made intelligible, not just overheard but understood, in order for learning to occur.

Another obvious flaw in the image is that liquid is conserved during pouring but knowledge is replicated in transmission. That is, if you teach me something that I did not know before, then knowledge has been doubled. You don't lose your knowledge by giving it to me. This fact suggests that knowledge should be depicted as an informing pattern, not an inert substance.

And there is a further problem with the pouring model. How can knowledge be acquired in the first place? While the pouring model does not in fact account for transmission, it cannot even pretend to account for any original acquisition of knowledge. New knowledge (if there be such) must be obtained without it being poured out by someone who already knows it. For anyone who seeks to think independently, anyone who strives to be a leader in any sense, this shortcoming is fatal. For even if education were pouring, a leader would have to be first in line on the bucket brigade, pouring out to others what has not been poured out before. That is, a leader must face novel situations, situations that have not been faced before. Some people in effect say that there are no novel situations, that everything has been faced and mastered. If so, then it is true that leadership simply demands fidelity to past insights. The insights of the elders are sufficient. But even if that were true, and I believe that it is not, the judgment of which past situation the present one resembles is not something that the elders can teach. The application of knowledge to circumstances is not part of the pouring model. The image purports to show how one acquires knowledge, not how one uses it. Whatever one must do to acquire judgment, it is not part of this process of teaching and learning. The pouring image implies that learning in school has little if any relation to learning on one's own out of school. It implies that learning by being taught is totally unlike learning on one's own, so it provides no insight into how to become one's own teacher, i.e., an independent learner.

Sowing

The pouring image, insofar as it seems plausible, seems so because of its confusion with a second, better, image. This better image is agricultural. The teacher is the sower, the knowledge is contained in the seeds, and the students are the soil into which the seeds are sown. The classic presentation of this image occurs in Jesus's Gospel parable:

> And he told them many things in parables, saying: "A sower went out to sow. And as he sowed, some seeds fell along the path, and the birds came and devoured them. Other seeds fell on rocky ground, where they had not much soil, and immediately they sprang up, since they had no depth of soil, but when the sun rose they were scorched; and since they had no root

they withered away. Other seeds fell upon thorns, and the thorns grew up and choked them. Other seeds fell on good soil and brought forth grain, some a hundredfold, some sixty, some thirty. He who has ears to hear, let him hear." Then the disciples came and said to him, "Why do you speak to them in parables?" And he answered them, "To you it has been given to know the secrets of the kingdom of heaven, but to them it has not been given. For to him who has will more be given, and he will have abundance; but from him who has not, even what he has will be taken away. This is why I speak to them in parables, because seeing they do not see, and hearing they do not hear, nor do they understand."[5]

The words of the teacher are the seeds, and the soil must make them grow into fully mature meanings or genuine knowledge. The soil is the condition for the growth of knowledge. Seeds take root and grow, and when the plants come to fruition they too can broadcast seeds, and thus knowledge propagates itself. The outcome depends in part on the quality of the seeds, in part on the ministrations of the farmer, and in part on the fertility of the soil. The fertility of the soil indicates intellectual capacity and receptiveness. Just as capacities differ across subject matters, so a given soil is not equally fertile for all crops. For some of us music will never flourish in our soil; for some of us mathematics will always be a struggle; for some of us history, or poetry, or natural sciences will always require careful tending and cultivation, while other subjects grow in us like weeds.

Jesus articulates a commonplace of growth when he says the more one has, the more that will be added. This accords with our understanding of the conditions for liberal education. The more one already has such an education, the more likely one is to profit from further exposure. If one has ears to hear, one can hear. If not, then all the talk in the world will strike one's ear as a parable not understood.

The use of parable itself points to the importance of correctly construing what one is engaged in. Jesus presents himself to the disciples as sent from the Father to tell about the kingdom of heaven. If his auditors think Jesus is an agricultural extension agent describing planting techniques, then "hearing they will not hear."

Soils can be prepared for planting, then watered and fertilized and weeded—these actions give us some control over the fertility of the soil (unlike the capacity of a container, which is fixed). We can "root away the noisome weeds which without profit suck the soil's fertility from wholesome flowers."[6] Whereas the pouring image depicts a homogeneous liquid of opinion, the sowing image permits us to distinguish the weeds of false-hood from the proper plants of truth. Preparing the soil, deciding what and where and when to plant, and tending the young shoots are all tasks for the farmer. While there is much that teachers can do, some things, like the weather, are out of their control.

As soil is prepared it is changed or "amended," as the gardeners say. Notice also that even if one forgets what one has learned, even if a plant grows only to die, still the dead plant can enrich the soil, and improve the growth of another like plant, or even a different plant if their requirements are similar. Thus not only can the soil be changed in preparation for learn-ing, but the process of growing knowledge itself can change the soil. Mind and knowledge are not independent. They are internally related, and forgot-ten knowledge leaves a trace. Even after factual details are lost, education can alter the power and tenor of a mind.

The agents at work in this image of learning are the agriculturist, the seed, and the soil. Each is necessary; each is a cause; each is responsible. The teaching art completes or perfects nature, but that means largely that it helps a good nature take its proper course. The best farmer cannot grow bad seed in poor soil. The best soil fails with poor seed, and the best seed fails in poor soil.

We distinguish the seed from the developed plant; the student must do something with what the teacher presents. A soil that merely retains a seed in the way that it is planted has failed. Nourished by an active mind, a seed will develop into something that is historically continuous with its origin but different in form and function. In fertile soil an idea will develop, and thereby multiply its relevance and potency, perhaps a hundredfold. One test of success is whether the grown plant can reproduce itself, that is, can the student under the proper conditions teach another? If not, then the plant is in some way immature, not fully developed.

Monoculture in the mind, or learning just one thing, has its limitations, as farmers often find. The natural ecosystem is a multiculture, which is usu-ally more resistant to pests and not so hard on the soil. The mind that grows only one kind of crop becomes exhausted easily and the prey of pests. Per-haps it only exaggerates a truth to say that the person who knows only one thing doesn't even know that thing.

Growing, unlike pouring, takes a long time, and there is a seasonal rhythm to it, just as there is a rhythm to education. Often the results of sowing seeds are hard to discern in the early stages. To tell whether any good will come is not easy. "You shall know them by their fruits" is right. There is no simple test, no tap-level kind of test, that can be applied immediately. We see sprouts, and we take that as a sign, but we really want fully matured flowering plants. We who are college teachers are in the position of nurserymen. Even our graduates are still only seedlings.

The best plants come from the best seed. The truly excellent books are the best seed, gotten from the best minds in the world. When liberal education is based on reading excellent books, the real teachers are the books, for the books contain the seeds. The difference between bad seed, mediocre seed, and superlative seed is not always evident to one who sees only the seed. Thus teachers who have seen the plants rather than students who have not should be responsible for choosing what to read. The teacher who is present in the classroom is largely occupied with choosing the books and preparing the conditions for implantation. The classroom teachers help to prepare the conditions, promote the occasion, but the learning is provided by the interaction between the students and the books. The high aim of teachers is to make the soil, the student's soul, able to cultivate itself or sustain itself as an ongoing ecosystem. Sustainable agriculture resembles life-long learning.

Midwifery

The third image of teaching and learning is drawn from the Platonic dialogue *Theaetetus,* in which Socrates compares himself to a midwife, an idea to an unborn child, and the student with whom he converses to an expectant mother.

> THEAETETUS: . . . I am myself incapable of either persuading myself that I say anything adequately or hearing some one else speaking in just the way you urge, and I'm incapable as well of getting rid of my concern with it.
>
> SOCRATES: The reason is, my dear Theaetetus, that you're suffering labor pains, on account of your not being empty but pregnant.[7]
>
> SOCRATES: . . . And whoever associate with me undergo this same thing as women in giving birth do. They suffer labor-pains and are filled with perplexity for nights and days far more than women are, and my art is capable of arousing this kind of labor-pain and putting it to rest.[8]

Just as a farmer knows what seed to plant in which soil, so the midwife knows what sort of unions to encourage:

SOCRATES: Have you perceived this, that . . . [midwives] are all-wise when it comes to getting to know what sort of woman must be with what sort of man to give birth to the best possible children?[9]

The unborn child is the idea that is hidden in the student. The task of the teacher is to assist in the birth of the student's conceptions—to help the ideas come out head first and right side up—and in the judgment of their value—to help decide whether the idea should be retained or cast away.

SOCRATES: . . . my art of midwifery . . . examines their souls in giving birth and not their bodies. But this is the greatest thing in our art, to be capable of assaying in every way whether the thought of the young is giving birth to an image and a lie or something fruitful and true.[10]

In this image learning is birthing. The teacher helps in the labor of the student, but clearly the student is the one expending the effort. The teacher assists, guides, cajoles, offers reassurance about the necessary pain and the often successful outcome. The teacher has seen many births, perhaps has given birth and knows the pangs. The teacher's calm and experience can be a great aid, yet in the end it is the student who brings an idea forth. The knowledge that will be the student's own is in the student, not in the teacher.

The outcome of a pregnancy cannot easily be foreseen. Today we have genetic testing, ultrasound and the like, but these give us signs and outlines of what remains hidden. Likewise with the testing of knowledge. We have signs and outlines, but that is all. Even the delivered baby has a long way to go to reach maturity. Having an idea and having a completely developed idea are very far from being the same. As in the sowing image, the wished-for outcome of the processes of teaching and learning cannot be completely foreseen.

The high aim of the midwife would be to have the mother learn to be a midwife, both for herself and for others. Helping others bring knowledge to birth can help you learn how to bring your own knowledge to birth. The best way to learn something is to teach it.[11]

Our first image was filling an emptiness. Our current image is emptying a fullness. We have arrived at the educational view of Jeeves, the butler in the P. G. Wodehouse stories, who reminds young master Bertram that "education is a drawing out and not a putting in." Notice the great difference between this image and the pouring image. The container does not change shape. Pregnant women do change shape. One is altered by having ideas quicken inside one. It may be frightening, overwhelming, to find yourself changing. One needs faith in the process, hope in the outcome, an outcome that for a long time cannot be seen clearly.

Both the organic images, as images, permit the creation of something that is novel. Whereas an inert liquid can only be lost in transmission, a living principle of knowledge can out of itself develop something new. Sports occur, variation occurs and if useful they may be retained, bred for, and thus established.

Filling an empty container, preparing the soil and implanting seeds, and bringing out into the light what is present but concealed—each successive image of teaching makes the student more active, more responsible, more involved. The final image of course is compatible with the second image. One may think of birth as the proper outcome of conception. In fact the combination of the last two images might depict the principles and practices of a liberal arts college. Find the best seed, the best books of the best minds, and ask students to conceive of these ideas. The faculty would try to create propitious conditions—an atmosphere that combines the dignity appropriate to the seriousness of the endeavor with an atmosphere of relaxation and fun appropriate to any process of conception. On this understanding education is serious play. But like farming—"In the sweat of thy face shalt thou eat bread"—and birthing—"in sorrow thou shalt bring forth children"—learning is not easy.

I prefaced these three images by saying that one obstacle to education is a misunderstanding of its nature. Wrong images are obstacles indeed. A student with the pouring model of education is likely to think that education will occur as long as teachers are competent and students are not disruptive. It won't. The pouring image encourages passive reception, static retention, and mindless reiteration. Even the better images can be perverted. If one fails to distinguish between the seed and the plant that springs from it, one can remain so tied to the literal words of the teacher that their extended range of meanings and implications is lost. Socrates distinguishes between viable and unviable offspring, but a student whose version of the birthing image lacks that critical feature may think that every idea extruded from the soul is a fresh-faced beauty. However, education does not consist in the public display and consensual or authoritative validation of whatever nonsense one happens to believe. It is rather an intense scrutiny of the value of what is within us. A picture of education that cannot admit the distinction of true and false or better and worse entails that there is no important difference between being educated and uneducated. Such a picture is not likely to further one's educational efforts.

THE DYING VINE—*IN VINO VERITAS*

Education, rightly understood, is thus a branch of agriculture. Now there are various theories of agriculture, and this leads me to my title, the dying vine. My brother is engaged in viticulture and enology, that is, he grows grapes and makes wine. He tells me that the French viticulturists have a saying: "To make a truly great wine grape the vines must suffer." The French believe this, and so, being rational, have made it the basis of a viticulture technique they call the dying vine. Vines are stressed almost to their limit, they are made to suffer, in order that they may produce something rich and wonderful. Pampered vines produce mediocre fruit. Vines that have been stressed call upon deep resources within themselves and produce the finest fruit.

Now it is my experience and my belief that the same is true of education. You might think that at the finest schools the students would work less hard, or at least no harder, than at more ordinary schools. After all, the students are presumably more gifted, the teachers presumably more expert, so more could be done in less time. In fact, however, the better the school, the greater the demands. Students at MIT and Cal Tech, for instance, routinely study 60 or 70 hours each week. They are stressed, and they often produce something rich and wonderful.

The dying vine teaches us that great demands are a condition for genuine education. It is also true that genuine education, deep education, education that makes a significant difference, makes great demands. I have said that liberal education consists in part in the acquisition of the arts of intentional inquiry, in part in the habit of employing those arts, and in part in the transformations of the soul that can result when such inquiry is directed at significant questions. "Transformations of the soul" point us toward a third factor in the difficulty of liberal education. We approach this factor through an explanation of the paradoxical fact that the pouring model is almost universally condemned in theory and almost universally employed in practice. Why should that be?

THE DANGER OF LEARNING

The answer is not hard, though it is various, since many factors concur. The weight of traditional practices is heavy. Logistics and resource limitations push practitioners toward the pouring model. But other reasons lie deeper. In the pouring model the roles are clear. The teacher tells the truth, the students receive the message. The teacher actively teaches, the students passively learn. The teacher is in control, and the students are relieved of responsibility for guiding the process. Imagine what it feels like for a teacher to give up that control. A teacher faces twenty students with no prepared script. What if nothing happens, or what if the wrong things happen? If the teacher doesn't teach, how will anyone learn? How can teachers, who feel responsible, give up control over a process whose outcome is their responsibility? To give up control is dangerous.

And for the students? There is a comfort in being told what to do by one who is in authority. The student wants to be told what to do. Responsibility is a burden. And how can one who is admittedly ignorant be expected to take responsibility for the process of learning? The student feels, when the pouring model is abandoned, that the teacher is throwing him into the deep end of the pool and calling that a swimming lesson. To give up authoritative guidance, to accept that education is one of the things that no one can do for you, is frightening.

Thus the pouring model persists because the alternatives are perceived as dangerous. The perception is accurate. Education is a dangerous business. Especially dangerous is liberal education, which aims at transformation. One problem we noted with the pouring model is that the liquid has no effect on the shape of the container. The learner is not transformed by the learning. Certainly there are things that one can learn that have just that null effect. There are things that one can keep in mind but at arm's length, so to speak. But when the liberal arts are addressed to significant questions, education becomes a more enveloping activity, an activity that embraces one's whole soul and whole life. Examining the beginnings and the ends of our whole life and thought, from the presuppositions upon which we direct our activities to the ultimate ends at which we aim, puts our whole lives at stake. And that is always a difficult and dangerous task. With so much at stake one cannot escape the sense of risk. The danger of having one's established order broken is the danger of learning.

The important distinction here is between learning as addition and learning as transformation. Adding a new item of information onto an existing cognitive structure need not be frightening or difficult. For the small price of paying attention one's knowledge is increased. One is unchanged but for knowing more. Transformation is otherwise. Imagine a glass breaking. What once was whole and solid shatters, its integrity gone, whatever it contained spilling out and escaping. Now imagine a cell dividing. What once was whole and single splits and changes, its simple unity lost, the unity to be regained only in a more complex form. Every transformation involves breaking. Since deep learning implies transformation, and transformation implies breaking, a condition for deep learning to occur is that the learner be willing to be broken. What divides the breaking of a glass from the breaking of a cell is that the latter, once broken, can regain its wholeness in a new form. The old form is broken and a new form emerges. The new form is better than the old. When something breaks and the result is an improvement on the original, we call it a lucky break. Liberal education, when successful, is a lucky break.

Not all breaks are lucky. Too often the initial form is abolished and replaced by something less good than the original. The half-educated person is one who, thinking himself sophisticated, is in fact merely sophistical. When Socrates was prosecuted by the Athenians as a corrupter of youth, a disbeliever in the gods of the city and a teacher of new gods, there was something in the indictment. The existence of the city—the social and political order—depends on forming the young in a certain way. Education as transformation requires examining and perhaps overturning rather than simply sustaining the existing formation. Even if ultimately the existence of the city depends on wise rule, and wise rule depends on deep education, still political concern over the danger of education is real. Sometimes it seems that an existing core of largely true opinions should be left alone, for too often when education starts but stops too soon the core will be broken only to be replaced by worse opinions instead of better. Since deep education is dangerous, political as well as psychological causes support shallower education such as the pouring model depicts.

Let us put to one side the traditional, logistical, and political obstacles to genuine education, and focus on the intrinsic danger of learning. Radical transformation is no picnic. I have used the Biblical image of sowing seeds, and the Platonic image of midwifery. What do the Bible and Plato say about transformation? In Christianity radical transformation appears as conversion. Jesus says "I bring not peace but a sword." We read in Acts that Peter speaks the Word and cuts them to the heart, for "how else but through a broken heart can Lord Jesus enter in?" In Plato we find a second image of education in which what is hidden in darkness is delivered into the light. I refer of course to the image of the cave in the *Republic*. As you will recollect, it goes like this.

> "[M]ake an image of our nature in its education and want of education, likening it to a condition of the following kind. See human beings as

though they were in an underground cavelike dwelling with its entrance, a long one, open to the light across the whole width of the cave. They are in it from childhood with their legs and necks in bonds so that they are fixed, seeing only in front of them, unable because of the bond to turn their heads all the way around. Their light is from a fire burning far above and behind them. Between the fire and the prisoners there is a road above, along which we see a wall, built like the partitions puppet-handlers set in front of the human beings and over which they show the puppets."

"I see," he said.

"Then also see along this wall human beings carrying all sorts of artifacts, which project above the wall, and statues of men and other animals wrought from stone, wood, and every kind of material; as is to be expected, some of the carriers utter sounds while others are silent."

"It's a strange image," he said, "and strange prisoners you're telling of."

"They're like us," I said.[12]

The education that liberates loosens the bonds, turns one around, and pushes one out into the light of the true day. It is the birth not just of this or that idea, but of the whole soul. This birth is traumatic.

Take a man who is released and suddenly compelled to stand up, to turn his neck around, to walk and look up toward the light; and who, moreover, in doing all this is in pain and, because he is dazzled, is unable to make out those things whose shadows he saw before. . . . Don't you suppose he'd be at a loss?[13]

"And if," I said, "someone dragged him away from there by force along the rough, steep, upward way and didn't let him go before he had dragged him out into the light of the sun, wouldn't he be distressed and annoyed at being so dragged?"[14]

Radical transformation as such, whether it be from worse to better or better to worse, is disorienting.

[T]here are two kinds of disturbances of the eyes, stemming from two sources—when they have been transferred from light to darkness and when they have been transferred from darkness to light. . . . [T]hese same things happen to a soul too. . . .[15]

The Christian convert has his heart cut open so that the seeds of salvation can be sown therein. The Platonic convert is twisted around, forced to rise, then pushed up and out so that the bright light breaks painfully into his eyes. Who is going to lay his heart open to that sword, or eagerly abet his expulsion from the familiar? Liberal education in these images comes to seem not merely difficult but impossible.

Liberal education is difficult because it is impossible. I find a melancholy satisfaction in that formulation. Of course it is not impossible in the way that squaring the circle is impossible. Liberal education demands whole-hearted, enthusiastic participation in a process that is inherently painful and disorienting. It is impossible in the way that psychoanalysis is impossible.

PSYCHOANALYTIC AFFINITIES

Whatever one thinks of the truth of psychoanalytic theory or the efficacy of its technique, one can recognize in the depth and seriousness of its aim an affinity with liberal education. Psychoanalysis too aims at a certain freedom of mind, a maturity that is not an inevitable achievement, and it too seeks its end by a re-orientation of the soul that has as cause and consequence an enlarged awareness. Analysis and education also have similar courses. Consider that the patient in psychoanalytic treatment willingly attends hour-long sessions several times each week for a period of years. The patient pays the analyst a fee that may be nearly two hundred dollars per hour. The commitment of time and money is considerable, even astonishing. What makes it more astonishing is that a good part of the treatment is taken up with what is called "the analysis of the resistance," which means the analytic exploration of the patient's resistance to the processes needed to get well.

The resemblance between psychoanalytic treatment and liberal education is striking—the same regular investment in time and money coupled with steady resistance to the process. Freud acknowledged that, like liberal education, analytic therapy is a long, slow, difficult process, and hence from a medical viewpoint is not ideal. Freud believed it to be the therapy of choice only because no other methods were effective.

> From certain of my remarks you will have gathered that there are many characteristics in the analytic method which prevent it from being an ideal form of therapy. *Tuto, cito, jucunde:* investigation and probing do not indicate speedy results, and the resistance I have mentioned would prepare you to expect unpleasantness of various kinds.[16]

Freud also said that from an analytic viewpoint most patients are not ideal candidates for the therapy, and thus full success is likely to be rare.

> The patients who are bound to be most welcome to him are those who ask him to give them complete health, in so far as that is attainable, and who

place as much time at his disposal as is necessary for the process of recovery. Such favorable conditions as these are, of course, to be looked for in only a few cases.[17]

Analytic therapy resembles liberal education also in that it is of uncertain outcome. The analyst attempts to initiate a process that he cannot completely control.

> The analyst is certainly able to do a great deal, but he cannot determine beforehand exactly what results he will effect. He sets in motion a process, that of the resolving of existing repressions. He can supervise this process, further it, remove obstacles in its way, and he can undoubtedly vitiate much of it. But on the whole, once begun, it goes its own way and does not allow either the direction it takes or the order in which it picks up its points to be prescribed for it.[18]

Like liberal education, the whole psychoanalytic undertaking is fraught with difficulties, and the demands on the practitioner are formidable. Freud summarizes in a famous statement written near the end of his life.

> Here let us pause for a moment to assure the analyst that he has our sincere sympathy in the very exacting demands he has to fulfil in carrying out his activities. It almost looks as if analysis were the third of those 'impossible' professions in which one can be sure beforehand of achieving unsatisfying results. The other two, which have been known much longer, are education and government.[19]

Rare, Unpopular, but Desirable

Educational fashions come and go, but the agony of radical transition abides. If, as I believe, the main obstacles to liberal education lie within the learner, it is there that educational efforts must be directed. In my university the current fashions are outcomes assessment, educational technologies, and online learning. These are externals that may be either useful or useless, depending on whether they can be brought to bear on the real issues, the most important of which is the degree to which students center themselves on, and so partially identify with, their intellectual curiosity.

Liberal education as I understand it is likely to remain rare and unpopular. Cognitive bootstrapping presents so many difficulties that fully successful liberal education is likely to be rare. The disorientation inherent in radical transformation conflicts with the universal desire to be comfortable and ensures that liberal education is likely to be unpopular. Given these facts, why, we may ask, should liberal education be desirable? I will touch very briefly on this question by way of conclusion.

Liberal education frees us from something and for something. It frees us from certain forms of enslaving folly. As F. H. Bradley said in defense of the study of philosophy,

> I think it quite necessary, even on the view that this study can produce no positive results, that it should still be pursued. There is, so far as I can see, no other certain way of protecting ourselves against dogmatic superstition. . . . [T]he mind which has thought sincerely on first principles . . . is too good to become a slave, either to stupid fanaticism or dishonest sophistry.[20]

But the prophylactic or disinfectant effects of liberal education, though real, are not I think anyone's real motive for aiming to develop a free mind. Where art completes nature, one acquires the art to attain fullness of being. Liberal education is to be desired because it realizes one of our high potentialities and thus makes us more fully and completely what we are. When the liberal arts are present and active and at work on serious questions, we see that liberal education can produce something rich and strange, namely, the activity of genuine thoughtfulness. Beyond the swirl of opinion and the accidental vagaries of circumstance, there is a world available to thought that fascinates us by its very being. The thinking of a free mind contacts that world, partially and intermittently perhaps, but truly, and such thinking is its own reward, for the activity of human thought is beautiful. When what is fascinating awakens our intellect and our minds are free to be drawn into fully engaged activity, we are held in a stillness alive with wonders, and taste the heady and intoxicating fruit of the dying vine.

NOTES

1 This notion of liberal education is drawn from a cluster of related notions. Traditionally liberal education meant acquiring the liberal arts, which are the arts proper to a free person, i.e., one who was politically free and also at leisure, free from the necessity of earning a living. When one is free to live as one chooses, the question of what life is worth living comes to the fore, so liberal education involves investigation of the proper ends of human life. The traditional seven liberal arts of grammar, logic, rhetoric, arithmetic, geometry, astronomy and music were the arts through which one pursued the intellectual activity proper to a human being. These arts (which today probably would be called arts of language, reasoning, communication, mathematics as the study of discrete and continuous quantity, physics, and music theory, respectively) were acquired

largely through the study of texts, and its textual base tied liberal education to literacy. As education in the sciences and humanities became more divided, the humanities retained the emphasis on texts and literacy, so often today liberal education refers to education in the humanities.

2   See, for instance, Noam Chomsky, *Language and Problems of Knowledge* (Cambridge, Mass.: MIT Press, 1988); Jerry Fodor, *Representations* (Lexington, Vt.: Bradford Books, 1981).

3   See Steven Pinker, *The Language Instinct* (New York: William Morrow, 1994).

4   Considerable evidence shows that without intentional learning adults reason coherently with abstractions only in limited domains; see P. R. Dasen, ed., *Piagetian Psychology: Cross-cultural Contributions* (New York: Garner Press, 1977).

5   Matthew 13.3–13.

6   Shakespeare, *Richard II,* 3.4.37–40.

7   Plato, *Theaetetus,* translated by Seth Benardete. Included in *The Being of the Beautiful* (Chicago: University of Chicago Press, 1984), 148e.

8   Ibid., 150c–151b.

9   Ibid., 149d.

10 Ibid., 150c.

11 When as a young physicist David Bohm complained that he didn't understand quantum mechanics, his mentor told him, "Then you should write a book about it."

12 Plato, *Republic,* translated by Allan Bloom (New York: Basic Books, 1968), 514a–515a.

13 Ibid., 515d.

14 Ibid., 516a.

15 Ibid., 518a.

16 Sigmund Freud, "On Psychotherapy," in J. Strachey, gen. ed., *The Standard Edition of the Complete Psychological Works of Sigmund Freud,* vol. 7 (London: Hogarth, 1905), 262.

17 Sigmund Freud, "On Beginning the Treatment. Further Recommendations in the Technique of Psychoanalysis," in J. Strachey, gen. ed., *The Standard Edition of the Complete Psychological Works of Sigmund Freud,* vol. 12 (London: Hogarth, 1913), 131.

18 Ibid., 130.

19 Sigmund Freud, "Analysis Terminable and Interminable," in J. Strachey, gen. ed., *The Standard Edition of the Complete Psychological Works of Sigmund Freud,* vol. 23 (London: Hogarth, 1937), 248.

20 F. H. Bradley, *Appearance and Reality* (Oxford: Clarendon Press, 1893), 4–5.

How Did Theaetetus Prove His Theorem?

Barry Mazur

Eva Brann has taught me many things, among which is the importance of cherishing something that can be called "the long conversation." This "long conversation" has a time-splicing seamlessness: it can be picked up at any time, even after long absences, and its themes are as fresh and vital as ever, and more resonant, more weighty. I have come to think of some of the great communal intellectual projects, mathematics, for example, as a long conversation that humanity has had, is having, and will continue to have.

I feel blessed for having—for still having—some long specific conversations with Eva. One of these has to do with the idea of "appreciation," that important word which characterizes many of Eva's writings, e.g. about Jane Austen, or Homer, for these are *appreciations* in the profoundest sense of that word.

Surely the art of *appreciation* is a great gift of the spirit. The ex-wife of a great contemporary mathematician once said to me, with equal measures of exasperation and dearly paid-for admiration, that her ex-spouse was somehow overcome with appreciative joy every time he proved the Pythagorean theorem. This, to me, is high praise.

Others would have a different view. André Weil, in discussing the passage from "intuition to certitude" in mathematics, writes

> as the Gita teaches us, knowledge and indifference are attained at the same moment. Metaphysics has become mathematics, ready to form the material for a treatise whose icy beauty no longer has the power to move us.

In its fullest sense, *appreciation* means continuing to get pleasure, and acknowledging that pleasure, from the things we *think* we already understand, and getting yet more pleasure facing the things we don't yet understand.

How thankful we should be—about numbers—that the first few of them, 1, 2, 3, are so immediate to our understanding, or at least seem that way, and are so ubiquitously useful to us. Beyond these numerical companions lies more and yet more, trailing into the bittersweet landscape of the

Kantian *mathematical sublime* with its infinities and profundities. Happily, the "sweet" comes after the "bitter," in that, first, we bitterly face this infinite prospect: we try to grasp that ungraspable infinite with our finite minds. Only by so trying are we prepared for the sweet afterthought, that we, with our merely finite minds, can miraculously manage to comprehend the impossibility of this infinite enterprise. We each emerge from this experience with our personal consolation prize: a "starry sky within," as Kant calls it.

What isn't acknowledged in the picture painted in the previous paragraph is the abundance of insights, and sheer joy, to be had en route. Why is there so much to understand about 1, 2, 3 . . . ? Why are so many stepping stones in the path of this understanding so often joyous to the soul?

1 THREE ANCIENT THEOREMS ABOUT NUMBERS

I want to discuss three mathematical gems of number theory—sources of joy, in my opinion—all three of them magnificently formulated in ancient Greek texts that have come down to us, and each of them pointing the way to far greater depths. I said *magnificently formulated* rather than *magnificently proved* but, in fact, two out of the three are both formulated and proved in Euclid's *Elements*. The third of these, Theaetetus's Theorem, alluded to in the title of this article, is formulated elegantly as Propositions 24, 25 of Euclid's Book VIII. But we will later be commenting on the proofs of these propositions as given in Book VIII (see Note 4).

The three gems are:

- Euclid's proof of the infinitude of prime numbers, as in Proposition 20 of Book IX of the *Elements*.
- The "Euclidean algorithm," as in Propositions 1, 2, and 34 of Book VII of the *Elements*.
- Theaetetus' theorem that—when put in modern terms—says that the square root of a whole number A is rational (i.e., is a fraction or a whole number) if and only if A is a perfect square. [So, $\sqrt{2}$, $\sqrt{3}$, $\sqrt{5}$, $\sqrt{6}$, $\sqrt{7}$, $\sqrt{8}$, $\sqrt{10}$, $\sqrt{11}$, $\sqrt{12}$, $\sqrt{13}$, $\sqrt{14}$, $\sqrt{15}$, $\sqrt{17}$, $\sqrt{18}$, . . . are irrational.]

2 THEOREMS THAT PROVE THEMSELVES

All three of these theorems are wonderfully stated in the ancient literature. But I want to make a mild reformulation of the first two, to advertise a principle that I feel helps to clarify things, whenever it is applicable. I'll call it the **self-proving theorem** principle. In effect, if you can restate a theorem, without complicating it, so that its proof, or the essence of its proof, is *already contained in the statement of the theorem,* then you invariably have

- a more comprehensible theorem,
- a stronger theorem, and
- a shorter and more comprehensible proof!

The first two theorems have "self-proving" formulations. Here they are:

3 Euclid's Proof of the Infinitude of Primes

"Infinite" is a word with a built-in *negative polarity.* It is *not* something, i.e., not finite. There is a vast ancient conversation about this, centering on the shades of intention behind the word *apeiron* meaning—variously —unbounded, unlimited, indefinite, . . . all of these translations having a telltale negative prefix. All the more remarkable, then, is Dedekind's positive-sounding definition of **infinite set** as a Hilbert hotel, so to speak; that is, as set S for which there is a one-one correspondence of S with a proper subset of itself.

Whenever we say we have proven a negative *something,* we have usually actually proven a positive *something else.* The see-saw aspect of Kant's antinomies in the *Critique of Pure Reason* has that quality, where you shift polarity (negative-to-positive, positive-to-negative) as you change viewpoint. But proofs and demonstrations by their very nature "accentuate the positive."

Often, perhaps always, when we translate a positive statement to a negative one, there is information—sometimes subtle, sometimes gross—that is lost in this translation. One sees this most poignantly in some important theorems that are actually packaged as "negative results" and "limits of reason," and yet, what they are directly providing—before being recast as negative—is some extraordinary affirmation of reason. One example of this is Matjasevic's famous proof that there is no algorithm to determine whether a polynomial equation in many variables with whole number coefficients has or doesn't have a solution in whole numbers. I've just stated it in negative terms, but what is actually proven is the richness of diophantine expression: roughly speaking, that *any* collection of whole numbers that can be algorithmically listed by a computer can also be described by diophantine means.

All this is preamble to my stating Euclid's theorem in a positive way, essentially as it is given in the *Elements*, i.e., as a self-proving theorem. It is helpful to put the theorem in an "exchange of gifts" mode; that is, a "You give me an *X* and I'll give you a *Y*" format.

If you give me any finite (non-empty, of course!) collection of prime numbers, I will form the number N that is 1 more than the product of all the primes in the collection, so that every prime in your collection has the property that when N is divided by it, there is a remainder of 1. There exists at least one prime number dividing this number N and any prime number dividing N is new in the sense that it is not in your initial collection.

The proof of this is essentially contained in its statement. My number *N* is contrived to have the property that all the primes of your collection cannot be prime divisors of *N*, for they each leave a remainder of 1 when one tries to divide my *N* by them. But *N*, being bigger than 1, has some prime dividing it.

For example, if you gave me the "collection" consisting only of the prime 2, the *N* that I would form would be 2 + 1 or *N* = 3, which is itself a "new" prime not on your list. If then, you gave me as list the primes 2 and 3, the N that I would form would be 2 · 3 + 1, or *N* = 7, again itself a "new" prime not on your list. If you gave me as list 2, 3 and 7, my *N* would be 2 · 3 · 7 + 1 = 43, and yet again it would be itself a "new" prime not on your list. If you enriched your list with this newly found prime, and give me 2, 3, 7, 43, I would form as "my" *N*, the number *N* = 2 · 3 · 7 · 43 + 1 = 1807. Now my *N* is not prime—as it had been in the previous cases— for it factors: 1807 = 13 × 139. Both factors, 13 and 139, are primes. At this point we have a bonanza, in that both of these primes, 13 and 139— as we would have known, from Euclid's proof even without looking back at our list—are "new," i.e., not on our list.

The general consequence, then, is that *no* finite list that you could give me will exhaust the totality of all prime numbers: I have shown you a way of finding new prime numbers that are not on *any* finite list. What a mixture we have here of simplicity and depth!

4 THE EUCLIDEAN ALGORITHM

When I talk of "number" I will mean positive whole number. A **divisor** of a number *N* is a number *d* that *divides N evenly*, meaning that it divides

N with *no remainder;* in other words, the number *d* is a divisor of *N* if, and only if, the fraction *N/d* is a whole number.

So, for example, 4 is a *divisor* of 12, for 12 divided by 4 is 3. But 5, for example, is not a divisor of 12: if you try to divide 12 by 5 you get a *remainder* of 2. In fact the only *divisors* of 12 are

1, 2, 3, 4, 6, and 12 itself.

We need only two other pieces of official vocabulary, *common divisors* and *greatest common divisor,* and they each have the meanings that you might expect: If you have a pair of numbers, a **common divisor** of them is just a number that is a divisor of each of them. For example, the common divisors of the pair 12 and 18 are 1, 2, 3, and 6. The **greatest common divisor** of a pair of numbers is the largest of their common divisors. So, the *greatest common divisor* of the pair 12 and 18 is 6.

This notion of *greatest common divisor* is pivotal in any dealings one has with numbers, and a major insight in Euclid's number theory—that is, his Book VII—is the recognition of the key role played by greatest common divisor, which is, nowadays, lovingly given the acronym GCD.

In our example, above, we easily worked out that the greatest common divisor of 12 and 18 is 6. But when the pair of numbers gets large, it is not immediately apparent how to compute their greatest common divisor. This is where the Euclidean Algorithm comes in. I'll state it in its splendid simplicity:

> *Suppose you are given a pair of numbers A and B with A greater than B. Any common divisor of A and B is a common divisor of B and A − B; and conversely, any common divisor of B and A − B is a common divisor of A and B.*

That's it! In the above modest sentence you have the working innards of the single most used algorithm in the history of algorithms. Not only is it, when spiffed up the tiniest bit, a fast-working process, but it is the very model of a fast-working process; its *rate of operation* sets the standard by which the speed of other algorithms is judged. And the proof of the Euclidean Algorithm? It depends on nothing more than knowing that if a number divides *A* and *B* then it divides *A* − *B* and *B*; and conversely. In a sense, the Euclidean Algorithm is simply stating its own proof.

Now its *proof* may be immediate, but its *use* is far-reaching. The beauty is that you can run this little machine first forward, and then backward, and in each of these runs you will get (different) important information.

Here is a brief "Manual for Use" of this Euclidean Algorithm (cast in a slightly more modern idiom than you will find in Euclid).

To get the *greatest* common divisor of any two numbers, A and B, you run the algorithm forward. I mentioned above that to get it to be speedy you should spiff it up a bit. Here's how. If A is greater than B, you may as well subtract B as many times from A as you can, all at once, to arrive at a number, A − nB, that is less than or equal to B. Then the numbers B and A − nB have the same GCD as A and B do. Repeated application of this Euclidean Algorithm will successively reduce the size of the pair of numbers whose greatest common divisor you are seeking.

This reduction of size of the numbers we are dealing with is a crucial point. *Any* process that has to do with (positive whole) numbers and whose application either reduces the size of the numbers being dealt with, or else terminates, *must terminate.*

This is the case with our Euclidean Algorithm. Moreover, the chain of iterated application of this algorithm *can only* no longer be repeated—indeed will terminate—when the pair of numbers (whose greatest common divisor you are reduced to finding) are *equal numbers,* for then no further subtraction of a B from an A is permitted. At this point, however, the answer stares us in the face, for the greatest common divisor of a pair of equal positive whole numbers is indeed that common number.

Try it on any pair of numbers you want; say A = 2975 and B = 221.

- (*First application of the Euclidean algorithm*) We can subtract B = 221 thirteen times from A = 2975 to get that the GCD of 2975 and 221 is the same as the GCD of 221 and 2975 − (13 × 221) = 102. So think of 221 as our *new A* and 102 as our *new B,* and to find their GCD, repeat:

- (*Second application of the Euclidean algorithm*) We can subtract B = 102 twice from A = 221 to get that the GCD of 221 and 102 is the same as the GCD of 102 and 221 − (2 × 102) = 17. So think of 102 as our *new "A"* and 17 as our *new "B,"* and repeat again:

- (*Third application of the Euclidean algorithm*) We can subtract 17 five times from 102 to get that the GCD of 102 and 17 is the same as the GCD of 17 and 102 − (5 × 17) = 17. And now, we're done, for the GCD of 17 and 17 is, of course, 17.

Conclusion: The GCD of the pair A = 2975 and B = 221 is 17.

But let us not turn this little machine off yet, for the even deeper application is to be had when we run it backwards: Looking at the "second application" above, we see that our GCD, namely 17, is 221 − (2 × 102), which I want to think of as (1 × 221) − (2 × 102); the *second application* above is telling us that 17 is a multiple of 221 minus a multiple of 102. Now looking at the "first application," we see that 102 is 2975 − (13 × 221), which I want to think of as (1 × 2975) − (13 × 221); similarly, the *first application* above is telling us that 102 is a multiple of 2975 minus a multiple of 221. Putting these together, we get that 17, our GCD of our initial pair of numbers 2975 and 221, is expressible as a difference of multiples of these two numbers; specifically:

$$17 = (1 \times 221) - (2 \times 102) = (1 \times 221) - 2 \times (2975 - 13 \times 221)$$
$$= (27 \times 221) - (2 \times 2975).$$

This, then, is what the Euclidean algorithm does for us: it computes the greatest common divisor of a pair of numbers elegantly for us, and then—when run backward—it expresses that GCD as a difference of multiples of those two numbers. This is precious information, for it is the key to some of the deep foundational results about numbers, as we shall see in section 10 below.

5 The Euclidean Algorithm, in Euclid

The account just given of Euclid's algorithm was reasonably faithful, I feel, to the spirit of Euclid's Book VII. But I did take liberties to make some shifts and changes. To appreciate the nature of Euclid's text, it pays to discuss these changes. You might wonder why when I gave a reference in Euclid to *the Euclidean algorithm,* I listed not one proposition, but rather three of them (Propositions 1, 2, and 34). Why did it take Euclid three propositions, two of them coming at the beginning of Book VII and one coming at the end of the book, to express his algorithm?

First, since Euclid makes a sharp distinction between "the unit" (i.e., what we would call the *number* 1) and numbers that actually denote a plurality (i.e., numbers ≥ 2), he is drawn to provide separate but similar accounts of his algorithm depending upon whether the result it gives, as greatest common divisor, is a unit (this is discussed in Proposition 1) or is what Euclid would consider to be a bona fide number—i.e., is 2 or greater (this is discussed in Proposition 2).

Second, in the discussion I gave in the previous section, the "Manual for Use" that was offered came immediately after the basic statement of the algorithm. This is not what happens in Euclid's Book VII. In rough terms, it is Proposition 34—only coming towards the end of the book—that tells us how to effectively use Euclid's algorithm.

That the explanation of how to make use of this marvelous algorithm ambles in so late in this little volume implies something quite curious about what occurs in the middle of Book VII, as we will see later.

Related to this, and altogether astonishing, is the strange fact that *not even a single specific numeral* makes its appearance in all of Book VII, the earliest profound treatise on numbers that we have. Much scholarly debate concerns itself with whether *diagrams* did or did not occur in early manuscripts of Euclid's volumes on geometry, and what role they played in the constructions and demonstrations in geometry. It might also be worthwhile to ponder the lack of numerical examples—or any specific numbers at all—in Euclid's foundational text on number theory, and to ask what this implies about the way in which the text was studied, or was meant to be studied.

6 THEAETETUS

A friend[1] once pointed out to me that the Platonic dialogue, *Theaetetus*, is framed in such a way that one might take its central text to be something of a legal deposition—fastidiously preserved and presented only thirty years or so after the trial of Socrates—giving evidence that Socrates had indeed *not* perverted Athenian youth. For we are given two intensely vivid portraits in the dialogue: of young Theaetetus, in focussed conversation with Socrates about the nature of knowledge; and of older Theaetetus, now an Athenian general, mortally wounded in carrying out his duties for Athens. The general refuses to take time to rest in Megara, for he is in a hurry to get home to Athens, desiring to die in his native city. The dialogue, then, is itself a testimonial to the commitment of philosophy to *long conversation* unrestricted by the time exigencies of the water-clock in Athenian law courts.

Here is the statement of young Theaetetus' theorem, as described in the dialogue (147, 148; Loeb transl.):

THEAET. We divided all numbers into two classes. The one, the numbers which can be formed by multiplying equal factors, we represented by the shape of the square and called **square** or **equilateral** numbers.

SOC. Well done!

THEAET. The numbers between these, such as 3 and 5 and all numbers which cannot be formed by multiplying equal factors, but only by multiplying a greater by a less or a less by a greater, and are therefore always contained in unequal sides, we represented by the shape of the oblong rectangle and called **oblong** numbers.

Soc. Very good; and what next?

Theaet. All the lines which form the four sides of the equilateral or square numbers we called **lengths,** and those which form the oblong numbers we called **surds,** because *they are not commensurable with the others in length,* but only in the areas of the planes which they have the power to form. And similarly in the case of solids.

In modern language:

> **The Theorem of Theaetetus.** The square root of any (whole) number that is not a perfect square (of whole numbers) is irrational. The cube root of any (whole) number that is not a perfect cube (of whole numbers) is irrational.

As I have already mentioned, we will be discussing the proof of this theorem, as it appears in the extant ancient literature. What is strange, though, is that a popular delusion seems to be lurking in the *secondary literature* on this topic. Specifically, you will find—in various places—the claim that Theaetetus' theorem is proven in Proposition 9 of Book X of Euclid's *Elements.* It doesn't serve any purpose here to list the places where you find this incorrect assertion, except to say that it is incorrect, and it remains a thriving delusion since at least one important article published as late as 2005 repeats it. It is an especially strange delusion since nothing subtle is going on here. Even a cursory glance at Proposition 9 of Book X will convince you that what is being demonstrated there—if you take it in a modern perspective—is an utter triviality. Proposition 9 of Book X stands, though, for an important issue in ancient thought if taken on its own terms, but it won't prove irrationality of anything for us, let alone irrationality of all the numbers that Theaetetus proves. One might imagine that Heath's commentary on this—which is perfectly clear, and says exactly what is indeed proved in Proposition 9—would dispel the misconception that Theaetetus' theorem about the irrationality of surds is contained in this proposition, but it seems that this has held on with some tenacity. I would guess that the source of this error is quite early, as early as the commentaries of Pappus, but I offer this guess timidly because that would seem to imply that poor Proposition 9 of Book X has been often cited but far less often read with attention since the fourth century AD.

7 PAPPUS

Here, then, are some curious statements of Pappus[2] on the subject; I hope some historian of mathematics will elucidate them for us.

> [Theaetetus] divided all numbers into two classes, such as are the product of equal sides (i.e., factors) on the one hand, and on the other, such as are contained by a greater side (factor) and a less; and he represented the first [class] by a square figure and the second by an oblong . . .
>
> Euclid, on the other hand, after he examined this treatise (or theorem) carefully for some time and had determined the lines which are commensurable in length and square; those, namely, whose squares have to one another the ratio of a square number to a square number, proved that all lines of this kind are always commensurable in length . . .
>
> [T]he difference between Euclid's proposition and that of Theaetetus which precedes it, has not escaped us . . .

Is Pappus referring to some proposition of Euclid not available to us? Is Pappus, in contrasting Euclid with Theaetetus, suggesting that Theaetetus has proven the deeper theorem, or that Euclid has? Or is the statement that "the difference between Euclid's proposition and that of Theaetetus which precedes it, has not escaped us" making no comment on the relative merits of the two results, but only that Pappus sees them as different? I know of no modern commentary on this sentence in Pappus beyond the remarks in the volume cited, which indeed refer to Proposition 9 of Book X; it is an especially confusing matter, because there are hints in loc. cit. section 11 (page 74) that Pappus believes that it is Euclid's result that is the deeper: Pappus notices there that the r and s of Euclid, being lengths, can themselves be irrational (relative to some unnamed, but stipulated unit measure, of course) and Euclid's proposition covers this, whereas Theaetetus' language, which is in effect about ratios of "numbers to numbers," precludes thinking about such a situation. To a modern, however, introducing an irrelevant extra unit—which is what Pappus claims Euclid is doing—is a red herring and not a whit more general. Pappus seems insensitive to this, but is focussed, rather, on the (important to him, of course) issue of transference, or translatability, of the notion of ratio from the context of *lengths* to that of *numbers*.

However one interprets this text, one has to admire the intensity of Pappus's convictions about the subject matter. Pappus writes that he holds ignorance of the fact that incommensurables exist to be:

a brutish and not a human state, and I am verily ashamed, not for myself only, but for all Greeks, of the opinion of those men who prefer to believe what this whole generation believes, [namely], that commensurability is necessarily a quality of all magnitudes.

8 Incommensurability of $\sqrt{2} : 1$ and the "Even and the Odd"

There are two well-known proofs of the irrationality of $\sqrt{2}$ that turn on the distinction of *even* and *odd*. So if the Pythagoreans were—as they are reputed to have been—involved in these matters, it is fair enough that Aristotle at one place refers to the Pythagoreans as (my rough paraphrase) "the folks of the even and the odd."

I will rapidly review both of these proofs; what may be worth bearing in mind is that the even/odd distinction in the first of these proofs has to do with the actual numbers involved, while in the second proof it has to do with the exponents of the factors involved.

(1) To prove: that the equation $\sqrt{2} = n/m$ is impossible with n and m (positive) whole numbers.

First assume that the fraction n/m is in "lowest terms," so that either the numerator or the denominator (n or m) is odd.

Next, by squaring (both sides of) that putative equation $\sqrt{2} = n/m$, you get the equation

$$2m^2 = n^2$$

which tells us that n^2 is even; since the square of an odd number can be seen to be odd, we get that n itself is even; so m must be odd.

Now use the even-ness of n, to know that you may write n as twice a whole number; say, $n = 2k$. Then substitute $2k$ for n in the displayed equation, to get:

$$2m^2 = (2k)^2 = 4k^2.$$

The coup de grace comes when you simplify this displayed equation by dividing by 2, and get $m^2 = 2k^2$ telling you that m^2, and hence m itself, must be even.

This is an absurdity because we know that both m and n are even, which contradicts the initial reduction of the fraction n/m to "lowest terms." The only conclusion one can make is that the initial supposition that there is an equation of the form $\sqrt{2} = n/m$ is wrong.

The second proof will give us the same kind of conclusion.

(2) **To prove: that the equation $\sqrt{2} = n/m$ is impossible with n and m (positive) whole numbers.**

As in the first proof, we come to the same equation, $2m^2 = n^2$. But now we argue

- that the "number of prime factors" of the number on the right-hand side of this equation is even, for it is a perfect square, and the number of prime factors of a perfect square is even, while
- the "number of prime factors" of the number on the left-hand side of the equation is odd for it is the product of the prime number 2 by a perfect square.

This would be a contradiction *if* we knew also that any number can be written as a product of prime numbers *uniquely* where the only possible variation is in the order of the prime factors. We would even get our contradiction if we only knew that you cannot write a given number as a product of an even number of prime factors, and also as a product of an odd number of prime factors. But we have to know *something* along those lines.

That initial *if* is a big *if*. It is in fact true that any number can be uniquely written as a product of prime numbers: this theorem is variously called the *unique factorization theorem,* or the *fundamental theorem of arithmetic.* Indeed, it is very decidedly fundamental, for much theoretical work about numbers depends critically on its truth. This *fundamental theorem of arithmetic* has a peculiar history. It is not trivial, and any of its proofs take work, and, indeed, are interesting in themselves. But it is nowhere stated in the ancient literature. It was used, implicitly, by the early modern mathematicians, Euler included, without anyone noticing that it actually required some verification, until Gauss finally realized the need for stating it explicitly, and proving it.

The relevance of proof (2) to our story is twofold. First, there is a proof of irrationality of $\sqrt{2}$ in Book X (Proposition 117), that is close in spirit to proof (2). This Proposition 117, a probable late addition, is not included in Heath's translation. Second, some of the known proofs of Theaetetus' theorem follow the general lines of proof (2). Here is a modern proof.

(3) **To prove (Theaetetus' Theorem): that the equation $\sqrt{d} = n/m$ is impossible with n and m (positive) whole numbers if d is a whole number not a perfect square.**

As in the previous two proofs, we contemplate the putative equation

$$dm^2 = n^2,$$

and wish to show that it leads to a contradiction.

Find a prime number p dividing d with the property that the exponent e of the maximal power of the prime p that divides d is odd. This means that we are looking for a prime p such that p^e is a divisor of d but p^{e+1} is not, and e is an odd number. So, if d were, say, 250, we could take p to be 5, because 5^3 divides 250 but 5^4 does not; so the (odd number) 3 is the exponent of the maximal power of the prime 5 that divides 250. It is important to us that we can, in fact, find such a prime number (i.e., whose maximal power dividing d is odd) *exactly* when d is *not* a perfect square.

We are now going to try to compute the exponent of the maximal power of p that divides the right-hand side of the displayed equation, and the exponent of the maximal power of p that divides the left-hand side of the equation. As you might guess, the first of these is even, and the second is odd.

We will be able to perform our computation (of the exponent of the maximal power of p that divides each side of the displayed equation) if we know, for example, how these "exponents of maximal powers of p dividing numbers" behave when you multiply two numbers. It seems reasonable to hope, for example, that the following rule applies:

The additive rule: *If p is a prime number, and A and B are numbers, the exponent of the maximal power of p that divides the product $A \cdot B$ is the sum of the exponent of the maximal power of p that divides A, and the exponent of the maximal power of p that divides B.*

If we use this additive rule, we can compute handily:

- If v is the exponent of the largest power of p that divides n, then (by the additive rule) $2v$ is the exponent of the maximal power of p that divides n^2, so the exponent of the maximal power of p dividing the right-hand-side of our putative equation is

$$2v,$$

which, of course, is even.

- If μ is the exponent of the largest power of p that divides m, then (by the additive rule) 2μ is the exponent of the maximal power of p that divides m^2, so the exponent of the maximal power of p dividing the left-hand-side of our putative equation, i.e., dm^2, is (by the additive rule, again)

$$2\mu + e,$$

which is odd, because e is odd.

To conclude our argument, we note the contradiction that we have one and the same number—the left-hand-side and the right-hand-side of an equation—such that the exponent of the maximal power of p dividing it is both *even* and *odd*. The culprit here is our initial assumption that we can find m and n (positive, whole) numbers forming an equation

$$\sqrt{d} = n/m$$

when d is a number that is not a perfect square. Such an equation is therefore impossible.

The same format will give us the addendum that Theaetetus, in the dialogue of the same name, muttered under his breath, at the end of his description of his theorem; namely, the cube root of a number is irrational if the number in question is not a perfect cube. Theaetetus could continue and prove a similar theorem for fourth roots, fifth roots, etc., if he wished to do so, and if he developed the vocabulary to discuss higher roots.

9 THE ENGINES OF PROOFS

I wrote earlier about theorems that prove themselves; but, strictly speaking, no theorem proves itself. Any demonstration that is interesting tends to have some *engine* in it, so it can proceed. I like the mechanical analogy here: an automobile must have lots of "stuff" to render it usable, but at its heart, there is its engine, a prime moving part, that gets it actually rolling.

I grant that it may be something of a subjective judgment, but I think of it often as an exercise helpful in appreciating the flavor of a specific theorem to decide what you think its engine is.

Sometimes the engine is pretty close to the theorem itself, as with the Euclidean algorithm, where there are two engines, to my way of reckoning. The first is a basic *distributive law* telling us that if a number, d, is a divisor of two numbers, it is also a divisor of their sum and difference. The second is that we are reducing a problem about two numbers to a problem about two "smaller" numbers, and such a process must terminate after only finitely many iterations, and we bank on this general fact.

With Euclid's theorem on the infinitude of primes, there are also at least two little engines at work: the concept of "remainder after division" and the fact that any number greater than one is divisible by some prime number.

I view the *additive rule* as the crucial *engine* in the proof (3) that we have just sketched. The additive rule, in turn, can be reconstructed from a crucial piece of information that I will refer to by the phrase *when a prime divides a product*.

When a prime divides a product: *If a prime p divides a product of two numbers, A · B, then p divides A or it divides B.*

This then is the basic "moving part" in the demonstration of proof (3). Its statement is essentially[3] Euclid's Proposition 24 of Book VII. What is its proof?

10 When a Prime Divides a Product of Two Numbers

We teach this, in some form or other, in any beginning course in number theory or algebra:

If a prime p divides A • B then p divides A or it divides B.

and we have our choice of various strategies for its proof. The *engine* behind its most standard proof is nothing more than the Euclidean algorithm—a tool perfectly at Euclid's disposal. Here is a sketch of this standard strategy.

If the prime p divides A we can go home, so suppose it does not. Since p is a prime number not dividing A, we can conclude that the greatest common divisor, i.e., the GCD, of the numbers p and A is 1. Now recall that by running the Euclidean algorithm backwards you can always express the GCD of two numbers as a difference between a multiple of one of the numbers and a multiple of the other. In this case, then, we would be able to express 1—the GCD of p and A—as the difference between multiples of one and multiples of the other. Allow me, then, to do this by writing

$$1 = s • p + r • A$$

where s, r are whole numbers (of which one and only one is negative). Multiply this equation by B to get

$$B = spB + rAB.$$

Now our prime number p divides the first summand on the right, spB, because p itself occurs as a factor in that number. The prime p

also divides the second summand *rAB* because, by our hypothesis, it divides *AB*. Therefore it divides the sum; that is, *p* divides *B*.

For proofs (1) and (2) in section 8 above all you would need is this displayed theorem for the prime number $p = 2$, which is of a lesser order of difficulty: it is simply saying that the product of two numbers is even only if one of those two numbers is even. This fact, which is just telling us that the product of two odd numbers is odd, can be demonstrated by expressing the two odd numbers as $2a - 1$ and $2b - 1$ where *a* and *b* are numbers, performing the multiplication, and noting that the product is again odd, being of the form $2(2ab - a - b) + 1$.

11 WHEN A PRIME DIVIDES A PRODUCT OF TWO NUMBERS, IN EUCLID

As I have mentioned, the statement that if a prime divides a product of two numbers, it divides (at least) one of them, is essentially Euclid's Proposition 24 of Book VII.

The engine driving Euclid's demonstration of Proposition 24, however, is Proposition 20 of Book VII. Our agenda then is

- first to review the statement of Proposition 20,
- then to show how it establishes Proposition 24,
- and then to focus our attention on how to establish Proposition 20.

Proposition 20 of Book VII says (my mild paraphrase):

If a/b is a fraction, i.e., a ratio of two whole numbers a and b, and if c/d is a fraction such that

$$a/b = c/d,$$

and such that among all fractions equal to a/b the fraction c/d has the smallest numerator c, then c divides a (and d divides b).

Accept this Proposition, and the essence of the proof in Euclid's Proposition 24 is easy enough to sketch:

If the prime number *p* divides the product *AB*, we write *AB* as a multiple of *p*, getting an equation of the form

$$AB = mp$$

where *m* is a number. Now form the ratios:

$$B/m = p/A$$

and let r be the rational number that is their common value. By Proposition 20, if c/d is the fraction equal to r where c, d are whole numbers and c is the smallest numerator of any fraction equal to r, then c divides all numerators of fractions equal to r. Therefore c divides p. But since p is a prime number we have only two possibilities. Either $c = 1$, giving us that p divides A, which would make us happy; or else, $c = p$, but since, as the displayed equation shows, B is also a numerator of a fraction equal to r, we would then have that $c = p$ divides B, which would also make us happy. That is, depending upon the two possibilities, $c = 1$ or $c = p$, we would have that p divides A, or B, as was to be proved.

The final item on our little agenda, then, is Proposition 20.

12 Proposition 20 of Book VII

Here, again, is the statement of that proposition.

Proposition 20: *Let r be a (positive) rational number. The smallest numerator of all fractions equal to r divides the numerator of any fraction equal to r.*

Now I don't quite follow Euclid's proof of this pivotal proposition, and I worry that there may be a tinge of circularity in the brief argument given in his text.[4] It is peculiar, though, that Euclid's commentarists, very often quite loquacious about other issues, seem to be strangely silent about Proposition 20 and its opaque proof, for it is an important piece of Euclid's number theory; even Heath, who is usually magnificently generous in his comments at problematic moments in the Euclidean text, seems not to flinch as he restates, in modern language, the step in Euclid's demonstration of Proposition 20 that is difficult for me to understand. A recent article,[5] however, discusses the logical insufficiency of the proof of Euclid's Proposition 20; Pengelley and Richman offer an elegant way of interpreting Euclid's text so as to, on the one hand, patch up Euclid's logic, and on the other hand, explain why so few commentators seem to have discerned the need for a patch.[6]

I too—with Euclid's permission—want to offer a way of "patching Euclid's Proposition 20" making use of the preparatory material Propositions 5 and 6 Book VII, and guided by the assumption that we have here a "laconic text" but not an inherently illogical one. I hope that what I will recount does not vastly violate the tradition of Euclid's mathematical thinking.

To prove Proposition 20, then, let a/b be the initial fraction and c/d be the fraction such that $a/b = c/d$ and such that the numerator c is the smallest numerator of any fraction equal to a/b.

Of course, if $a = c$ we are done, so c is strictly less than a. Find the largest multiple of c, $m \cdot c$, that is strictly less than a. Then we have that $a - m \cdot c$ is less than or equal to c, for if it were strictly greater than c, then the next multiple in line, namely $(m + 1) \cdot c$, would be strictly less than a.

For example, if a were 7 and c were 3, then twice 3, which is 6, is the largest multiple of 3 strictly less than 7; and $a - m \cdot c = 7 - 6 = 1$ is indeed strictly less than $c = 3$.

At this point we shall make use of the information in Propositions 5 and 6 of Book VII—put in modern terms they are some of the standard algebraic rules for manipulation of fractions. To paraphrase their statements:

If we have an equality of two fractions

$$S/T = U/V$$

with S larger than U then the fraction whose numerator is the difference of the numerators of S/T and U/V, and whose denominator is the difference of the denominators of S/T and U/V, is also equal to the common value of S/T = U/V. In symbols:

$$S/T = (S - U)/(T - V).$$

Since

$$a/b = (m \cdot c)/(m \cdot d)$$

and a is larger than $m \cdot c$ we can conclude that the fraction whose numerator is the difference of the numerators of a/b and $(m \cdot c)/(m \cdot d)$, and whose denominator is the difference of the denominators of a/b and $(m \cdot c)/(m \cdot d)$, is also equal to a/b. In symbols:

$$a/b = (a - mc)/(b - md).$$

But $a - mc$, which is now exhibited as a *numerator* of a fraction equal to a/b, is also, by construction, less than or equal to c. Since c is the smallest such numerator, we had better have $a - mc = c$, or, in other words, $a = (m + 1) \cdot c$, i.e., a is a multiple of c, as was to be demonstrated.[7]

13 MAKING TWO PROOFS TALK TO EACH OTHER

It is time to take stock of what we have done so far:

- We contemplated the statement of Proposition 24 of Book VII *if a prime divides a product it divides one of the factors* as an important engine.

- We gave one of the standard modern proofs of this statement. This proof makes essential use of the Euclidean algorithm, so I'll refer to it as the *Euclidean algorithm proof.*

- We reviewed the route that Euclid offers us, as a strategy for the proof of his Proposition 24; namely via his Proposition 20.

- We gave a sketch of a correct proof of Proposition 20, culling material from earlier in Book VII (specifically, Propositions 5 and 6), in hopes that we have remained within the compass of Euclid's vision of number. I'll refer to this proof as the *"smallest numerator" proof.*

Although the Euclidean algorithm is surely one of the strategies palpably available to Euclid, the very structure of his Book VII would keep Euclid from employing the *Euclidean algorithm proof.* For Proposition 24 is comfortably in the middle of his text, and although the text begins straightaway with a *formulation* of the Euclidean algorithm (Props. 1, 2), information critical for the use of this algorithm is kept to the very end (Proposition 34).

As a result, we now have two quite different demonstrations of the statement *if a prime divides a product it divides one of the factors;* namely, via the Euclidean algorithm, and via the proposition regarding the smallest numerator, as we described above.

Whenever we have two proofs of the same thing, we have three questions in front of us:

- Are they "really" different proofs?
- Do they "really" prove the same thing?
- Is there a way of synthesizing them, forming something larger, more clarifying than either of them?

A preliminary chore sometimes needs to be done, to be able to compare the two proofs at all. Sometimes we must rephrase one, or both of them, in slightly different language, so that they are capable of "speaking to each other." This is necessary here, so let me refashion, and sharpen, the statement of the *smallest numerator proof* ever so slightly, to prepare it for its encounter with the *Euclidean algorithm proof.*

The Smallest Numerator Proposition, recast. *If a positive rational number r is expressed as a fraction in two ways r = A/B = C/D then it can also be expressed as a fraction r = E/F where the numerator E is the greatest common divisor of the numerators A and C.*

The reason why the recast proposition implies the fact that the smallest numerator divides all numerators of fractions equal to a given rational number is that (using the notation we have at our disposal) the greatest common divisor E divides A and C; now if C *were* the smallest numerator, it would be necessarily the case that $C = E$, and therefore C divides A, and A could have been taken to be *any* numerator of a fraction equal to r. This latter statement is just our old version of the "smallest numerator proposition."

The recast version of the smallest numerator proposition has a more concrete aspect than the original formulation, and no wonder: it has engaged as a resource the mighty Euclidean algorithm, thereby moving a step closer to the *Euclidean algorithm proof*. If we were to follow this further, we would find our two proofs merging into one unified understanding of *when a prime divides a product*. But, of course, we would not, even then, be done.

14 Turning Things Around

Sometimes, when we have defined a concept P and then have proven, by a proposition, that P is equivalent to Q—that Q *characterizes* P—we find that we have a remarkable option open to us. We can turn the tables on the *definition* and the *proposition* by "starting over again," so to speak, and redefining that same concept as Q, and then regarding the proposition as affirming that Q is indeed equivalent to P.

We see shades of this turn-around strategy in other disciplines: we wish to define the almost ungraspable notion of *intelligence,* for example, and we have a sense that, whatever it is, it is—if not equivalent to—at least somehow related to performance on a certain curious *test*. We then, it seems, formulate a definition in terms of performance on that test, refashioning the name of what we're after as *Intelligence Quotient*. We don't do this capriciously, of course: we are not, after all, hellbent on confusing ourselves. We would not, I imagine, do such a strange thing—put the responsibility of earmarking such an extraordinary concept as *intelligence* onto the shoulders of a single number—if we had a more straightforward definition—or measure—of intelligence. Perhaps we shouldn't do this, with any confidence, in any case.

The "turn-around tactic" in mathematics has quite a different flavor. There, we assume that we have a perfectly clear definition of the concept P to begin with. We only turn around and redefine the same concept as Q if doing so sheds light—a new light—on the concept that is already grasped.

One of the most striking "turn-arounds" in modern mathematics is in the very definition of prime number. The property satisfied by primes, for which we have given two proofs, namely *when a prime divides a product it divides one of the factors* is a characterization of prime numbers: A prime number *p has* this property, as we have seen. A composite number N *does not have* this property (factor N as N = A • B with both A and B less than N, and here we have a case where N divides, and in fact is equal to, a product, but doesn't divide either factor).

Not only is this property a characterization of prime number, but it reflects a fundamental feature of prime numbers; in fact, such an important characterizing feature of primality that there is much to be gained in our understanding if we simply turn the tables on the the way we introduce primes into our discussion, and make the following new

> **Turn-Around Definition:** *A* **prime number** *is a number greater than 1 that has the property that whenever it divides a product of two numbers, it divides one (or both) of the numbers.*

What we have done in the preceding sections, from this vantage, is, effectively, to have shown two proofs of the fact that this table-turned definition of prime number coincides with our usual definition.

This new definition, expressed in the language of the modern notion of ideals, is the gateway to the modern conception of algebra, and the profound link between geometry and algebra. But that is another story, and will only deepen our appreciation of *when a prime divides a product* as the somewhat laconically addressed glorious center of Euclid's Book VII, and as a possible engine to Theaetetus' demonstration of his theorem.

15 Reading Euclid

In a prior section we forced one aspect of Euclid—his algorithm that frames Book VII like a pair of book-ends—to talk with another aspect of Euclid—the somewhat terse middle of Book VII. It seemed to me that this glorious text deserves to have such a face-to-face internal encounter. Of course, all reading is a more external encounter between at least two subjects, reader and writer, as aided by a speechless and speechful messenger, namely the material book. Most of the time, when we refer to our reading, we may quote the author at length, discuss chapters, sections, and page numbers, but we rarely refer to the physical presence of the book itself, ever in front of us as we contemplate its contents.

In my case, I have a copy of Sir Thomas Heath's three-volume paperback series that translates and comments on the thirteen books of *Euclid's Elements,* published by Dover in 1956, but now lacking some of its front covers. This set was originally used as a school text by my young sister-in-law Ali, Alexandra Dane Dor-Ner, when she studied Euclid at St. John's College in Santa Fe in the mid-1960s, and the books were passed to me when she died some fifteen years ago. My copy of Book VII is especially invigorated by Ali's marginal notes, recording her extraordinarily vivid encounter with Euclid. I'm intrigued to see that it is around Propositions 5 and 6 that Ali's pencil notes have reached a crescendo. So, when I read, the three of us are in "the room" together: Euclid, Ali, me. Her questioning of Euclid has its intense moments, and when this happens, I find that I can sit back and imagine Euclid—distracted from gazing upon beauty bare—responding.

"Unproved"—Ali writes at one point, and on reading this I'm taken, at the same time, with a sense of pride for my (then teen-age) relative, and a sense of admiration for the accomplishment of Euclid, who had instilled such a high level of scrutinizing question-asking and question-answering that halfway through his thirteen books, a reader will have learned this intimately so as to demand it, vigorously, of Euclid himself.

Eva Brann, in her essay "The Second Power of Questions," talks of the different kinds of *questions, problems, dilemmas* and *mysteries.* The lesser categories of problems, dilemmas and mysteries, Eva says, "belong to a type of question that calls for the answer to do away with the question." Eva pinpoints the distinction between *mysteries* and *problems* by quoting a fourth-grader who, in *Thinking: The Journal of Philosophy for Children,* says: " If I were to find myself on the moon, it'd be a mystery how I got there but it'd be a problem how to get back."

The title question of this article, for example, lives somewhere in these lesser categories. But there exist also the "true" questions, about which Eva writes:

These are never resolved nor do they lapse, but they collect about themselves an ever-live complex of reflective results.

Euclid's inquiry about numbers deftly points us to some of the most abiding questions in mathematics:

- Euclid has convinced us of the important role that prime numbers and the notion of *relative primality* play in our understanding of arithmetic, and yet we are still only at the beginning of our understanding of the laws governing prime numbers, and even more specifically, governing the placement of prime numbers among all natural numbers.

- Euclid has introduced us to "his" algorithm, and now—especially with the advent of electronic computing—algorithmic thinking is ubiquitous in our theoretical and our practical studies.
- Euclid has inspired us to organize our sciences as discursive, rational, structures—with articulated *definitions, axioms,* and *propositions,* so that when we come to our conclusions we can truly hold them "beyond a shadow of a doubt."

These are examples of the "true" questions that Eva is celebrating: questions that provide nourishment for long conversations, inviting anyone to enter, to think afresh, to converse.

NOTES

1 Robert Kaplan.

2 "The Commentary of Pappus on Book X of Euclid's Elements," Arabic text and translation by William Thomson (Cambridge, Mass.: Harvard University Press, 1930), section 10, page 73.

3 Euclid phrases this slightly differently, but the essence of the statement hasn't been significantly modified by our recasting of it. He formulates the property as saying that if a number is relatively prime to A and divides $A \cdot B$ then it divides B.

4 This problematic Proposition 20 of Book VII is cited, for example, in the proofs of Propositions 20 and 21 of Book VIII, these being cited, respectively, in the proofs of Propositions 22 and 23 of Book VIII, which, in turn, are cited in the proofs of Propositions 24 and 25 of Book VIII. These latter propositions are a formulation of the result of Theaetetus.

5 David Pengelley and Fred Richman, "Did Euclid Need the Euclidean Algorithm to Prove Unique Factorization?" *American Mathematical Monthly* 113 (March 2006): 196–205.

6 Pengelley and Richman formulate two concepts; the first they call *Eudoxian proportionality,* which is the elementary proposition that says that $a : b = c : d$ if and only if $ad = bc$; the second they call *Pythagorean proportionality,* which is the significantly deeper statement about whole numbers that says that $a : b = c : d$ if and only if there are whole numbers $x, y, m,$ and n such that

$$a = mx, \quad b = nx, \quad c = my, \quad d = ny.$$

It is this deeper statement that contains the essence of Proposition 20. Their argument is that ellipsis in Euclid's text leads us to misread a reference to

Pythagorean proportionality as a reference to the more elementary statement. The bibliography of Pengelley and Richman's paper contains references to much of the modern commentary on these issues, and the text of their article contains some interesting reflections on this commentary. I am thankful to them and to David Mumford for conversations regarding issues in this article.

7   I am thankful to Mark Schiefsky, from whom I learned that Wilbur Knorr, in his *The Evolution of the Euclidean Elements* (Dordrecht, Holland: D. Reidel, 1975), 225–33, proposes that Theaetetus' Theorem might have been proved in antiquity via Euclid's Proposition 27 of Book VII. This indeed is plausible, since Proposition 27 asserts that for a and b whole numbers, their squares, a^2 and b^2, are relatively prime if and only if a and b are relatively prime, from which Theaetetus' Theorem follows directly. The proof of Proposition 27 in Euclid's text, however, threads its way through Propositions 24 and 20, and therefore leads us to the same problematic Proposition 20.

THE WORLD OF FICTION AND THE LAND OF THE DEAD

Grace Dane Mazur

I. THRESHOLDS AND INSTABILITIES

WE CURL UP WITH A NOVEL. The very verb implies a spiraling inward of the field of our attention. If all goes well we soon enter into an altered state of consciousness in which we tumble into a world not our own. What are these other worlds, and how do we make the descent? What do we find when we're down there?

Stories begin with instabilities. The opening pages of many novels show the protagonist in a condition of both liminality and entrancement, liminality being the state of being on the threshold.[1] They seem to say, *Look, reader, the same thing that is happening to you—now that you are coiled around this book and are about to fall into the fictional world—is happening to this character, who is at the edge of his own altered consciousness, at the edge of adventure.*

If we look closely at the openings of certain masterpieces of contemporary American fiction, we can see a sort of intricate imbalance leading to what I would call structural instability—that state where things are so precarious that something has got to happen. This structural instability can come from being on the edge, or simply being *on edge,* and is accompanied often by uneasiness, excitement, fear. Often, Time is a preoccupation as well. As an example of what I mean, consider the first few sentences of Paula Fox's novel, *The Widow's Children:*[2]

> Clara Hansen, poised upright in her underwear on the edge of a chair, was motionless. Soon she must turn on a light. Soon she must finish dressing. She would permit herself three more minutes in her darkening apartment in that state that was so nearly sleep. She turned to face a table on which sat a small alarm clock. At once, a painful agitation brought her to her feet. She would be late: buses were not reliable. She could not afford

---

A slightly different version of this paper was given at The MFA Program for Writers at Warren Wilson College in July 2005.

a taxi to take her to the hotel where her mother, Laura, and Laura's husband, Desmond Clapper, were expecting her for drinks and dinner [. . .]

A few drops of rain slid down the windows as she passed through the living room. She turned on a light to come home to, and for a brief moment, it seemed the evening was already over, that she had returned, consoled by the knowledge that once Laura was gone, she hardly need think of her. After all, the occasions of their meetings were so rare.

Clara is *poised* (the word implies the necessity of action or change)—she's on the edge of her chair, not quite on, not quite off. Not asleep, but nearly, neither dressed nor naked, in the apartment that is neither light nor dark, on an afternoon that is turning into evening. The first few raindrops have just appeared, signs of the leading edge of the storm. Both the weather and the season are on edge, that cruelty of late spring when it should be warm but neglects to be.

Clara is at the edge of sleep, but also in a turmoil over time, and Time words are ticking like some furious vexed clock all through these opening pages. Finally Clara does something so strange and so lonely: she turns on "a light to come home to." This preemptive strike against the dark shows her solitary existence: *she* is the one who greets her when she comes home, she provides light and warmth—but notice also how she's looping together two separate points in time, before and after the interaction with her mother, as though, if she could, she would loop it out of existence.

So many instabilities—postural, psychological, diurnal, seasonal, meteorological—and we read on, teetering, waiting for something to topple or crash.

While the opening of Fox's *The Widow's Children* shows Clara dozing when she should be waking, in the beginning of Charles Baxter's *The Feast of Love*,[3] we find that our narrator, Charlie Baxter, is abruptly waking when he shouldn't—panicked in the middle of the night:

The man—me, this pale being, no one else, it seems—wakes in fright, tangled up in the sheets.

The darkened room, the half-closed doors of the closet and the slender pine-slatted lamp on the bedside table: I don't recognize them. On the opposite side of the room, the streetlight's distant luminance coating the window shade has an eerie unwelcome glow. None of these previously familiar objects have any familiarity now. What's worse, I cannot remember or recognize myself. I sit up in bed—actually, I *lurch* in mild sleepy terror toward the vertical. There's a demon here, one of the unnamed ones, the demon of erasure and forgetting. I can't manage my way through this feeling because my mind isn't working, and because *it,* the flesh in which I'm housed, hasn't yet become *me.* [. . .]

Then I feel her hand on my back. She's accustomed by now to my night amnesias, and with what has become an almost automatic response, she reaches up sleepily from her side of the bed and touches me between the shoulder blades. In this manner, the world's objects slip back into their fixed positions.

Charlie has lost who he is, for a moment, until his wife stabilizes him into self-recognition by putting her hand on his back. He gets up, goes to the study, and then descends the stairs, at the bottom of which he passes a large looking glass that does not reflect. The reason he gives for this is that the mirror is so old, but we have to wonder, too, if he has somehow gotten to the other side of that looking glass. He goes out into the Ann Arbor night and wanders through his neighborhood forest, which has turned disgusting with an infestation by gypsy-moths. Back out on the street, on the far side of the woods, the traffic light blinks red in both directions—collapsing space, or perhaps slightly forbidding all things. From there he trespasses into the football stadium—where no one is supposed to be. Down below, right on the fifty-yard line, is a young couple, in the throes of sex.

Charlie finally comes across a man sitting on a park bench; this is his neighbor Bradley—who looks like a toad. Bradley has a dog which is disconcertingly also named Bradley. Bradley, the man, tells Charlie that it's illegal for him to be out so late in Ann Arbor without a dog.

All these temporal and psychic perversities combine to put us in an unstable situation in which something, everything, is bound to happen. We, and the characters, have tumbled into the story, and the story clearly takes place in Nighttown, which I will talk more about below.

II. DESCENTS TO THE LAND OF THE DEAD

The altered state of consciousness brought about by reading fiction or epic transports us to the domain that the ancient Greeks referred to as the realm of Hades. When we enter the place that fiction carries us to, we are in some way enacting the descent of the classical hero to the Land of the Dead. I should emphasize that this is the case whether or not the fiction we are reading has anything to do with Hades' realm or the analogous regions.

Although all the works that I discuss here do contain descents to one sort of underworld or another, my general claim about what happens to us as readers has to do with the nature of literary entrancement, and not with the contents of any particular narrative.

What I am calling "descent" often has nothing to do with altitude relative to ground level. The way to the Land of the Dead does not always lend itself to rational mapping and often the journey is one of infinite horizontal distance, as though if one goes far enough—to the edge of the world, for example—space will buckle and *far* gets folded onto *under.*

The territory of the Dead is so well protected from the living that the journey there should not be undertaken alone if one hopes to come back alive. In some cases there are two sorts of guides, the first having to do with transport—a ferryman or charioteer—then an immortal, or a seer, or the goddess of the Underworld herself. The usual goal of such a descent is to bring back a beloved, or a monster, or treasure, or ideas, in the form of religious instruction, wisdom, or revelation. It is this last goal of bringing back ideas that interests me here, and the heroes we will follow are all on such a quest.

Related to these journeys is the trip to *Nighttown,* which I think of as the urban, living equivalent of the Land of the Dead. A long descent or crossing infinite distances is not always necessary to get there: sometimes we find Nighttown in the soft underbelly of our own hometown. Nighttime is not always a prerequisite for Nighttown. One of the most intense and beautiful fictional accounts is Eudora Welty's long short story, "Music from Spain," where Nighttown is in San Francisco, in broad daylight.

How do we know if we, or a set of fictional characters, are in our world or in Hades' realm or one of the other worlds such as Nighttown or Wonderland? There are many markers for these other worlds, and one of the most important is that the boundaries between categories that are usually kept distinct—man and beast, male and female, human and divine—become blurred. Time often appears distorted in the other world and language, too, becomes strange.

In general, our world consists of the known and the normal, while Hades' realm, Nighttown, and other examples of the other world are full of the unknown and the abnormal. Some of the indicators that tell us Baxter's *The Feast of Love* takes place in Nighttown include the hero's waking instead of sleeping, mirrors that refuse to reflect, the dog who shares the name of his owner, and the dog's owner who is like a frog. In a final transgressing of classical literary boundaries, it is the character of this froglike man, Bradley, who tells Charlie Baxter, the narrator and author, how to write his book.

Before we follow the hero to the Land of the Dead, I would like to set the mood by recounting the descent my husband Barry and I took with Eva Brann.

The year is 1988. The place is the prehistoric caves at Lascaux. Though the hills are not far away, the land nearby is flat, and we can't see any cave openings as we stand by the fence. The *Laissez-passer* that came from the Ministry of Culture directed us to this unmarked gate in the middle of nowhere in the Dordogne valley in southern France. We wait, in the soft rain, wondering if it is the right fence, the right rusted gate, but we don't mention our doubts to each other. Instead, Eva talks about the people who painted these caves 17,000 years ago. "Do you think we would know them as *us?*" she asks.

Finally a man dressed in blue denim ambles toward us, from the other side, jingling his keys. Without greeting us he unlocks the gate and silently leads us to a stone hut. There he examines our papers with ecstatic grimness, as though hoping our documents will not be in order so he can send us away again. But he changes into an army fatigue jacket and tells us to leave our sacks on the table. I proudly show him our new flashlights and he tells us to leave them behind as well. *"C'est moi qui prendra la lampe,"* he says. "I'll be the one taking the lamp. I'm the guide, I'll be showing *you* the cave. It's better like that, no?"

Out of the hut and down some cement steps into a bunker with a heavy steel door. As we descend, Eva whispers, "What if one of them were coming out?" We don't have time to answer her. Our guide motions us inside and steps into a footbath, demonstrating how deeply we should shake our shoes in the disinfectant. This is meant to kill any hitchhiking microorganisms, as molds and bacteria brought in by travelers have tended to encrust and eat the paintings in the cave to such an extent that Lascaux has been off limits to the public for decades. One has to apply for special permission to get in. The room smells of the sweetly vicious odor of formaldehyde.

Steel doors clang shut behind us and lock with a thud. Our guide herds us down steep iron-grill stairways, barely lighting our way with the narrow beam of his lamp. Then he positions us by the cave wall and turns off his flashlight, saying that it is time for us to become adapted to the dark. The blackness is thick and velvety and sudden. Behind us, somewhere, is a slow drip of water.

As we stand there bewildered in the darkness, the man talks to us, telling us that the cave was discovered in September, 1940, by four schoolboys. We are about to ask which of the two discovery legends is the correct one—the four boys out hunting were chasing after their dog which had fallen down a hole made by an uprooted tree . . . or the four boys were following the instructions of an old woman who told them of a cave with what she called medieval drawings—but he admonishes us to keep quiet until we emerge. Our time below is limited, he says, and he will be doing all the talking. We stand in the darkness, obedient children, unnerved.

Finally he turns on his light and points out two types of cave wall: the smooth part, generally used for incised drawings, and the rough part, encrusted with microcrystals of calcium carbonate. This is the canvas used for the paintings of Lascaux, and it is part of the reason they have lasted for 17,000 years. The hard needle-like projections of the tiny crystals capture and hold the pigments. Like a sort of mineralized velvet, this surface doesn't allow any erasures: what was drawn is what you see.

Down a narrow passage to the Chamber of the Bulls. Five or six bulls follow each other, facing into the cavern, with the first one we meet, the one closest to the exterior, having a somewhat different shape and two long straight horns with round blobs at the ends. The whole beast looks a bit saggy and off somehow. Our guide tells us to keep this one in mind: he will talk of it later.

Except for this first animal, throughout the cave the sureness of line and form is astounding, as is the freshness of the painting, the intensity of the pigments. The cavern's own projections and recesses are used to play into the volumes of the painted forms. Sometimes a hollow in the rock is reverse shaded to give the optical illusion of the bulging side of a cow. Some animals extend around corners in the rock, so that painting one end of the beast the artist could not see the other end, and yet a nubbin of rock at the head is used for the eye, a spine of rock towards the tail is used for the line of the haunch, and the whole animal is in perfect proportion.

Five reindeer swim across a river, their heads raised to keep their muzzles out of the water, their antlers graceful and precise.

A horse falls off a cliff, the cliff being a natural outcropping of the rock: the horse is upside down, its legs stiff in the air, its ears back in fear, its mouth open in a sharp whinny.

Our guide turns off his light again and has us walk downhill along the slippery path. Then he tells us to turn around as he illuminates:

Everywhere, on every surface of the folded walls and ceilings, there are cows, bulls, goats, reindeer, horses, bison—dancing, billowing like clouds. This is the Sistine Chapel of Lascaux. By this time, all three of us are weeping, and seeing that we are properly moved, our guide has warmed and gentled toward us.

Finally he leads us back to the first animal in the cave, back in the Chamber of the Bulls. There he shows us how, if you cover the top of the muzzle of this being with your hand, you can suddenly see the whole figure as a bearded man, wearing an animal skin and ritual horns. For those long straight horns with blobs on the tips belong to no known beast and the eye is a human eye, not an animal one. Our guide has saved this figure for the very end of his tour when we have seen enough to realize that the artists down here are in total control of their craft, their art. So, there's a reason for the apparent clumsiness of the skin on this first bull: it is not his own skin but a ritual costume of a skin, worn by a shaman.

Our guide leads us up into daylight again. When I get my voice back, I ask him how long he has been taking people through the cave.

"*Je prends ma retraite dans deux ans,*" he says. "I'll retire in two years. I've been at it for 47 years."

"Ah, then you're the master of the cave," I say glibly.

"*Ah, non non non.*" he corrects, gesturing back toward the cave entrance. "*They* were the masters."

Late that afternoon, back at our hotel, leafing through a small booklet on Lascaux, I notice a recent picture of our guide, tending some hygrometric machinery having to do with the preservation of the cave; his name is given as Jacques Marsal. On page one of the same booklet is a picture of the four boys who discovered the cave in 1940: Jacques Marsal is one of the four. He never left it.

Our trip with Eva to the cave at Lascaux took place in the late twentieth century, but stories of the Netherworld and the regions at the Edge of the World are found all the way back to the earliest Sumerian tablets soon after the invention of cuneiform writing in about 3000 B.C. Perhaps the most intense of these ancient Babylonian tales is the Epic of Gilgamesh, in which the brash, overactive, youthful king discovers mortality when his beloved companion Enkidu dies. Grief-stricken, Gilgamesh then voyages to the End of the World looking for a way to avoid death.

When Gilgamesh has finally crossed the Waters of Death, with the necessary help of the ferryman Urshanabi, he finds Uta-napishti, the only human immortal, the Babylonian Noah figure who lived through the great flood. Uta-napishti shows Gilgamesh how hard it is to become immortal by giving him a simple test: as a model of avoiding death forever, can he do without sleep—that analogue of death—for a week? Of course, Gilgamesh fails miserably, falling into a narcoleptic slumber the minute he hunkers down on his haunches. Uta-napishti has his wife bake a loaf of bread each day and put it beside the sleeping Gilgamesh, so that there will exist incontrovertible proof of the time he has slept as shown by the progressive staleness and moldiness of the loaves. When he wakes up a week later and understands that he has no hope of avoiding death, Gilgamesh howls.

Although Odysseus is middle-aged, he too is a king who seems more interested in adventure than in responsibility. By the time of his return to Ithaka, he has stayed away for a decade and has succeeded in losing all of the men under his care. I will just touch on a couple of aspects of the *Odyssey,* and it will be obvious, but should be stated, how indebted my discussion of it is to Eva's astonishing and wonderful *Homeric Moments.*[4]

In the middle of the *Odyssey,* in Book XI, Odysseus travels to the Land of the Dead. For this journey he has two guides. Circe, the witch, tells him how to get there and how to behave so that his second guide, Teiresias, will appear. Teiresias, the blind Theban seer, tells Odysseus how to get home, and instructs him in how to deal with the Dead, how to make them tell their stories in an intelligible manner, one at a time, without gibbering. As Eva notes, Teiresias's instructions take up only one of the twenty odd pages of Book XI. All the rest is stories, the myths of the Greeks, and these are what Odysseus brings back from the Land of the Dead. Eva calls this land *the safe-depository of tales, the treasure house of myth.* And these stories are Odysseus' booty, his wise findings, his revelations.

In contrast to Gilgamesh and Odysseus, Parmenides is not a plundering king but a young philosopher. He goes down to the Land of the Dead and comes back with ideas he recounts in the form of a grand poem in three parts. In the Proem, or introduction, he tells of his voyage to the underworld.

The Proem[5]

The mares that carry me as far as longing can reach
rode on, once they had come and fetched me onto the legendary
road of the divinity that carries the man who knows

through the vast and dark unknown. And on I was carried
as the mares, aware just where to go, kept carrying me
straining at the chariot; and young women led the way.
And the axle in the hubs let out the sound of a pipe
blazing from the pressure of the two well-rounded wheels
at either side, as they rapidly led on: young women, girls,
daughters of the Sun who had left the mansions of Night
for the light and pushed back the veils from their faces with their hands.
There are the gates of the pathways of Night and Day,
held fast in place between the lintel above and a threshold of stone;
and they reach up into the heavens, filled with gigantic doors.
And the keys—that now open, now lock—are held fast by
Justice: she who always demands exact returns. And with
soft seductive words the girls cunningly persuaded her to
push back immediately, just for them, the bar that bolts
the gates. And as the doors flew open, making the bronze
axles with their pegs and nails spin—now one, now the other—
in their pipes, they created a gaping chasm. Straight through and
on the girls held fast their course for the chariot and horses,
straight down the road.
And the goddess welcomed me kindly, and took
my right hand in hers and spoke these words as she addressed me:
"Welcome, young man, partnered by immortal charioteers,
reaching our home with the mares that carry you. For it was
no hard fate that sent you traveling this road—so far away
from the beaten track of humans—but Rightness, and Justice.
And what's needed is for you to learn all things: both the unshaken
heart of persuasive Truth and the opinions of mortals,
in which there's nothing that can truthfully be trusted at all.
But even so, this too you will learn—how beliefs based on
appearance ought to be believable as they travel through
all there is."

This translation is by the classical scholar and philosopher Peter Kingsley, who points out a number of strange things about the passage.[6] The first is that though Parmenides is the founder of Western philosophy—the creator of metaphysics, the inventor of logic, and the teacher of Plato—in this voyage to the goddess who will teach him all these subjects, he doesn't say that his path proceeds from darkness into light; rather he says he was taken from our world of light through the vast and dark unknown down to where Day and Night reside.

This passage into darkness becomes easier to understand if we note that Parmenides describes himself as "the man who knows," meaning an initiate or seer. According to Kingsley, Parmenides was part of a long line of healer-prophets that lasted for about five hundred years. These healers were masters of the technique of *incubation*. They were priests of Apollo—Apollo not in his later aspect of light and clarity, but in his earlier aspect of the God of Darkness, when he was associated with healing, with snakes, with death and the underworld, and with caves where the incubation rites took place.

Incubation as performed by these healer-prophets was a meditative practice involving prolonged stillness and silence leading to a trance state resulting in visions or dreams. Because caves lack sensory stimuli, these meditations were often performed there. Although the master healer-prophets such as Parmenides, and before him Pythagoras, would incubate alone, ordinary people required such a master to guide them in their practice, to watch over them in their trances, and keep them from being eaten by bears or other beasts.

Incubation can be thought of as a magical/religious analogue to the hero's voyage to the Land of the Dead, an echo or re-enactment of the descent, complete with spirit guide and with a goal of attaining of wisdom, religious instruction, or revelation.

Like Odysseus on his journey, Parmenides is surrounded by females who serve as helpers and guides: mares pull his chariot; maidens guide the way; Justice opens the gates; and finally it is the Goddess, Persephone,[7] who greets and will teach him. Peter Kingsley points out something else going on in the Proem; he calls it the Noise of the Whistling Roar. Kingsley says that Parmenides is an extremely careful poet, and when he uses insistent repetitions of words, like the verb "to carry," he does it for incantatory effect: the poem is both describing and enacting a trance induction of the sort practiced in the ritual of incubation. Parmenides uses the Greek word *syrinx*, which means "pipe" or "sound of a pipe," and he repeats this word when he tells how the huge doors spin open, rotating in hollow tubes or pipes. This instance in the Proem is the only time in Classical Greek, Kingsley says, that *syrinx* is applied to doors or parts of doors, and it is supposed to give a sense of the sound that the doors make.

There is often something alarming about change of state, what one might call the groan of the liminal. Think of the Gates of Hell in Milton's *Paradise Lost:*

> (. . .) on a sudden, open fly
> With impetuous recoil and jarring sound

> Th'infernal doors, and on their hinges grate
> Harsh thunder, that the lowest bottom shook
> Of Erebus . . .

Think of the screech of the doors of the haunted mansion in any good horror movie; but think too of birth pangs; throes of ecstasy; the death rattle—crucial thresholds often announce themselves by a particular sort of voice.

According to Kingsley, this syrinx sound of piping and whistling of the hinges of the doors of Hades was also the sound of snakes who were sacred to Apollo. In Ancient Greek accounts of incubation one of the signs that mark the entry into another world—into the trance state—is that one becomes aware of a rapid spinning movement; another sign is the vibration produced by a piping, whistling, hissing sound. Of course, this sound is part of ancient (and current) exercises in breath control; and it is also the ancient —as well as contemporary—call for silence: Pssssst! Kingsley cites Greek mystical texts, which explain that this hissing or piping sound, this sound of silence, is the sound of creation: the noise made by stars and planets as they coil and spin.

There is some terror involved here, in these celestial orbitings. I wonder if there isn't also terror just in the idea of rotary motion: circling about a static core, that empty center of non-being and stillness,[8] while the rim which is rotating is all motion and everywhere *becoming*. The only *being* is when the whole thing is viewed from outside, or described by the philosopher/poet. Thus the whistling roar can also come from the friction between the moving and the still, as non-being rubs up against becoming, invoking the idea that BEING IS, which is the primary philosophical finding that Parmenides brings back to us from the underworld.

To what extent do the stories of these three classical heroes exhibit the blurring of boundaries, the distortions of time, or the distortions of language that I mentioned as signs that one is in the other world?

For Gilgamesh there are many blurred boundaries: guardians are part human, part scorpion; a garden has flowers made of minerals; the human survivors of the flood are immortals. There is no distortion of language, but there is something strange going on with time. In one episode, Gilgamesh races the Sun God through the Sun's mountain and comes out before the Sun God does. He has gotten to the morning of the next day before the sun, going, in our terms, faster than light.

When Odysseus visits the realm of Hades, there isn't much of a concern with time, but there is a great problem with language, for the ghosts will gibber incomprehensibly, "rustling in a pandemonium of whispers," unless Odysseus gives them access, one at a time, to drink the sacrificial blood he has poured in the votive pit.

Parmenides travels to the domain of both Night and Day and is thus beyond time. There is no apparent distortion of language, as far as he is concerned, but the philosophical ideas he brings back from the goddess and recounts in parts two and three of his poem are so difficult that for us they are much in need of interpretation.

III. "THE GARDEN PARTY"

Keeping the ancient travels of Gilgamesh, Odysseus, and Parmenides in mind, we can now turn to a brilliant twentieth-century narrative, Katherine Mansfield's "The Garden Party."[9] This is the story of Laura Sheridan, a girl on the cusp of womanhood, who helps prepare for her family's party and then, when it is over, takes the bounty of leftovers to the impoverished and grief-stricken cottagers down the hill. This errand of Laura's can, I think, be thought of as a voyage to the underworld, to talk with the dead. Following the tradition of such visits, she brings gifts, elegant sweetmeats and sandwiches, and comes away with new and ineffable knowledge.

And after all the weather was ideal.

The first half of this story is taken up with the preparations for the party. The grounds shimmer with new-mown grass and daisies; hundreds of roses have blossomed overnight, "bowed down as though they had been visited by archangels." Mrs. Sheridan has decided that her children should take over the running of the party this year. When the workmen come to put up the grand tent in the garden, Mr. Sheridan and his son, Laurie, have already left for "the office," Meg has just washed her hair, and Jose is in her usual silk petticoat. So it is the youngest girl, Laura, who goes out to confer with the men. Unsettled as to her status, and unused to talking to laborers who are not her family's servants, Laura's diction shifts and cracks like the voice of an adolescent boy.

In my view, Laura and Laurie are twins—why else would one name them thus? They seem to me to be sixteen or seventeen, and according to the customs of upper-class New Zealand of the early 1920s, Laurie is already a man, going off each day into the real world of the office with his father, while Laura remains sheltered and a bit infantilized among the women.

Anyway, the Sheridans are rearranging everything to increase delight: the tent is erected, the piano is moved—making a chuckling noise—the whole world seems golden and alive with "soft, quick steps and running voices," with faint playful winds, and warm reflections of the sunlight from all the silver. Into all this plenty, more is brought: two trays of pink canna lilies "wide open, radiant, almost frighteningly alive on bright crimson stems." Almost deliriously sensuous these preparations, even down to writing out the labels for the fifteen kinds of sandwiches—cream cheese and lemon curd; egg and olive—and then the tasting of the cream puffs from Godber's pastry shop.

Jose and Laura are just licking the whipped cream of those puffs from their fingers when Death appears at the back door. Halfway through the story, the delivery man from the pastry shop tells the cook, the maid, and the manservant that an accident has happened: a man who lives nearby has been fatally thrown from his cart when his horse shied at a steam engine.

Laura is aghast: "But we can't possibly have a garden party with a man dead just outside the front gate."

This is not geographically correct as the man lives in the shanty town down the hill, but it is emotionally correct as, in Laura's sudden awareness, death is looming. The next five pages of the story are given to arguing about the party and death: Laura's mother chides her to use common sense rather than emotion, arguing that if a normal death had occurred among the poor cottage-dwellers, and the Sheridans hadn't happened to hear about it, they would still be having their party. Finally, Mrs. Sheridan takes off the new hat she has been trying on and bestows it on Laura in a sort of rite of initiation to adulthood:

> . . . the hat is yours. It's made for you. It's much too young for me. I've never seen you look such a picture. Look at yourself.

But Laura refuses to look. Mrs. Sheridan accuses her of being both extravagant and a spoilsport: "People like that don't expect sacrifices from us." Uncomprehending, Laura walks into her own room, and catches herself in the mirror, unintentionally:

> this charming girl in the mirror, in her black hat trimmed with gold daisies, and a long black velvet ribbon. Never had she imagined she could look like that.

Against Laura's will and her beliefs, her mother's extravagant gift jolts aside the notion of death, and Laura decides to "remember it again after the party is over."

One of the great surprises of this story is the way the actual party in the garden is over before we know it, almost before it begins, taking up less than a page. The guests,

> like bright birds that had alighted in the Sheridans' garden for this one afternoon, on their way to—where? Ah, what happiness it is to be with people who all are happy, to press hands, press cheeks, smile into eyes.

One of the guests tells Laura she looks "quite Spanish" in her hat, meaning: romantic, sexual, foreign. Laura basks in the compliments and offers tea and passion fruit ices.

> And the perfect afternoon slowly ripened, slowly faded, slowly its petals closed.

The afternoon is a flower, and the party itself only a small stopover on the migration of the birds, just as human life, of the individual or the species, is a moment in the life of the cosmos. The party takes up such a small portion of the whole story that we begin to wonder if life itself might be what is referred to in the title: Life is the garden party we prepare for, experience, reel away from. We grow into our adult costumes, revel in them, and just down the hill is death.

After the guests have gone home the Sheridans sit down in the deserted tent in the garden; Mr. Sheridan munches on the leftover sandwiches and brings up the news of the death of the carter. Mrs. Sheridan now has "one of her brilliant ideas." She takes the leftover sandwiches, cakes, cream puffs and heaps them into a big basket and tells Laura to take it down to the grieving family of the dead man. Mrs. Sheridan considers adding lilies, but their sexual parts would stain Laura's dress, so no lilies. She starts to give motherly warnings: "Don't on any account . . ." she trails off and does not finish, not wanting to plant ideas, but hoping to warn against contamination by ingestion, sex, dirt. Above all, though, this unfinished sentence warns against contact with the numinous. Laura, in her lace frock, her exotic hat, and carrying her basket full of bounty, sets off alone like the young goddess Persephone, to the underworld.

> It was just growing dusky as Laura shut their garden gates. A big dog ran by like a shadow. The road gleamed white, and down below in the hollow, the little cottages were in deep shade. How quiet it seemed after the afternoon.

Just as in ancient descriptions of the other world distinctions and boundaries are lost or blurred, here too, once Laura crosses "the broad road" to the dark, smoke-filled lane: the women are wearing men's caps, the shadows of people from within the cottages are "crab-like." An old woman with a crutch puts her feet up on a newspaper, as though reading matter were for the feet not the head. Laura is nervous, wishes she were dressed anyhow but the way she is, wishes to be away, utters a prayer, "Help me, God."

As is often the case in the other world, language, too, is distorted. The widow's sister does not understand what Laura says, and instead of letting her flee at the doorstep, the woman acts as psychopomp, leading her further and further into the house of death. In the heart of the house, the smoky wretched kitchen, Laura finds Mrs. Scott, the new widow, beside the fire. Mrs. Scott is beyond language of any sort, she is a gorgon of grief,

> Her face, puffed up, red, with swollen eyes and swollen lips, looked terrible. She seemed as though she couldn't understand why Laura was there. What did it mean? Why was this stranger standing in the kitchen with a basket?

In her desperation to flee this Medusa, Laura goes back into the passage, opens a door, and finds herself in the bedroom with the dead man. Again Mrs. Scott's sister misreads the young girl's wishes and draws back the sheet, uncovering Mr. Scott's face:

> So remote, so peaceful . . . he was wonderful, beautiful. While they were laughing and while the band was playing, this marvel had come to the lane. Happy . . . happy . . . All is well, said that sleeping face. This is just as it should be. I am content.

Instead of the gasp of horror we expect, it is as though the archangel who visited the rose bushes in the beginning of the story has passed by again: Laura is overcome by the peace and beauty; she feels the need to cry and to say something to the dead man. She sobs, childishly, and then says the wonderfully bizarre and fitting prayer, "Forgive my hat." This is properly reminiscent of *forgive us our trespasses,* for her hat was both the cause of Laura's forgetting about the death and the extravagant insignia of her own coming into sexual flower. It is a mark of her liveliness and fertility, and of her ability to travel back to the world of the living.

Having looked death in the face, having sobbed and spoken to it, Laura can now find her way out of the house without a guide. At the boundary of the underworld she finds her brother, Laurie, waiting in the shadows. He asks her if it was awful, and she replies that it was marvelous, but her experience and her new insight are so far beyond her capacity for words that all she can do is stammer, "Isn't life . . . isn't life?"

Laurie, being her twin, understands completely, and is only able, himself, to say, "Isn't it, darling?"

I noted earlier that the language of the other world differs from the language of our world in that often it is distorted, unintelligible, gibbering, or sibylline; often it needs an interpreter. Laura and Laurie, standing on the boundary of that world, are not able to be completely coherent, and the adjective that she needs, that they both need, is not utterable. For any single word would be too finite, too constricting and mortal for the concept that she is struggling to recount. As though in answer to her mother's unfinished sentence warning her to avoid all contact with the numinous, Laura's echoing and broken sentence to her brother demonstrates that she has in fact just collided with it.

Another way of looking at their enigmatic words: Having gazed on death in the underworld, Laura reverses Death's negating statement, *Life Is Not,* to give the affirming and infinitely open-ended question, *Isn't Life?* This is perhaps her version of what Parmenides finds in the underworld, his startling discovery that *Being Is.*

At the end of the story Laura and Laurie stand in each other's arms at the junction of the lane and the broad white road that separates this world from the domain below; in the darkness her black hat and its black velvet ribbon would no longer be visible, but the daisies circling its rim would glow in whatever light remains, seeming to form a crown of gold.

IV. The Other World of Fiction

It is time for me to revisit my original claim: that our entrance into the other world when we read fiction is in many ways analogous to the hero's descent to the underworld. I base this on the three qualities that seem most indicative to me about such journeys: the blurring of boundaries, the distortion of time, and the distortion of language.

If the fiction is good enough, we *lose* ourselves; we lose our *selves* as we lose all sense of what is going on around us. While we are entranced, we shift from our personal sense of time as narrative time takes hold.

Like dream time, narrative time is non-linear, with no metric unless one is imposed. It is elastic, stretching and contracting, with flash-backs and flash-forwards imposed at will. Perhaps narrative time echoes what I would call "mind time," or the time of our imagination, where—although our bodies are embedded in actual time—our thoughts flicker, multi-layered and multi-stranded, looping back, not at all one-at-a-time, but singing over and through one another like birds in the forest at dawn.

Narrative language too is distorted, partly because we are taking it in through our eyes instead of through our ears, and partly because the author's or narrator's voice is so strangely married to our own.[10] This is another way in which the border of the self can become indistinct, another blurring of boundaries.

Reading, we come up alongside perceptions that are often more vast or illuminating or crazed or perverse than our own limitations permit. But to what extent these perceptions are revealed to us depends also on what *we* bring. The experience, thoughtfulness, and intellect of the reader informs the text, imparts intelligence, if you will, to the text itself, as well as the other way around.

So we descend into story, tumbled into that underworld by the unstable geometry of the nature of openings in general and by any particular instabilities that may be present. In the ensuing silence and stillness of reading to ourselves, under the guidance of a master-seer, also called "authorial instruction," we enter a state where time and language take on new properties. There we see visions, hear voices, and perhaps converse with the Dead. This curling up with a book, this incubation, is not at all a passive undertaking, but is an enactment of the hero's trip to the realm of Hades, and if we prepare ourselves properly, if we pour the dark wine into the votive pit, if Right and Justice are in conjunction, if the deities or the Dead decide to speak to us, we might just emerge with a revelation or two.

NOTES

1   I am indebted to Philip Fisher for pointing out to me this coupling of liminality and entrancement, which he examines in the context of early novels.

2   Paula Fox, *The Widow's Children* (New York: Norton, 1999).

3   Charles Baxter, *The Feast of Love* (New York: Pantheon, 2000).

4   Eva Brann, *Homeric Moments: Clues to Delight in Reading* The Odyssey *and* The Iliad (Philadelphia: Paul Dry Books, 2002), chapter 30, "Odysseus in Hades."

5   The best translation of the Proem, and the one I use here, is from Peter Kingsley's *In the Dark Places of Wisdom* (Inverness: The Golden Sufi Center, 1999).
     For parts 2 and 3 of the poem, probably the best translation is by David Gallup, *Parmenides of Elea: Fragments* (Toronto: University of Toronto Press, 1984).

6 For a complete examination of Parmenides and incubation, see Peter Kingsley's *In the Dark Places of Wisdom.*

7 Although she is unnamed in the text, Kingsley notes that because she is Queen of the Dead, Persephone is very rarely called by name in Greek texts and that whenever someone is referred to as simply "the Goddess" it is understood to be Persephone.

8 If we look back to the Proem, we see these rotary motions not only in the chariot wheels and the doors to the Mansions of Night and Day, but also in the more complete rotations of the keys to the gigantic doors held by Justice, as they turn in one direction to open, and the other to lock; I would claim also in the pivoting of her scales, which are unmentioned. Perhaps it is going too far to say there could also be a quarter rotation when the maidens are pushing back the veils from their faces.

9 Katherine Mansfield, "The Garden Party," in *The Garden Party and Other Stories* (London: Penguin, 1922; reprint, 1983).

10 Tom Lux has a wonderful poem about this, with a slightly different take on the matter. See "The Voice You Hear When You Read Silently," from Thomas Lux, *New and Selected Poems* (Boston: Houghton Mifflin, 1997).

ON THE PERPETUATION OF OUR INSTITUTIONS

Christopher B. Nelson

> The two communities that I love, the country and the college, have
> both had a founding and a re-founding, and I suspect it's always so.
> The first founding is bright, the documents are fluently enlightened,
> the negotiations are lustily assertive, the institutions are confidently
> devised. The second founding is a work of nostalgia for bright begin-
> nings, sadness for tainting tragedies; there's experience, sophistication,
> deeper delving into the philosophical and providential roots: from
> Jefferson to Lincoln.
>
> —*Eva Brann,* Open Secrets/Inward Prospects *(123)*

No one has given St. John's College a finer public voice than Eva Brann. For
that matter, there may be no better voice anywhere for liberal education
itself. Certainly my own way of speaking has been shaped by hers. From
time to time, I receive copies of remarks she has delivered elsewhere, always
with a little "post-it" attached telling me that it's for my "cannibalistic use."
I have eaten those pieces up, digested them, and tried to make something
new of them that I may call my own. Every now and then, I see that some
particularly felicitous expression has found its way into my concoction—
and I know it when I see it as something that is purely Eva, but something
that now belongs to me, too. I carry a little of Eva with me whenever I speak
about the college to friends and colleagues beyond our halls. I won't be able
to hide that in this essay, and I've even encouraged a few Eva-isms to appear
without reference. It is her distinctive voice on behalf of liberal education
in the larger world that has inspired this essay in tribute.

The question I wish to address here is shared by every president of a
small liberal arts college (and probably by their governing boards and faculties too): how do we perpetuate what is distinctly ours in a world that
cares less and less about making thoughtful distinctions? The times are
highly charged, the speed of communications lightning quick, and the
expectations of a wealthy society growing beyond bounds. Business practices and focus groups are replacing learning communities. Commercial
sound bites are drowning out our attempts at conversation about the old

educational truisms. We are facing pressure to reshape our campus communities and retool for a new age. How do we choose the path that is right for each of our schools?

Eva Brann's reflection quoted above suggests a way. Each of our country's liberal arts colleges has had a luminous founding, with expansive and optimistic founding documents and enlightened leadership. Some of us, like St. John's College, have had a refounding that was every bit as luminous as its original founding in the radical changes it brought about. But most refoundings, those that must take place in the hearts of each generation of a school's defenders, are efforts to recapture the original spark. They require a healthy application of good sense learned from years of experience in applying the original idea to a practical reality. The passion needed to spark a new beginning wanes and must be replaced by some kind of institutional framework lest the entire enterprise die out entirely with the passing of an earlier generation.

The question for us is how to keep our flame burning, long past the founding days. Our institutions of learning are, or ought to be, radical in relation to our traditions. We ought to know enough about our past to understand how we have been shaped by it. But we also need to be free enough to ask whether and how that past ought to continue to shape our future, whether it holds enough truth that we should be guided by it.

We are communities of learning, first and foremost. Our colleges exist to promote learning activity and to protect the conditions of learning. It is not enough that we may have built a grand edifice, a reputation for excellence, or even a faculty renowned for its scholarship. We want classrooms teeming with energy and conversation that come from students who wish to learn because learning is desirable for its own sake. We would banish passivity from the classroom, in order that students might find their own paths to learning. Otherwise, we risk becoming antiquarian museums and libraries, rather than centers of learning. Libraries and museums are protectors of our heritage and contain the means and equipment for learning in our schools; they may even contain all that's worth preserving, but they are preservative, conservative institutions, useful to our purposes but not identical with them. We must remember that as learning communities we belong to the present, not the past.

We must keep alive to our purposes, promoting liberal learning in the ever precarious present, threatened by the Scylla of institutional atrophy and antiquarian tendency on the one side and the Charybdis of consumerism on the other. On the one hand, we risk losing all desire to challenge the world, which is the spark to learning. On the other, we risk fueling the desire to sell only what is wanted at the expense of what is needed by the students who come to us for help in shaping their education. Our very virtues and strong foundation stories can lead us to defensiveness and stagnation; we can come to believe that we already have the answers that our founders set out to seek, particularly when we see about us so many others who have lost their way. Yet, if we keep ourselves too open to the intellectual fancies of our age, we lose our identity. If we fear to fight the outside challenges to those things we cherish most, we risk becoming what we least want to be: a mere cipher among the indistinguishable mass of schools who do what they are told (by their governments, their students or the marketplace) rather than what they believe to be right.

Let me offer a few suggestions to avoid our crashing upon those rocky shoals—suggestions offered to help liberal arts colleges maintain their place of distinction in the world of higher education:

I. Recall Your Place and Maintain Your Ground

Stand for liberal education, but abandon the effort to find one, broad, bland, expansive way of speaking of it as if we must reach agreement with one another. We should hail our distinctive voices and let them all be heard. The better any one of us is understood, the better for all of us. Our publics need to hear voices that are anchored in a real place and time, inhabited by real people. Truth-telling then becomes possible. When we speak with one voice we risk speaking falsely or without sufficient conviction to be convincing.

Distinguish liberal from utilitarian learning. Earning a living is about means; making a life worth living is about ends. Liberal education is concerned with ends; mechanical, utilitarian, professional or vocational learning is about means. We don't live in order to work; we work in order to live a good life. It is, thus, a higher form of education that helps us understand just what a good life might look like, in order that we might live it well.

Defend the search for truth—or at least avoid foreclosing the possibility of truth. We don't have to have the truth to believe it is there, to have some sense that one thing is better than another for a reason. For learning to take hold, the student must find some way to make the lesson his or her own. To make it one's own requires that something be at stake for the student. The student is driven then to ask, not just what something means, but whether it makes any difference what something means (i.e., whether it is true or not).

Acknowledge that liberal learning is about foundations and elements. Liberal education is elementary education in the highest sense. For this reason, what we teach is important. We should explain and defend the choices we make to give our students subject matter that is worthy of their study and contemplation. Give our students material that will give them practice at thinking, rather than pretend we can teach them how to think.

Promote the desire to learn over the mania to test performance; success in passing tests will follow the former as night does the day. Therefore, we should construct academic programs that encourage the desire to learn for its own sake rather than for the sake of the grade. This requires that we give attention both to the quality of the materials we use to teach from and our ways of giving them life in the classroom. Let us give our students matter that will be worthy of their love. After all, it is love that moves us to the good in this world, including all the good that can be learned. We might even consider using the desire to learn as the principal criterion for admission to our colleges, for that desire will better determine a student's ability to learn than a high SAT score.

Abandon the language of the marketplace. We are not delivery systems; students are not consumers; and education is not a product that can be bartered, going to the highest bidder. Socrates had it right when he reminded us that the power of learning is in the soul of each of us and cannot be put into us, just as one cannot put sight into blind eyes.

Own up to our commitment to serving the interest of the individual soul. Our duty is to the health of the individual. Good citizenship and well-paying jobs should never be seen by us as more than useful byproducts of our central activity.

Reclaim the argument that our colleges serve the public good. We do this by helping to bring thoughtful adults into the world—adults who are free to think for themselves and free to choose paths of action they consider to be best rather than those that are easiest or most popular. It is only incidental to our purposes that our graduates earn better salaries and contribute more to the global economy.

II. Remain High-Minded but Practical

Fight only the fights worth fighting. There are a thousand chimeras in the world. Some are hideous but will never threaten; ignore them. Some can be fought collectively by our collegiate associations; support those groups.

Others come in an endless stream of constituent complaints about issues peripheral to our central purposes. As most of those issues can be resolved by giving them some attention, attend to them; develop a plan with a timeline and a set of priorities. We are all stronger for attending to things that have been ignored, and our alumni, friends, students and faculty will be happier for it. As to those that threaten the very identity of our schools, take them head on. This requires that we have some sense of who we are. Self-knowledge is the key to self-preservation. My experience here suggests that we will gain respect and strength by defending what is truly of the essence, so long as we're flexible when our first principles are not at stake.

Embrace institutional self-examination but beware of external means of assessment. With our students, we accept the wisdom of Socrates, that the unexamined life is not worth living. Another way of putting this is that our students might as well be dead if they are not asking themselves who they are, what kind of world they inhabit, and what their place should be in the scheme of things. The institutional equivalent of death is atrophy and stagnation. We have unlimited ways to come to know ourselves better and to improve our campuses. We should admit this publicly and seek the support we need to improve ourselves. On the other hand, we should not fear to fight those silly rankings and so-called science-based measurements that take no account of the liberal arts we are trying to help our students acquire.

Balance is required in all things. To paraphrase a favorite expression of Eva Brann's, the president and the board ought to be concerned with existence ("keeping us in being"), while the faculty ought to be concerned with essence ("keeping us being who we are meant to be"). The one without the other is death. Keep the two intertwined by every possible device. This suggests balance at the practical level, too. The whole organization improves best when all of its parts are getting some attention, not just those who have shouted the loudest, had the most success, or claimed the greatest need.

We are perpetual institutions. This should not be an excuse for delay in attending to things, but rather a reminder that time is on our side. We will be here tomorrow. Therefore, careful planning is required, and all good things will be redeemed in time. Ideally, we should want to give to the next generation at least as much as we have had to work with in this one. Our financial people call this intergenerational equity. Do not spend down capital today that will be required to preserve the college tomorrow, but do not spend so little that you have sacrificed the essence of the college today. This is a healthy tension to carry with us.

III. Maintain Institutional Practices That Preserve Institutional Ideals

Champion and fund the cause of broad and affordable access to our colleges, and provide the means to complete the course of study with us. A liberal education does not recognize class or economic distinction. We are sometimes challenged for being elitist, providing an education to the rich and the powerful. For most of us, this charge is simply false. The best education is available to everybody with the desire and the ability to learn; no segment of higher education has done more to provide the economic means to those without the financial wherewithal than the national liberal arts colleges. If a student has the desire to enroll and meets our entrance requirements, we provide the way and the means.

Accept and explain the high cost of education. Education is expensive because it requires the giving of the life of one well-educated human being to another, a devotion of time that cannot be compromised without being cheapened. (Now, there's another Eva-ism.) Let's not apologize for that. Rather, explain why it's a veritable bargain. After all, none of us charges what it costs to educate a student, even one who is able to pay the full tuition.

Encourage intellectual freedom among the faculty; it stimulates intellectual growth. Freedom is required for institutional health. In our governance structures and leadership constraints, we should leave enough room for the freedom to grow and change. The alternative is defensiveness, stagnation, or unhealthy strife. A liberal education is grounded in the conviction that humility of intellect and humility of spirit are required for wisdom: we understand that we are still seeking the answers we don't have and still aching for something we desire. Faculty who are not engaged in their own learning cannot hope to help free their students. To encourage intellectual freedom among the faculty, we need to provide the funds and the opportunity for leisure study. Our faculty need the renewal that comes from discovering, over and over, what they don't know and improving their understanding of what they purport to know.

Encourage in our students the freedom to be at leisure. Freedom requires that students have some time to look at, contemplate, and talk about fundamental questions. This requires that they get some break from the practical pressures, even from paid work, if possible. School is "time out" to study (Eva again!); it's not just another job, another test, more work. We are loading our students with more and more work, and giving them less and less time for "leisure" in its highest sense.

Encourage all opportunities for learning together: faculty, students, and staff. Learning is a social activity and a cooperative art. Support the many ways we might come together on campus and we will remain vital and close to our fundamental purposes. One way to attend to community health is to try to treat all community members, students, faculty and staff, as ends in themselves, not simply as means to our institutional purposes. This is impractical at its limit, but is nonetheless a worthy object of pursuit.

Acknowledge all shortcomings. This will keep us from taking ourselves too seriously. It will also help us attend to our faults. Eva Brann: "Few things are as harmful to community as terminal idealism."

IV. Be Flexible

If we anchor ourselves to unshakeable principles, we may find it difficult to consider changes that might be healthy for the college. We should concern ourselves less with the principles behind our actions and instead satisfy ourselves that we have adequate reasons for everything we do. It is easier to make a change and easier to undo one if we are giving reasons for our actions rather than trying to find an underlying principle for everything.

The essential problem I have tried to address here is how to organize ourselves best for the freedom we wish to encourage in our lively colleges. It's easy to become more complex and hard to become simpler, easy to add things and hard to take them away. Simplicity is more likely to come from an attitude that encourages freedom than one that is so rigid that a rule is required for every action.

Where is the path through all the obstacles? That remains the big question. And that question has to be rediscovered and re-answered with each generation. We should not look back to our founders for anything but the big picture, because we have to live with our present condition. We cannot live in the past and expect that we will retain our most radical characteristic: that we value the question more than the answer, the search more than its end . . . not because we don't want the truth or an end to our toil, but because experience tells us that the end of each search is the beginning of the next, the answer to each question the occasion for another. Questions alone make learning possible.

I close with an appeal to the final lines from the fourth of T. S. Eliot's *Four Quartets:*

> We shall not cease from exploration
> And the end of all our exploring
> Will be to arrive where we started
> And know the place for the first time.
> (*Little Gidding*)

To rediscover our origins is to refound our institutions and to remake our foundation stories. If we are alive to learning, it is impossible that we will not remake those stories over and over again. Like anything else, we start with something we think we know, and discover in our study of it that we only knew it as a child might. We find that we never really understood it at all, or that we now see something altogether new that we were sure was never there in the first place. That is when we come back to the place where we started and find that we now know it for the first time. That is what liberal learning should be: a continual rediscovery and deeper understanding of what is right there before us but only barely known. We need to practice such liberal learning in the very activity of refounding our communities of learning.

The trick seems to be that we must find ways to stay young as we grow old. This will allow us the wisdom, will and delight to continue the search for happiness which is at the heart of liberal education.

THE WORK OF IMAGINATION: SUNDRY AND SUMMARY

Joe Sachs

Wherever you go, you will not
find the limits of the soul,
though you travel every road,
so deep a *logos* it has.

—*Heracleitus*

EVA BRANN'S AREA of special interest is everything that has to do with thinking, imagining, and speaking. This makes writing something appropriate to her life's work akin to hitting the side of a barn. In order to narrow the scope of my contribution to this celebratory collection, I have decided to confine my discussion to the thinking, imagining, and speaking that is done by those who are not human beings. I am talking not about alien intelligences, but just the reverse, about those other intelligences that are most familiar to us and with whom we are most at home, the animals we share our lives with.

That animals have intelligence is not granted by everyone, but the denial of this fairly obvious fact can stem from very different motives. One variety of denial comes from those who only grudgingly grant that they themselves possess intelligence, as opposed to mechanical reflexes; animals comfort them with what they take to be evidence that highly complex behavior can be displayed by mere machines. The opposite kind of denial comes from those who are concerned to protect a conception of human uniqueness; they do this by attributing to mere instinct anything animals do that seems intelligent. My hope in this discussion is to clarify a few aspects of animal intelligence that should pose no threat either to our self-esteem or to our humility.

As presiding spirits for our discussion, we might call upon the figures of Rene Descartes and Thomas Aquinas. Thomas, though he is willing to grant animals a share of rationality, minimizes it by saying that they participate in reason only by *aestimationem naturalem*, translated by the Dominican Fathers as natural instinct (*Summa Theologiae* I, Q. 96, art. 1), and he makes it clear that they are thereby remote from the divine image (Q. 72).

But Descartes famously announces in his first published work that animals have no reason at all, but are only mechanisms no different in any important way from pieces of clockwork (*Discourse on Method,* Part V). Where Thomas looks upon all things as parts of a hierarchical scale in which animals are near us in having souls but more distant from the provident creator, Descartes ruptures being into the well-known duality of mind and body. Descartes takes pains to remove all traces of soul from body, with the result that the remnant of soul (*anima* in Latin) becomes reduced to mind (*animus*). If one follows his lead—and anyone who sees the primary distinction among phenomena as between the mental and the physical has wittingly or unwittingly followed it—there is no longer any way in which the experience of things other than ourselves can present evidence of anything other than body.

These two ways of assessing animal intelligence are consequences of deeper opinions, fundamental attitudes that govern the way any evidence will be interpreted. But at the beginning of the twentieth century a set of experiments was reported which was widely taken as demonstrating the truth of the Cartesian view. Ivan Pavlov, in experiments begun in 1901 in the township of Koltushi on the outskirts of St. Petersburg, "conditioned" dogs to salivate in the absence of food when presented with arbitrary stimuli such as the sound of a bell or a metronome or the sight of an ellipse projected on a screen. There seems then to be no need to assume any mental event between the sensory stimulation of a dog's nervous system and its motor response, since no animal that could think at all would think the sound of a bell or sight of an elliptical shape was something to eat.[1] Pavlov's dogs are evidently machines into which he has introduced a malfunction. But then it would seem that we too must be machines, since a human being might salivate at the sight of a pair of golden arches, or the sound of a radio jingle, even when no food is at hand. Pavlov did not shy away from this extension of his conclusions, but his work did not rule out the possibility that we exhibit other kinds of behavior as well. As for animals, though, he understood his experiments to be a display of their "higher nervous activity," in which the entire psychological life of the dog became objective and measurable. Henceforth, there could be no reason to consider an animal as anything other than an input-output, stimulus-response machine.

But it is interesting that Pavlov chose to speak of the arbitrary sensory inputs to which he conditioned his dogs to respond as signals. Erwin Straus, in the book *The Primary World of Senses* (The Free Press of Glencoe, 1963, a translation of *Vom Sinn der Sinne*), argues that the usual interpretation of

Pavlov's experiments was not only mistaken but just the opposite of what those experiments in fact made evident. It was a failure to reflect on the nature of signals that caused the misinterpretation. The English word "signal" had come to be used in the late 19th century for transmissions by radio or along telegraph wires, and that is clearly the sense in which Pavlov uses his word (which, when transliterated into the Roman alphabet, is also "signal").[2] But does a flickering streetlight transmit a signal? From whom? To whom? We can answer those questions about the light transmitted in accordance with "one if by land and two if by sea," and by so doing distinguish that transmission from the innumerable others with which the world is filled. What are the conditions that determine whether Pavlov's lights and sounds become signals? The answer to that question is there to be found in his reports of his work, but it was not remarked on by him.

Straus points out that, in the quarter-century during which Pavlov's experiments became known and celebrated around the world, before Pavlov's own description of them was translated into any of the world languages other than his own, one particular false summary of them came to be accepted and enshrined in textbooks. It was believed that Pavlov conditioned his dogs to respond to audible or visible signals by displaying them at the same time that he fed the dogs. Pavlov himself perpetuated this misunderstanding by summarizing the cause of a conditioned reflex as "a coincidence in time of the action of any previously neutral stimulus with some definite unconditioned stimulus" (I. P. Pavlov, *Conditioned Reflexes*, Dover, 1960, p. 27), but he immediately modifies this to mean not an exact coinciding but an overlap in time with a necessary order. Only when the arbitrary stimulus appeared before the feeding began did it ever become a signal; without that order of appearance of the stimuli, even 427 repetitions could not produce a conditioned response. But if the association of the arbitrary stimulus with the act of feeding was only an event in the pathways of the nervous system, why would not simultaneity of reception associate them even more strongly? The assumption that it must do just that is clearly what led to the false reports of what Pavlov had done. But the temporal order of events might very well be important if what is at stake is whether an arbitrary sensation will be taken by the dog as a signal. Signals carry meaning. An open-minded reflection on Pavlov's experiments would have to raise the question whether, under differing circumstances, the same stimuli *mean* something different to the dog. That question in turn requires that one keep open the possibility that, like ourselves, the dog can assess the meaning of things that are presented to it.

If we are to give serious consideration to the meaning the sound of a bell or the sight of a bright ellipse might have to a dog, we must take into account the whole of the circumstances in which it is heard or seen. In Pavlov's experiments, the stimuli were presented to a dog that was standing on a table, held in harnesses tied to a rigid frame, in darkness and silence, in a room from which all living things other than that one dog had been excluded. Otherwise, says Pavlov "we should get hopelessly lost as soon as we began to seek for cause and effect among so many and various influences, so intertwined and entangled as to form a veritable chaos" (p. 20). But while conscientiousness of this sort would not bother a machine, it might alter the reactions of a dog. If the dog has a state of mind—and whether it does must be in doubt prior to the experiment—that state of mind might be greatly affected by sensory deprivation, forced immobility, and solitude. If the dog is also hungry, the sudden arrival of food in its mouth through a mechanical device might be an event of such importance that it would prevent the dog from paying any attention to the sound of a bell heard simultaneously. Presumably, though, the sound of the bell, whether attended to or not, would have no different an effect in the sensory neural pathways. It is only in the consciousness of the dog that it could go unregistered, even when heard 427 times. But suppose what first emerged from the silent darkness was the bell, and the mechanically conveyed food followed it. Might the bell then soon, after only a few repetitions, come to be heard as a signal that food is about to appear in its mouth? Signals bear significance. They signify something other than themselves to some being that can experience not just the bare objects present to it but their significance in its world.

One more fact, also absent from the original reception of the news of Pavlov's research, makes this conclusion even less escapable. Not only were no conditioned reflexes formed unless the temporal order of events permitted the arbitrary stimuli to become signals, but no conditioned reflexes were ever formed, no matter what was done to a dog, until the dog had been in isolation in the laboratory for days. The dog's nervous system would be the same mechanism on day one as on any subsequent day. If we were talking about human subjects, we would have no hesitation about saying what would be different: the state of mind of someone subjected to such drastic psychological deprivation must have an effect on all of that person's experiences. I have no doubt that dogs too can become resigned and demoralized, desensitized to a monotonous environment and hypersensitive to sudden novelties. Pavlov explains that time was needed to overcome the "freedom reflex" brought on by the dog's restraints and the "investigatory reflex" evoked by unfamiliar surroundings (pp. 12–13); one might say instead that the dog's spirit of independence and curiosity had to be broken or at least quelled before Pavlov's conditioning could begin.

Erwin Straus begins his discussion of Pavlov's work by observing that Christopher Columbus, after three voyages to the Americas, always insisted that he had reached India. Straus has allowed me to see that Pavlov demonstrated, in spite of himself, that dogs occupy, along with ourselves, a world in which there is not a mere mechanical registering of objects but an experience of meaning. There is of course more than one sense in which things can carry meaning. A sequence of dots and dashes, or short and long buzzes, is a signal only to someone who understands the code. The sound of a bell that heralds the one bit of relief (or new torment) in a bleak existence requires no understanding to be perceived as a signal, but it does require an imagination. The circumstances in which no conditioned reflex can be formed prove that the linkage between sensory input and motor output in Pavlov's dogs took place not in their nervous systems but in their imaginations.

Now even if Pavlov's experiments proved that dogs do in fact have conscious lives, the behavior consequent upon the signals of which they became conscious in those experiments was still entirely involuntary. This sort of passive relation to one's own behavior is just what people mean by speaking of instinct. The question then arises whether animals are capable of taking conscious control and direction of any of their behavior. In the decade following that of Pavlov's work, a series of experiments was conducted that is less widely known, and was designed to shed light on just this question. Wolfgang Köhler, stranded during World War I at the anthropoid research station of the Prussian Academy of Science at Tenerife in the Canary Islands, worked primarily with nine chimpanzees. He did not bring them into a distorted environment alien to their lives, but introduced new elements, of interest to them, into a place where they were accustomed to be. He set up practical problems for them to solve in a large enclosed outdoor playground, and paid attention to what they did. His effort was never to force the chimps to behave in ways he had thought through in advance, but to give them surroundings that contained goals they would want to achieve and a variety of materials to work with, letting them display intelligence if they had any, and requiring of himself that he display the intelligence needed to understand what he saw.

The experiments are described in detail in his book *The Mentality of Apes* (Harcourt, Brace, 1927), and many of them were filmed. I saw some of these films about thirty years ago, and retain vivid memories of them. In the experiments, a bunch or basket of bananas was suspended out of the reach of the chimp, with sticks and boxes lying around the playground. In some cases a chimp tried to climb a stick but fell over. In others a chimp used a long stick to knock some bananas down. In others, boxes were piled up, well or badly, and climbed successfully or unsuccessfully. In the experiment that made the greatest impression on me, a chimp named Sultan took one of the human beings present by the hand, led him under the bananas, and climbed onto his shoulder, where he could pick the fruit with ease. In another experiment that in some respects perhaps should have impressed me even more, this same Sultan pushed a thinner bamboo stick into the end of a thicker one to make a pole long enough to knock down the fruit. The chimps appear to have been approaching a goal by trial and error, but not blindly. What is characteristic of all their attempts is that they met some obstacle, paused, looked around, looked back and forth from something in the playground to the fruit, and eventually undertook some new procedure in a directed way. They give every appearance of having come up with a solution to the problem in the imagination before attempting it in practice. Köhler concludes that the chimps were learning by means of insight, the familiar experience in which the elements of a situation suddenly come together for us in a new pattern.

Köhler's work was a variation on an earlier series of experiments by Edward Thorndike, a student of William James and an investigator admired by Pavlov; Thorndike had set up for dogs and cats the sort of "intelligence tests" sometimes given to human children. Köhler quotes Thorndike as concluding "I failed to find any act that even *seemed* due to reasoning." From Köhler's point of view, Thorndike's experiments were designed in an unimaginative way, and the only thing important about his conclusion is its implied acknowledgment that it is possible for some pieces of behavior to seem intelligent. Köhler's chimps certainly seem intelligent, and among them Sultan seems particularly intelligent. And Köhler himself seems to me to have displayed great intelligence in finding ways to let the thinking of his chimps make an appearance. But ought one to conclude that chimpanzees are uncharacteristic of animals in general, near the human borderline, evolutionary precursors of a kind of life utterly different from the common animal pattern? We might be cautious about such an opinion simply because Köhler's example teaches us that we need to learn how to look for and recognize intelligence in any other beings. And I can supply, for what it is worth, one piece of evidence that dogs may not be incapable of figuring something out in the same way the chimps did. I once had a dog named Peanut, of no determinate breed, that I was able to take for walks without a leash. She liked to bring home a stick from a walk, usually the longest one she could find and always held in her mouth near one of its ends. One day she was trotting along the sidewalk with an unusually long stick protruding into the street on her right. As she approached a parked car she began to slow down, and before reaching the car she stopped and dropped the stick. She looked back and forth from car to stick a couple of times, then bent down, picked up the stick by its other end, and trotted rapidly and confidently on with the stick projecting into the front yards on her left.

It is the interval between the recognition of an obstacle to a goal, and the attempt to surmount the obstacle, that is crucial to any consideration of animal instincts. When Thomas Aquinas calls the source of an animal's rational behavior an *aestimatio naturalis,* I take him to mean that the assessment of the situation confronting the animal must be already implanted by nature, so that an appropriate bodily response can be automatic. It is the going awry of such an assessment that is usually given as the strongest proof that behavior is merely instinctive. In *On Aggression* (Bantam, 1967, p. 114), Konrad Lorenz cites a case in which an airplane, flying low over a silver-fox farm, caused all the mother vixens to eat their young. But then what do we say about the situations in which Sultan or Peanut paused and came up with a successful solution of a problem? Is there a meta-instinct that selects one from among an array of conflicting instinctive responses? Or is there an assessment that has not been made already by nature but is newly arrived at by the animal on the spot? An account Donald McCaig gives in *Eminent Dogs, Dangerous Men* (Harper Perennial, 1991, p. 39) of a situation once encountered by a sheepdog is worth quoting in full:

> The trainer Tony Illey has said, "The most difficult thing I ever saw a dog do was bring a ewe who'd just lost her lamb through a field full of lambing ewes."
>
> Let me offer a gloss: Ewes with new lambs are extremely protective of their lambs and often charge a dog. When they lose sight of their lamb, they assume the dog has killed it, and despite his teeth will try determinedly to trample him. A ewe who's lost her lamb will rush back and forth seeking it, bleating to other newborn lambs trying to collect one. The other mothers are confused by this, and when the dog gets near them they, too, go on the attack.
>
> Unlike Tony Illey, I don't think what this dog did was difficult. It was impossible. Knowing that the dog can read sheep better than any man and can react quicker than any man, what commands would you give him?
>
> Correct answer: his name.

I offer the further gloss that the meaning of the correct command is "Stay alert. Continually reassess." But even if we grant that animals can assess and deal with the things around them in non-instinctive, purposely chosen ways, can animals ever introduce new components into their environments to change their relations to those things? Köhler devoted two chapters of *The Mentality of Apes* to the making of implements by his chimps, and Sultan's double stick seems incontrovertible evidence that they did exactly that, but it was only a half-century later that the world at large was willing to accept the fact that animals can make tools. In practice, anthropologists had come to use tool-making as the criterion for declaring skeletal remains to be those of primitive humans as distinct from advanced apes. But Jane Goodall put an end to that authoritative belief in the 1960s when she reported observing chimps engaged in "termite fishing." Goodall went where the chimps were and watched them live their lives as they naturally do. In the Gombe Stream National Park on the shores of Lake Tanganyika she made the massively detailed observations reported in her book *The Chimpanzees of Gombe* (Harvard U. P., 1986). She found that termites were an important part of their diet, but were generally inaccessible in the recesses of nests or rotten logs. What the chimps regularly did was take some thin flexible object and modify it so that it would serve as an eating utensil. They would strip leaves off a twig, or strip the edges off a stalk of grass, to make a suitable tool to poke into the places the termites were, pull it back out with termites clinging to it, and draw it through their mouths to leave its tasty occupants behind. When I saw a film of a chimp enjoying himself in this way, I was reminded of the flourish with which Charlie Chaplin, radiating pride in his own ingenuity, drew a nail from his boiled shoe out of his mouth in *The Gold Rush*.

Now most people who have been associated with St. John's College will be aware of other and deeper criteria for distinguishing humans from animals. One of them is well articulated by Hans Jonas in the book *The Phenomenon of Life* (Harper & Row, 1966) in a chapter called "Image-making and the Freedom of Man." The claim is that only a human being can ever see an image as an image. For a bird, a scarecrow is either sufficiently like a human figure to fool it, or sufficiently unlike one to be ignored. We humans have the unique capacity to see an object as same and other at once, in the sophisticated recognition of something as an image of something else. But while the nature of an image is a topic worthy of our wonder, its human exclusivity is by no means clear. I have in mind watching a cat play with a ball of yarn. When it pounces on the yarn, does that mean it has mistaken it for a mouse? Does its subsequent behavior reflect the discovery of a mistake? If it continues to play, does that mean the cat takes the ball of yarn to be at once the same as and other than a mouse? In a chapter on carefreeness in his book *Man, Mutable and Immutable* (Greenwood Press, 1975), Kurt Riezler observes that all play, because it involves semblance, is present only in the subjective attitude of the one playing (pp. 163–167). It is, like signal-recognition, possible only within an interior, conscious life. And I can report that Hans Jonas was well aware of the nature and importance of play. He used to recount with pleasure the fact that, on each of his early shipboard crossings of the Atlantic, there came a moment when a group of dolphins would surround the ship and play. He was convinced that dolphins play and sharks do not. What the dolphins take the ship to be, I cannot guess, but Jonas's belief was that it is for them at such times not a dangerous large obstacle and not a potential source of food, but the occasion for a carefree frolic. That means that their imaginations must be capable of investing an object with more than one kind of significance.[3] I conclude that cats and dolphins, and any other animals that play, see images as images. To her great credit, she in whose honor this essay is written acknowledged in print that she would welcome reasons to be convinced that animals share that capacity with us (Eva T. H. Brann, *The World of the Imagination, Sum and Substance,* Rowman & Littlefield, 1991, p. 651).

Vivid evidence that chimps recognize images as images was reported by E. S. Savage-Rumbaugh in her book *Ape Language: From Conditioned Response to Symbol* (Columbia U. P., 1986). She described what happened one day at Georgia State University in Atlanta, when a chimp named Austin was being videotaped sorting colored blocks: "After calmly sorting for about 30 minutes, Austin casually glanced over at the television monitor and suddenly appeared to recognize himself. He began staring intently at the screen while bobbing up and down and making funny faces. Next he approached the TV and positioned himself just inches from the screen and began to scrutinize his lip movements as he ate a muscadine and drank ice water. . . . For the next twenty minutes, Austin continued to watch himself on the screen as he experimented with different body postures, facial expressions, and methods of eating" (p. 308). In this special case of self-recognition, the dual nature of the image for the one seeing it is undeniable.[4] One might want to argue that even though the cat does not mistake the ball of yarn for a mouse, but playfully treats it as a mouse, it is merely ignoring for awhile conflicting evidence that it is not a mouse and never viewing it in both ways at once. But if Austin recognized a flickering piece of glass as himself, there is no way that he could suppress or ignore the fact that it was also not himself. "That's a mouse" is make-believe, an interplay of possible meanings of an outward object, and one might legitimately wonder whether those meanings are simultaneous or sequential in the imagination of the one playing. "That's me" can be nothing other than an inward recognition of sameness in an outward experience of an object that remains distinct. The very act of facing an object, that places oneself at one pole of the experience, in this instance finds that same self in the opposing pole. And if the structure of experience that permits self-recognition in an image can be present in an animal, it is hard to see why one would want to deny that any other sort of image can be recognized as such by any being with an imagination.

But now we can no longer avoid considering the primary criterion that has perennially been understood as distinguishing human beings from animals. It is not tool making or image recognition but speech. But what should count as speech? Even Aristotle says, at 1253a 12–14 of the *Politics,* that animals signify things to one another (*sêmainein*), and in Bk. IV, Chap. 9, of the *History of Animals,* he acknowledges that the vocal articulation made by some of them might be called a language (*dialektos*). What Aristotle says belongs to humans alone is the power of *logos.*But if this can be absent from significant vocal utterances, then the connection between it and that medium is not a necessary one, and an animal might be thought to have the power of *logos* but not display it by that means. Karl von Frisch discovered that the dances of bees can convey complex information non-vocally.[5] Should they be considered a form of *logos*? How are we to decide? I propose, rather than attempting to begin by defining the word *logos* even provisionally, that we look instead at some instances in which animals have been taught language skills, just to see whether any important ground of distinction seems to present itself.

I first became aware of the work being done on language learning by animals almost thirty years ago when Duane Rumbaugh gave a lecture at St. John's. He had taught a chimp named Lana (because she was being taught a *lang*uage *a*nalogue) to use a large keyboard to display visible symbols for things she wanted. His lecture built up to an announcement that on one momentous day, when Lana was first shown an orange, she said, via her keyboard, "Give me the apple which is orange." He interpreted this to mean that she had subordinated the thing in front of her to a genus and defined it by a difference, all contained in a grammatical sentence. In the question period he was pressed by many of those present to give more details about what had taken place. For one thing, how did Lana signify what he had translated by the words "which is"? He explained that there was a special symbol that she was required to use when combining a name with a modifier, and that she was not given what she requested unless she used it in the order name/special symbol/modifier. Under long and persistent questioning, he finally revealed that the string of symbols he had translated as "Give me the-apple which-is orange" was not a spontaneous response to the sight of the desirable new object, but something like the fortieth string of symbols she produced when she saw it. Clearly Lana had the impressive ability to signify things, actions, and colors by the names of their kinds, but to claim that she had any grasp of the relation "which is" was far-fetched at best. Clearly too, she could give signals of her desires and combine them into compound signals. But the fact that the selection and order of the constituent signals seemed to be a matter of indifference to her, a fact omitted from Rumbaugh's lecture, suggested to me that the string of signals was for her not a sentence but an aggregate or heap. For me, that suspicion was strengthened many years later, when I read about projects other than Rumbaugh's in which apes have been taught the American Sign Language for the deaf. Donald Griffin, in the 1992 book *Animal Minds* (p. 223), tells of a chimp named Nim who signed "Give orange me give eat orange give me eat orange give me you," and a gorilla named Koko who signed "Please milk please me like drink apple bottle."[6]

We have, then, a first candidate for a distinction between animal language use and human speech. To this day, the biography of Lana on the website of Georgia State University's Language Research Center (at gsu.edu) asserts that she "could form syntactically adequate sentences . . . such as '? You give Lana banana which is black'". This assertion is true only if syntax is taken to mean a set of rules for combining things in a required order. Even so, it is not clear from the similar example of the orange that Lana had learned those rules, though it is technically accurate to say that she could form one syntactically adequate combination of symbols among many syntactically inadequate ones. The rules governing her performance are extraneous restrictions something like the one that prohibits a child playing a game from taking a step forward until it first says "Mother, may I?" The symbols for apple, banana, orange, and black clearly have meaning for Lana. But does she understand "banana black" as having a meaning different from "black banana"? And does the symbol which the human experimenters translate as "which is" have any meaning to her at all? If Lana's strings of symbols truly had any syntax, then she would grasp them as wholes, not as aggregates. Syntactical ordering in human speech reflects an inherent order among the ideas of the things signified. We recognize the primary sort of unity in a string of words as a sentence, for which, incidentally, the name in ancient Greek is *logos*. The ordering of a sentence is hierarchical, since its unity is of a different kind from that of the words and phrases within it. If the ordering of Lana's strings of symbols makes no difference to her, she has achieved no new level of meaning by their combination, and it could never make sense to her why 39 ungrammatical requests for an orange went unrewarded. She might or might not eventually learn to string symbols together in the ways the humans want her to, but she would still never grasp a change in meaning in such a change in order.

So on the basis of the available evidence of the Lana project and of sign-language use by apes, I would have to conclude that, while the primary unit of human speech is not the word but the sentence, the primary unit of animal language is the single signifier or signal. It is nonetheless amazing that animals have the capacity to recognize, learn, and use a great variety of such signals intelligently, and that certain imaginative humans have found ways to make evident what the animals were doing all along. There was a day when I realized that Daisy, an impure border collie of mine, had for years known the difference between "Come here" (or "Come'ere") and "Come on." I had never trained her to distinguish those sounds, or in fact to do anything, but she had picked up on her own that when I uttered the former I wanted her to approach me, and when I uttered the latter I merely wanted her to move along in more or less the same direction I was going. One of the two of us was very perceptive, and the other was a slow learner. And most of us perhaps have been slow to recognize that it is not just the "higher" apes and highly trainable dogs that have language abilities. Since 1977, Irene Pepperberg has been vividly demonstrating that the sounds that come out of the mouths of parrots are not all merely parroted. Alex (named for the *a*vian *l*earning *ex*periment) was then a year-old African Grey parrot in a Chicago pet store, but he has gone on to become an honored resident at Purdue, Northwestern, the University of Arizona at Tucson, and now M.I.T. With at least 80% accuracy, Alex can recognize and name at least 30 kinds of objects, seven colors, and five shapes, and count numbers of objects up to six, and he can answer simple questions and express feelings. He has been seen on television performing these feats; what startled me most when I saw him was a moment when he dropped something, looked up at Professor Pepperberg, and said "Sorry."

What seems to me particularly worth noting here is the way in which Alex was taught to speak. The method used was a variation on what was called the model/rival technique, and it is described by Pepperberg in "A Communicative Approach to Animal Cognition," in the book *Cognitive Ethology; The Minds of Other Animals: Essays in Honor of Donald R. Griffin* (Erlbaum, 1991, pp. 161–164). Two humans do the training, and they reverse their roles from time to time. One asks what something is, such as a group of popsicle sticks, and the other gives an answer such as "Five wood." The first then gives the second praise, and hands over the sticks. But sometimes the responding human deliberately gives an incorrect answer or mispronounces a word. The asker then scolds the responder and puts the objects out of sight. Alex is present watching, and frequently butts in to imitate an answer or correct one. Like a typical human child, Alex wants to be in on the action, and to show he can outdo someone else. One striking thing about this technique is the absence of food rewards. Alex is never given a piece of food for a correct answer; at most he is allowed to ask, in words, for such a reward. Most of the time he gets two things: whatever he identified and a word of praise. I would suggest that the former is a way of feeding curiosity rather than bodily hunger, and the second a way of feeding a pleased self-consciousness of achievement. If these interpretations seem extreme, I remind you that even Pavlov in his own way granted the existence of curiosity in dogs. The "investigatory reflex" he had to overcome before beginning his experiments was also referred to by him (on p. 12 of the work cited earlier) as a "What-is-it?" reflex. Surely Lana too was curious about the orange, but the design of Rumbaugh's experiment makes it impossible to disentangle her interest in what it is from her interest in eating it. Alex uses language, at least in part, for the undiluted satisfaction of the desire to find something out.

The behavior of this wonderful bird seems to me finally to show us something common to animal language use and human speech. The *logos* is the medium in which understanding comes to be. That understanding can be subservient to other ends, but it is also an end in itself. We want to know, at least sometimes, for its own sake. I have no hesitation in saying that Alex does too. But the difference we noted when considering Lana's language use is not overcome by anything apparent in that of Alex. There is no evidence of a set of immanent connections among Alex's words that could guide him to learn anything about five wooden sticks. He learns that by biting them or pecking at them. His acquisition of words must enlarge and enhance the content of his world in ways that can hardly be overestimated, but there is no reason to believe that his words gain him entry to a *logos* in which exploration and discovery could continue through the act of thinking. Every one of his acts of language production or comprehension may begin and end in an image, and have no other ground of coherence with the rest. All his thinking may be confined to that realm. Alex appears to possess and deploy *logoi* that belong to no *logos*.

This distinction between *logoi* and a *logos* is relevant within human speech as well, at least as a matter of emphasis. It is at the root of the self-revelation of the two men Gorgias and Socrates in their extended conversation (448 D–461 B) in Plato's *Gorgias*.Gorgias, a teacher of rhetoric, boasts that he knows how to handle words to become master of any situation while Socrates, a philosophic inquirer, repeatedly insists that they try to follow the *logos* they are engaged in to see where it leads. For all his language skills, Gorgias is either unable or unwilling to follow the *logos* very far, and he cannot achieve mastery of his discussion with Socrates. He is in fact the topic under discussion, since the question that initiates this dialogue is playfully introduced by Socrates at 447 C as "What is Gorgias?" It expands to become a complex inquiry into what a human being is, centering on the rhetorical and philosophic relations we may have to our power of speech. If rhetoric is taken in an extended sense to mean not oratory but any use of words to elicit desired actions from those who hear them, we might be tempted to consider Alex and Lana and all the other language-using beasts rhetorical animals. Like Gorgias's, their skill would consist in manipulating words for ulterior ends, not in following the connections among the meanings those words reveal. What you and I are doing now, for the sake of no end beyond understanding, would be beyond their reach. But this conclusion does not quite ring true to me. It does not leave room for the fact that Alex began to appropriate words out of imitation, rivalry, and curiosity rather than in the way Sultan or the chimpanzees of Gombe began to appropriate sticks and twigs with an eye to an end already envisioned. The picture of animals as using but not being led anywhere by words may be a consequence of the limitations of the projects that have studied them.

What seems to me finally most important about Irene Pepperberg's work with Alex is not that she taught a parrot to be like a human being, but that she let human beings learn something about the interior life of a parrot. Alex's language use allows him to display some of that inner activity in ways accessible to us. There is a world of difference between Pavlov's squashing a dog's natural curiosity so that certain kinds of training can be imposed on it, and Pepperberg's arousing a parrot's natural curiosity in order to invite it into learning. For these same reasons, the most interesting work now being reported on language use by an animal is Savage-Rumbaugh's project with a bonobo named Kanzi. (A brief description of the early years of this project can be found in her book cited earlier, on pages 386–397.) Sometimes called pygmy chimpanzees, bonobos are the least known of the four species of great apes. In the wild, they live only in a small region on the left bank of the Congo in what was formerly Zaire, in a food-rich area that allows them a lot of leisure. Their faces are a little more like ours than are those of chimps, and they seem to communicate in a more varied and extensive way among themselves.

Kanzi's "training" in language use began as an accident. His adopted mother, Matata, was not a very good language learner, but from the time he was six months old, Kanzi was always around, watching and listening to what she was doing. He soaked up words and meanings for a long time before he ever found any reason to use them to communicate; it was only when he was separated from his mother for a while at the age of two and a half that he spontaneously began to use the keyboard. His early life turned out to have been an unintended and nondirective model/rival learning situation, in which he took his mother as a model on whom he improved but never as a rival to compete with. Kanzi, now in his twenties, uses a set of keyboards like Lana's, but with a larger vocabulary and technical enhancements such as a voice synthesizer. Unlike Lana, who was kept in one room while being trained by someone in another room, Kanzi was always able to see human gestures and hear human speech along with the visual symbols on the keyboard. This is the antithesis of a controlled experiment, with so many factors reinforcing one another, but it is much nearer to the way human children learn to speak. Lana's training had been controlled to eliminate any suspicion of the "clever Hans fallacy," by which subtle cues from a trainer's body language once made credulous observers believe that a horse had done arithmetic. But Kanzi's learning was a natural response of his own innate capacities to a rich variety of stimuli.

When Kanzi communicates with humans he reveals something of himself, and not just a persona tailored to the preconceptions that guided the experimenters to construct a certain training regimen. A tabulation of his most frequent two- and three-word combinations at age three had no food requests in the top 25 items on either list. By contrast, about two-thirds of the items on similar lists for the chimp Nim were requests for food. Most of Kanzi's utterances have something to do with play. Of the extended exchanges in which Lana had produced her "syntactically adequate sentences," Savage-Rumbaugh says, "The topics of these exchanges were nearly always the same—that of somehow making food accessible to Lana" (p. 245). But the combinations of words that Kanzi puts together are incomparably more interesting than Lana's orange apples and black bananas. Once, when he had pulled a folded blanket out from under the head of a sleeping human, he signified "Bad surprise." On another occasion, when he had been heard popping a balloon in another room, a human asked him where the pieces were; he pointed to his mouth and then to his stomach and signified "Bad balloon." It may simply be that Kanzi is a more interesting person than any of the other language-using apes, but it is more likely that his trainers have stumbled onto the fact that the best learning is the kind that originates in the learner.

With the other language-trained apes, it was always possible to report the precise sizes of their vocabularies—Lana 80, Nim 125, Koko either 224 or 246—but Kanzi is off the charts. The experimenters arbitrarily stopped adding symbols to his keyboard at 256, since it became too complicated even for humans to find and use them beyond that number, but he understands at least twice that many words. His language use never began with the performance of producing words. All such acts by him were preceded by a learning of meanings, out of which he chose to use those he had reasons for using. And he spends as much as possible of his time not in the laboratory but in a fifty-acre forest adjacent to it. In those surroundings, his "keyboard" is not the high-tech one indoors, nor a portable computer that had first been tried, but what appears in pictures to be a folded piece of cardboard with three 8x8 arrays of symbols. He communicates simply by touching the symbols, reinforcing his meanings with gestures and with vocal sounds that indicate his feelings. Sometimes he uses the board not to communicate but to talk to himself, deliberately shielding what he is saying from observation. There are various accounts of his accomplishments, written by Savage-Rumbaugh alone or with others. The best of them seems to me to be the first chapter of the book *Apes, Language, and the Human Mind* (Oxford U. P., 1998), in which she argues that he must have a rudimentary grasp of syntax, since, for example, he can reliably tell that a request to throw a potato at a turtle does not ask him to throw a turtle at a potato. But she knows that this argument is not persuasive enough, since Kanzi might be thought to be figuring out what to do from the situation as a whole, and not from the sentence alone. So she gave him a test (p. 68), with 660 odd-ball requests, made by her when he could not see her, and she could not be heard by anyone else, with each request stated only once. Habit or a sense of the situation would not help him with such requests as "Put the chicken in the potty" or "Go vacuum Liz." He did well, a little better than a two-and-a-half-year-old human child who was given the same test. But it was his failures that were the most interesting, and they seem to me to offer the first decisive piece of evidence I have seem that an animal participates in something that has to be considered a *logos*.

Savage-Rumbaugh discusses (pages 71–73) three similar requests that were made of Kanzi: (a) Give me the ball and the cereal. (b) Put the ball in the cereal. (c) Get the ball that's in the cereal. Kanzi responds correctly to requests of types (b) and (c) more than three-fourths of the time, but he has difficulty with those of type (a), to which he responds correctly only one-third of the time. When the request is merely compound, he generally forgets one part of it. When it is grammatically complex, he holds it in mind with ease. What holds together the two objects in sentence (a) is nothing but an "and," which gives the string of words the quantative unity of an aggregate or heap. The unity of the two objects in sentence (b), though, depends upon grasping a relation, or what might be called a qualitative ratio. And the unity of the two objects in sentence (c) is of a purely intelligible kind, depending on grasping a meaning within a meaning—in fact, the "which-is" structure allegedly used by Lana. The requests Kanzi understands best are those that are held together in the hierarchical unity of a sentence rather than in the arbitrary additive unity of a string of symbols. All three requests are delivered as sentences; the question is how they are received. In those to which Kanzi responds most reliably, there is a wholeness that transforms the meanings of their parts to such an extent that they can only be taken in as sentences. To grasp them, Kanzi must be thinking not just in compound images but in sentences. Emily Sue Savage-Rumbaugh has made a *prima facie* case for an understanding of sentences by Kanzi, a case that Duane Rumbaugh failed to make for Lana, and the whole discussion of animal intelligence seems to me now to have reached a new level.

But I doubt that the spirit of Descartes would be much impressed by Kanzi, or by any of the other evidence of animal intelligence noticed here. In general, the attitude of Descartes is that, if experience runs counter to theory, so much the worse for experience. I suspect, though, that any open-minded consideration of the handful of examples we have gathered would lead anyone to conclude that there are serious reasons not to reject a natural inclination to regard them as evidence of conscious thinking. Only a reflexive mechanomorphism would lead anyone to say that they prove nothing, rather than that they suggest that we should widen and deepen our own sense of the possibilities in things. From the other side, the spirit of Thomas seems to me also to be too attached to a rigid scheme of the way things are. Richard McKeon, in the glossary to his two-volume *Selections from Medieval Philosophers* (Scribners, 1930), indicates that Thomas's word *aestimatio,* along with its synonym *existimatio,* had become a technical term for the highest capacity of the animal soul. But Aristotle, from whom Thomas borrowed his ranking of souls, was much more flexible about where their capacities begin and end. Early in *On the Soul,* Aristotle says that the animal's soul causes motion "by some kind of thinking and choosing" (406b 24–25), and late in the same work he says of the perceptive power all animals share that "one could not easily place it as irrational or as having *logos*" (432a 30–31). Thomas is powerfully attached to a conception of an eternal law that sets clear boundaries to all things, and of a hierarchical ordering of them in which every possible rank is occupied by creatures with corresponding powers; he is as confident of what animals cannot do as he is of what angels can do. Thomas and Descartes are thinkers of great philosophic depth, but neither of them wants to remain long in a philosophic attitude. Neither the faith of the one in what is above the human realm nor the certitude of the other about what is below it leaves us any room to find anything of ourselves if we experience a continuing fascination with the lives of animals.

We can borrow a distinction from Thomas, though, that may help us reconcile the various motives we might have for paying close attention to animals. Researches into the mechanisms underlying animal behavior reveal what Thomas called second causes. Nowhere among them is there to be found an origin of any effect. Without a recognition of a cause capable in some way of being first in a chain of causation, there can never be an adequate understanding of anything that happens, but without an account of second causes any such understanding is at best deficient. The latter point is vividly illustrated by Johannes Kepler, who in his *Epitome of Copernican Astronomy* (Bk. IV, Part II, Chap. 2) asks how intelligence could cause the motion of a planet, since the planetary globe has no feet or wings. The other side of the coin is captured in an unforgettable example given by Socrates, who in Plato's *Phaedo* (98C–99A) asks how his bones and muscles could have caused him to be on death row in Athens, when, if he had thought it was good, those same bones and muscles would have rested at ease in Megara or Boeotia. Socrates does not even call the instrumental mechanism a secondary cause, but calls it instead that without which the cause could not be a cause. Nothing compels us to reject the spirit of inquiry that drives either a Kepler or a Socrates. A philosophic standpoint can welcome every kind of exploration that helps make the world more fully understood, and a truly philosophic standpoint keeps the question of its own presuppositions always in view. It is only the premature decision to turn away from a philosophic openness that makes any evidence inadmissible or incapable of more than one interpretation. The evidence suggestive of animal intelligence need not be summarily explained away as mechanical motion or instinctive action. If we have sufficient imagination, exploring that evidence can help us keep the activity of the human *logos,*as well as our attempt to understand the human *logos,* alive.

NOTES

1 It should be noted that what arrived in the dog's mouth in some experiments was a squirt of an acid, since the consequent "mild defence reflex" to a poison in the mouth caused saliva to flow in exactly the same unconditioned way as the alimentary reflex aroused by a piece of bread. For a variety of reasons, we will continue to speak of feeding or food for all cases.

2 I have not succeeded in confirming from the original Russian texts that this is the word Pavlov used, but I am advised by Dr. O. V. Vishnyakova that it is a very common word and was so in Pavlov's time, that there is no other word that would fit his uses so well, and that, with the adjectives *zvukovoi* and *svetovoi*, the Russian word *signal* would be the usual way of referring to all the sounds and lights he employed.

3 Jacques-Yves Cousteau begins the book *Dolphins* (New York: Doubleday, 1975, written with Phillipe Diolé) with a description of the same phenomenon that captivated Jonas, and he reflects on its implications on pages 20 and 176–7.

4 The fact that chimps recognize themselves in mirrors was demonstrated cleverly by George G. Gallup, Jr., as first reported in the journal *Science* (1970), 167, p. 86. He put colored spots on their faces while they slept, and they discovered them when they awoke.

5 *The Dance Language and Orientation of Bees* (Cambridge: Harvard University Press, 1967).

6 This similarity is all the more striking in that Koko's trainer (Francine Patterson) appears to overstate all her pupil's achievements, while Nim's trainer (Herbert Terrace) became convinced in 1979 that what apes were learning in all such projects is not language but tricks.

SUN AND CAVE

Eric Salem

NEAR THE END of book five of the *Republic,* and at the very center of the dialogue as a whole, Socrates makes his famous—or infamous—claim

> Unless the philosophers rule as kings or those now called kings and chiefs genuinely and adequately philosophize . . . there will be no rest from ills for the cities, my dear Glaucon, nor I think for human kind, nor will the regime we have now described in speech ever come forth from nature, insofar as possible, and see the light of the sun. (473d)

Fortunately for us, Glaucon and Adeimantus have the courage to call Socrates' bluff. They demand that Socrates justify this claim and he does, over the course of more than two books. In the middle of his justification, between his account of the nature of the philosopher and his account of the education proper to him, Socrates sets out three strange and strangely haunting images. In the image of the sun, he posits a source that somehow yokes together knower and known, and calls this source the good or the idea of the good. In the image of the cave, he describes our nature and condition in light of that source. In the image of the divided line, Socrates characterizes the ascent to the good and the human powers required for that ascent.

I want to think about—or rather to think *through*—these images, by first raising and then attempting to answer the questions about them that I suppose any serious reader of the *Republic* would raise.

Now doing this, confronting Socrates' images on their own terms, will require me to abstract, for the most part, from the context I have just sketched out. However, I want to urge you to keep this context in mind. In particular, I urge you to keep asking yourselves what light Socrates' images

---

This essay—a revision of a lecture delivered at St. John's in Annapolis and the Thomas More Institute in Nashua, N.H.—was first published in "The St. John's Review," in 1996. It is dedicated to Charlie Salem, whose eager questions about images got me started, and to Eva Brann, whose "Music of the Republic" is in my view the gold standard in these matters. In this as in so many other things Eva has served as both Muse and Fairy Godmother for me. Quotations from the *Republic* are from the translation by Allan Bloom, Basic Books, 1968.

might shed on his central claim that the philosopher is the solution to the problem of human community. I myself will turn to this question at the end of my essay. There I hope to show you that Socrates' strange and apparently apolitical images form the true center of the *Republic*. That is, I hope to show you that Socrates' images are the key to understanding why and in what sense the philosopher should rule.

I. QUESTIONS

Socrates introduces his description of the good in book six with the claim that the good is the chief and universal object of human desire: it is "what every soul pursues and for the sake of which it does everything" (505d). Very near the end of book seven, while describing the final stages of the philosopher's education, Socrates further claims that the good, once known, can serve as a pattern or paradigm for the life of a man or a city: "Lifting up the brilliant beams of their souls, they must be compelled to look toward that which provides light for everything. Once they see the good itself, they must be compelled, each in his turn, to use it as a pattern for ordering city, private men, and themselves for the rest of their lives" (540a–b).

I find neither of these claims about the good particularly problematic. The claim that everyone somehow desires the good is at any rate a familiar Socratic dictum, and one that seems to be amply borne out by the drama of the *Republic*. Glaucon's longing to see the conversation continue, Cephalus' willingness to absent himself from it, even Thrasymachus' angry wish to put a stop to it—all seem to be rooted in a desire to secure the good for oneself. The drama of the *Republic* also seems to support the claim that the good could serve as a pattern for human action. For instance, viewed in retrospect, Glaucon's desire to know whether justice is good can be seen as a desire to know the good so that he might shape his life in accordance with it.

What I find puzzling, then, is not these claims themselves, but the relation of the good as Socrates describes it to them. It would be one thing if the good were, say, pleasure or knowledge. (These, by the way, are the alternatives that Socrates explicitly rejects just before he begins his own description.) I can easily convince myself that pleasure is what everyone desires most, and on some days I can almost convince myself that the same is true of knowledge. I can also see how thinking that either pleasure or knowledge were the chief good would shape and inform a life. But what of the good as

Socrates describes it? What would it mean to take what yokes together knower and known as a pattern for the life of a city or a man? And even if someone could do this, what sense could it make to say that it is the chief object of desire for anyone, much less for "every soul"?

In different ways these questions both concern the applicability of Socrates' image of the good to ordinary human concerns. Both questions arise because Socrates' image confounds our ordinary sense of what should count as an answer to the question, "What is the good?" My next question is of a different sort. It concerns the very existence of the good as Socrates describes it. As you may remember, that description draws heavily on an analogy with sight. Seeing and being seen, Socrates observes, differ from, say, hearing and being heard in a decisive respect. Hearing, the capacity to hear, depends only on the presence of something to be heard for its completion, and vice versa. Put someone who can hear in the presence of a sound; he will hear and the sound will be heard. But put someone with good eyes in a darkened room full of the most brilliant colors and nothing will happen. Seeing and being seen depend on a third thing or rather on two things: light and a source of light. So, too, Socrates claims, in the case of knowing and being known. The capacity to know and the capacity to be known depend on an external source for their completion; this source, this yoke, as Socrates calls it, is the good or the idea of the good.

Yet why, we might ask, should we suppose that knowing is sight-like rather than hearing-like? After all, as Socrates himself admits, seeing is the exception and hearing is the rule. That is, in nearly all cases—and I suppose he is thinking particularly of smelling, touching and tasting—no third thing seems to be required for the completion of a capacity to do something and the corresponding capacity to suffer. Why then does Socrates insist on putting knowing in the class defined uniquely by sight rather than in the common class—the economy class—characterized by hearing? Is there some feature of our experience which would allow us to infer that there must be some mediating principle between knower and known? If there is, Socrates does not mention it. Do we perhaps encounter this principle directly in the ordinary course of our learning and knowing? Again, if we do, Socrates does not say so—and in any case, if we did, it is difficult to see why he would resort to an image to bring that principle into view.

Our bafflement about this most basic matter can only increase as we enter further into the details of his image. For Socrates does more than merely posit a principle that mediates between knower and known. He likens the ability to see to an overflow dispensed to us by the sun, and draws the corresponding consequence for our ability to know: the good is not only a necessary condition for our knowing, but the very source of our capacity to know. He then goes on to make parallel claims about the objects of our knowledge. He likens the truth to light, and makes it somehow a feature of those objects: "[T]herefore say that what provides truth to the things known and gives the power to the one who knows is the idea of the good" (508e). And then, as a final step, he claims that the good is responsible for the very existence of the things we know: "[T]herefore say that not only being known is present in these things as a consequence of the good, but also existence and being are in them besides as a result of it" (509b).

It seems to me that each of these additional features of Socrates' image is worthy of question. I, at any rate, would have liked to hear some reason given for each of them, some reason that is not dependent on the initial (and questionable) analogy with sight. However, once again, this is just what Socrates does not provide. Yet suppose we were to accept, in principle, every detail of Socrates' image of the sun. Suppose, that is, that we were to admit, as genuine, the possibility that knower and known are yoked together by some external source, that the knowable things are always aglow, lit up by that source, and that we as knowers are somehow akin to these things by virtue of our common heritage. It seems to me that just here we encounter a difficulty at least as great as any I've described. We need only reflect on our own experience as learners and knowers.

On balance it seems to me that we know—really know—very little and that what little we do know we know only as the result of great and unremitting labor. The things most worth knowing are not luminous, not to us at least. Perplexity with respect to them is for most of us the most we can manage, and in truth most of us prefer the dull comfort of well-worn opinion to knowing that we don't know. Is there room in this world of ours for the good as Socrates imagines it? Is there room in Socrates' sun-drenched world for the darkness of our own experience as knowers? It would hardly seem so. And yet, the picture I have just drawn of our condition as learners and knowers is largely in accord with another picture put forward by Socrates, his image of the cave. The human-all-too-human preference for opinion over perplexity, the painfulness of that perplexity, the arduousness of any ascent to true knowledge—these are all features of Socrates' own image. To say that Socrates' image of the sun is not in accord with our experience is to say that it is not in accord with his own image of the cave; it is perhaps to say that Socrates is not in accord with himself. Are we willing to say this? Is there some way to reconcile the two images with one another?

Here is a possible solution. Someone might argue that Socrates' image of the sun is meant only to characterize us and the world as it is for us *as knowers*. But we are not simply knowers. And our capacity to know is continually distracted, continually drawn away from its proper objects by other parts of the soul, by what we like to call our passions. As a consequence, we find ourselves bound in darkness, our knowing part forced to content itself with shadows rather than substance, with mere images of things rather than the things themselves. Thus, according to this argument, there is no important sense in which the image of the sun is at odds with the image of the cave. The one simply describes our initial—and for most people, normal—condition; the other, the condition to which we should aspire.

There is, I think, something to be said for this argument. Socrates himself seems to say that distraction is at the root of our ignorance in these lines from his description of the cave: "[B]ut the present argument indicates that this power [to know] is in the soul of each, and that the instrument with which each learns—just as an eye is not able to turn toward the light from the dark without the whole body—must be turned around from that which is coming into being together *with the whole soul* until it is able to endure looking at being and the brightest part of being. And we affirm that this is the good, don't we?" (528d). Still, the very way in which Socrates makes his point, his spatial metaphor, points to the inadequacy of the solution I have just sketched out. If coming to know is a matter of turning around, if it somehow involves directing our vision aright, then there must be parts of the world which are dark, dark beyond any human making, and these dark regions must be somehow populated by shadows, again not of our making. In short, although our ignorance, the human condition, has something to do with the condition of the soul, it also has to do with the condition, indeed the very structure, of the world.

This is what I mean when I say that the image of the cave and the image of the sun are at least apparently at odds with each other. The ordinary sun is sometimes present, sometimes absent. It rises and sets. Here we have a perfectly satisfactory explanation for ordinary darkness. But the sun as good never sets; the lights are always on in the world disclosed by Socrates' image of the good. How, then, are we to explain the presence within it of the shadow-filled darkness of the cave? Once again we must ask: Is there some way to bring the images of sun and cave together, a way that will also point us toward answers to the other questions we have raised? Let us see.

II. IMAGE AND ORIGINAL

Let us reflect, for a moment, on one obvious feature of Socrates' image of the cave. The shapes which the inhabitants of the cave delight in observing are shadows. What difference does this make? What is a shadow? In the image of the divided line, Socrates puts shadows first in his list of natural images; he thus suggests that shadows constitute the lowest order of images. This seems reasonable. The shadow of a face reveals far less about a face than, say, its reflection in still water or in a mirror. The shadow of a thing reveals only the boundary of a thing. The interior of the thing, its texture, its depth—all these are absent from the shadow. The darkness which forms the interior of a shadow itself seems to be an image of its lack of revealing power. And yet a shadow *is* an image. To know the boundary or limit of a thing is to know something of that thing. The inhabitants of the cave thus encounter the things that truly are in a peculiar fashion. They dwell—we dwell—among the shades of things.

Here is something else that might seem to distinguish shadows from other types of images. A shadow can only exist if at least three other things are present. There must be a thing to be shadowed. There must be light. And the light must be directed light: It must stem from a source or at least a finite number of sources. Otherwise the light will not be blocked and no shadow will be produced.

How peculiar are these conditions to the kind of images we call shadows? (I am speaking here of natural images, the sort that Socrates associates with the first level of the divided line, and by natural images I mean not images of natural things, but images that do or can arise without human intervention.) Clearly *all* images presuppose originals: an image is always an image of something. And clearly all visual images presuppose light. By this I do not mean that there must be light for them to be seen, though this is of course true. I mean that light produces—or at least co-produces—say, the reflection of a tree in water. Now it is less clear in such cases than in the case of shadows that all visual images are also dependent on a source. On a cloudy day, when light is diffuse, there are no shadows, but one can still see reflections in water. Still, without a source of light to be diffused, no reflection can exist.

What, then, of images which are neither visual nor manmade? Do they also depend for their existence on the equivalent of light and sources of light? Let me answer by turning the question around: Are there such images? We can be deceived—or deceive ourselves—about the things we touch and hear and taste: we can mistake the voice of an enemy for the voice of a friend; a bitter medicine can be disguised by the taste of honey. But it is one thing to say this and another altogether to say that there are natural images *in* the world of smells, tastes and so on. My sense is that there are none or none worth mentioning, and my guess is that Plato and Socrates would agree with me. (I might mention here that in the *Sophist,* the only dialogue I know of in which an explicit distinction is made between natural and manmade images, the only examples given of the first class are visual [*Sophist* 266b–c]. Likewise in the divided line image.)

On the other hand, the world is full of visual images that are not of human making. In fact, it is precisely *when* the conditions for seeing *things* are most fully satisfied—when the sun is at its brightest and things seem to be aglow of themselves—that the world is most full of such images. Where there is sun, there is shade. And the converse is also true—where there are natural images, where there are shadows and reflections, there must be sun or at least some source of light. Perhaps we can now see another reason why Socrates puts shadows first on his list of natural images: They may reveal least about the things they image, but they are exemplary in the way they display the dependence of such images on a source of light.

No doubt you have already seen where I mean to go with this argument. The more we think about images—natural images—and the conditions for their existence, the less strange at least two of Socrates' claims sound. We wondered earlier why Socrates chooses to liken knowing and being known to seeing and being seen and why, in particular, he insists that knowing and being known depend upon some external source, namely, the good. In a somewhat different context, we found ourselves wondering how Socrates can *both* claim that such a source exists *and* claim that most men spend their lives absorbed in the play of shadows not of their own making. But if *within* what we ordinarily call the world, if *within* the world of visible, tangible, audible things, all natural images depend for their being on some third thing, *beyond* their originals and *beyond* those who perceive them, and if, in addition, things in what we ordinarily call the world are themselves images of purely intelligible objects, then it makes sense for Socrates to suppose that there must be an external source of *these* images as well, a source other than those who perceive them and other than their intelligible originals. Moreover, if *within* what we ordinarily call the world, images arise only in those contexts where the perception of the original also depends on an external source (as in the case of sight), and if, furthermore, in these contexts the source of the image is always *also* the source of the perceiving and being perceived of the original, then it makes sense to say that knowing and being known, intellection and intelligibility, depend on a source external to themselves *and* it makes sense to say that this source is the same as the source of the images we take to be things. In short, the relation of seeing and being seen *does* make sense as a paradigm for the relation of knowing and being known. It makes sense to suppose that knowing and being known depend on an external source—that is to say, it makes sense to suppose that the good exists—and it *also* makes sense to suppose that *this* source is the very source of what we ordinarily call the world. The cave is the offshoot, the inevitable byplay, of the illuminating activity of the good. The shadow-play that surrounds us, the unintelligibility that suffuses the lives of most of us most of the time, is simply the price—high, but non-negotiable—that must be paid for supreme intelligibility.

Clearly there are a number of "ifs" in this argument that require further examination. What's more, there is at least one crucial condition for the production of shadows that I have glossed over entirely, a condition that strongly suggests that life in the cave is the offspring of more than one parent: no shadow can exist in the absence of a *surface* upon which it is cast. I haven't mentioned this condition until now—and won't mention it again—because to consider it adequately would take us too far afield: at the very least we'd have to think about the correspondence between the wall of the cave and what's called the Other in the *Sophist* and variously called Mother, Nurse, Receptacle and Place in the *Timaeus*. Rather than take upon myself this limitless task, I propose to spend much of my remaining time looking closely at two other assumptions I have made.

III. POETRY AND MATHEMATICS

The first supposition I want to look at is the claim that the things around us, which most of us take to be freestanding, are themselves images of intelligible originals *(noēta)*, that is, ideas or forms *(eidē)*. Now since Socrates so frequently and so freely employs this supposition in the *Republic* and elsewhere, and since in certain dialogues, notably the *Parmenides,* the supposition appears to lead to great, if not insuperable difficulties, we might expect to find a proof of it somewhere in the dialogues. But to my knowledge no proof of the supposition is to be found, if by a proof is meant an attempt to reason one's way to it from grounds that are prior to and clearer than it. I can think of two reasons why this might be so.

First, it is at least suggested in certain dialogues that, however problematic the supposition of intelligible originals may be, that supposition is what first makes reasoning (and hence proving) possible. Or, as Parmenides puts it to the young Socrates, just after subjecting the ideas to a devastating critique, anyone who denies the ideas ". . . will have nowhere to turn his thought," for that denial will ". . . utterly destroy the power of conversation" and hence philosophy (135b–c). In other words, the ideas or forms are the always problematic, yet ever indispensable condition for the possibility of serious inquiry. About them the philosopher could say: Can't think with them, can't think without them.

A second reason for the avoidance of any attempt at proof emerges from Socrates' own image of the cave. Life in the cave is so absorbing—our devotion to shadows is so complete—that the effects of the cave linger long after an initial turning around. Witness the desire of the man who's been turned around to flee back to his state of bondage and witness, too, his tendency to regard what he's seen as less true, less revealing than the shadows he loves. Given this state of affairs, it is difficult to see how a general proof, however certain, would do any or at least much good. What seems to be needed instead are illuminating experiences, paths by which the potential learner might gradually find his way from the shadows he finds so absorbing—that is, from his everyday experience of the world—to the intelligible originals upon which they depend.

What experiences are likely to provide this much-needed illumination? Socrates points to one answer through his image of the divided line. Let me remind you of some of the details of that image. Socrates has Glaucon cut a line unequally. He then has him cut each of its parts in the same ratio as the whole was cut. (Thus $A + B : C + D :: A : B :: C : D$.) Socrates goes on to assign certain kinds of beings and certain powers of the soul to each of the produced segments. The larger segments produced by the first cut (that is, $A + B$ and $C + D$) correspond respectively to what is intelligible and what is visible (Figure 1). Of the four segments produced by the second set of cuts, D corresponds to the natural images we spoke of earlier, C to the things of which these images are images, B somehow to mathematical objects, and A to the forms themselves.

Now perhaps the first thing we should glean from this image is the following: To say that $C + D : A + B :: D : C$ is to say that the visible world has the same relation to the intelligible world that ordinary images within the visible world have to their visible counterparts. This is, of course, just the claim we are examining, the claim that the things around us are somehow

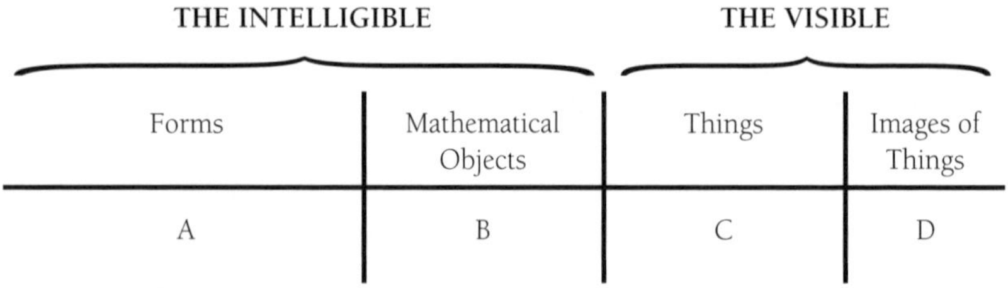

THE INTELLIGIBLE		THE VISIBLE	
Forms	Mathematical Objects	Things	Images of Things
A	B	C	D

Figure 1

images. The second thing we should notice is that B has to A, mathematical objects have to the forms or *eidē* just this same relation. Such objects are, in other words, the intellectual equivalent of reflections or, perhaps better, shadows. Socrates partly unpacks and partly amplifies this thought in his discussion of the divided line.

Mathematicians and their objects have a curious relation to objects in the visible world. As Socrates says,

> Don't you know that [the mathematicians] use visible forms and make their arguments about them, not thinking about them but about those others that they are *like*? They make arguments for the sake of the square itself and the diagonal itself, not for the sake of the diagonal they draw and likewise with the rest. These things that they mold and draw, of which there are shadows and images in water, *they now use as images,* seeking to know those things themselves, that one can see in no other way than with thought. (510d–e)

Mathematical objects thus occupy an intermediate position between the *eidē* or forms and things in the world. Like the *eidē* they are accessible only to thought. And yet the mathematician is constantly forced to see things in the world *as images* of them in order to make the mathematical objects accessible to himself. They may be mere images or shadows of the things that truly are. Still, shadowy though they may be—or perhaps precisely because they *are* shadowy—they seem perfectly suited to introduce the learner to the intelligible realm. It is for this reason that Socrates goes on, in book seven, to make the first education of the philosopher kings a mathematical education. For it is precisely through the study of mathematics that we first come to see the shadowy, the image-like character of the things about us.

Or at any rate, mathematics is one way. I think that Socrates' account of mathematical experience is right on the mark. One cannot study mathematics seriously without at least wondering from time to time whether the objects we draw and count—and by extension all things insofar as they possess shape and number—are not images of objects accessible only to thought. And yet my sense is that there are other ways of arriving at this thought, and that Socrates knows it. I will have occasion to speak about these alternatives later. But first I need to address at some length a second sticking point in the argument I sketched out earlier.

Someone might be willing to agree with Socrates' claim that the things about us are somehow images. He might also be willing to admit that the things about us can only be images if there exists some source external to the originals of those images, an image-casting source. But this someone might deny that the source is the good as Socrates describes it and might also deny that the originals of the images we see are the forms or *eidē*—on the grounds that Socrates himself does! For *Socrates* makes the shadows on the wall of the cave images of artificial things carried about by human beings and *he* has them projected on the wall, not by the good itself, but by a fire *within* the cave.

What are we to make of these peculiar features of Socrates' image? What are the artificial things here? What is the fire? And who are the human beings? I think it is very hard to say. At one point Socrates himself interprets his image as follows: "Well, then, my dear Glaucon, this image as a whole must be connected with what was said before. Liken the domain revealed by sight to the prison home, and the light of the fire in it to the sun's power" (517a–b). Yet this interpretation is very strange. How can Socrates suggest that we see only shadows or images of the things illuminated by the ordinary sun? Whatever the status of the visible things turns out to be, we see those things directly, don't we?

Another interpretation of this peculiar middle realm comes to mind when we begin thinking, for instance, of Socrates' criticism of Homer and other poets in books two and three of the *Republic*. There are certain human beings—we might call them image makers or opinion makers—who so dominate our thinking, our imagining and our lives that we might almost be said to inhabit worlds of their making. We can certainly be said to live in their shadows. What we cherish and revile, what we weep about and laugh at—all are governed by the images they put before us. Might such men, poets of the first rank and perhaps founders and great statesmen as well, not be the human beings who occupy this middle realm? Indeed, couldn't this be why Socrates himself suggests that we see only shadows or images of the visible things—that we never see even such things directly?

The extraordinary influence of, say, Homer on our thinking about moral and political affairs seems clear enough: I, for one, can never think about courage and honor without being haunted by the figure of Achilles. But in a certain sense that influence seems to be equally present in our viewing of natural things: Who, having read Homer, can look at the Mediterranean and not see wine or look at the sunrise and not see rosy fingers?

If everything we see we see through the eyes of such image makers, if the world is image for us in *this* sense, then much of what I've been saying thus far would seem to be simply false. There might be a good which somehow yokes together knower and known, but it would not also be responsible for the images we take to be true things. The casting of shadows would be a merely human affair. Moreover, the very existence of the good would seem to be called into question by this reading. At any rate, my attempt to argue from the image-like character of the world about us to the existence of the good would seem to have been misguided. Must we draw these consequences? Or is there some way to incorporate what I am calling the middle realm of Socrates' image into those earlier arguments about the good?

I think there is such a way, and I think that Socrates himself points to it several times in the course of book seven. The first hint comes at the very beginning of the book. Here Socrates notes, as if in passing, that the entrance to the cave is both large and "open to the light across the whole width of the cave" (514a). I take this curious remark—echoed in the great final myth of the *Phaedo,* where the *many* hollows or caves are said to be more or less open to the surface of the true earth (108D–111D)—to mean something like the following. The light of the good may not make its way into the cave; it may not be *directly* responsible for the shadows we see or for our ability to discern them. And yet the cave is not altogether closed to the light, not a self-enclosed, self-contained whole. It is somehow open to the light, and open to it at every point. Perhaps it would not be going too far to say that the light of the good is potentially present throughout the cave, in this sense: Every image, every shadow, is potentially an occasion for the ascent from cave to sun. Less metaphorically, every opinion or image put before us by the opinion or image makers, once seen *as* an opinion or image, can be an occasion for the ascent to true knowledge.

Why this should be the case Socrates hints at elsewhere in book seven. First, he suggests that the objects carried before the fire should not simply be regarded as originals of the shadows that most men see. They are themselves images. Indeed, at least some of the words that Socrates uses to describe them—*andrias, zōon* (man-image, animal-image) and later *agalma* (image of divine being)—seem to underscore just this, to emphasize that each object carried before the fire points beyond itself, to some further original, presumably to some intelligible object (514c–515a; 517d–e). Moreover, Socrates suggests that what holds for the objects carried before the fire holds for the fire as well. For instance, in the very passage in which he identifies the light of the fire with the sun's power, he claims that anyone who sees the idea of the good must conclude that "this is in fact the cause of all that is just and beautiful in everything—in the visible it gave birth to the light and its sovereign, in the intelligible, itself sovereign, it provided truth and intelligence" (517c). Again, in the passage I have already cited from the end of book seven, Socrates seems to claim that all seeing, all discerning—even the discerning of shadows that takes place in the cave—ultimately depends on the light of the good: the good is "that which provides light for *everything*" (540a).

If the originals of the shadows in the cave are themselves images of the *eidē,* and if the fire, the shadow-casting and shadow-discerning source, is itself derived from and an image of the good, then it makes sense to say that an ascent from cave to sun can begin anywhere. What's more, it becomes possible to return to a modified version of our initial conclusion that sun and cave form an elemental pair, with each implying the presence of the other.

The modification consists, in effect, in the admission that the good is not *directly* responsible for the shadows that surround us. The good is present in the cave by proxy, as it were; it is present—somehow—in the image-casting activity of image makers. Does this suggestion make sense? Let me be clear, first, about what I do not mean to say. I do not mean to say that the shadow casters portrayed by Socrates knowingly imitate the good. Nor do I mean to say that the quasi-originals with which they cast shadows are known by them to be images of the truly knowable things. On the contrary, I think we are meant to see that most image makers are unwitting mediators between the sun and the cave. A sign of this is the fact that the human beings in Socrates' picture—I mean the ones who carry objects before the fire—neither look at nor tend the fire. Instead they scurry about, shifting their image-producing images from place to place. The very condition of their activity—which is also the condition of the activity of the prisoners in the cave—is as unknown to them as it is to their prisoners.

If the image makers portrayed by Socrates are not knowing mediators, in what sense can they be said to mediate? Perhaps this question can best be addressed by way of another image, that of the mathematicians of the divided line. As we saw earlier, Socrates suggests through his image of the divided line that mathematical objects must be regarded as shadows or images of the *eidē*. Let me now add to this that Socrates emphasizes in his discussion of the divided line that the mathematicians, like the image makers, tend not to be aware of this: They treat images of the *eidē* as originals. Strange as it may sound, this would seem to mean that when the mathematician inquires, say, into the relations between figures or between numbers, he is in fact engaged unawares in a purely formal study of the possible relations among the forms. In other words, something like the possible structures of the eidetic realm are made visible *in shadow form* in the more or less accessible speech of the mathematicians. Now, might something similar be said of those we've called image makers? To found a regime or to craft a great poem is to fashion a comprehensive vision of what is just and unjust, beautiful and base, good and bad. But to do this, I am suggesting, is to figure in speech a possible configuration of the eidetic realm; it is to make visible the boundaries or limits, the shadowy outlines, of the just, the beautiful, the good.

Perhaps you find disturbing my suggestion that poetry and mathematics are closely related. I confess I find it a little disturbing myself. Still, my sense is that Socrates means us to see their kinship with one another. In fact my sense is that he means us to see that the third section of the divided line and what I have been calling the middle realm of the cave are images of the same *place*, the proper home of mathematicians and poets alike. If I am right about this, the occupational disease—or rather, temptation—of those who dwell within this region would seem to be the temptation to regard their activity and their objects as freestanding, as originals, rather than as the images they are.

Let me explain why I speak here of an occupational temptation rather than a disease. In part it is because Socrates himself seems to envision the possibility—a possibility that Euclid will later set out to fulfill—of a mathematics that knowingly points beyond itself, that invites its students to reflect on its formal foundations even as it moves them forward. That is, the harshness of his critique of mathematicians at the end of book six seems to be offset by his suggestion in book seven that mathematics is a necessary preparation for the study of dialectic and the ascent to the good. Yet in the end it is the *figure* of Socrates rather than his description of a quasi-dialectical mathematics that inclines me to use the language of temptation rather than disease.

What I mean is this: My sense is that if the Socrates of the dialogues belongs anywhere on the divided line, it is on the third level, with the mathematicians and the image makers. We rarely, if ever, see him engaged in the pure dialectic he associates with the highest level of the divided line. And we certainly see him producing a great number of images. Consider the evidence of the *Republic* alone. The bulk of the dialogue is an elaborate image of a city, which we are meant to see at the same time as an image of the soul. It ends—after a harsh criticism of image making—with another elaborate image of the soul and its choices. And right at the center of the dialogue Socrates sets out the very images we have been considering. It is these images, above all, which display the possibility of a knowing mediation between sun and cave. For here we see Socrates making and conveying images—two of them "poetic," one mathematical—which are intended precisely to point Glaucon and us beyond the realm of images and human image making. The images of Socrates announce themselves *as* images; they are transparent in the highest degree. Such images could only be the work of a man aware, supremely aware, that his image-making activity was itself an image of a more fundamental, more original activity.

I will have more to say about Socrates a bit later. In particular, I will want to bring the figure of Socrates to bear as we circle back to the first set of questions I raised about the good, namely, how the good as Socrates describes it could be the good for us and could furnish a paradigm for human action. But before we can treat this first set of questions, we must return to Socrates' own characterization of the good.

IV. Weaving Together

We would do well to remind ourselves at the outset that the feature of the good we have been focusing on for some time, its image-casting power, is not at the heart of Socrates' description here. It is certainly mentioned: the sun, the image through which we are to glimpse the good, is called "the child of" as well as "most like" the good it images (506e). But as I said, image-casting is not at the center of Socrates' description.

What is? The good yokes; it gathers; it brings things together—this seems to be its primary feature. Now thus far we have been supposing that the gathering of the good is limited, that knower and known are the only things it brings together. But Socrates says nothing here to make us think that he means to restrict the gathering power of the good to this relation alone. And indeed, later on, as he attempts to describe what it would mean for someone to dwell outside the cave, he insists that the good is not only "in a certain way the cause of all those things that the man and his companions had been seeing," that is, somehow the source of shadows in the cave but also "the source of seasons and of years [outside it]," that is, the overarching source of order among the intelligible objects (516b). The good, we must now understand, is responsible for all collectedness, all being together, within the intelligible realm. It brings together knower and known; but it also makes the known, the realm of intelligible objects, *a* realm, an articulated whole rather than a heap of objects

What does the word "whole" mean here? The word "yoke," used by Socrates in various forms three times in the course of his image, might seem to imply the violent imposition of order, subjugation. But this is clearly not Socrates' meaning (or, at any rate, not his primary meaning). The good is a ruling source, an *arché,* but its rule is not arbitrary. Rather, as the example of knower and known makes manifest, the good brings together, not indifferent elements, not indistinguishable monads, but things that *belong* together. In other words, the collections it produces are *well-ordered* collections, and the good is a source of wholeness in at least this sense.

There is, however, another and perhaps more fundamental sense in which the good is a source of wholeness. Once again, it is the relation of knower and known that points the way. It is not the case that the power to know is, as it were, somewhat better off for being conjoined with a knowable object. On the contrary, the power to know *is,* is wholly itself, only in the presence of what is knowable. Or, as Socrates himself observes, the power to see is barely distinguishable from blindness in the absence of illuminated objects. The very identity of the power to know would therefore seem to depend on its being joined with a knowable object—and the same might be said of the knowable object. Perhaps this is why Socrates insists that the good is in some way responsible for the very existence of knowable objects: In bringing knower and known together, in making a pair of them, it makes each one just the one that it is. The good, in this sense, might also be called the same, the source of all identity—and indeed this may be just the name that is given to it in the *Sophist,* in a discussion where the community and integrity of the *eidē* is at issue.

I have just suggested that the good is a source of identity insofar as it brings together things that can be fully themselves only in being together. But perhaps we need to go further. Socrates' image suggests that the good is also the source of the very power of such things to come together, and that it acts as a source by granting those things a share of its own being. This is made particularly clear in the case of the knower; through the analogy with sun and sight, Socrates characterizes the power to know as an overflow and gift of the good. That a strict parallel to this is intended in the case of the objects of knowledge becomes clear when we see that light—that is, truth—is not here a medium through which we see. Instead the good "provides truth to the things known" (508e). The *eidē* do not simply *reflect* the light of truth; they are radiant. They shine forth with a light that is somehow their own. In the end, the yoking together with which we began may amount to this: Out of the fullness of its being, the good renders each being in the intelligible realm fit for the activity and community which complete it.

Where are we in this picture? In what sense can *this* good be said to be *our* good? And what would it mean to take *this* good as a pattern for our lives or the life of our city?

Let me venture a first answer to the first of these questions. Suppose we were all, at bottom, lovers of wisdom. Suppose the longing at the bottom of all the great variety of human longing were a longing to dwell, somehow, among the most knowable objects. Then it seems to me that there might be two senses in which the good would be our good. It would be the very condition for the activity we prized most. For it would be that which fits us for the activity of knowing and makes our objects fit to be known. That is, the good would be the most beneficial or most needful thing, the good for us in this sense. But as the source of the knowability, the truth, the radiance, of the knowable things, the good would itself be the most knowable, most radiant, hence most alluring of the knowable things. It would be the chief object of human desire, "what every soul pursues," *the* good for us in this sense.

It would be, that is, if we were all at bottom lovers of wisdom. But are we? Would Socrates say that we are? His image of the cave would seem to suggest that we are not. It is true that the inhabitants of the cave take a certain delight in discerning and distinguishing the shadows before them. Indeed, this activity of discerning and distinguishing seems to be in some sense at the center of their lives. And yet, the violence with which they resist being turned around toward the truly discernible and distinguishable things suggests that something else, some other desire, is at the core of their being.

Not all human beings, then, are lovers of wisdom, and yet I still think it can be said that the good is somehow the good for us. First I must tell you what I think *does* lie at the core of human desire: I think it is the desire to be complete, either by being a whole on one's own or by participating in a larger whole. It seems to me that this desire for completion or wholeness is, for instance, the thread that binds together the two great speeches about love by Socrates and Aristophanes in the *Symposium:* The philosopher and the poet disagree about what constitutes and makes possible human completeness; they do not disagree about the depth of the desire for it. It also seems to me that this desire is at the root of the resistance of the inhabitants of the cave to being turned around: the cave is after all a dwelling, an *oikēsis;* to give up the cave is to give up a kind of home; it is to give up a kind of being at home in the world (514a). Finally, it seems to me that this desire is just what the image makers in the cave are serving and satisfying through their images. The image makers are at bottom homemakers. The visions embedded in their poems and laws, the visions of what is good and evil, noble and base, right and wrong—these visions give order to the lives of men. They make a common life possible. They make human being a being together: it is no accident that the word *nomos,* usually translated as law, also means song and at bottom means distribution and order.

Do we not see just here at least one sense in which the good is somehow our good, and at the same time glimpse an answer to our other question, namely, how the good could serve as a pattern for human and political action? The image makers are unwitting images of the good in a double sense. *As* makers of images they imitate the image-casting power of the good, and *in this very activity* they imitate its community-making power. But in so doing, in making dwelling places for men, they make possible— or at least aim to make possible—the satisfaction of what I am suggesting is the deepest human desire, the desire to be whole or complete. The good, and such men as imitators of the good, are good for us in just this sense.

But of course most human communities fall short. Most men may find them homey enough to resist the ascent to the good. But they fail to find in them the full satisfaction of their desire for completeness. Thrasymachus' violent rejection of the claim that justice is good, that being just is to one's advantage, is one sign of this lack of satisfaction. The terrifying tale of political strife and disorder that forms the backdrop for the *Republic*—a tale narrated in part by Thucydides—is another: Just think of what happens in Corcyra. As Socrates himself says in the passage with which I began this essay, "[T]here is no rest for ills for the cities, my dear Glaucon, nor I think for humankind . . ."

Of course, Socrates goes on to complete this sentence by suggesting that the ills of cities and mankind could be put to rest if only the philosophers were to rule. We are now in a position to see what this would mean. The philosopher, taking as the model for his activity as king the very thing that makes possible his activity as a lover of wisdom, would order the citizens of his city in accordance with their natures. He would yoke them together both by casting before them the right images and by rendering each of them fit for the activity proper to his nature. In so doing he would bring to fruition the definition of justice arrived at in book four: Each citizen would mind his own business—literally, do his own things—and in doing them achieve the satisfaction of being one with himself in being one with the city.

Now I say "would" here because by the end of book nine Socrates and Glaucon seem to have abandoned the possibility that such a city could ever be founded "in deed." The pattern for it, Socrates says, is laid up in heaven. Perhaps a man who looked to it could "found a city within himself on the basis of what he sees" (592b). But the city he spent nearly six books of the *Republic* talking about is just this, a city in speech. In other words, the true city, the true community, is the heavenly community presided over by the good; it is the community of the *eidē* or perhaps the community of the *eidē* in communion with the one who knows them. Such a knower might be able to shape his own life and his own soul in the image of that city. But the possibility that a human community might arise that was more than the merest shadow of the true city—this possibility has been abandoned.

At any rate this is how things look if we focus only on the argument of the *Republic*. If we look to its drama—and above all if we look again to the figure of Socrates himself—we see something quite different. For in the *Republic* we see Socrates founding not one but two cities in speech. There is the city he talks about with Glaucon and others. But there is also the city—or at least the community—that arises in the course of the talk about it. Here, as elsewhere in the dialogues and *like the dialogues themselves*, Socrates is at work as the visible image of the good, uniting within his own person, the person of the philosopher, the powers of weaving together and image making delimited in the *Sophist* and the *Statesman*. He gathers up and distinguishes the young men around him, taming Thrasymachus, spurring Glaucon and Adeimantus on, helping each to find his proper place and work within their city in speech. He does this in part by collecting and distinguishing in speech the forms of things, by practicing the art of dialectic. But Socrates' casting forth of wondrous images lies at the center of his gathering, and at the center of these images stand his images of sun and cave. Here his intellect, itself the overflow from the sun's treasury, becomes the fire that illuminates the cave. Here he lets the young men sitting around him see, if only for a moment, what it would mean to stand up, turn around, and make their ascent from the cave. If, then, we turn the words of Socrates' central claim into a question, if we ask whether the "regime traversed now in speech" can ever "blossom forth and see the light of the sun," we can say, "Yes"—it can, it *has,* because the philosopher, for a time, has become king.

THE HAZARDOUS FUTURE OF DEMOCRACY IN AMERICA: TOCQUEVILLE & LAWYERS IN AMERICA

Harrison Sheppard

ALEXIS DE TOCQUEVILLE, who wrote *Democracy in America* during the second quarter of the nineteenth century, believed that American lawyers of his time were "the most powerful existing security" against the potential excesses of democracy. By "excesses of democracy," Tocqueville meant a tendency toward either a kind of anarchy or "mob rule," or an oppressive tyranny of the majority leading to despotism. In the course of this essay, we will examine the reasons for Tocqueville's beliefs. We will then consider the significance of Tocqueville's views as they relate to the prevailing character of American lawyers today. The real subject of this lecture, therefore, is the likely future of the United States of America as it may be affected by the habits and practices of twenty-first-century American lawyers.

Significant discourse about lawyers or "speakers of the law" in America should include, and may perhaps best begin with, a clear understanding of the nature of the "law" that American lawyers are supposed to speak.[1] In this country, the U.S. Constitution and federal laws "enacted in pursuance thereof" are declared to be "the supreme Law of the land" (*U.S. Constitution,* Article 6), indicating that American lawyers should at least partly be governed in what they say about the law by their understanding of the provisions of the U.S. Constitution and its guiding purposes. We should, however, consider the most fundamental definition of "law" in a reasoned discussion of the kind of law American lawyers are supposed to speak. For this purpose, I choose to refer to the seminal definition of "law" given by St. Thomas Aquinas in his *Treatise on Law* in the *Summa Theologica:*

> Law is an ordinance of reason, for the common good, promulgated by those who have the care of the community. (Thomas Aquinas, Treatise on Law, Question 90, "Of the Essence of Law.")

I suggest that this definition states a proper understanding of authoritative American law as the authors of our Constitution would have understood it. The definition accords with John Locke's view, reflected also in the writings of Blackstone (with which most of the Founders were familiar), that "the life of the law is reason." A political "ordinance" that fails to conform substantially to the Thomistic definition of law is something other than "law" properly understood; it is, rather, usually a mere *edict,* like a royal decree in antiquity, pronounced by those who have the *power* to enforce their will in a given polity, without necessarily possessing the authority of either reason or care for the common good.

It is with these premises that I introduce my discussion of what Alexis de Tocqueville had to say in the second quarter of the nineteenth century about American lawyers in his enduring and often prophetic work, *Democracy in America.*

I. Tocqueville's Fears About the Future of Democracy

Tocqueville's consideration of the part American lawyers play, or should play, in the American polity is, for the most part, highly complimentary, even flattering. This may come as something of a surprise to those familiar with the critical literature, both ancient and modern, condemning the character of the typical lawyer and the way he works.[2] Here is Tocqueville's seminal statement about lawyers in *Democracy in America:*

> I am not ignorant of the defects inherent in the character of this body of men; but without this admixture of *lawyer-like sobriety* with the democratic principle, I question whether democratic institutions could long be maintained; and *I cannot believe that a republic could hope to exist at the present time, if the influence of lawyers in public business did not increase in proportion to the power of the people.* (*Democracy in America,* Everyman's Library [hereafter "Everyman"], Alfred Knopf, NY, 1994, Vol. I, Chapter XVI, "Causes Which Mitigate the Tyranny of the Majority in the United States," p. 276, emphasis added)

To understand the meaning of this apparent heterodoxy, we have to understand, first, what Tocqueville feared about the possible future of democracy in America as it might prefigure ever-more pervasive democracy in the world; and, second, what he meant by "lawyer-like sobriety" in the context of the sentences I have just quoted.

In the Introduction to the first volume of *Democracy in America,* after surveying the history of Western civilization, Tocqueville concluded that the steady development of democracy—by which he meant "a general equality of [social] condition among the people"—was an "irresistible revolution" and a "providential fact."[3] He eloquently summarized the reasons for this trend as follows:

> From the time when the exercise of the intellect became a source of strength and of wealth, we see that every addition to science, every fresh truth, and every new idea became a germ of power placed within the reach of the people. Poetry, eloquence, and memory, the graces of the mind, the fire of imagination, depth of thought, and all the gifts which Heaven scatters at a venture, turned to the advantage of democracy; and even when they were in the possession of its adversaries, they still served its cause by throwing into bold relief the natural greatness of man. Its conquests spread, therefore, with those of civilization and knowledge, and literature became an arsenal open to all, where the poor and the weak daily resorted for arms. In running over the pages of our history, we shall scarcely find a single great event of the last 700 years that has not promoted equality of condition. (Everyman, Vol. I, p. 5)

Tocqueville was a nineteenth-century French aristocrat who confessed some sadness at the passing of the old order. An evidently pious, if not conventionally religious, Catholic who declared "I believe, but I do not practice,"[4] he sought to find and accept reasons to rejoice in what he characterized as the will of a just God. The whole of *Democracy in America* was written, he said, "under the influence of a kind of religious awe . . . of that irresistible revolution which has advanced for centuries in spite of every obstacle . . ." (Everyman, Vol. I, p. 6). As a political scientist, he undertook by coming to America, where democracy as he understood it was most fully developed, to study and to understand it, and then consider how its inevitable human imperfections could best be mitigated. He is explicit about this:

> I confess that, in America, I saw more than America; I sought there the image of democracy itself, with its inclinations, its character, its prejudices, and its passions, in order to learn what we have to fear or to hope from its progress. (Everyman, Introduction, Vol. I, p. 6)[5]

Like many of the Founders of the American Republic, Tocqueville feared what common people—the *demos*—might do with their power in democratic society. He feared—one might even say correctly he predicted—that the democratic outlook would lead to the following political developments:

First, a highly centralized government tending toward a diminished concern for individual rights; second, an enormous expansion of governmental power in regulation of private enterprise and in providing for the public welfare; third, a consequent need for the development of countervailing aggregations of private power to prevent the government from becoming too oppressive; fourth, an increasing tendency toward political apathy, following an almost complete absorption in private business and affairs on the part of people generally; fifth, a reluctance of the people to withdraw their confidence in the government "in the midst even of its excesses and errors;" and, sixth and lastly, agreeing with Thomas Jefferson (whom Tocqueville regarded as "the most powerful advocate democracy has ever had"), a greatly expanded power in the Presidency "at a distant period."

Tocqueville's fears about the future of democracy may be seen as focusing upon two main concerns: the possible development of a welfare state, which he eloquently condemns as a "despotic" polity promoting material well-being at the price of spiritual impoverishment,[6] and the exercise of a "tyranny of the majority" oppressively disregarding the rights of minorities and of individuals.[7] (These at least echo, as you will recognize, the prognosis for failed democracy in Plato's analysis of polities in the *Republic*.[8]) Tocqueville's fears were, however, overridden by his faith that the flourishing of democracy was the result of "Divine Providence." He declares in his Introduction that, though he is "ignorant" of God's designs, he "shall not cease to believe in them because [he] cannot fathom them, and [he] had rather mistrust [his] own capacity than [God's] justice."

Throughout *Democracy in America,* Tocqueville therefore looks for elements at work in American society that may operate to prevent the degeneration of democracy into anarchy, or into a benevolent but wholly materialistic despotism, or into a complete tyranny of the majority. He finds five American institutions that give him such hope, in most of which lawyers may play a substantial part:

1. Private Voluntary Associations
2. A Free Press
3. Trial by Jury
4. The American Legal Profession Itself
5. The "Spirit of Religion"

Let us *briefly* consider each of these in turn, maintaining our focus upon what Tocqueville has to say about the American legal profession.

II. Tocquevillian Safeguards Against Democratic Anarchy, Despotism, and the Tyranny of the Majority

1. *Private Voluntary Associations.* At the beginning of the nineteenth century, Tocqueville could accurately say that the United States was "the only country on the face of the earth where the citizens enjoy unlimited freedom of association for political purposes" (Everyman, Vol. II, Chapter VII, p. 115). Tocqueville begins a chapter in Volume I titled "Political Associations in the United States" (Everyman, Chapter XII, p. 191) with this observation:

> In no country in the world has the principle of association been more successfully used or applied to a greater multitude of objects than in America. . . . In the United States associations are established to promote the public safety, commerce, industry, morality, and religion. . . .
>
> At the present time the liberty of association has become a necessary guarantee against the tyranny of the majority. In the United States, as soon as a party has become dominant, all public authority passes into its hands. . . . There are [therefore] no countries in which associations are more needed to prevent the despotism of faction or the arbitrary power of a prince than those which are democratically constituted. (Everyman, Vol. I, Chapter 12, pp. 191–195)

Tocqueville considers private voluntary associations, and private associations with a public purpose, as constituting "a separate nation in the midst of the nation, a government within the government." He views their continued existence as indispensable to the preservation of minority liberties by exercising collective, vocal power outside of government. We should judge for ourselves the extent to which private voluntary associations continue to function as safeguards against either oppressive government or the tyranny of the majority in the United States; but we need also to consider the extent to which they may presently operate to entrench, rather than disperse, centralized power in the use made of them, for example, in political campaign financing. Might Tocqueville have had too narrow a view of the potential effects of private voluntary associations in America for good *and* ill? The growing public apathy about politics Tocqueville feared as a likely development in American society seems to have been realized. May that not operate to diminish the extent to which the most effective voluntary associations today are, on the whole, more likely to be associated with, rather than distant from, the axes of established political power, thus diminishing their Tocquevillian function as countervailing forces against the power of government?

2. *A Free Press.* In Tocqueville's day, a "free press" meant mainly the liberty of *newspapers* to publish independent opinions. Tocqueville was restrained in his appreciation of liberty of the press. "I confess," he wrote:

> that I do not entertain that firm and complete attachment to the liberty of the press which is wont to be excited by things that are supremely good in their very nature. I approve of it from a consideration more of the evils it prevents than of the advantages it ensures. (Everyman, Vol. I, Chapter XI, "Liberty of the Press in the United States," p. 181)

This restraint was no doubt born in part from his awareness of how irresponsible and misleading the American press could be—perhaps even more in his day than in ours. It was also partly the result of an observation he makes in the very first sentence of his chapter on liberty of the press:

> The influence of liberty of the press does not affect political opinions alone, but extends to all the opinions of men and modifies customs as well as laws. (Everyman, *ibid.*)

In his admiration of a free press for "the evils it prevents," Tocqueville associates a free press closely with the salutary power of voluntary associations. Given the likely geographic dispersion of the membership of voluntary associations large enough to exercise significant power, he argues that

> There is a necessary connection between public associations and newspapers: newspapers make associations, and associations make newspapers. . . . Thus it is in America that we find at the same time the greatest number of associations and of newspapers (Everyman, Vol. II, Chapter VI, p. 112).

We need not dwell on the importance of a free press for preservation of political liberty, its special power to help promote the security of minorities and the rights of individuals by providing the public with the information it needs, and to which it is entitled, if it is to be able to assess the actions of its government. It is, I think, enough to note that the *First* Amendment to the U.S. Constitution, which is, accordingly, the first of its "Bill of Rights," is the Amendment that says in relevant part:

> Congress shall make *no* law . . . abridging the freedom of speech, or of the press, or the right of the people peaceably to assemble, and to petition the Government for a redress of grievances (emphasis added).

We do need to ask, however, how the provisions of the First Amendment have been interpreted and both restricted and expanded over the past 215 years; by whom it is authoritatively interpreted (lawyers and judges, of course); how the addition of radio, television, and the internet as means of communication subject to First Amendment protection have changed what we understand by a "free press"; whether, or to what extent, these modern media effectively enhance, or compromise, or even distort, the political functions of a free press as envisioned by the Founders. Consider, for example, Tocqueville's concern about the effects of a free press on social custom when, as at present, they include the cultural effects of television.[9]

In the 1930's, public hearings were held to consider federal issuance of radio licenses. David Sarnoff, President of RCA, testified that it was "inconceivable" that the public airways would be used for commercial purposes. One is tempted to ask whether the "public airways" are, in effect, now being used for any other purpose, even in the context of considering network television news broadcasts. In considering America's free press as a safeguard to liberty and check on governmental power, we should also ask these questions: Has the substantial decrease in the number of newspapers in the United States since Tocqueville's day—during the past half century especially—coupled with the increasing concentration of major mass media generally, operated to reduce the availability to Americans of the range of readily available, politically significant information? Has private censorship of the "public" airways significantly reduced the extent to which the American press represents and advocates minority political opinion? Does the public continue to have sufficient access to the information it needs to judge the extent to which our government, in Lincoln's formulation, remains a "government of the people, by the people, and for the people"?

3. *Trial by Jury.* Speaking of the centuries-long establishment, in English law, of the institution of trial by jury, Tocqueville says:

> A judicial institution which thus obtains the suffrages of a great people for so long a series of ages, which is zealously reproduced at every stage of civilization, in all the climates of the earth, and under every form of human government, cannot be contrary to the spirit of justice (Everyman, Vol. I, Chapter XVI, "Causes Which Mitigate the Tyranny of the Majority in the United States," p. 281).

Tocqueville has a very high opinion of the effects of trial by jury—in both civil and criminal cases—on the people of a democracy. He considers the institution as important an incident of the sovereignty of the people as the right to vote. Trial by jury decisively affirms the sovereignty of the people in their most important encounters with governmental power.[10] Jury service is, moreover, in Tocqueville's view, an institution that educates and elevates people to exercise their democratic powers with greater prudence and regard for justice by imbuing

> all classes with a respect for the thing judged and with the notion of right. . . . It teaches men to practice equity; every man learns to judge his neighbor as he would himself be judged. And this is especially true of the jury in civil causes; for while the number of persons who have reason to apprehend a criminal prosecution is small, everyone is liable to have a lawsuit. (Everyman, Vol. I, p. 284)

The process of selecting a jury in both civil and criminal cases in the United States is generally in the hands of the judge and the attorneys on each side of a case. In high-profile criminal cases, and in civil cases where a great deal of money is involved, this has become a sophisticated art. The recent Hollywood movie, *Runaway Jury,* may portray an exaggerated picture of this process, but it is suggestive of the extraordinary lengths to which contemporary American lawyers may go in their efforts to ensure that the "right" jury is selected for their respective purposes. This brings us to the heart of our subject: Tocqueville's view of the part American lawyers may play in avoiding the excesses of democracy and mitigating the tyranny of the majority. Recall Tocqueville's expressed opinion that without "lawyer-like sobriety" as a factor in American society, *he could not imagine* that American republican institutions would continue to exist.

   4. *The American Legal Profession Itself.* It would be difficult to overestimate the importance that Tocqueville attached to the conduct of members of the legal profession as the guardians of freedom in American democratic society. "If I were asked where I place the American aristocracy," he reports, "I should reply without hesitation that it is not among the rich [whom the people are apt to mistrust and] who are united by no common tie, but that it occupies the judicial bench and the bar" (Everyman, Vol. I, p. 278). The first sentence of his address to this subject, in the chapter titled "Causes Which Mitigate the Tyranny of the Majority in the United States," reads as follows:

> In visiting the Americans and studying their laws, we perceive that the authority they have entrusted to members of the legal profession, and the

influence that these individuals exercise in the government, are *the most powerful existing security* against the excesses of democracy. (Everyman, Vol. I, p. 272, emphasis added)

Here is the reason Tocqueville gives to explain why he views lawyers as "the most powerful existing security against the excesses of democracy":

Men who have made a special study of the laws derive from this occupation certain habits of order, a taste for formalities, and a kind of instinctive regard *for the regular connection of ideas,* which naturally render them very hostile to the revolutionary spirit and the unreflecting passions of the multitude. (Ibid., p. 273, emphasis added)

Tocqueville is explicit in his association of American lawyers with the old aristocracy. "Some of the tastes and the habits of the aristocracy," he says, "may be discovered in the characters of lawyers" (*ibid.*). For example, "the habit of directing to their purpose the blind passions of parties in litigation inspires [American lawyers] with a certain contempt for the judgment of the multitude. . . . They participate in the same instinctive love of order and formalities; and they entertain the same repugnance to the actions of the multitude . . ." (*ibid.,* pp. 273–74). Tocqueville does not, however, assert that

all the members of the legal profession are at *all* times the friends of order and the opponents of innovation, but that *most of them are usually so.* In a community in which lawyers are allowed to occupy without opposition that high station which naturally belongs to them, their general spirit will be eminently conservative and anti-democratic. (*ibid.,* p. 274, emphasis added)

"Most of them," he asserts with confidence, "are usually so." "Lawyers," he goes on to say, "are attached to public order beyond every other consideration, and the best security of public order is authority" (*ibid.,* p. 275). Tocqueville goes so far as to say that lawyers generally value legality even above freedom, and fear tyranny less than disorder; that they are even willing to accept limitations upon individual freedom so long as they are properly authorized by the duly constituted legislature. He accurately observes:

The government of democracy is favorable to the political power of lawyers; for when the wealthy, the noble, and the prince are excluded from the government, the lawyers take possession of it in their own right . . . since they are the only men of information and sagacity . . . who can be the object of popular choice. (p. 275)

Six of the first ten U.S. Presidents were lawyers, including three of the six Presidents preceding the date *Democracy in America* was written. In fact, until 1952, about two-thirds of our American presidents were either lawyers or had some formal legal training. Why would American lawyers command such a position in democratic society at least until the middle of the twentieth century? Tocqueville tells us why. Lawyers, he says,

> like the government of democracy without participating in its propensities and weaknesses; whence they derive a twofold authority from it and over it. *The people in democratic states do not mistrust the members of the legal profession,* because it is known that they are interested to serve the popular cause; and the people listen to them without irritation, *because they do not attribute to them any sinister design.* . . . Lawyers belong to the people by birth and interest, and to the aristocracy by habit and taste; *they may be looked upon as the connecting link between the two great classes of society.* (Ibid., pp. 275–76, emphases added)

The conservative, aristocratic tendencies of the habits of English and American lawyers as Tocqueville perceived them is fortified by Anglo-American reliance upon legal *precedent,* which is not as binding on their French equivalents. In marked contrast to Jonathan Swift's condemnation of the use of precedent "to justify the most iniquitous opinions,"[11] Tocqueville approves of habitual reliance upon precedent as a brake on democratic excess. The deference an American lawyer pays to the opinions of his forefathers, Tocqueville points out, "necessarily give him more timid habits and more conservative inclinations . . . than [a lawyer] in France" (*ibid.,* p. 277). Here, then, is Tocqueville's summary of the reasons he has concluded that American lawyers "as a body, form the most powerful, if not the only, counterpoise to the democratic element":

> When the American people are intoxicated by passion or carried away by the impetuosity of their ideas, they are checked and stopped by the almost invisible influence of their legal *counselors.* They secretly oppose their aristocratic propensities to the nation's democratic instincts, their superstitious attachment to what is old to its love of novelty, their narrow views to its immense designs, and their habitual procrastination to its ardent impatience (*ibid.,* at p. 278, emphasis added).

We need to consider how Tocqueville's assessment of the character of the typical American lawyer of the 1820's relates to what we may observe about the character of contemporary American lawyers. Before doing so, however, we will briefly consider what Tocqueville has to say about the "spirit of religion" as the fifth check upon the excesses of democracy.

5. *The Spirit of Religion.* Tocqueville feared that the tendency toward materialism he found in the democratic spirit might lead to a despotic welfare state. (In this he might be regarded as foreseeing the possibility of a Soviet-style regime.) He also observed among Americans a spirit of individualism of a kind he thought most congenial to despotism.

> No vice of the human heart is so acceptable to [despotism] as selfishness; a despot easily forgives his subjects for not loving him, provided they do not love one another. . . . Despotism, then, which is at all times dangerous, is more particularly to be feared in democratic ages. (Everyman, Vol. II, Chapter IV, p. 102)

In contrast to this tendency, Tocqueville congratulates Americans for the way that their free political institutions combat "the tendency of equality to keep men asunder" (*ibid.,* p. 103). But it is *materialism* that Tocqueville fears and hates most. It is his view that democracy in America will succeed in avoiding the worst of its excesses only so long as the "spirit of religion" remains widely diffused. In his summary formulation, Tocqueville states his opinion that "liberty cannot be established without morality, nor morality without faith" (Everyman, Vol. I, "Author's Introduction," p. 12). The faith of which he is speaking, however, is not one of adherence to any particular religious dogma. It is the *spirit* of religion, a capacity for faith in the value of higher things, in which Tocqueville places his hopes, for the following reason:

> It must be acknowledged that equality, which brings great benefits into the world, nevertheless suggests to men some very dangerous propensities. It tends to isolate them from one another, to concentrate every man's attention upon himself; and it lays open the soul to an inordinate love of material gratification.
>
> The greatest advantage of religion is to inspire diametrically contrary principles. There is no religion that does not place the object of man's desires above and beyond the treasures of earth and that does not naturally raise his soul to regions far above those of the senses. Nor is there any which does not impose on man some duties toward his kind and thus draw him at times from the contemplation of himself. (Ibid., p. 22)

American civil law, like religion, is also concerned with one person's duty to another; and lawyers, like clergymen interpreting their bibles, are, or should be, deeply devoted to interpretations of what may be called "civil scripture," and their "regular connections of ideas." Abraham Lincoln implicitly noted this parallel in his *Address to the Young Men's Lyceum of Springfield, Illinois* in 1838 with the following words:

> Let reverence for the laws . . . become the political religion of the nation; and let the old and the young, the rich and the poor, the grave and the gay, of all sexes and tongues, and colors and conditions, sacrifice unceasingly upon its altars.
>
> While ever a state of feeling such as this, shall universally, or even very generally prevail throughout the nation, vain will be every effort, and fruitless every attempt, to subvert our national freedom.

In Tocqueville's day, lawyers could rightly be termed "the secular ministers of American democracy," especially in their function as counselors of restraint and respect for the spirit of the law. This may be the chief reason Tocqueville so much admired the American legal profession as he perceived it.

III. A Comparison of 21st-Century American Lawyers as a Body with American Lawyers Praised by Tocqueville

How relevant are Tocqueville's observations about the redemptive character of American lawyers to the American legal profession today? I am unhappy to say that, while they may remain highly relevant to consideration of what we may *need* to preserve our civil liberties, they are no longer accurate characterizations of the American legal profession—except perhaps for Tocqueville's observation about a tendency toward procrastination. The degeneration of the American legal profession from the model Tocqueville had in mind has a long history, beginning as early as the post-Civil War period.[12] Since the 1960's, however, the character of the American legal profession as Tocqueville admired it has not been just further eroded; it has virtually disappeared. Signaling this catastrophic loss, a number of books were published in the 1990's by authoritative authors with titles and subtitles such as these:[13] *The Lost Lawyer: Failing Ideals of the Legal Profession; The Betrayed Profession: Lawyering at the End of the Twentieth Century; The Death of Common Sense: How Law is Suffocating America; A Nation Under Lawyers: How the Crisis in the Legal Profession is Transforming American Society.* The authors of these books include a Yale Law School dean, a distinguished member of the

Harvard Law School faculty, and a former chairman of Xerox Corporation who was also ambassador to the Organization of American States.

Lawyers are no longer generally educated, trained, or employed to cultivate a love "for the regular connection of ideas." Though each of them swears an oath upon admission to the bar to uphold the Constitution and laws of the United States (and their respective states), they are not likely to take those oaths very seriously. Very few American lawyers today are likely to be able to quote the words, or even summarize the sense, of the *Preamble* to the U.S. Constitution in substantial part—which would probably not have been the case in Tocqueville's day. Lawyers are no longer generally inclined to fulfill their function as Tocquevillian *counselors*, skilled in checking their clients' passions or the impetuosity of their ideas—where money is to be made by indulging their passions and impetuosity. The practice of law in America has become much more of a business—with the applause of some American economists—than one of the three traditional "learned professions" that distinguished the practice of law from a merely commercial enterprise. The present dominant *ethos* of American legal practice is the will to win at any cost that the client can afford, including the cost of truth.[14]

There are many reasons for these sad developments. Some of them may be manifestations of the very character of American democratic culture and materialism, as Tocqueville himself perceived and feared. There have, however, been a number of specific institutional developments during the past quarter century or so that have clearly contributed significantly to the present situation. Chief among these, in my judgment, are, first, the U.S. Supreme Court's authorization (on First Amendment grounds!) of commercial advertising by lawyers in *Bates vs. State Bar of Arizona,* 433 U.S. 350 (1977), which had been generally prohibited by State Bar ethical rules of practice before 1977; second, the spectacle of Watergate, in which the Attorney General of the United States and the Counsel to the President were successfully prosecuted for violations of law demonstrating their contempt, while in office, for faithful execution of the laws of the United States and fidelity to their Constitutional oaths; and third, the proliferation of large *and very large* law firms (a rarity before the 1970's). This development has been especially pernicious. The growth of large law firms in the U.S. has had the effect of both eliminating the ethical mentoring of young lawyers and creating virtually irresistible pressures for the generation of "billable hours" as a higher priority than pursuit of prudent measures designed to resolve disputes efficiently (let alone achieve justice).

Fourth and finally, though a passion for justice, equity, and right may yet animate most students *entering* law school, such aspirations are virtually mocked by typical law school training as naïve and simplistic, and are then usually entirely crushed as law graduates quickly learn that the will to win at any cost—while billing the maximum amount of hours possible—is now the dominant *ethos* of typical legal practice in America. The need for radical change in legal education has become increasingly apparent since it was urged as a necessity early in the twentieth century—a necessity which I have been personally advocating in my own writings for the past decade.

What might Tocqueville say about all this? I seriously doubt that Tocqueville would find that "lawyer-like sobriety," in the sense in which he intended that phrase, now typifies American lawyers, either in how they practice and "speak the law," or in the way most Americans perceive them. The great founding organs of the American polity—*The Declaration of Independence* and the Constitution—were intended to harmonize a diverse people through the music of their law of reason. Tocqueville considered American lawyers, the chief exponents of that law, to be essential *harmonizers,* a "connecting link between" different factions of American society. They have now, however, generally become agents of its *division* as they cash in on its conflicts.[15] Nor can we say that most people today "do not mistrust members of the legal profession," or "do not attribute to them any sinister designs."[16] In short, the essential attributes of American lawyers Tocqueville thought made them the "most powerful security against the excesses of democracy" do not appear to be operating in the United States today.

Tocqueville was not alone in fearing that democracy in America might end in some form of despotism. Benjamin Franklin in fact *predicted* that would be its outcome. At the conclusion of the constitutional convention, he had this to say:

> I agree to this Constitution with all its faults, if they are such: . . . there is no *Form* of government but what may be a blessing to the people if well administered; and I believe farther that this is likely to be well administered for a Course of Years and can only end in Despotism as other Forms have done before it, when the People shall become so corrupted as to need Despotic Government, being incapable of any other. (As quoted by Gore Vidal, *Inventing a Nation,* Yale U. Press, 2003, at pp. 30–31, punctuation and emphasis in original)

But I do not wish to end this lecture without some notes of hope—for this audience in particular.

IV. CONCLUSION: THE NEED FOR RENEWAL

On December 27, 1938, Walter Lippman, one of the most distinguished journalists of the twentieth century, who was one of President Woodrow Wilson's most trusted young advisors at the Versailles Peace conference, published a column in *The New York Herald Tribune* titled "The St. John's Program." In that column, Lippman compared the institutions of the American polity to "a great and noble pipe organ" capable of producing the most beautiful music by those who knew how to play it. He told a story of how this pipe organ had been carefully constructed by its owner; how, as the organ was passed to the maker's son and grandson, it fell into disrepair, so much so that, in the course of time, no one could even find the parts needed to repair it. Lippman then made the point of his tale explicit:

> This sad tale will serve, I think, as a parable of the history of the free peoples during the past three or four generations. For they have inherited great and noble institutions from their forefathers. But because they have not inherited the knowledge which enabled their forefathers to make these institutions, they do not really know how to preserve them, repair them, and improve them.

"Men are ceasing to be free," Lippman continued, "because they are no longer being educated in the arts of free men," the classical liberal arts. Lippman saw in the St. John's program the possibility of a "seedbed of an American renaissance" of understanding the *design, purpose, and rationale* of the American republic.

The principal Founders of our American polity—Washington, Adams, Jefferson, Madison, Hamilton, Franklin, and Gouverneur Morris—all regarded the democratic republic they had created as a great "experiment."[17] In his *Gettysburg Address,* Lincoln reasserted this view by stating that we are a nation "dedicated to the *proposition* that all men are created equal," and that the Civil War was testing whether a government "of the people, by the people, and for the people" could "long endure." The experiment has so far endured for more than 200 years; but it may yet fail. It is more likely to fail if its chief safeguards wither away, and are not renewed. One of the authors read at St. John's College anticipated Walter Lippman's prescription for American renewal by over 400 years. That author is Machiavelli, a passionate republican who, in his *Discourse on the First Ten Books of Livy,* written in 1521, had this to say about the renewal of republics:

There is nothing more true than that all the things of this world have a limit to their existence; but those only run the entire course ordained for them by Heaven that do not allow their body to become disorganized. But keep it unchanged in the manner ordained. . . . And as I speak here of bodies such as republics, I say that those changes are beneficial that bring them back to their original principles. And it is a truth clearer than light that, without such renovation, these bodies cannot continue to exist; and the means of renewing them is to bring them back to their original principles. (*Discourses on Livy*, Book III, Chapter 1, 1521)

Machiavelli's reference to Heaven may remind us of Tocqueville's belief in the providential future of democracy, and the "spirit of religion" he thought indispensable to the preservation of American liberties. The kind of faith of which Tocqueville was writing was demonstrated by a young law school graduate during a period when "loyalty oaths" and confessions of political affiliations were requirements for admission to some State bars. In 1950, George Anastaplo graduated at the top of his class at the University of Chicago Law School. In his examination for admission to the Illinois State Bar by a "Committee on Character and Fitness," he refused to answer a question about his political beliefs, relying upon his faith in the political principles enunciated in the *Declaration of Independence* and his First Amendment rights under the U.S. Constitution. The young Anastaplo *personally* argued his case before the U.S. Supreme Court when his admission to the Illinois Bar was denied because of this refusal. He *lost* his case in a 5–4 decision against him (366 U.S. 82, 1961).[18] In a truly eloquent dissent to the majority opinion on that occasion by Justice Hugo Lafayette Black, Justice Black said that Anastaplo's main fault, if any, was that he had taken too much responsibility upon himself to protect the integrity of the bar and the duty of American lawyers to uphold the U.S. Constitution. Justice Black implicitly applauded Anastaplo's courage in the concluding, resonant words of his dissent, words which he asked be read at his own funeral as his political testament: *"We must not be afraid to be free."* Though not a practicing lawyer, George Anastaplo demonstrated not only his courage, but his understanding of the first virtue—*Justice*—and the final good—*Liberty*—referred to in the *Preamble* to the U.S. Constitution. In doing this, Anastaplo also exhibited the *redemptive character* of the American lawyer as Tocqueville understood it.

In large part, Tocqueville was led to admire the American lawyers of his day because of their characteristic admiration of the classical virtues and aspiration toward them through their education and intellectual habits.

Study of the classical virtues of courage, prudence, justice, and temperance—virtues that sustain and enable one another—is, in effect, part of the St. John's College curriculum. Students of this curriculum are entrusted with some special duties: the duty to help keep the American experiment alive; the duty to use the power of their acquired understanding of its original principles and design to help restore them, whether as a doctor, or a manufacturer, or a computer technologist; but especially as an American lawyer. To these students and future alumni of St. John's College, I repeat Justice Black's admonition: "You must not be afraid to be free."

NOTES

1 Members of the American legal profession are designated by three different titles signifying three different functions. A "lawyer" is "one who speaks the law." An "attorney" is "one who stands in the place of another"; that is, represents another. (Thus one can be an "attorney in fact" and not an attorney at law.) A "counselor" is one who gives advice. In most situations, counseling is, as a practical matter, the most important service rendered by an ethical lawyer.

2 For a collection of complaints about lawyers in great secular and religious literature, see Harrison Sheppard, "American Principles and the Evolving *Ethos* of American Legal Practice," 28 *Loyola University Chicago Law Journal* 237 (Winter 1996): 246–49, notes 20–28. Hereafter referred to as *Loyola*.

3 Everyman, vol. 1, p. 6.

4 See Doris S. Goldstein, *Trial of Faith: Religion and Politics in Tocqueville's Thought* (New York: Elsevier Scientific Publishing Company, 1975); and John Lukacs, "The Last Days of Alexis de Tocqueville," *The Catholic Historical Review* 50, no. 2 (July 1964), explaining Tocqueville's refusal to take communion on his deathbed and the significance of Tocqueville's declaration of faith without practice.

5 For a highly informative discussion of Tocqueville's political—as opposed to merely philosophical—purposes in writing *Democracy in America*, see Marvin Zetterbaum, *Tocqueville and the Problem of Democracy* (Stanford: Stanford University Press, 1967).

6 See Everyman, vol. 2, chapter 6, "What Sort of Despotism Democratic Nations Have to Fear," 316 ff.

7 See especially Everyman, vol. 1, chapter 15, "Unlimited Power of the Majority in the United States and its Consequences."

8 Plato's *Republic*, Bk. 8, 555 ff., especially 561–64.

9 For an instructive discussion of the deleterious effects of mass media, and television in particular, on American political life, see George Anastaplo, *The American Moralist: On Law, Ethics and Government* (Athens, Ohio: Ohio University Press, 1992), in the section titled "The Use and Abuse of the First

Amendment," especially chapter 17 at 261–73, which includes the following observations at p. 261: "The modern mass media tend more toward centralization of power, while the old fashioned press tended to be more localizing in its efforts and effects . . . [With the nationalization of mass media] is there a tendency toward homogeneity of tastes and opinions as well as a general lowering of effective moral, political, and intellectual standards? . . . [With modern industrialization and] its marvels-laden technology . . .. one is forced into a passive role: not the role of the alert observer, but that of the pampered slave."

10   For a discussion of the relationship between trial by jury and the "Blessings of Liberty" under the U.S. Constitution, see George Anastaplo, *The Constitutionalist Notes on the First Amendment* (Dallas, Tex.: Southern Methodist University Press, 1971), chapter 8, "The Blessings of Liberty."

11   Jonathan Swift, *Gulliver's Travels* (New York: Alfred A. Knopf, 1991), 265–66.

12   See, e.g., John Dos Passos, *The American Lawyer* (Littleton, Colo.: Fred B. Rothman & Co., 1996), 12–13: "I am drawing a line between the period before and after the Civil War, and I put the old generation of American lawyers on the farther side, and the new ones on this side of the line. . . . The fundamental difference between the old and new regime of lawyers is this: the great aim of the old lawyers was to master the elements of law; they depended upon an eloquent presentation of their causes; the judges had the time, and it was their pleasure, to listen to the advocates; 'commercialism' did not exist; there were less legal tricks or technical legerdemain to resort to, because the dire plague of codification had not yet spread itself over the profession, and destroyed its science, as it existed under common law, where, while form was strictly observed, the substance or merits of a controversy, were principally sought for. The lawyers of today are case and code lawyers. The search for *principle* is subordinate to an investigation for *precedent*. The right or justice, or the merits of controversies, disappear under a mass of irreconcilable decisions and forms. It requires a different kind of intellectual development to be a lawyer than it did in the days long gone by" (emphases in original). Dos Passos' first prescription for reform of the American legal profession is to correct "deficiencies, imperfections, and looseness in the preliminary, elementary, and legal education of law students" (ibid., p. 165).

13   A more complete list, fully cited, may be found in *Loyola*, p. 246, n. 19.

14   See William T. Braithwaite, "Why Lawyers Lie," in *The Great Ideas Today,* edited by Mortimer J. Adler (Chicago: Encyclopaedia Britannica, 1994), 231.

15   See Sheppard, "Cashing in on Conflict," *The Washington Post* (June 6, 1996): A23; David Luban, "The *Noblesse Oblige* Tradition in the Practice of Law," 41 *Vanderbilt Law Review* 717 (1988): 724: "The common good will be realized in a society such as the United States, by blunting or mitigating conflict, especially class conflict; Brandeis espoused this theme as did de Tocqueville." Luban also points out that the reconciliation of conflicting interests "is one of the most ancient conceptions of the function of law, appearing originally in *The Laws* of Plato. . . . Because factionalism and class war will inevitably destroy a city

unless it is governed by the rule of law, not of men, the lawmakers must attempt to reconcile the conflicting elements of society" (ibid., n. 31).

16 To the contrary, American Bar Association polls and surveys of the last decade show that "the more contact people have with lawyers, the less favorably they look upon the legal profession"; see the sources cited in *Loyola,* 261, n. 48.

17 See *Loyola,* 253, n. 38, quoting, *inter alia,* Washington's statement in his first inaugural address that the "preservation of the sacred fire of liberty, and the destiny of the republican model of government are justly considered as *deeply,* and perhaps as *finally* staked, on the *experiment* entrusted to the hands of the American people" (only the last emphasis is added).

18 The *Anastaplo* decision may have been effectively overruled in later cases; see, e.g., *Konigsberg v. State Bar,* 366 U.S. 36 (1961). One consequence of Anastaplo's denial of admission to the Illinois State Bar is that Professor Anastaplo (now at the Loyola University of Chicago Law School) has produced as prolific a body of writings on the American Constitution as any contemporary American; his bibliography occupies more than 80 printed pages in the two-volume tribute to him titled *Law and Philosophy: The Practice of Theory, Essays in Honor of George Anastaplo,* edited by John A. Murley, Robert L. Stone, and William T. Braithwaite (Athens, Ohio: Ohio University Press, 1992). These notably include *The Constitutionalist: Notes on the First Amendment* (Dallas, Tex.: Southern Methodist University Press, 1971); *The Constitution of 1787: A Commentary* (Baltimore, Md.: The Johns Hopkins University Press, 1989); *The Amendments to the Constitution: A Commentary* (Baltimore, Md.: The Johns Hopkins University Press, 1995); and *Abraham Lincoln: A Constitutional Biography* (Lanham, Md.: Rowman & Littlefield, 1999).

SIGHTS AND INSIGHTS: IN GREECE WITH HOMER AND EVA

Robin Chalek Tzannes

WHEN I WAS a student at St. John's College, I wanted to get to know Eva Brann. Happily that was not difficult: among a faculty that makes itself particularly available to students, Eva is even more accessible than most. She once wrote, "Our students can ask us anything and do." Sensing this, I stopped her on campus one day and asked, "How can a student get to know her tutors better?" She replied, "Invite them to tea."

Tea in my Campbell dorm room was slightly awkward, but it broke the ice; thirty-six years later Eva and I are still friends.

After I graduated from St. John's I married George Tzannes, an artist with Greek roots. He brought me to his father's birthplace, the Ionian island of Cythera, and I brought the *Odyssey*. It was definitely the right place to read Homer, especially as I found myself at leisure—"a laid-back listener" being what Eva says the epics require.

George and I contrived to spend a good deal of our time on Cythera, and in the late 1980s Eva came to visit. To our delight she felt right at home, and became a great favorite with our boys (both of whom would become Johnnies two decades later). When her deaning days were over, Eva began visiting us regularly on Cythera, in what has become an annual idyll for us all.

I don't know how many times I would have reread the epics if it hadn't been for Eva's influence, but whenever I know she's coming, I brush up my Homer. For Eva, "Reading Homer's poems is one of the purest, most inexhaustible pleasures life has to offer." For me, that pleasure has been greatly enhanced by the lucky coincidence of having Homer and Eva together in Greece.

The general consensus at St. John's is that one can profit greatly by reading Homer in Greek, but not much is to be gained by reading him in Greece. Both the life and the language of Greece have changed considerably in 3000 years, and anyway, the real value of Homer is in the poems, not in the place. Eva expressed this view in *Open Secrets*, reflecting on the time she spent as a young archaeologist. "The Greeks came to life not in the excavations of the ancient marketplace of Athens where I worked but in the texts of a little college in Annapolis where I teach."

Still, there is a great benefit to be reaped: living on Cythera provides rich material for what Eva calls the "book-illustrating imagination." Being in this place enables me to visualize Homer's world and to illustrate the epics vividly in my imagination.

Eva, too, when she first came to Greece, formed similar, indelible, illustrative images: "the glowing red crepe of blown poppies by a fragrant footpath, an ivory temple pediment rising like a wing over far crests, spires of poplars in primordial landscapes—the real profit, deposited in the treasure house of unforgettables."

My Illustrated Homer

Homer's Ithaca sounds a lot like Cythera.

> It's a rugged land, too cramped for driving horses,
> but though it's far from broad, it's hardly poor.
> There's plenty of grain for bread, grapes for wine,
> the rains never fail and the dewfall's healthy.
> Good country for goats, good for cattle, too.

Cythera and Ithaca are Ionian neighbors, both members of the *eptanissia* or "seven islands." Cythera is beautiful but cramped, without any wide-open, flat spaces. The valleys are lush and fertile, the hillsides rugged and rocky; there's plenty of water and plenty of dew, perfect for growing wheat and olives and grapes. Most of the island is crisscrossed with dry stone walls that divide the fields and hold up the terraces, weathered, gray limestone walls probably very similar to the dry retaining wall in Odysseus' own terraced vineyard.

In springtime, Cythera is a riot of wildflowers. We read in the epics that violets and parsley grow on Calypso's island, vitex in the land of the Cyclopes, crocuses and hyacinths in heaven, asphodel in hell, and poppies in gardens on earth; all of them grow on Cythera. The ancient forests of alder and oak have vanished, but we still have the fruit trees Homer names: pear, pomegranate, apple, fig and olive. Alas, the lions, deer, and wild boar disappeared with the forests, but Homer's farm animals remain, along with snakes and cicadas, hawks and cranes. Sometimes we see bird signs: once a falcon swooping down to snatch a swallow from the air, once a buzzard flying across the valley with a snake in his talons.

Even beyond the landscape, beyond the flora and the fauna of Homer's world, I have discovered on Cythera many of the things that Homer talked about: foods, farm implements, household tools. The names are familiar, too: we have friends called Phoebus, Philoctectes and Athena, an Aunt Eurycleia, and a neighbor Odysseus. The butcher's wife is Aphrodite.

In the 1970s, Cythera, remote and hard-to-reach, had not quite entered the modern age. Eva reminds us in *Homeric Moments,* "The Homeric world is considerably different in its circumstances from ours." Among the differences, "all the appurtenances of culture are handmade." Yet I was lucky enough to find some of those handmade, pre-industrial objects still intact and still in use on Cythera.

When we first lived here, our little hamlet had no plumbing, no electricity, no telephone. We drew our water from a well, and spent our evenings by candlelight. Every family had a donkey, and I saw village boys struggling with uncooperative donkeys just as they did in Homer's day. Many families had working looms, and women still wove their blankets and rugs. Farmers still used the old stone threshing floors set on windy hilltops just as they did in ancient times.

On Cythera people gather their salt from the craggy rocks along the shore, where seawater collects in pools over the winter and then evaporates in the dry summer heat, leaving behind shallow pockets of clear, sharp crystals. This is the same unprocessed, Mediterranean seasalt that Odysseus must have eaten. I think of it when I read the instructions for his last journey:

> Carry your well-planed oar until you come
> to a race of people who know nothing of the sea,
> whose food is never seasoned with salt.

The salt that we eat on Cythera was more than a seasoning to Homer. It was an emblem of seafaring civilization, one of the things that identified the people who live near the sea, and separated them from the inland races.

Other foods have survived from Homer's day. In addition to gathering sea salt, Cytherians press their own olives for oil and stomp their own grapes for wine. And they still eat souvlaki, as Homer tells us the heroes did:

> . . . they carved the rest into small pieces, pierced them with skewers,
> roasted them thoroughly, and drew them all off.

Another Homeric food is the farmer's cheese called *mizithra*. This soft, mild cheese is still available on Cythera; in fact, Eva and I once concocted an exquisite dessert of *mizithra* with fresh strawberries. The curdling agent for *mizithra* is fig sap, obtained simply by stirring a pot of boiling milk with a fresh-cut fig branch. Homer described this in Book 5 of the *Iliad,* after the War-god Ares was speared in the gut by Diomedes. Screaming in pain and gushing ichor, Ares flew to Olympus for relief.

> Paeeon spread soothing ointment on the wound and healed it, for Ares was not made of mortal stuff. Indeed, he made the fierce War-god well in no more time than the busy fig-juice takes to thicken milk and curdle the white liquid as one stirs.

Homer chose this homely simile to show us not only how fast the god was healed, but also how the cure worked to thicken the running ichor. The image we see is, literally, Ares' blood curdling.

Throughout the epics there is mention of one more thing that survives on Cythera, and that is the color purple. To the Mycenaeans, purple was as precious as gold, and so costly that only royalty could afford it. Kings wore it:

> A fleecy cloak of purple did goodly Odysseus wear.

Palaces and royal tents were draped in it:

> Achilles led them in and made them sit on couches and rugs of purple.

Queens worked with it:

> She found Helen in her palace, at work on a great purple web.

Purple dye was made from the glandular excretions of a sea snail called the Spiny Murex. Its manufacture was a messy, laborious process that took several days. After the murex were fished from the sea, the snails and their shells were crushed, mixed with sea salt and then boiled. Snail glands being rather small, only one part of dye was obtainable from sixteen parts of the pungent brew—which explains the high cost of purple.

The Spiny Murex is plentiful in the waters around Cythera, and the island became a bustling center for the manufacture of purple dye in ancient times. Dye workshops were set up around the Cytherian city of Scandia, where huge deposits of murex shells have been uncovered by archaeologists. We still find plenty of murex snails on Scandia beach today.

Scandia grew into a thriving, cosmopolitan center and international trading post, a city important enough to be mentioned by name in the *Iliad.*

A Place in the Epics

There are few passages in the epics that mention Cythera by name. The first is about a strange helmet.

> Meriones gave Odysseus a bow, a quiver and a sword, and set a leather helmet on his head. . . . The outer rim was cunningly adorned . . . by a row of white and flashing boars' tusks. This helmet originally came from Eleon, where Autolycus stole it from Amyntor son of Ormenus by breaking into his well-built house. Autolycus gave it to Amphidamas of Cythera to take to Scandia. . . .

Odysseus was given the famous helmet the night he went on a dangerous mission into enemy territory. It must have been quite valuable if Autolycus went to the trouble of breaking and entering to get it. Autolycus then sent the helmet to Scandia, maybe in order to sell it—why else would anyone send such a valuable object to a trading post?

The strange cap changed hands again and again, but when it was needed by Odysseus it returned as a sort of family heirloom—for we know that the thief Autolycus was Odysseus' own grandfather. I like to think that this stolen helmet magically conferred the power of thievery: with it, Autolycus protected his grandson and empowered him to steal. And steal he did—big time! Odysseus and Diomedes raided the Thracian camp, slew the warriors in their sleep and rustled their matchless, magnificent horses.

The second time Cythera appears in the *Iliad* is in the story of Lycophron.

> With that, he flung a shining lance at Ajax, but missing him, struck Lycophron son of Mastor, a Cytherian squire of Ajax, who had come to live with him after killing a man in sacred Cythera.

Despite the fact that he was a murderer, Lycophron is written about and looked upon with pride by modern Cytherians, being their only native son to have fought at Troy.

In the Lycophron passage, Cythera is called "sacred" in reference to the goddess Aphrodite, who arose out of the foaming sea just off our coast. According to local legend, she came ashore on Scandia beach. Acknowledging her birthplace, Homer calls Aphrodite by the name "Cytherea" twice in the *Odyssey.*

The island itself appears only once in the *Odyssey,* and then as a mere geographical detail. Cythera faces the southernmost tip of the Peloponnesus, opposite the treacherous Cape Malea. The winds and weather at Cape Malea are famously fierce. Both Agamemnon and Menelaus, returning home separately from the Trojan War, were given rough sailing around Cape Malea, and it was from that same cape that Odysseus was swept into his fantastic odyssey. This single event delayed Odysseus' homecoming for years; for him it was a moment of supreme frustration, but for us it is the wonderful moment when the real adventure begins.

> And now, at long last,
> I might have reached my native land unscathed,
> but just as I doubled Malea's cape, a tide-rip
> and the North Wind drove me way off course
> careering past Cythera.

Just before being thrown into his incredible adventure, Odysseus' last glimpse of the known world was the sight of Cythera.

I treasure these passages, slight as they are, simply because they mention Cythera. When my boys were reading Homer as freshmen at St. John's I'd ask them: Did you get to the part about Lycophron yet? Did you read about Meriones' hat? These passages reassure us that our little island was really a part of Homer's world.

Eva commented about Homer's mention of Athens, "It must have given an Athenian a thrill to hear his city so named in the work that united Hellas. . . ." When I was a student, I found the famous Catalog of Ships pretty tedious; but after I came to Greece I read it hungrily, looking for familiar place-names. I'm certain that modern-day inhabitants of Aegina or Zakynthos are deeply gratified to hear their islands listed in the Catalog; the fact that our island doesn't appear on the list doesn't bother me: it's a thrill to know that Homer spoke the name of Cythera at all.

EVEAN MOMENTS

But knowing about all the real places and objects in Homer's world is not the key to Homer. These things are fun to find and interesting to think about. Sometimes seeing them transports us back to the world of the heroes; but not always.

One spring Eva came just as the poppies had finished blooming. We were walking up the drive when she stopped and looked down at a cluster of poppies whose petals had blown off, leaving their naked pods heavy with seed. Being with Eva, I naturally thought of the beautiful Homeric simile she had translated:

> And like a poppy he let fall his head to one side, a poppy that is in a
> garden,
> Laden with fruit and the showers of spring,
> So he bowed to one side his head made heavy with helmet.

I said something about the soldier with a helmet-heavy head, but Eva didn't bite. Instead she looked up and said brightly, "These pods are full of seeds. Let's bake with them!" Well, sometimes a poppy is just a poppy.

When *Homeric Moments* arrived I devoured it. Reading it was almost like listening to Eva talk, and it left me bubbling over with insights, questions and ideas. I couldn't wait for Eva's next visit so we could discuss it.

I was eager to tell Eva my theory about the goatherd. In her chapter "Suitors and Servants," Eva discussed the loyal swineherd Eumaeus, the faithful cowherd Philoetius, and the evil goatherd Melanthius. As a passing comment, Eva wondered "why swineherds and cowherds should be more given to loyalty than goatherds." I had a hunch.

On Cythera cows are kept in stables right in the village. The cowherd lives with his family in town, and spends his evenings at the cafenio, socializing with his neighbors. I think he can live and work in town because cows smell all right, and so do cowherds.

Pigs, however, get pretty stinky. The law on Cythera—an ancient law, no doubt—requires that pigs be kept outside the village, far from anyone's house. A swineherd like Eumaeus, with hundreds of smelly pigs, would have to live way out of town and couldn't be as urban as the cowboy. But he would still have a home with a table and a hearth, the symbols of comfort and civility that Odysseus, visiting Eumaeus in disguise, refers to when he swears "by this table of hospitality" and "by Odysseus' hearth."

Now, goats are both smelly and uncivilized. Here on Cythera they climb the rocky hillsides, eating scrubby bushes, watched over by rough and also smelly goatherds. These goatherds spend long stretches of time camped out beside their pickup trucks, far from table and hearth. In Homer's day, too, goatherds lived on the wild side.

> Here in Ithaca, goatflocks, eleven in all, scatter
> to graze the island, out at the wild end,
> and trusty goatherds watch their every move.

I guessed it was this life on the edge of civilization that made Odysseus' goatherd so crude and uncivil, and in the end, so disloyal. Eva found it plausible.

Knowing the things that Homer wrote about might afford some insight, but not knowing them doesn't prevent us from understanding the poems. In Eva's words, "Let it be granted that the Homeric world is full of conditions and objects very different from those of our world. It would follow that Homer's people think about different things, not that they think differently." Living in Greece has helped me understand some of the things Homer's people think *about*; but knowing Eva has helped me understand *how* they think. And you don't have to be royal, or ancient, or even Greek to understand them. Eva assures us, "The poet made a world that we are authorized to enter and enabled to inhabit by the mere title of our humanity. . . . If you're human, Homer is home territory."

Eva and I like to talk about people. We talk about Helen and Penelope, Telemachus and Hector, almost as though we knew them. But what's more gratifying is to recognize Homeric traits in the people we really do know. No matter how much the world has changed, people haven't, and we can find Homeric characters all around us.

George and I live in a 300-year-old stone farmhouse, purchased as a ruin, that George restored and rebuilt on his own. The first time Eva saw the finished house, she took a tour with George, asking questions about how he had planned this and crafted that, praising his skill in designing and inventing. Then she said to me, "You know, he's like Odysseus."

Odysseus was famous for making things. He invented an ingenious eyeball-poker in the cave of the Cyclops, and built a sturdy raft to leave Calypso's island. Like George, he could build houses.

> I built my room round this with strong walls of stone and a roof to
>   cover them,
> and I made the doors strong and well-fitting.

When Eva compared the two men, I saw that they do share a certain characteristic, one that goes far beyond being handy and that has nothing to do with their both being Greek. Rather, it's a way of taking the world in hand, of ordering and managing things, of fashioning material to suit their needs. Seeing this helped me understand both my husband and Odysseus a little better.

In *Homeric Moments* Eva talked about the way Athena transformed Odysseus' appearance, making him look younger for his meeting with

Nausicaa, taller and stronger for his reunion with Penelope. Transformations can occur, she said, even without divine intervention. "Nothing happens to him that does not happen to us all. We too glow and crumble and have our alternating moments. . . . Even in our world these transformations are wonderful."

When I read the chapter about transformations, I remembered something that had happened the year before. Eva, George and I were visiting a favorite site, the ruined city of Paliochora. The approach was narrow and steep, and we had to pick our way carefully among loose stones. At a particularly rough spot, George reached back and gave Eva his hand; just at that moment, I looked up. The thought actually crossed my mind that George had never looked better: the evening sun cast bronze on his hair and complexion; he seemed somehow stronger, more solid and capable. But I couldn't stand there gazing. They were moving ahead and I had to watch my footing. So I looked down again, keeping my eye on the backs of Eva's feet in their neat, blue sneakers as I followed her footsteps along the path.

The people in our village admire Eva's energy, knowing that she sets out early every morning on a long walk across the valley. One neighbor, perhaps a little envious, asked me suspiciously, "Was she ever married?" When I said no, she gave a derisive little snort. "Well, that explains it. No achos!" I had to laugh. The word achos is used casually in Modern Greek to mean "stress." More literally, it translates as angst, anguish, ache. In Homeric Moments, Eva said that achos is the grief-sound we hear in the name "Achilles." I realized how apt my neighbor's observation was: Eva has no achos. In fact, no one I know is less angst-ridden, less dwelling on pain and anguish, less given to fury and resentment—in short, less like Achilles— than Eva.

When I can manage it, I accompany her on her walks. And as we walk, we talk. One time we were discussing a novel she'd given me, set in 1920s Peking. As we wound our way through the valley, I paused to look around: olive orchards to the right, vineyards to the left, and in the distance the wine-dark sea. The setting couldn't have been more Greek. Yet there was nothing strange about two American women walking in Greece and talking about China. If there's one thing I learned at St. John's, it's that you can read any book anywhere. We're perfectly comfortable talking about Canterbury Tales in Santa Fe, War and Peace in Annapolis, or Don Quixote in New York. The place really doesn't matter. Ah, but what an incomparable pleasure it is to be visited by Eva, here in Homer's own country.

NOTES

Note: Line numbers for *The Iliad* and *The Odyssey* correspond to the Samuel Butler translation (Medford, Mass.: Tufts University Perseus Digital Library Project, 2005); www.perseus.tufts.edu

When I Was a Student: 1969–1973

"Our students can ask . . .": Eva Brann, "In Memoriam Alice E. Kober," 2005

"laid-back listener": Eva Brann, *Homeric Moments: Clues to Delight in Reading* The Odyssey *and* The Iliad (Philadelphia: Paul Dry Books, 2002), 18.

annual idyll: Eva Brann, dedication to *Open Secrets/Inward Prospects: Reflections on World and Soul* (Philadelphia: Paul Dry Books, 2002).

"Reading Homer's poems . . .": Brann, *Homeric Moments,* 3.

"The Greeks came to life . . .": Brann, *Open Secrets/Inward Prospects,* 199.

"book-illustrating imagination": Brann, *Open Secrets/Inward Prospects,* 76.

". . . the glowing red crepe . . .": Brann, *Open Secrets/Inward Prospects,* 201.

My Illustrated Homer

"It's a rugged . . .": *Odyssey* XIII.242; Robert Fagles trans. (New York: Penguin Books, 1996), 294.

dry retaining wall: *Odyssey* XXIV.225.

violets and parsley: *Odyssey* V.72.

vitex: *Odyssey* IX.427.

crocuses and hyacinths: *Iliad* XIV.349.

asphodel: *Odyssey* XI.539.

poppies: *Iliad* VIII.306.

alder: *Odyssey* V.64.

oak: *Odyssey* XIV.425.

pear, pomegranate, apple, fig, olive: *Odyssey* VII.115.

lion: *Odyssey* XVII.129.

deer and wild boar: *Odyssey* VI.105.

farm animals—sheep and cattle: *Odyssey* XV.386; swine: *Odyssey* XIV.410.

snakes: *Iliad* XII.203.

cicadas: *Iliad* III.155.

hawks: *Odyssey* XV.525.

cranes: *Iliad* II.460.

bird signs: *Odyssey* XV.533.

names—Phoebus: *Odyssey* III.279; Philoctectes: *Odyssey* VIII.219; Eurycleia: *Odyssey* XVII.33; I won't even bother footnoting the names Athena, Odysseus and Aphrodite.

"The Homeric world . . .": Brann, *Homeric Moments,* 24.

uncooperative donkeys: *Iliad* XI.553.

looms: *Iliad* III.125.

threshing floors: *Iliad* V.495.

"Carry your well-planed oar . . .": *Odyssey* XI.120, Fagles trans., 253.

". . . they carved the rest": *Iliad* I.465, E.V. Rieu trans. (New York: Penguin Classics, 1950), 35.

"Paeeon spread . . .": *Iliad* V.899, Rieu trans., 116.

as precious as gold: Richard M. Podhajny, *History, Shellfish, Royalty, and the Color Purple* (Greenwood Village, Colo.: Primedia Business, 2002)

"A fleecy cloak . . .": *Odyssey* XIX.225, Butler trans.

"Achilles led them . . .": *Iliad* IX.199, Butler trans.

"She found Helen . . .": *Iliad* III.125, Rieu trans., 67.

a laborious process: G.L. Huxley and J.N. Coldstream, *Kythera: Excavations and Studies Conducted by the University of Pennsylvania Museum and The British School at Athens* (Park Ridge, NJ: Noyes Press, 1973), 37.

Dye workshops: Peter D. Vanges, *Kythera: A History of the Island of Kythera and its People* (Sydney: Kytherian Brotherhood of Australia; 1993), 29.

archaeologists: Huxley, *Kythera,* 36.

A Place in the Epics

"Meriones gave Odysseus a bow . . .": *Iliad* X.256, Rieu trans., 187.

Autolycus: *Odyssey* XIX.395.

"With that, he flung . . .": *Iliad* XV.430, Rieu trans., 283.

written about: Vanges, *Kythera,* 35, and Lydia Bell, "Of Myths and Migration," *Athens News* (September 26, 2003), A24.

Cytherea: *Odyssey* VIII.289; *Odyssey* XVIII.19.

Agamemnon: *Odyssey* IV.515.

Menelaus: *Odyssey* III.286.

"And now, at long last . . .": *Odyssey* IX.79, Fagles trans., 214.

"It must have given . . .": Brann, *Homeric Moments,* 224.

Catalog of Ships: *Iliad* II.485–875.

Aegina: *Iliad* II.562.

Zakynthos: *Iliad* II.634.

Evean Moments

"And like a poppy . . .": *Iliad* VIII.306, Brann trans., *Homeric Moments,* 15.

". . . why swineherds and cowherds . . .": Brann, *Homeric Moments,* 268.

"by this table . . .": *Odyssey* XIV.159, Fagles trans., 306.

"Here in Ithaca, goatflocks . . .": *Odyssey* XIV.103, Fagles trans., 304.

"Let it be granted . . .": Brann, *Homeric Moments,* 27.

"The poet made a world . . .": Brann, *Homeric Moments,* 20.

eyeball-poker: *Odyssey* IX.320.

a raft: *Odyssey* V.244.

"I built my room . . .": *Odyssey* XXIII.192, Butler trans.

younger: *Odyssey* VI.238.

taller and stronger: *Odyssey* XXIII.153.

"Nothing happens to him . . .": Brann, *Homeric Moments,* 50.

achos: Brann, *Homeric Moments,* 143.

a novel: Ann Bridge, *Peking Picnic* (London: Akadine Press, 2000).

Not Is Not

Stewart Umphrey

EVA BRANN'S TRILOGY leads us away from the periphery of human inwardness (which she identifies with sense perception), first to the space of visual imagination, then to time as we experience it, and finally to discursive thought, the restless heart of "the human center."[1] Things imagined are absent as well as present. The now implicates the not yet and the no longer. Hence imagination and inner time both involve negation.[2] The same is true of the thinking in which naysaying originates.[3] Brann's trilogy thus brings to light the entwined ways in which negation pervades our inwardness.

Naysaying itself occurs in many ways, with notable differences in illocutionary force and in object or point. Brann collects them under six headings. Is there something in common to all of them, or should we say instead that they exhibit a family resemblance? The latter, I think. But can we pick out the family head—as Aristotle, while considering the various ways in which being is declared in speech, found them all to be ordered *pros hen*? Brann claims that naysaying gains its "proper object" in nonbeing, and that "Thinking the Unsayable: Philosophic *Nonbeing*" is the central chapter in her book on the subject.[4] Does she then take *thinking* to be principally philosophical, and philosophical thought to be principally about nonbeing together with being? I'm not sure. In any case, nonbeing is somehow the focus of her discourse on naysaying. But how is that possible? Parmenides famously and plausibly denied that nonbeing could be thought or said, and the goddess of his poem prohibits any attempt to do so. Of course, whatever our age, we don't like people telling us what to do; every prohibition from on high is naturally a temptation to go for it. No wonder subsequent philosophers tried to think nonbeing and declare it in speech. In fact, Parmenides quite unintentionally launched "the thought of nonbeing" in our philosophical tradition. Brann recounts the conception, birth, and recent eclipse of this great thought. I wonder, though, whether it was conceived in error. Might it not be a gigantic wind-egg to which we are but the latest heirs? Should thinkers have resisted more firmly the temptation that comes with Parmenides' prohibition? To find out, we must turn back once more to his poem, to review yet again the evidence it presents. I now do so.

1. The Parmenidean Critique and Its Impact

In the poem as we have it, an anonymous young man recounts a fantastic journey at the end of which he received not a vision but a speech. This speech, delivered without interruption by an anonymous goddess, has two main parts. The first, called "Truth" by later commentators, highlights the only acceptable way of inquiry for thinking. It is about being or truth, described as ungenerable, imperishable, indivisible, in need of nothing to be complete. The way of nonbeing is ruled entirely out of bounds, and so too the way of mortals, an aimless indecisive tribe for whom being and nonbeing are the same and not the same. The other part of her speech, called "Doxa," presents a phony little physics designed to keep the young man from being outstripped by mortals while he lives among them.

Before describing being in some detail, the goddess tells him to judge by *logos* her much-contending *elenchos* (B7.5).[5] That philosophers of the time regarded her speech as a hard-hitting critique is clear from the imprint it left in their writings. Its impact can be sketched as follows:

(1) Thanks to Parmenides' poem, nonbeing established itself in philosophical thought as being's "unwanted shadow," "its unwelcome but unshakable doppelgänger."[6] According to Aristotle, nonbeing is but one of the many ways in which being is declared in speech; and it is something in the world, either as privation or as unactualized potentiality. According to Plato's *Sophist,* nonbeing is but one of several greatest genera; his Eleatic stranger calls it "the Other," and says that it *is* by sharing in Being, another coordinate genus. From this it follows that there can be the non-beautiful as well as the beautiful, the spurious as well as the genuine. Sophistry therefore is possible, and so too dialectic, for as Brann observes, it is in virtue of the Other that things are distinct from one another and yet conceptually interrelated.[7] Philosophy like sophistry relies on the otherness of things; they both have the same basis in reality. No wonder we can hardly tell them apart.

(2) Thanks also to Parmenides, philosophy came to be regarded as ontology above all. According to Aristotle, philosophy is primarily the science of beings as beings and of that being to which all other beings are ordered. Hence, in his view, "metaphysics" is principally ousiology, or rather theology understood as knowledge of that *ousia* identified first as the immobile mover, then as thinking of thinking itself, and finally as the highest good. This being, rightly called "god," is ungenerable, imperishable, indivisible, and in need of nothing beyond itself to be complete. According to Plato, it's not clear that philosophy is about being above all; it may instead be about

the Good. In any case, his dialogues distinguish strictly between being and becoming, and tend to identify the former with a hyper-pantheon of Forms or Ideas, each of them ungenerable, imperishable, etc. And Plato even more than Aristotle took his bearings by *logos* in contradistinction to sense perception. The Parmenidean critique thus plainly had an effect on the thinking of both.[8]

(3) It also compelled natural philosophers to tighten up their conceptions of nature (*phusis*). Neo-Ionian philosophers agreed that there could be no absolute nascence or evanescence; what human beings call "becoming" and "perishing" are nothing more than the mixing and unmixing or combining and separating of things that have always existed and will always exist. Though meaning different things by the term, Empedocles and the early atomists agreed that everything occurs in accordance with necessity (*anankê*). And it may have been in response to the Eleatics that Anaxagoras not only separated mind from matter ("the all-together"), but also insisted that matter was divisible without limit and that stuff of any kind is in stuff of every other kind.[9] The monism of the earlier Ionians—Thales, Anaximenes, Heraclitus, and perhaps Anaximander—now seemed quite unable to explain the *genesis* and *phusis* of natural things.

I submit, however, that the influence just now described was due more to the rhetorical power of Parmenides' poem than to the *logos* it presents. For consider:

(1′) The goddess makes no distinction between nonbeing (*mê eon*) and nothing (*mêden*). To think or say nonbeing is to think or say nothing at all —to be logically silent, paralyzed in thought. The negative route, as she describes it, more nearly resembles an abrupt abyss than a way of inquiry. It is, she says, unintelligible and anonymous. From it there are no tidings.[10] Democritus agreed that nonbeing is to be distinguished strictly from being, but having identified nonbeing with the void in which particles combine and separate, he could plausibly maintain that nothing (*mêden*) *is* no less than thing (*den*).[11] And watch how Plato moves within the dialogue *Sophist*. His anonymous stranger is helping young Theaetetus track down the sophist when suddenly, it seems, their prey has taken refuge in nonbeing. This puts the zetetic duo into a grave impasse, for as the stranger makes clear, absolute nonbeing (*to mêdamôs on*) cannot be an object of speech or thought.[12] How then are they to go on? The stranger, being far and away the more experienced, recommends that they "push" their way somehow through being and nonbeing. Theaetetus agrees, naturally, and within minutes nonbeing has come to light as the Other, an existing genus whose *phusis* is surely if subtly intelligible.[13] But then "nonbeing" and "nothing" are to be strictly distinguished, since one has become a genuine name while the other remains no name at all. We suddenly realize that Plato's Eleatic stranger never identifies the Other with absolute nonbeing. He seems in fact to have forgotten what he said just fifteen pages earlier. Or to put it more vividly, he appears to have killed his father. What looks like parricide, however, is really a turning away from the Parmenidean command to decide between *is* and *is not*, and back toward a more human way of thinking about human affairs. This backward turning began with a push, and the push (he later admits) involved compulsion.[14] Plato's stranger from Elea no longer judges by *logos* alone. There are unsettling consequences. One is that being becomes a genus coordinate with nonbeing. Another is that "vertical" otherness has been assimilated to "horizontal" otherness: the distinction between spurious and genuine is now taken to be on a par with the distinction between non-beautiful and beautiful. Is this, according to Plato, the sort of thing that inevitably happens when you domesticate nonbeing in order to capture wily humans in speech?[15]

(2′) Parmenides' goddess takes being to be one, unique, indivisible, in no way generable, perishable, mobile or incomplete. Aristotle maintains that the being (*ousia*) of a natural entity is primarily its form, essence, or actuality. So conceived, natural being is not divisible (except in speech), not mobile (except incidentally), and not the sort of thing that could be in a process of becoming or perishing.[16] He also maintains that the highest being (god) is absolutely ungenerable and imperishable, in no sense mobile or incomplete. Yet thinking, he claims, is a way of being alive; god is just thinking of thinking itself; hence even the highest being is living (*zôon*).[17] According to Parmenides' goddess, being could not be alive: so much for philosophical theology.[18] Nor does she allow for different ways of being, whatever mortal discourse may suggest. Nor, I think, would she admit a plurality of beings.[19] Platonic Forms are not the sort of thing that could be mobile or alive, nor are they causal in any ordinary sense, but surely there are many of them (just how many remains disquietingly unclear). Some of them also appear dimly as objects of human concern—namely the just, the beautiful, and the good—about which we dispute vehemently and indecisively. Our ignorance of things so important to us could hardly be more obvious, and yet, for Plato's Socrates, their perplexing appearances are signs directing us away toward what *is*. Parmenides' goddess would certainly have disagreed. In her view, the Socratic turn guarantees endless muddle. Do we disagree?

(3') Nor does the goddess admit any such thing as nature; she seems rather to preclude it, to deny its very possibility. It would be more accurate, however, to say that she finds a place for *phusis* only within the framework of Doxa, where seemings have their home.[20] Human beings seek to understand all such things in terms of Light and Night, she says, but in positing this duality they have already made an error.[21] The error is likely because we mortals are profoundly "double-headed." Absent any guidance from without, we're simply going to go on the assumption that everything is full of these two "shapes" as a pair. Natural philosophers are paradigmatic mortals, and the expressly deceptive physics presented in Parmenides' poem is a model of what they say and think. Consequently, as Odysseus used the Moly plant whose nature was revealed to him by Hermes, so may we use this model as a diagnostic tool to prevent our own bewitchment. Take for instance Heraclitus, who said that this cosmos is everliving fire, and that everything happens in accordance with the *logos*. We now see what he's doing: he's construing everything in terms of Night-Light! Likewise Empedocles, for whom everything is formed out of four elementary masses or "roots," all mixing and unmixing necessarily in accordance with a great, unexplicated oath. Likewise Philolaus, for whom nature is out of the Unlimited fitted together with the Limited; and Aristotle, for whom every natural entity is composed somehow out of matter and form; and Newton, for whom natural phenomena are to be understood in terms of inertial matter and deterministic force laws.[22] Were the history of natural "science" a description of one man's intellectual career, we would regard it as the odyssey of a brilliant wanderer who seems destined never to get home. In his wanderings we would find moreover the same basic error, the same doubletalk again and again in ever-new reiterations. The nature of nature always involves two principles, one rather light-like (a principle of intelligibility), the other rather night-like (a principle of obscurity), whose togetherness in natural things is at once necessary and mysterious. The task for natural philosophers appears twofold. On the one hand, they need to clarify the murkier principle without explaining it away. On the other hand, they need to understand just how these principles can be both two and one.[23] The task is urgent, immense, and fundamentally misconceived. Those who take it up remain wedded to the way of mortals. Thus natural philosophers are like people so fond of their own faults that their repeated efforts to improve themselves are doomed from the start. We're all like that, insofar as we think mortal thoughts.

Being human we naturally construe being itself in terms of Light, non-being in terms of Night. Should we then find that being and nonbeing are for us the same and not the same, and that our vagrancy in inquiry has its source here, we might decide to separate being from nonbeing and reduce Night to nothing, so that Light alone *is*. But this too would be a mistake, since Light is merely a contrived echo of being. So being-like is it in fact that the goddess describes them in very similar terms; that's why we're so easily deceived by it. To remain undeceived, we must hold on to the thought that Light resides wholly within Doxa, a place rich in seemings, teeming with life, where naturally we feel at home. It is impossible to follow the *logos* and remain human in our outlook. Physicists have "decided" to remain human. So too have most ontologists. Of course they try to have it both ways by domesticating being and nonbeing so as to make them coordinate principles to which Doxa is not entirely closed. Thus humanized, as it were, these principles have profound explanatory power in one's investigation of the world. They seem indispensable as well whenever one tries to elucidate the nature of imagination, time, and thought. How otherwise could one say anything illuminating about our inwardness? Do we not find utterly incredible the claim that all such inquiries are wrongheaded in principle? Yet we also feel the strength of the Parmenidean critique. Indeed, insofar as we follow the *logos* and not *doxa*-laden experience, Parmenides appears not only to have been right about being and nonbeing, but also remarkably prescient about the way in which his poem would be received then and now.

2. Initial Objections Rejected

I have so far taken the side of Parmenides in order to make clear that the other side is radically questionable. Our entire philosophical tradition carries a notable burden of proof. That this burden has been little noticed shows how readily philosophers have shied away from dealing straightforwardly with fundamentals. And while it's interesting that Parmenides appears to be the odd man out, it's also irrelevant insofar as we are seeking the truth and not counting votes. Better to face the fact that he's offered a critique of natural philosophy (and by implication almost every other philosophy) that is plausible at least, and devastating if correct.

One need hardly add that Parmenides, too, has a burden of proof. We must examine his side as well. Some commentators have already done so and concluded that the speech of the goddess is unacceptable on philosophically acceptable grounds. Let us examine their counter-critiques in the following order.

First Objection. Parmenides identifies truth with being, which he takes to be ungenerable, indivisible, in need of nothing, etc. An ontology so restrictive cannot account for falsehood or fakery. Nor can it elucidate what Brann in her trilogy calls "the human center." Nor indeed can it explain the possibility of philosophical inquiry. If Parmenides is right about being, he cannot say how it is that he might ever have come to be right about being. Any account of his "journey" would in truth be sheer poetry, a tall tale, as his in fact is.[24]

Rejoinder. Parmenides would not disagree. He would observe, however, that this argument has a suppressed premise and a missing conclusion. The missing conclusion is that his ontology is therefore unacceptable. The suppressed premise is that an ontology is acceptable only if it allows for an explanation or elucidation of such things. This premise Parmenides would reject. For his ontology implies that sophistry, philosophy, and the human center all belong to Doxa, and about such things there can be no "true trust." Therefore, one must either keep silent about them or wander vaguely in speech and thought. Elucidations and explanations, whether causal or not, are in principle no less fantastic that the journeys recounted in his poem, and to think otherwise shows unwitting fidelity to the way of mortals.[25] That's Parmenides' position. It rests on his having decided between *is* and *is not*. The objection now before us rests on an implicit refusal to make that decision. The refusal may be justifiable, but one cannot assume that it is without begging the question against Parmenides. The objection does assume as much. Therefore it's no refutation at all.

Second Objection. The poem refutes itself. For if the ontology it presents were true, no goddess or mortal could have uttered it or written it down. But it was written down. Fragments of it still exist. Therefore, the ontology it presents is too restrictive to be tenable.[26]

Rejoinder. As an argument, this counter-critique seems complete. Before judging its strength, however, we must distinguish between logical and pragmatic self-refutation. A statement refutes itself logically just in case it contains a logical contradiction. The statement that all statements are untrue is arguably an example. Another is this. **A**: statement **B** is true. **B**: statement **A** is not true. Taken in conjunction with **B**, **A** is true if and only if it is not true. Therefore, the conjunction of both logically refutes itself. A statement refutes itself pragmatically, on the other hand, when it entails that the statement itself could not have been made. The same holds for arguments. Zeno's motion "paradoxes" are good examples. For if any of these arguments is sound, he could not have made it since the making of an argument or statement requires some motion, if only "in the head." But notice: Once made logically valid,[27] Zeno's argument refutes itself *only* pragmatically. And such arguments or statements are not really *self*-refuting, since the incoherence lies not within the *logos* itself, but only in its relation to pragmatic conditions under which alone it could have been made or expressed.

The objection before us finds Parmenides' ontology to be pragmatically and not logically self-refuting. Parmenides might well agree that "Truth" rules out of bounds the very existence of the poem in which "Truth" occurs, but he would deny that his ontology is therefore untenable. For seemings (*dokounta*) are not just nothing. Instead, says the goddess, they needs must *dokimôs* be.[28] The word *dokimôs* usually means "genuinely" or "acceptably." Here, though, I take it in context to mean "seemingly." Seemings needs must *seemingly* be.[29] For mere mortals, who tend to confuse what seemingly is with what really (*ontôs*) is, the word *dokimôs* usually means "acceptably." But for the goddess, who never confuses them, it cannot mean simply that; there is no necessity that she accept *any* seemings as *being*. Now Parmenides' poem is among the things that seemingly are. He seems to have written it. Parts of it seem to have survived the ravages of time. And, as a matter of fact, it does seem that some motion must have occurred when Zeno proved that motion is impossible. From these facts alone, however, one cannot infer that motion or generation is really possible, or that these fragments of verse really *are*. Parmenides may then deny that his ontology refutes itself pragmatically, and he would deny it. The objection before us says the opposite, because it accepts the pragmatic turn in philosophy. But it fails to show that the facts or *pragmata* to which it appeals are beings (*onta*) and not mere seemings. Therefore it too begs the question.

From our examination so far I draw the following lesson. Being human, we are only too ready to refute Parmenides by presupposing that his ontology is incorrect. It's got to be wrong, in our view, because we simply assume that most if not all *pragmata* are real. Human agents, their practices and productions, the concrete situations in which they live and die: that's reality! So when Parmenides consigns all such things to Doxa, we balk and set out to prove he's wrong by appealing to the existence of the poem before us, the actuality of a motion whose very possibility has been denied, or the like. In doing so, moreover, we think we're following the *logos*. That's how foolish we are. To appreciate how radical the Parmenidean critique is, we might do well to begin by agreeing with Montgomery Furth and others when they say that anyone who takes Parmenides seriously is insane.[30] To be insane is have an outlook so different from our own that it makes one unfit for the business of the world. Parmenides, then, seems quite insane. That's a good start. Of course it won't do as a refutation, since objections *ad hominem* are not arguments at all, and to suppose otherwise is to be logically deaf and dumb.

Third Objection. Early in her speech, the goddess discerns two ways of inquiry: "how [it] is and how it's not possible that [it] not be," and "how [it] is not and how it's necessary that [it] not be."[31] The first, positive way turns out to be about truth or being. The second, negative way turns out to be unsayable and unthinkable. In her subsequent discourse about being, however, the goddess describes what *is* in terms of what is *not:* it is not generable or perishable, not divisible, not in need of anything, etc. So, having as it were banished nonbeing by reducing "it" to nothing, she proceeds to describe being in terms of nonbeing. Parmenides, it seems, is yet another mortal trying to have it both ways. At any rate, his ontology both rejects and relies on the negative way. It both rules out any appeal to nonbeing and requires some appeal to nonbeing. Such incoherence makes it untenable.[32]

Rejoinder. Parmenides' ontology is pervasively negative. How could it be otherwise, given the decisive role of negation in discursive thought? Yet superficially at least, it could have been otherwise earlier in the poem, when the goddess first articulated her preferred way of inquiry. For instead of saying, "how [it] is and how it's not possible that [it] not be," she might rather have said, "how [it] is and how it's necessary that [it] be." Why does she put the "positive" way negatively? Good question! Yet, whatever the answer, Parmenides would surely deny that recourse to negation entails recourse to nonbeing. And he would be right to do so. For consider the several ways of naysaying exemplified in his discourse about being. First, there are many instances of the predicate form "non-F"—"ungenerable," "imperishable," "immobile," etc.[33] Second, there are a few instances of the propositional form "Not-*p*"—among them, "Nor is it divisible."[34] Third, there is at least

one modal form—namely, "It's not right that being be incomplete."[35] These
are the principal ways of naysaying in Parmenides' ontology. They are conspicuous, indispensable, and obviously in need of interpretation. For now,
though, it suffices to note that none of them involves any recourse to non-
being. How so? It's true that we could not begin to understand what Parmenides is saying here if we had no acquaintance at all with things that
come to be and perish, that are mobile, divisible, or incomplete. All such
things belong to Doxa, the realm pervaded by seemings.[36] Therefore, in
saying that it is ungenerable, denying that it is divisible, and affirming that
it could not be incomplete, Parmenides is describing being in terms of non-
seemings. But again, seemings are not just nothing. Nor in fact does the
goddess ever say or imply that things becoming and perishing are non-
beings (*mê eonta*). To describe being in terms of non-seemings is not necessarily to describe it in terms of non-nonbeings.[37] So, while Parmenides'
ontology does require the negation of seemings that must "acceptably" be,
it involves no recourse to nonbeing, no tacit commitment to the unthinkable "negative" way. The objection before us says otherwise. Therefore it too
should be set aside.

It's not easy to refute Parmenides by means of *logos*. To try, we must
step onto his own turf, as it were, where he holds a commanding position.
We've gone three rounds with him and lost. His ontology may after all be
correct, or incorrect, we don't know. We're up in the air—which is progress
of a sort, if being undecided in this way is indeed better than being of two
minds on the way of mortals. We'll go on being undecided, however, unless
we get a better grip on what exactly the goddess is doing in her discourse
about being. Let us now try.

3. On the Way About Being

She begins her "trustworthy" account of the *way* how [it] is by saying:
"On it there are very many signs, how being is ungenerable, imperishable,
[a] whole unique and untrembling . . . neither was it once nor will it be,
since it is now altogether one, cohesive."[38] She then proceeds to a demonstration, in the course of which she mentions still more signs, deploys some
rather picturesque metaphors or analogies, and makes a couple of tantaliz-
ing remarks about thinking. I'll begin by trying to interpret three facts about
these signs: (1) They are on the way, (2) there are indefinitely many of them,

and (3) most if not all are negative. I'll then try to explicate (4) the distinction she seems to make between discursive and noetic thinking, that is to say, between rational discourse (*legein*) and insight (*noein*). We should then be in a better position to understand and assess her argument.

(1) According to Aristotle, *being pale* is an attribute of some material beings. Every such being has indefinitely many attributes, which fall naturally into distinct categories. According to Parmenides, *being ungenerable* is not an attribute of being. Being has no attributes. Yet "being ungenerable" is predicable of being, otherwise it would not be an acceptable sign. Adopting the modern view that every predicate represents a property or relation, we may divide all properties into two classes: those that are real and those that are not. Those that are not I call "transcendental." Every sign on the way about being is a transcendental property. Or perhaps we should say that they all figure in transcendental facts about being, which together mark out the only acceptable way and distinguish it from every other way.

Transcendental properties or facts are very strange objects. On the one hand, they are not real. Indeed, to reify or entify them would be to involve ourselves in those Light Night fantasies from which we have tried so hard to free ourselves. On the other hand, they are not unreal. Indeed, to regard them as non-entities would put us on the shortcut to unintelligibility that we are trying so hard to avoid. Should we then assign them to Doxa? The goddess has just said that *there are* (*easi*) many such signs. That she would use the verb "be" locatively in this context is remarkable. It puts one in mind of her prior acknowledgement that seemings must "acceptably" be. So perhaps we may say that there is about being a nimbus-like framework of seemings, a sort of atmosphere or corolla in which being is transcendentally situated.

These transcendental signs demarcate a way that locks one's thinking onto being. They are *uniquely* descriptive; they circumscribe being.[39] So if we accept the goddess's claim that being is like the bulk of a well-rounded ball,[40] we can also say (following Aristotle) that the place of being is the innermost boundary of the transcendental situation about it. And if, moreover, we take the necessity that "binds" being to be represented by its spherical surface,[41] it would seem to follow that the necessity proper to being and the necessity proper to discourse about it are both to be located at the interface between being and its transcendental situation. Are they not then one and the same necessity viewed in two different ways? But I'm afraid we're getting carried away by the picturesque analogies we have assembled. There is no evidence that Parmenides would have identified logical necessity with ontic necessity. Nor, however, do they appear to differ in number. The distinction between them is itself transcendental. I call it "the ontological difference." It belongs with the distinction, already drawn, between being and the semantic field of signs (*sēmata*) about it, as does the traditional distinction between the truth and evidence or criterion of truth.

Parmenides' ontology may have been the first openly transcendental philosophy.[42] Certainly it was not the last.[43] Indeed, every ontology must be transcendental. For it must be an *account,* not merely the sentence "Being!" And an account *of* being has to be in terms of something *beyond* or *about* being. It's no great surprise, then, that soon after the publication of Parmenides' poem there appeared a robust strain of skepticism which sought to preclude all cognitive access to truth by driving a wedge between the two sides of the onto-logical difference, thus splitting apart the epistemological from the metaphysical. Radical skepticism is not the opposite of transcendental philosophy, but its ineluctable shadow.

It was Kant who first divided all ontologists (metaphysicians) into those who are robust realists and those who are not. Among those who are not are some he called "transcendental idealists."[44] I prefer to call them "irrealists." Transcendental realists and irrealists agree that, apart from its transcendental situation, the discursive mind would be flying blind in its effort to know being or reality. But they have very different conceptions of the ontological difference, for the realists deny that being itself depends on its transcendental situation, whereas the irrealists affirm it. All ontologists before Kant were transcendental realists. Following Kant, there have been transcendental irrealists as well. The debate between these two branches of ontology is ongoing. It is our "gigantomachy."[45]

(2) There are, the goddess says, many signs on the way about being. But when we try to count them, we find that we cannot. Our preliminary list would certainly include *whole, untrembling, one,* and *cohesive.*[46] But then we come upon *not divisible, immobile, not incomplete, not needy,* and *complete.*[47] *Not divisible* and *cohesive* may be two names for one sign. But what about *one:* is it identical in number with any of them? Are all of them identical with it? Commentators disagree in their tallies. There appears to be no textual basis for settling the matter.

The same is true of the ways themselves. We quickly single out the way about being, the way "about nonbeing," and the way of mortals who know nothing.[48] So far, then, we count "one, two, three." Should we not add as a fourth the way on which the young man was led to the goddess?[49] And what about the way back: is it the same or not the same? But is the way of mortals really distinct from the first two ways taken together? But is the second way really a way at all if no one could take even the first step along it without falling into unintelligibility? We're lost. Better, it seems, to stop counting and admit that, while our situation is certainly many-wayed, there is no fact of the matter enabling us to tell how many there are.

The same is true of the deities with which Parmenides populates our world. Those mentioned are mostly female and non-Olympian. About each we can say very little, since the poets have given us so little to go on. Yet plainly there are many of them: polytheism is fitting. Once again, however, we find ourselves unable to assign a number.[50]

One might take this to be a sign of indifference on Parmenides' part. After all, why should he care how many deities there are, or how many ways, or how many signs? The question is a reasonable one. Yet, as we have seen, Parmenides was very interested in the situation that makes it both possible and difficult to apprehend being and give an account of it: ontology, though properly monistic in his view, must nonetheless admit a transcendental domain. Furthermore, he seems deliberately to have presented this situation as being full of indefinitely many indefinite pluralities: he took the transcendental domain to be vaguely pluralistic. Were it not pluralistic at all, ontology would be impossible. Were it not vague as well, why would physics still be impossible?

Parmenides' ontology is explicitly transcendental, and the situation in which alone we can discourse about being he took to be richly indeterminate. He chose moreover to present all this in a poem full of striking images and metaphors. Why this choice of medium for his message? Parmenides, I suggest, made a distinction similar to Wittgenstein's between saying (telling) and showing.[51] Roughly: being can be declared in a *logos,* whereas the transcendental situation of being can only be "shown" poetically in a *muthos.* Ontology is therefore implicitly if not explicitly mythological.

As followers of the *logos,* we are receptive to the claim that what can be shown cannot be said, but we balk at the further claim that what can be said must also be shown. There is in Parmenides' poem a passage that invites us to test this very issue. Upon saying that being is ungenerable, the goddess gives a two-fold reason. The first part goes as follows: "If being were generated, from what did it grow? Not from nonbeing. And what need would have urged it to grow later or sooner, starting from nothing? It must then be altogether or not at all. [The latter is impossible. Therefore . . .]"[52] The other part follows immediately: ". . . since Justice did not, by releasing her bonds, let being become or perish, but she holds. . . . Thus becoming has been extinguished and perishing unheard from. . . . Becoming and perishing are banished far afield, driven out by true Trust."[53] The first part adumbrates a reductio proof, a *logos,* whereas the other seems to be an imaginative reworking of the first, a *muthos.* Both together I call a *mutholegomenon.*[54] Why does the goddess pair them, when the first alone would suffice? But look more closely at the terms she uses in this proof. The supposition to be reduced refers to nature, time, and becoming. Without these references it could not be stated, and if they meant nothing to us we could not follow the proof. True, she might have used other terms instead. But if the proof is to be a reductio, and one that finds being to be not this or that seeming, then the supposition to be reduced would have to refer (seemingly) to things that can only be shown imaginatively in a *muthos.* But what if the proof were not simply a reductio? It would still have to be expressed in some language *L.* The goddess speaks Greek, and Greek, like every other "natural" language, is thoroughly if only inchoately poetic. One might then try to construct an ideal language in which to reformulate one's ontology, so as to free it from all that binds our speech and thought to the rough ground of ordinary usage, the discursive way of mortals. Russell tried, but the results, while interesting, have not shown that discourse about being could ever be "logical" simply, not "mythical" as well. Indeed, they suggest the contrary, as does Parmenides' poem.

Parmenides took our situation to be inherently vague. It is likely, moreover, that he took the relation between counting (*arithmein*) and accounting (*legein*) to be such that if the former is impossible, so is the latter.[55] We are reminded once more of Plato's *Sophist,* where Socrates gets things started by asking the stranger from Elea whether he counts the sophist, statesman, and philosopher as one, two, or three. As three, says the stranger, who then sets out to give a *logos* of each. Parmenides, were he listening, might well infer that the "parricide" has already occurred, long before the sophist slips away into "nonbeing." Socrates is unexpectedly quiet.[56]

(3) Signs on the way about being are mostly negative—primarily of the form "non-F," secondarily of the form "not-*p.*" And as promised, the supporting proofs are elenctic: the goddess shows indirectly that being is ungenerable and complete by proving that it could not be anything generated or incomplete.[57] The way about being appears to be a *via negativa.*

Without negation there would be no discernment.[58] If "being" were not a term of distinction, it would mean nothing to us. Hence every ontology involves a negative way. Most of them sort out objects into those that are real and those that are unreal. In antiquity, Platonists were inclined to regard as real certain Ideas and denigrate as unreal all physical things, whereas Aristotelians were inclined to do the opposite. In our era, some are antirealists with respect to numbers, realists with respect to material continuants, whereas others are antirealists with respect to continuants, realists with respect to four-dimensional occurrents, or universals, or sets. Kant, the first irrealist, was emphatically an empirical realist with respect to such things as roses, an antirealist with respect to such things as the color and fragrance of roses. Parmenides, the first openly transcendental realist, abjured any division of objects into beings and nonbeings (entities and non-entities), so he was no antirealist in the usual sense. But he did distinguish strictly between being and seemings. For him, the acceptable way in ontology is positive in directing one's thinking about being alone, negative in directing one's attention away from everything that must seemingly be—the cosmos, bodies, living things (including human beings and gods). It is moreover a *via negativa* insofar as the positive in it depends on the negative.

If wholly negative, an argument will not enable one to know what *is*. Take for example Cantor's reductio proof that $2 \wedge \aleph_0 > \aleph_0$. Because it did not exhibit what he sought to demonstrate, Cantor still had no idea whether $2 \wedge \aleph_0$ is the next transfinite cardinal, no reason even to believe that it exists. Indirect proof is the *via negativa* in mathematics. It can take one a long way into unfamiliar territory. Being merely negative, however, it is insufficiently deictic. Consequently some mathematicians (called "Intuitionists") have tried to purge it from their discipline. A similar difficulty arose in philosophical theology. The way most appropriate to the aim of knowing God would appear to be a radically negative one. But again, finding *that* He is *not* this or that sort of thing does not amount to finding out *what* He is. Philosophers were therefore reluctant to accept the negative way in theology.[59] Still less attractive was the positive way, which belittles God by making Him commensurate with our finite mind. So they sought a middle way, one that would enable them to slip between the Skylla of unqualified sameness and the Charybdis of unqualified otherness. They found it in analogy.

Parmenides' way about being is not simply negative. In the first place, some of the signs are positive: *whole, unique, one, cohesive, complete.* And some of the negative signs appear to negate something inherently negative —*imperishable, not divisible, not incomplete*—and one may argue that the negation of a negation yields a positive. Finally, there is the analogy made between being and the bulk of a well-rounded ball.[60] I must say, however, I find this evidence to be little more than suggestive. First of all, the signs that look positive may not be positive. That being is whole cannot mean that it has parts. So what might "whole" mean besides *not-divisible*? And what does "complete" mean? The goddess proves that "not-incomplete" is predicable of being. But "not-incomplete" does not entail "complete" any more than "not-immortal" entails "mortal." So perhaps "complete" just means "not-incomplete." But then it's not the positive predicate we thought it was. Finally, what are we to make of this enticing but slippery analogy? It presents being as a mass fettered by Necessity—a paradigmatic case of Light-enclosed Night. About it we could write a short tragedy entitled "Being Bound." All this imagery, however, belongs to the attendant disanalogy. If we are to see the analogy aright, we must disregard everything in it that is unlike. What's left when we do? A bare "subject" "governed" by a logical "operator"? But what is that? And how exactly did the goddess, by following these signs, reach the conclusion that being is "logically" definite? Parmenidean discourse about being is not simply negative, but how exactly it is positive proves very difficult to explicate. In this respect, if no other, it closely resembles Socratic elenchus.

Let us review what has become reasonably clear about the Parmenidean way. (1) The signs marking it out are transcendental properties or facts about being. They belong to the transcendental situation without which discoursing about being would be impossible. (2) There are several such signs, several conditions of the possibility of knowing being discursively, but it's hard to tell just how many of them there are. (3) The signs are mostly negative, the arguments manifestly elenctic. They determine a way that resembles a *via negativa*. We found moreover that transcendentality, indefinite plurality, and negativity are all proper to ontology in general. Parmenides was not only the first openly transcendental philosopher, he also showed the way for the rest of us. His poem remains exemplary for ontologists as well as students of natural philosophy.

(4) Twice explicitly, and elsewhere implicitly, the goddess couples speaking and thinking (*legein* and *noein*), speech and thought (*logos* and *noêma*).[61] But she also distinguishes them. Consider these two passages: "It is [the] same for thinking and for being," and, "It is the same for both thinking and for the sake of which there is thought."[62] What the goddess means here is far from clear, yet scholars generally agree that the sentences form a pair, and that together they say something like this: "Thinking has its proper object solely in being. Indeed, the 'two' are really one and the same."[63] But she never says that *legein* and being are one and the same. To the contrary, she strongly suggests that while its proper object is being, the home of rational discourse is the way about being rather than being itself.

What is it to think noetically? The goddess doesn't say. The following, however, is consistent with what she does say: Noetic thinking is less like judging something to be the case, more like seeing things as they are.[64] Call it "noetic insight." Unlike speaking, noetic insight is non-discursive and immediate. It thus resembles touching.[65] But what it "touches" is being and being alone. And unlike any mode of sensing, noetic insight could not be opinion-fraught, nor could it be intermittent insofar as it is identical with what it "touches." Should we then say that *noein* is the very intelligibility of being? But if so, how is your thinking or mine related to it?[66] And how exactly are we to understand the coupling of noetic insight with rational discourse?[67] Does *noein* complement *legein* about being? Must we think discursively about being if we are ever "to achieve noetic insight" (whatever that means)?

To such questions the goddess offers no answers. Nor does she offer any account of what thinking noetically might be insofar as it can be distinguished not only from thinking logically about being, but also from being *qua* being. It's clear, however, that Parmenides had some part in forming the tradition according to which *noêsis* is the supreme mode of knowing. Also formative were Plato and Aristotle, and though, like Parmenides, they wrote very little on the subject, their scant remarks had a great influence on epistemology down into the early modern era. But then it declined. Today, philosophers disparage old-fashioned appeals to a "God's eye view," or simply ignore them. This strikes me as a great loss to ontology in particular, but I won't belabor the issue here.

4. Proof?

Having now reached some understanding of what the goddess is doing in her discourse about being, we are in a better position to examine her argument. Remember, we are to examine it by means of *logos*, not by recourse to experience or custom, nor it seems by appeal to noetic insight alone. If she's right, we too will conclude that of the two ways of inquiry available to us—the "positive" way *how it is* and the "negative" way *how it is not*—the one is to be accepted as trustworthy, the other rejected as unintelligible.

Now, if my interpretation is correct, there is right away a difficulty: We don't know how to lift the argument out of its poetic medium, to purge the *logos* of the *muthos*. Yet let it have been done. There is still another difficulty: Her argument (such as it is) is manifestly indirect. One may thus be able to find that the negative way is unacceptable, but finding this indirectly is not tantamount to finding that the positive way is acceptable. For all we know so far, they're both unacceptable. Hence, to make the decision she asks us to make, we need some positive argument as well. She hints at one, but we were unable to make it out. Yet suppose we have. There is still another difficulty: She goes on to conclude that being is ungenerable and complete, like a spatially delimited solid symmetrical from all points of view, and for this further conclusion her positive argument (such as it is) is manifestly incomplete. Perhaps, when she told the young man to judge by *logos*, she was urging him to fill in her sketch and clarify its terms, that he might then be able to find that the argument is logically valid. That is no small task. Yet suppose we have completed it. We then know that the conclusion follows necessarily from well-articulated premises. But now we confront the greatest difficulty of all and one of greatest interest to philosophers: Are the premises and presuppositions all acceptable? We have anticipated some reasons for doubt. For one, the transcendental framework within which Parmenides makes his argument is open to skeptical attack aimed at the ontological difference, i.e., at the transcendental distinction between being and seeming, truth and evidence. If the skeptic can succeed in driving a wedge between the two sides of this difference, we will have to abandon all hope of ever knowing whether or not being is as Parmenides described it. Also doubtful is the presupposition that thinking depends transcendentally on being, not the reverse. That Parmenides, most rigorous of realists, did not foresee the Kantian alternative is understandable. We, however, cannot overlook it, for while Kant's own brand of irrealism is deeply and perhaps terminally problematic, no one has yet refuted transcendental irrealism in general. A third reason for doubt concerns the fact that Parmenides' ontology could not be more paradoxical. We had trouble refuting it without tacitly begging the question, yet there remains a reasonable ground for suspicion. For if the way about being is cognitively so remote from the way of mortals, if ontological knowledge is so foreign to human opinion, how do we get from here to there? Parmenides' poem makes the transition appear miraculous. Philosophers, though, are not inclined to rely on miracles.

I conclude that the jury is still out. We are not yet ready to agree that being is ungenerable, indivisible, and complete. Nor are we ready to disagree. We must for the time being remain undecided.

If this result seems anticlimactic, that's because it is. It's also no surprise, for where in philosophy have we found an argument that we know to be sound? There may be some, but the more interesting ones all have premises and presuppositions that remain in question. Parmenides' argument is certainly no exception, nor is the strongest argument that we might now launch against it. We're still up in the air, unable to make anything like the decision we would like to make. Indeed, we find ourselves at an impasse, in *aporia*.

To be in *aporia* is not to be paralyzed: we still have the freedom of indecision, not to say indifference; we can still inquire. There are in fact as many degrees of freedom for us as there are ways in which we may go on. How many are there? We can't tell, yet plainly our situation is many-wayed. The possibilities for further movement in thought radiate away from us in many directions. Though too unclear and indistinct to fall neatly into discrete classes, they nonetheless adumbrate a few major options. One is to continue thinking about being, using Parmenides and other ontologists as argumentative guides. Another is to study nature, to become natural philosophers or scientists. The goddess ruled this option out of bounds, but we have to rule it back in until further notice. A third major option is to study things human. After all, why not examine ourselves? Are we not the name-givers, lawmakers, and opinion-laden beings for whom there must seemingly be seeming things as such? Parmenides supplied a few hints along these lines,[68] but it was Socrates who first made what's first for us the starting point and ongoing focus of philosophical investigation. The Socratic turn established an alternative tradition, one that has undergone considerable modification down into our era. It is to this modified tradition that Eva Brann's trilogy belongs. We are free now to let her take us by the hand and lead us into the labyrinth of "the human center." I cannot think of a more resourceful guide. We should bear in mind, however, the possibility that Parmenides is right, that we will in fact be wandering in circles like wayward mortals who know nothing. But that's a risk we cannot avoid, no matter how we choose to proceed or not to proceed. The uncertainty, difficulty, and risk inherent in our situation are all proper to philosophy in general.

NOTES

1 Cf. E. Brann, *The World of the Imagination: Sum and Substance* (Savage, Md.: Rowman & Littlefield, 1991), *What, Then, Is Time?* (Lanham, Md.: Rowman & Littlefield, 1999), and *The Ways of Naysaying: No, Not, Nothing, and Nonbeing* (Lanham, Md.: Rowman & Littlefield, 2001). For her account of the three books as trilogy, cf. *The Ways of Naysaying*, Preface.

2 Cf. *The Ways of Naysaying*, xi–xiii, 211, 216–18 with *The World of Imagination*, 389 ff., and *What, Then, Is Time?*, 163–65, 189 ff.

3 Cf. *The Ways of Naysaying*, xi.

4 Cf. *The Ways of Naysaying*, xiv–xv.

5 All references to Parmenides' poem employ the ordering in Diels-Kranz, *Fragmente der Vorsokratiker*, 6th edition (Dublin: Weidmann, 1972), volume 1, chapter 28.

6 Cf. E. Brann, *The Ways of Naysaying*, 123–24, 133.

7 *The Ways of Naysaying*, 138–44, and Aristotle, e.g., *Metaphysics* 1003b10, 1030a26–27, 1047b1–2. In Plato's *Sophist*, nonbeing is called *to heteron* (contracted to *thateron*), never *to allo*. In ordinary Greek, something is called *heteron* when it is the other of two that together constitute a pair. So, for example, the left hand is the other (*hetera*) of the right hand.

8 Cf. Aristotle, *Metaphysics*, e.g., IV.1–2, VI.1, XII.7–10; Plato, e.g., *Republic* 475–480a, 505d–511e. Even in those Socratic dialogues said to be early, being is distinguished strictly from becoming. For example, in the *Euthyphro*, where Socrates asks "What *is* the holy?" and encourages Euthyphro to look away to the *ousia* of the form in question (5d7, 6e4, 11a7), the distinction shows up right in the surface of the text: of the 21 instances of the verb *gignomai*, 5 occur before that what-is-it question is first asked, 7 occur in interludes or at the dialogical meta-level, and the remaining 9 are in sentences that present illustrative examples, analogies, or the like.

   Although being remained paramount in philosophical thought for over two thousand years, Brann gives reasons for thinking that in our era it has been supplanted, on the one hand by the absolute nothingness of the nihilists, on the other hand by existence as conceived in the writings of Russell or Meinong (*The Ways of Naysaying*, 75–81, 164–66, 180–83).

9 Cf. Empedocles B8–9, 11–14, 17.13, 26.3, 35; Anaxagoras B4, 10, 17; and for the early atomists, cf. Aristotle, *de Caelo* 303a3–b8, *Generation and Corruption* 324b35–326b6, and Cicero, *de Finibus* I.6.17. Empedocles B115.1, 116, Leucippus B2, Democritus B181. Anaxagoras B11–12. For his influence on the cosmology presented in Plato's *Timaeus*, cf. E. Brann, *The Ways of Naysaying*, 148 n34.

10 Cf. Parmenides B6.1–2, B8.7–9. On the meaning of B2.6–8, cf. A. P. D. Mourelatos, *The Route of Parmenides* (New Haven: Yale University Press, 1970), 75–76, 99–100.

11 Cf. Democritus B156.

12 Cf. Plato, *Sophist* 237b7, 240e2, e5 (also 237e2, 240b2, 241a3) with 249e–250e.

13 *Sophist* 251a2. The word *phusis* clusters in the stranger's rather brief account of the greatest kinds, where it is used most frequently in describing the Other.

14 Cf. Plato, *Statesman* 284b7–c3.

15 The distinction between vertical and horizontal otherness is rightly emphasized by E. Brann (*The Ways of Naysaying*, 216), though she makes no use of it

in her discussion of the *Sophist*. She nonetheless asserts (xiv) that in the *Sophist* Plato domesticates nonbeing.

16 Cf. Aristotle, *Metaphysics* VII.4–16, *De Anima* I.3.

17 Aristotle, *Metaphysics* 1072b26–30.

18 That being could not be alive is an implication of her account, but in the extant fragments, at least, she leaves it unstated. Why? Is it because she and the young man are presumably among the living? Be that as it may, for the ancient Greeks, and I suspect for human beings generally, to be is especially to be alive either as immortal or as mortal: C. Kahn, *The Verb BE in Ancient Greek* (Boston: Reidel, 1973), 233–35, 240–45. Aristotle does not diverge radically from this common understanding: *Generation of Animals* 731a35–b4, together with the passages cited in notes 16–17.

19 Compare A. P. D. Mourelatos, *The Route of Parmenides*, 130–33, and J. Barnes, *The Presocratic Philosophers* (London: Routledge & Kegan Paul, 1979) I: 204–10. Other commentators, too, do not find their arguments in favor of Eleatic pluralism to be very persuasive. It may also be worth noting that if Parmenides was indeed a monist, he had this much in common with the earlier natural philosophers such as Thales, Anaximenes, and Heraclitus. They were then on the right track, but fell short because they confused being with the nature of nature.

20 Growth (*phuein*) is expressly ruled out in B8.10, but returns, so to speak, in "Doxa" (B10.6, B19.1). The word *phusis* occurs only in B10.1, 5, B16.3. Its occurrence in B16 is just one of several reasons for refusing to allocate this fragment to "Truth."

21 The proper interpretation of B8.54 is a matter of ongoing controversy. Some commentators, focusing on the passage itself, argue that the error consists in positing Night as well as Light. Others, focusing more on the context in which the passage occurs, argue that the error consists rather in positing both of them as a single pair. I'm inclined to accept the latter interpretation, and will presuppose it in what follows. Another source of controversy is the fact that "Fire" and "Light" are both used as names for one of the two principles. I prefer the latter on the ground that it's more revealing, but here too I may be mistaken.

22 Cf. Heraclitus B1, 30–31, 67, 72; Empedocles B6, 17, 26, 35, 115; Philolaus B1; Aristotle, *Physics* II.1 and *Metaphysics* VII.3ff.

23 Consider Aristotle, *Physics* 192b13ff with 194a16, *Metaphysics* VII.3 with VII.17; and I. Newton, *The Mathematical Principles of Natural Philosophy*.

24 This objection has become rather common in the scholarly literature. Cf., e.g., A. A. Long, "Parmenides on Thinking Being," *Proceedings of the Boston Area Colloquium in Ancient Philosophy* 12 (1996): 125–62, and S. Trépanier, *Empedocles: An Interpretation* (New York: Routledge, 2004), 140–44, 152 ff. If Trépanier is right, a sketch of this argument can be found in Empedocles' poem.

25 Parmenides' poem is silent about the beginning and the end of his search for truth—or in other words, about the *archê* and *telos* of philosophy. But not every

philosopher has kept quiet about them. I challenge readers to examine their accounts, to see whether they are really superior to Parmenides' silence.

26   This objection is commonly made by students in discussions of the poem.

27   This can be done in the case of Zeno's arguments against the possibility of motion.

28   Parmenides B1.30–32. I take the goddess here to be speaking of seemings in general, not of each and every seeming. The word *dokimôs* does not occur in the extant works of Homer or Hesiod.

29   This interpretation, too, is controversial. For references to the relevant literature, cf. D. Gallop, *Parmenides of Elea* (Toronto: Toronto University Press, 1984), 21, 37 n64, 53.

30   Cf. M. Furth, "Elements of Eleatic Ontology," *Journal of the History of Philosophy* 6.2 (1971): 111–32, reprinted in *The Pre-Socratics: A Collection of Critical Essays*, 2nd ed., edited by A. P. D. Mourelatos (Princeton: Princeton University Press, 1993), 241–70.

31   Parmenides B2.3–5. How to interpret these lines is a subject of ongoing debate. The principal questions are these: (1) Does *hôs* mean "how" or "that"? (2) Is the verb *estin* solely or even primarily existential? (3) Does this verb have a so-called unstated subject, or should we regard it as complete in itself? (4) Does the second clause, in each case, modify or merely clarify the first? Readers will note that my translation here is far from being interpretation-free.

32   Cf. E. Brann, *The Way of Naysaying*, 134.

33   Parmenides B8.3–4, 26–27, 48. The word *alêtheia* is one of Parmenides' two names for the object of rational discourse (B8.51). Did he regard it, too, as an alpha-privative?

34   Parmenides B8.22.

35   Parmenides B8.32. For a detailed analysis of the ways in which negation occurs in B8, cf. S. Austin, *Parmenides: Being, Bounds, and Logic* (New Haven: Yale University Press, 1986), chapter 1.

36   Parmenides B1.32. I adopt the reading favored by most recent commentators: cf. D. Gallop, *Parmenides of Elea*, 53.

37   For convenience I have not tried to make explicit the modalities involved. To do so, one might begin with *agenêton* (*ungenerable*), first explicating it as *not-possibly-something-possibly-becoming* (*coming-into-being*), then trying to clarify the difference between the more logical *not-possibly* and the more naturalistic *possibly-becoming* or *possibly-coming-into-being*. Good luck.

38   Parmenides B8.2–6.

39   The way is *amphis alêtheiês*, about truth, she says at B8.51.

40   Parmenides B8.43.

41   Cf. Parmenides B8.30–31, 36, 42.

42 Commentators have noted that his poem is manifestly logical (epistemological, methodological) as well as straightforwardly metaphysical.

43 Two examples from Aristotle: (1) Early on in the *Categories* he distinguishes between *being-present-in* and *being-said-of*, but these relations do not fall within the category of relations or any other category. They belong rather to the trans-categorial framework within which Aristotle discerns categorial ways of being. (2) In the *Metaphysics*, near the end of Book IX, he divides all entities into two classes: those that are composite and those that are not. Those that are not he calls "simple." *Being simple* is not a real attribute, for if it were, simple entities would not be simple. Instead, it is a transcendental property in terms of which Aristotle can begin to describe god, for example, without implying that it (god) is in any way composite.

Two contemporary examples: (1) Near the beginning of *Being and Time*, Heidegger undertakes to disclose *Sein* (being) by recourse to an "interrogation" of *Dasein*, the existing questioner himself. (2) In the *Tractatus Logico-Philosophicus*, Wittgenstein tries to declare the logical structure of the world. This structure is not itself in the world, but rather about it. Its transcendental character reminds one of Parmenides' way about being: G. E. L. Owen, "Eleatic Questions," *Classical Quarterly* 10 n.s. (1960): 84–102, reprinted in *Studies in Presocratic Philosophy*, edited by R. E. Allen and D. J. Furley (London: Routledge & Kegan Paul, 1975), II: 48–81. But Owen exaggerates the degree of resemblance. For one thing, Parmenides' poem does not imply that our *logos* about being is finally to be discarded, as one might kick away a ladder once one has used it to attain the desired vantage point.

44 Cf. Kant, *Critique of Pure Reason*, B52, A369–71, B519–20. Kant rightly emphasizes that transcendental idealism is quite compatible with "empirical" realism.

45 Cf. Plato, *Sophist* 246a4. The two parties in this debate are often called "realists" and "antirealists." But these antirealists are mostly "internal" realists with respect to certain classes of objects. Consider, for example, the works of Panayot Butchvarov, Hilary Putnam, or Nelson Goodman. I have tried to adjudicate this debate in three writings: "The Meinongian-Antimeinongian Dispute Reviewed," *Grazer Philosophische Studien* 32 (1988): 169–79; *Complexity and Analysis* (Lanham, Md.: Lexington Books, 2002), chapter 7; and "Rethinking the Subject Matter of Protometaphysics," in *The Philosophy of Panayot Butchvarov*, edited by L. L. Blackman (Lewiston, N.Y.: Mellen, 2005), 27–50.

46 Parmenides B8.3–6.

47 Parmenides B8.22, 26, 32–33, 42.

48 Parmenides B2.2, B6.4, 9 (cf. B1.23), B8.1, 17–18.

49 Parmenides B1.2, 21, 27. Is the way described in B1 upward or downward? Parmenides has made it impossible to tell.

50 Parmenides, e.g., B1.3, 9, 14, 22, 26, 28, B8.28, 30, 32, 37, B10.6, B13. To judge from the extant fragments, this is an epic poem in which no Muse is ever invoked.

51 Cf. Wittgenstein, *Tractatus Logico-Philosophicus* 4.022, 4.1212, 6.51–53.

52 Parmenides B8.6–13.

53 Parmenides B8.13–21. On the language of this and similar passages, cf. S. Benardete, "The Grammar of Being," *Review of Metaphysics* 33.3 (1977): 493–95, and A. P. D. Mourelatos, "'Nothing' and 'Not-Being': Some Literary Contexts," in *Essays in Ancient Greek Philosophy,* edited by J. P. Anton and A. Preus (Albany, N. Y.: SUNY Press, 1983), II: 59–69.

54 Cf. Plato's *Phaedo* 61e2, also 70b6, *ApSoc* 39e5, *Republic* 376d9, 392c2, 415a3, 501e4. Right before Socrates uses the word *muthol(o)geô* at *Phaedo* 61e2, he offers a double construal of pleasure and pain that resembles the double reason offered by the goddess in Parmenides B8.6-21. See note 56 below.

55 The words *legein* and *logos* do not occur in Parmenides B9-19, where the goddess presents her "physics."

56 Cf. Plato, *Sophist* 216c4–217b3. Compare *Theaetetus* 189a10, *Republic* 478b12–c1. In *Phaedrus* 229d2–e4, Socrates warns against trying to rationalize (rectify, straighten out) the ambient myths. In *Phaedo* 60a3–c7, he presents two ways of construing the relation between pleasure and pain. According to the first, what men call "pleasant" and "painful" and regard as opposites are in their nature an indissoluble pair. According to the second, a god joined pleasure and pain together at the head in an effort to reconcile them. On the first construal, "they" can hardly be counted as two. On the second, an external agent has partially concealed the fact that they are certainly two. The second, moreover, is explicitly poetic, whereas the first is not. Now, when the stranger counts philosopher and sophist as two, is he or is he not unwittingly telling a tale?

57 Ancient Greek mathematical works contain many indirect proofs. In these proofs, the supposition to be "reduced" is found to have a consequence that is impossible (*adunaton*) or absurd (*atopon*). The word *atopon* means *out of place,* which suggests that the "reduced" supposition has no place within the system of truths; it has been banished far afield, cast out by apodictic necessity. The word *adunaton* means *impossible,* which suggests a notion much less picturesque. Notice, however, that *adunaton* belongs to a large family of words all having to do with (in)capacity or (im)potence. So once again we are reminded of the twofold reason given in Parmenides B8.6-21 and the double construal given in Plato's *Phaedo* 60a–c. Whether this was in the minds of Euclid and other early Greek mathematicians I have been unable to discover.

58 Cf. E. Brann, *The Ways of Naysaying,* 26.

59 It may of course serve to strengthen the attitudes of submission and reverence. As philosophers, however, the principal aim is always to know or understand.

60 Parmenides B8.3–49.

61 Parmenides B6.1, B8.50.

62 Parmenides B3, B8.34. Only here and at B6.1 does the verb *noein* occur. All are in "Truth." In "Doxa" there are only the nominalized forms *noos* ("mind") and

noêma ("thought"): cf. B16, 19. It is probably no coincidence that the second instance of *noein* occurs in the context of establishing that being is complete. Unfortunately for us, the other key instance occurs in a single line (B3) now bereft of its original context.

63 As many scholars have noted, this is a statement of extreme realism with respect to thinking, and thus very far removed from Berkeley's identification of *esse* with *percipi*. Notice, too, that in the extant fragments of the poem, these are the only "material" identity statements, of the form "A = B" rather than "A = A." That all such statements are transcendental: P. Butchvarov, *Being Qua Being* (Bloomington: Indiana University Press, 1979), 39–63.

64 Cf. K. von Fritz, "Nous, Noein, and Their Derivatives in Pre-Socratic Philosophy (Excluding Anaxagoras)," *Classical Philology* 40 (1945): 223–42 and 41 (1946): 12–34, reprinted in *The Pre-Socratics*, edited by A. P. D. Mourelatos, 23–85.

65 Cf. Aristotle, *Metaphysics* 1051b24, 1072b21, and Plato, *Phaedo* 65b9, *Republic* 511c7.

66 Consider Aristotle, *De Anima* III.4–5.

67 Consider Plato, *Republic* 511b4, c5, d8, and context.

68 Cf. Parmenides B6.8, B8.39, 53, B9.1, B19.

Twelve Poems for a Reader of Novels

Elliott Zuckerman

1 Teaching at Night

I teach at night in a marble building
set on the heights between converging rivers.
The greater river lies strangely to the east.

The corridors are wider than they need be,
as are the staircases. Through years of use,
edges, once straight, are trodden into curves,
like modulated phrases. In the halls
the heavy wooden doors, once table tops,
appear at intervals. One doesn't know
what lies behind a given door.
But I know where my classrooms are.

I teach three courses. Two are going well.
I'm popular without pandering to tastes,
or using the latest expressions,
or hinting that I hold certain opinions.
These are, after all, night students.
True, I tend to sit on top of my desk,
and fold my legs, with little care
of how my trousers are arranged.
I'm diligent and never miss a meeting.

The third class casts a shadow
over all my life and all my happiness.
For never once have I attended it.

I know what hour they say the class takes place.
But I never even look into the room,

except at times when no one could be there.
By now I'm afraid to set foot on that floor
during any time close to the right hour.
If the students were to be there, waiting,
what would they say? What would I say?
I have no excuse, not even a reason to give.

I would, however, like to know
whether they're still attending, faithfully waiting.

2 SETTLEMENT SCHOOL

Ear at the doorcrack, we could hear a lesson.
Some mumbling, then a fragment of Etude
would speak its cranky phrase. Our eyes
were forced to study the chipped paint on the door,
where the cream and eggshell densities recorded
years of tenementary living.

In nineteen forty music had a smell.

Once pushcarts parked in front. Now postings
told teen-age soloists, still unknown,
of openings uptown. Rewards were small,
but so were expectations of reward.
No movie camera would be zooming in
on mother and her sister in their seats,
the poise on the piano bench
at last worth all the aggravation.

Meanwhile the fingerings for all toccatas
were settling in, no easier to remove
than ancient underpaint,
the tics and knacks of digitation
becoming sedimentary.
We learned our moves, or let them take us over —
the rhythmic wink of eyelid,
the purse of lips, as for a kiss,

the properly seated haunch, the hunt, the hover,
the aim for high notes in a single bound —
all acts of practice giving us the grace
to recognize, wherever we might settle,
what can't be done and what can't be undone.

3 THE POET AT SIXTEEN

He could not hide.
The mere glimpse of an earlobe was enough
to tell us where he was.
Not that we could in any way forget him
after that morning when,
quartering potatoes for our frugal lunch,
he whispered, breathless with mock discovery,
that the skin of his spud was as delicate in hue
as any rain-drenched sunset.

From then on he would go off for siesta
on a grassy square he called the Green,
treeless behind the buildings, well beyond
the back recesses where we peeled and sang.
Bordering his lawn were woods
where intricate brambles barred the doors of nature.
The shadings were too dense,
hyperboles too striking to be useful,
and animals—Lord knows what animals!

And so he lay on his lawn alone, unshaded,
until the elevating shine would drive him
back to our clan of peelers and exchangers.
He'd hang around for the snack of fried potatoes
and then at last he'd settle down to work.
Scumbling a landscape with translucent milk,
he brushed an inlet in, a bush, a sky,
and asked us each to parse the finished scene,
taking our measure.

4 Ostrich

Where were *you* when I created ostrich?
And when I made the emu were you there?

Oh Challenger, you know I wasn't there.
The hatch of even birdlet is beyond me.
Nor can I force a seedling into flow.

But when you looked my way,
you did allot an oval space to me,
and down, down from the skies there swoop
a horde of avian invaders
who peck and scratch and screech and bite and coo
and bring to nest, along with straw and spew,
perpetuating worms,
wriggling enigmas of anger unallayed.

Should bird and wormlet quit the scene,
they leave behind the artificial pigeons
inherited from a mosaic past.
They're painted greener than nature's green,
and they can fly.
Listen as they articulate my needs
from their enamel pigeon-holes.
They coo so well that I can do
without the ostrich.

5 The Corner Flat

Schopenhauer at Home, circa 1840

Observe the wall of books,
a hundred copies of the World as Will
once remaindered at the Frankfurt fair,
and folios of bel canto tunes
arranged for solo flute.

Deep, at his ego's core, he felt the basses
moving in fifths and fourths,
akin to rocks, he theorized.
The rocks feel pain, but do not suffer much.
They share in the Idea, but only faintly.

He played the flute in imitation of a voice
stepwise and florid, feminine yet human.

In the world's theater, music will take a turn
away from the hopping bass.
Heavy ladies will do without
the cuckoo coloratura,
and risk a thrall that better suits his thesis —
that Night of Love
when a hundred members of the Philharmonic
perform the sexual act.

Yet he already knew that music mimes
the will itself, probing beneath mimēsis.
He learned it from the sisters of Cinderella,
from Norma and from all those English Queens.

In the street outside, the careless carriage drivers
turning the corner
cracked their unnecessary whips.

6 Even Little Things

The last days of Hugo Wolf

Today he thinks he's Jupiter, in charge
of weather for the world.

Never before had he been larger than life.
But then a month ago he burst
into this very room and told us all
he'd been appointed impresario

of the Vienna Opera. We thought
that was a joke. But one perceptive friend
suspected, sighing, with sadness in his eyes,
that here was the beginning of the end.

Next thing we know, he said, he'll be
Napoleon, another Thunderer,
but short, like Richard Wagner, our puppet-master,
now the demigod who ruled our circle.

We all knew melody was infinite.
But when the weather gave our Hugo breath,
and when the water of our winter storms
had settled into quiet pools,
Hugo at his keyboard found the frames
scorned by the Master's other minions.
When they, like Humperdinck,
were draping fairy tales in velvet,
Hugo settled for a song
and etched the syllables of chosen poets
in pointed celebration of the small.

7 My Ancient Informant

You asked how one could learn about love
from a wizened woman?
Her wisdom may be tarnished
but I can summon fragments up
and leave them here for what they're worth as tips
to you boys who are waiting at the table,
waiting with torsos tanned from the sand and the surf
of your islands. Lust seems to matter less
to you, with your quaint illustrative ways,
than it still matters to me. I burn with age,
haunted by that age-old interview.

At times I've tried to generalize desire.
Even now I'm trying.

But then there comes a pang
a sudden pluck of gust
that sets the Harp into an oscillation
and scatters on the veranda's marble floor
petals of yellow roses.

Yes, what stirs me and spurs me is pungent still.
It is a chaste elopement when the ladder
hits higher than the window, and anyhow
there's no one waiting at the windowsill.

8 NORTHERN TOUR

One winter's day I toured the sculpture garden.
Workmen played the lift and thrust of life
with maids who also served as midwives.
All were topped by snow,
by undiscriminating snow.

Inside the castleyard I toured the fort,
hewn out of logs they'd gathered in the arctic
and hauled on shoulders to the city.
There laws were ratified, and there they housed
the famous scream.

In nearby neighborhoods the poets were learning
apartment living. They double-locked their doors
and sat at windows facing windows
where other poets sat regarding them.
At dinner all the bearded bachelors
put on their matching hats.

At the early end of day I sought
the hostelry. Over the wireless came
a masterpiece in E, the key of cherries,
burnt and bitter, wild and sour.

On warmer tours there's far too much to see.
The laws here are enough, the neighborhoods,
the bachelors, the Phrygian symphony,
the statues in the snow.

9 An Enclave in the Hospital

He counted every step, and knew
that she was counting too. One metronome
compelled them both.

His mother, suddenly widowed, was suddenly young,
and young together they climbed the winding stairs,
summoned by the family justices,
for gossip and review.
He saw her for the first time as a niece,
eager to be comforted herself,
no longer old enough to comfort him.

White were the steps and risers, hospital white,
spread with a thick enamel cream.
The suite of rooms above
had once been set aside
and stuffed with rugs and cabinets and chairs
to serve as home for his mother's aunt,
the widow of the hospital Intendant.

Here was the prototype of future towers:
a pad for plump Buck Mulligan, and a cell
where mad Bavarian Kings could entertain
imaginary Lohengrins.

Great aunt Teresa wore her hair rolled tight,
a judge bewigged in golden bolsters.
On either side the spinster sisters sat,
Ada and Uta in grey, their pompadours
asserting righteousness.

Three chins displayed the family chin,
like Hapsburg bites improved by Titian.

They served a coffee cake, a wreath
of nuts and currants, saved by the dribbled icing.
He sat himself beside the Chinese urn.
In a household less than musical
he didn't have to earn his keep.
There was no wallspace for a Steinway,
no room for Flügel.
And after a while he was allowed to wander.

At the end of the long hall there were two doors,
a choice as in an epic.
The first was heavily chained and cast in shadow,
sealing off the kin from where, beyond,
the corridor continued:
a length of sickrooms, closets, nurses' stations,
patients and their envious keepers.

The other door led to a world within,
yet opened without a key,
without a sign, without a magic word.

Here were the books of the hospital Intendant.
One book was waiting for him, high in a case
and bound in water-stained magenta.
In paragraphs of small italic print
a hyphenated doctor had collected
vignettes of neurasthenics at the end
of a weary century. Most of the men were frail
but some were hefty. A few had played piano.
In upright collars and decorative cravats,
they too had climbed the stairs.
They too confessed to privacies
that only Latin could decently describe.

He learned that Heaven, in mordant craftiness,
had given these men a name:

Ouranus, Father of Titans, Consort of Earth.
Neptune would be next, then distant Pluto –
the furthest planets that we knew so far.
The dreaded dive into the ebbing ocean,
and then the steep ascent to being judged.

Sickrooms were sealed behind the other door.
Back in the parlor, ladies laid their plans.
Somewhere between, his harrow had begun.
He felt the rhythm and continued counting.

10 An Incident on Clare Bridge

In Memoriam R. C. P.

The gates are stately here. Parades
of lanterns guard the yard beyond the crossing.
The beech displays a darker tone of copper.
The garden is a water-color.

Under the bridge their cold white necks
are floating by in silly dignity,
the sludgy Cam concealing all propulsion.
You say to me 'There's one that always wins,'
and watch her take the lead,
and toss the bread to that particular swan.

You are the athlete and the soldier,
I the dark-haired stranger.
As backdrop to us both
the indestructable display
where paneled windows plead for numbering.

11 Early Teacher

At the end of seven years of Saturdays
we reached B minor for the second time

and celebrated having mimed
all forty-eight.

We knew Bach's questions asked for tonal answers,
nodded in fellowship when anyone
worked out a stretch of double counterpoint
without forbidden fifths.
And when Bach strettoed, we would stretto too.

Your talk of music was our sermon.
There was no point in art without revenge.
We learned who cheated, who mis-spelled,
who settled without struggle, who would sin
by striving for success
with chords of the eleventh and thirteenth.
We were shown
how tawdriness intrudes upon
the overblown.

We learned that movements searching for an end
were riddled with death.

You often said that lovers sick
of music should consult
a doctor of music. It was your only joke.

Once out of nowhere you announced
that to be handsome is a curse.
You didn't even look at me, alas,
but at the bud among us in the class,
a boy named Max, original and blond,
ready to bloom but not prepared to beware.

And with you I was there
when Mary Garden in a single day
sang Melisande at a matinee
and after dark reversed her character
to cast the veils of Salome.

What did we say
when later we walked the length of East Broadway
to drop you at the El and then go on
to eat Chinese, or Spanish on Fourteenth?
Even now I contemplate your power with fear.
There are subjects, there are answers, to this day
on which no possible opinion
no earlier or later influence
no irritable reach for fact and reason
can shake my certainty, can shake
your certainty.

12 THE DANCE

The window shows a march of trees. Between
each pair of sturdy trunks where it has snowed
the squares of whitened lawn are also marching.

Much of the world does come on evenly,
as with the waves, as with the waves. When not,
planters with foresight learn to interfere

by scattering seeds in paced-out intervals,
and training the new greenery to grow
like lined-up spears in scenes of victory.

Players can make the waltzers trip
by tossing in a four among the threes.
Or surer still, upsetting symmetry
with just one extra measure, funny, perilous,

hilarious. Yes, counting matters. Now
I'm counting step by step
when climbing to the attic lookout where,
within my chosen pane, parades are framed.

ENVOI

Did somebody ask my opinion?
When I want loveliness, I dwell
in other people's rose-gardens.
What I learn each day
is always what I've often heard before.
And for feelings of home, beyond
all metrical nostalgia, I depend
upon the steady rain in foreign cities.

Contributors

Laurence Berns taught for forty years at St. John's College in Annapolis. He translated Plato's *Meno* (with George Anastaplo), and published articles on philosophy, political philosophy, Shakespeare, and American Government. He is completing a translation of Aristotle's *Politics*.

David Bolotin is a tutor at St. John's College in Santa Fe, where he has been teaching since 1982. From 1974 to 1982, he was a tutor on the Annapolis campus.

Chester Burke has taught at St. John's College in Annapolis since 1984 and has played in the Baltimore Chamber Orchestra since 1982.

James Carey is a tutor and former Dean of St. John's College in Santa Fe. He has recently occupied the position of Distinguished Visiting Professor of Philosophy at the United States Air Force Academy.

Mera J. Flaumenhaft has taught at St. John's College in Annapolis since 1976. She has published essays about Homer, Aeschylus, Euripides, Machiavelli, and Shakespeare, as well as a translation of Machiavelli's *Mandragola*. She is the author of *The Civic Spectacle: Essays on Drama and Community*.

Richard Freis, a graduate of St. John's College, is Professor of Classics at Millsaps College. He has published studies in classical and modern literature and is also a poet, translator, and librettist.

Burt C. Hopkins is Professor and Chair of Philosophy at Seattle University, founding co-editor of *The New Yearbook for Phenomenology and Phenomenological Philosophy*, and author of articles on Jacob Klein's thought, especially in relation to 20th-century phenomenology and hermeneutics.

Peter Kalkavage has been a tutor at St. John's College in Annapolis since 1977. He has collaborated with Eric Salem and Eva Brann on translations of Plato's *Sophist* and *Phaedo*. They are currently working on the *Statesman*.

Susu Knight taught at St. John's College in Santa Fe from 1974 until she retired in May 2006. She welcomes the chance this brings to pursue art even more actively than she has in the last eight years.

Sam Kutler is a faculty member emeritus at St. John's College in Annapolis, where he served as academic dean in the early 1980s. He and Eva Brann have been colleagues at St. John's since 1961. Over the years they have led numerous seminars together.

David Lawrence Levine has taught at St. John's College in Santa Fe since 1986. He was Director of the Graduate Institute from 1997 to 2001 and Dean of the college from 2001 to 2006.

Paul W. Ludwig teaches at St. John's College in Annapolis. He is the author of *Eros and Polis: Desire and Community in Greek Political Theory.*

Chaninah Maschler has been a tutor at St. John's College in Annapolis since 1976. She and Eva Brann became acquainted as graduate students at Yale.

Ronald Mawby, a graduate of St. John's College, has taught for the past twenty years in the Honors Program at Kentucky State University.

Barry Mazur is a mathematician and is the Gerhard Gade University Professor at Harvard University.

Grace Dane Mazur is on the faculty of the MFA Program for Writers at Warren Wilson College. She was a research biologist studying the micro-architecture of silkworms before switching to writing fiction.

Christopher B. Nelson has been president of St. John's College in Annapolis since 1991. He is also a graduate of the college. A frequent speaker on national educational public policy, he is the immediate past chair of The Annapolis Group, a consortium of the nation's leading liberal arts colleges.

Joe Sachs taught for thirty years at St. John's College in Annapolis.

Eric Salem has been teaching at St. John's College in Annapolis since 1990. He has collaborated with Peter Kalkavage and Eva Brann on translations of Plato's *Sophist* and *Phaedo.* They are currently working on the *Statesman.*

Harrison Sheppard, a graduate of St. John's College, is a frequently published political essayist. Following a career as a U.S. government lawyer, he has maintained a solo civil law practice in San Francisco since 1991.

Robin Chalek Tzannes graduated from St. John's College and now writes advertising copy, children's books, and occasional book reviews. She is currently working on a book about the island of Cythera, to which she hopes to retire before long.

Stewart Umphrey teaches at St. John's College in Annapolis. Present interests include: what is it to be a natural kind (about which he is writing a book), and objectivity of fictional objects (about which he is not).

Elliott Zuckerman began teaching at St. John's College in Annapolis in 1961. He is now retired, painting and writing songs.